Neo-Scholastic Essays

Neo-Scholastic Essays

EDWARD FESER

St. Augustine's Press

South Bend, Indiana

Manufactured in the United States of America.

1 2 3 4 5 6   20 19 18 17 16 15

Library of Congress Cataloging in Publication Data
Feser, Edward.
[Essays. Selections]
Neo-scholastic essays / by Edward Feser.
pages cm
ISBN 978-1-58731-558-9 (paperback: alk. paper)
1. Neo-Scholasticism. I. Title.
B839.F47 2015
149'.91 – dc23   2015005657

∞ The paper used in this publication meets the minimum requirements of the
American National Standard for Information Sciences - Permanence of Paper
for Printed Materials, ANSI Z39.48-1984.

St. Augustine's Press
www.staugustine.net

Table of Contents

Preface

In a series of publications over the course of a decade, I have argued for the defensibility and abiding relevance to issues in contemporary philosophy of Scholastic ideas and arguments, and especially of Aristotelian-Thomistic ideas and arguments. This work has been very much in the vein of what has come to be known as "analytical Thomism," but the spirit of the project goes back at least to the Neo-Scholasticism of the period from the late nineteenth century to the middle of the twentieth. I am happy to own the "Neo-Scholastic" label, and would be happier still if my work helped encourage others to own it as well.

Much of this work has been in the form of books. *Philosophy of Mind* (2005) argues for a revival of Aristotelian hylemorphism as the key to resolving the deadlock in contemporary philosophy of mind between materialism and Cartesian forms of dualism. *Locke* (2007) criticizes modern empiricist metaphysics and epistemology and Lockean political philosophy from an Aristotelian-Thomistic point of view. *The Last Superstition: A Refutation of the New Atheism* (2008) is an exposition and defense of the classical philosophical tradition from Plato and Aristotle to the Scholastics, a critique of the moderns who supplanted the Scholastic tradition, and a defense of the traditional Thomistic arguments for the existence of God, the immortality of the soul, and the natural law conception of morality. *Aquinas* (2009) provides a more in-depth exposition and defense of St. Thomas's central ideas in metaphysics, natural theology, philosophical psychology, and ethics. *Scholastic Metaphysics: A Contemporary Introduction* (2014) offers an even more in-depth exposition and defense of Scholastic, and especially Thomistic, ideas and arguments in metaphysics, as well as a detailed treatment of ideas and arguments in contemporary analytic metaphysics which recapitulate Aristotelian and Scholastic themes.

Much of the work in question has also been in the form of essays which have appeared in academic journals and anthologies, and which pursue in greater depth than I have in the books various specific topics. The aim of the present volume is to make those essays more easily available to readers who lack access to an academic library. I have also included three papers presented at academic conferences which have not been previously published. My personal blog *Edward Feser* (edwardfeser.blogspot.com) has since 2008 also provided a forum for the discussion of Scholastic ideas. I have included here a post from the blog entitled "The Road from Atheism," which recounts the various philosophical influences that gradually led me in the late 1990s to give up the atheism and philosophical naturalism to which I had been committed for about a decade and to adopt the Scholastic brand of theism I now defend. As of this writing it has gotten by far the most page views of any blog post I have written. Academic philosophers, and others too, may find it of interest as a counterexample to the cliché that no one is ever led to religion via rational arguments.

I would like to thank Bruce Fingerhut at St. Augustine's Press for his interest in this project. As always, I thank my beloved wife and children—Rachel, Benedict, Gemma, Kilian, Helena, John, and Gwendolyn—for their patience in tolerating the many hours I devote to research and writing. And I thank my readers for the kind interest they have taken in my work over the years. I dedicate this volume to them.

Acknowledgments

"Motion in Aristotle, Newton, and Einstein" originally appeared in Edward Feser, ed., *Aristotle on Method and Metaphysics* (Basingstoke: Palgrave Macmillan, 2013).

"Teleology: A Shopper's Guide" originally appeared in *Philosophia Christi,* vol. 12, no. 1 (2010).

"On Aristotle, Aquinas, and Paley: A Reply to Marie George" originally appeared in *Evangelical Philosophical Society Online Article Library* (June 2011).

"Natural Theology Must Be Grounded in the Philosophy of Nature, Not in Natural Science" was presented at a conference on the theme *Can Science Inform Our Understanding of God?* held at Franciscan University of Steubenville from December 2–3, 2011. It is published here for the first time.

"Existential Inertia and the Five Ways" originally appeared in *American Catholic Philosophical Quarterly*, vol. 85, no. 2 (2011).

"The New Atheists and the Cosmological Argument" originally appeared in *Midwest Studies in Philosophy*, vol. 37 (2013).

"Between Aristotle and William Paley: Aquinas's Fifth Way" originally appeared in *Nova et Vetera,* vol. 11, no. 3 (Summer 2013).

"Why McGinn is a Pre-Theist" originally appeared in *Theoretical and Applied Ethics*, vol. 1, no. 4 (2012).

"The Road from Atheism" originally appeared at the blog *Edward Feser* (edwardfeser.blogspot.com) on July 27, 2012.
"Kripke, Ross, and the Immaterial Aspects of Thought" originally appeared in *American Catholic Philosophical Quarterly*, vol. 87, no. 1 (2013).

"Hayek, Popper, and the Causal Theory of the Mind" originally appeared in Leslie Marsh, ed., *Hayek in Mind: Hayek's Philosophical Psychology*, a special issue of *Advances in Austrian Economics,* Vol. 15 (2011).

"Why Searle *is* a Property Dualist" was presented at the American Philosophical Association Pacific Division meeting held in Pasadena, CA from March 24–28, 2004. It is published here for the first time.

"Being, the Good, and the Guise of the Good" originally appeared in Daniel D. Novotny and Lukas Novak, eds., *Neo-Aristotelian Perspectives in Metaphysics* (London: Routledge, 2014).

"Classical Natural Law Theory, Property Rights, and Taxation" originally appeared in *Social Philosophy and Policy,* vol. 27, no. 1 (2010).

"Self-Ownership, Libertarianism, and Impartiality" was presented at a symposium on the theme *Impartiality and Partiality in Ethics* held at the University of Reading, England, from December 1–2, 2006. It is published here for the first time.

An excerpt from "In Defense of the Perverted Faculty Argument" was published under the title "The Role of Nature in Sexual Ethics" in *The National Catholic Bioethics Quarterly*, vol. 13, no. 1 (Spring 2013).

Metaphysics and philosophy of nature

1
Motion in Aristotle, Newton, and Einstein

I. The purported contradiction

In Book VII of the *Physics*, Aristotle famously maintains that "everything that is in motion must be moved by something."[1] This serves as a crucial premise in his argument for an Unmoved Mover. Aquinas's related First Way of arguing for the existence of God rests on a variation of the premise, to the effect that "whatever is in motion is moved by another."[2] Let us call this the "principle of motion."[3] Newton's First Law states that "every body continues in its state of rest or of uniform motion in a straight line, unless it is compelled to change that state by forces impressed upon it."[4] Call this the "principle of inertia."

It is widely thought that the principle of motion is in conflict with the principle of inertia, and that modern physics has therefore put paid to Aristotelian natural theology. The assumption is that Aristotle, followed by Aquinas and other Scholastics, held that an object cannot keep moving unless something is continuously moving it, but that Newton showed that it is simply a law of physics that once set in motion an object will remain in motion without any such mover.[5] Hence Anthony Kenny judges that "it

---

1   *Physics* 241b34, as translated by R. P. Hardie and R. K. Gaye in Aristotle 1930.
2   *Summa Theologiae* I.2.3, as rendered by the Fathers of the English Dominican Province in their original 1911 edition of the *Summa Theologica*. The revised 1920 edition instead reads "whatever is in motion is put in motion by another." The change was no doubt motivated by considerations about inertia of the sort we will be discussing.
3   Here I follow Wippel 2000, p. 453. The premise is labeled the "motor causality principle" by Wallace (1983). It is called the "mover causality principle" by McLaughlin (2004).
4   This is a common rendering of Newton's statement in Latin of his First Law in *Philosophiae Naturalis Principia Mathematica* (London, 1687).
5   DeWitt (2004) contrasts Newton's principle of inertia with what he calls the "Pre-1600s Principle of Motion," according to which "an object in motion will come to a halt, unless something keeps it moving" (p. 109).

seems that Newton's law wrecks the argument of the First Way" (1969, p. 28).

Common though this view is, it is not only mistaken, but unfounded. To think otherwise requires reading into each of the principles in question claims they do not make. When we consider what Aristotelian philosophers have actually said about the principle of motion and what modern physicists have actually said about the principle of inertia, we will see that they do not contradict one another. Indeed, when we consider the philosophical issues raised by motion, by the idea of a law of nature, and so forth, we will find that there is a sense in which the principle of inertia *presupposes* the principle of motion.[6]

II. Why the conflict is illusory

There are at least five reasons to think that any appearance of conflict between the two principles is illusory:

II.1. No formal contradiction: Suppose that "motion" is being used in the two principles in the same sense. Even given this assumption, there is no *formal* contradiction between them. Newton's law tells us that a body *will* in fact continue its uniform rectilinear motion if it is moving at all, as long as external forces do not prevent this. It does not tell us *why* it will do so. In particular, it does not tell us one way or the other whether there is a "mover" of *some* sort which ensures that an object obeys the First Law, and which is in that sense responsible for its motion. As G. H. Joyce writes:

> Newton, indeed, says that a body in motion will continue to move uniformly in a straight line, unless acted upon by external forces. But we need not understand him to deny that the uniform movement itself is due to an agency acting *ab extra*; but merely [to deny] that it is produced by an agency belonging to that category of agents which he denominates "external forces" … forces whose action in each case is of necessity confined to a particular direction and velocity. (1924, p. 100)

Of course, one might ask what sort of "mover" an object obeying the principle of inertia could have if it is not an "external force" of the sort Newton

---

6   For a useful survey of some earlier treatments of the relationship between Aristotle's principle and Newton's, see Augros 2007, at pp. 68–78.

intended to rule out. One might also ask whether such a mover, whatever it might be, really serves any explanatory purpose, and thus whether we ought to bother with it given Ockham's razor. Those are good questions, and we will return to them. But they are beside the present point, which is that the principle of motion and the principle of inertia do not actually contradict one another, *even if* we assume that they are talking about the same thing when they talk about motion.

II.2. Equivocation: In any event, we shouldn't make that assumption, because they are *not* talking about the same thing, or at least not exactly the same thing. "As usually happens when science appears to contradict philosophy," notes Henry Koren, "there is here an ambiguity of terms" (1962, p. 95). Newton's principle of inertia is concerned solely with *local* motion, change with respect to place or location. When Aristotelians speak of "motion," they mean change of *any* kind. This would include local motion, but also includes change with respect to quantity, change with respect to quality, and change from one substance to another.[7] More to the point, for the Aristotelian all such change involves the actualization of a potency or potential. Hence what the principle of motion is saying is that *any potency that is being actualized is being actualized by something else (and in particular by something that is already actual)*.

So understood, the principle of motion is, so the Aristotelian would say, something we can hardly deny. For a potency or potential, being merely potential, can hardly actualize itself or anything else. In any event, the principle is, we see once again, not in formal contradiction with the principle of inertia because they are not talking about the same thing. When the Newtonian principle states that a body in motion will tend to stay in motion, it isn't saying that a potency which is being actualized will tend to continue being actualized. Even if it were suggested that the principle *entails* this claim, the point is that that isn't what the principle of inertia itself, as understood in modern physics, is *saying*. Indeed, modern physics has defined itself in part in terms of its eschewal, for purposes of physics, of such metaphysical notions as act and potency, final causality, and the like. So, it is not that modern physics has falsified the principle of motion so much as that it simply makes no use of it.

---

7   To be sure, there is in Aristotle and Aquinas a narrow sense of "motion" in which substantial change does not count as motion, though there is also a broader sense in which it does. For discussion of these senses and of whether substantial change is included in the scope of what Aquinas's First Way is meant to explain, see Wippel 2000, pp. 445–47.

Now one might ask whether modern physics has not for that very reason made the principle of motion otiose and of nothing more than historical interest. We will return to this question as well, but it is also beside the present point, which is that there is no *necessary* conflict between the principle of motion and the principle of inertia.

II.3. The "state" of motion: Having said all that, we must immediately emphasize that there is a sense in which the Newtonian principle implicitly *affirms* at least an aspect of the Aristotelian principle it is usually taken to have displaced. To see how, consider first that modern physics characterizes uniform motion as a "state." Now this has the flavor of paradox. Reginald Garrigou-Lagrange objects:

> Motion, being essentially a change, is the opposite of a state, which implies stability. There is no less change in the transition from one position to another in the course of movement, than in the transition from repose to motion itself; if, therefore, this first change demands another cause, the following changes demand it for the same reason. (1939, p. 273)[8]

Yet the modern physicist would respond to this objection precisely by collapsing the distinction between repose and motion. As Lee Smolin writes:

> Being at rest becomes merely a special case of uniform motion—it is just motion at zero speed.
>
> How can it be that there is no distinction between motion and rest? The key is to realize that whether a body is moving or not has no absolute meaning. Motion is defined only with respect to an observer, who can be moving or not. If you are moving past me at a steady rate, then the cup of coffee I perceive to be at rest on my table is moving with respect to you.
>
> But can't an observer tell whether he is moving or not? To Aristotle, the answer was obviously yes. Galileo and Newton were forced to reply no. If the earth is moving and we do not feel it, then it must be that observers moving at a constant speed do not feel any effect of their motion. Hence we cannot tell

8   Cf. Joyce 1924, p. 95.

whether we are at rest or not, and motion must be defined purely as a relative quantity. (2007, pp. 21–22)

Now, this sort of move raises philosophical questions of its own. As Smolin goes on to note:

This is a powerful strategy that was repeated in later theories. One way to unify things that appear different is to show that the apparent difference is due to the difference in the perspective of the observers. A distinction that was previously considered absolute becomes relative ...

Proposals that two apparently very different things are the same often require a lot of explaining. Only sometimes can you get away with explaining the apparent difference as a consequence of different perspectives. Other times, the two things you choose to unify are just different. The need to then explain how things that seem different are really in some way the same can land a theorist in a lot of trouble. (2007, pp. 22–23)[9]

Indeed, I will suggest later on that the attempt to explain away what Aristotelians mean by "motion" by means of such relativizing moves faces limits in principle.

But the point to emphasize for the moment is that, precisely because the principle of inertia treats uniform local motion as a "state," it treats it thereby as the *absence* of change. Moreover, it holds that external forces *are* required to move a thing out of this "state" and thus to bring about a change. One more quote from Smolin:

There is an important caveat here: We are talking about uniform motion—motion in a straight line ... When we change the speed or direction of our motion, we do feel it. Such changes are what we call *acceleration*, and acceleration *can* have an absolute meaning. (2007, p. 22)

But then the Newtonian principle of inertia hardly conflicts with the Aristotelian principle that "motion"—that is to say, change—requires something

---

9   For an illuminating discussion of the explanatory strategy in question and its application to motion, see Simon 2001, chapters II and III.

to cause the change. The disagreement is at most over whether a particular phenomenon *counts* as a true change or "motion" in the relevant sense, *not* over whether it would require a mover or changer if it *did* so count.

II.4. Natural motion: If Newton is closer to the Aristotelians than is often supposed, so too are the Aristotelians (or at least Aristotle and Aquinas) closer to Newton than is often supposed. As James A. Weisheipl (1985) has shown, the idea that Aristotle and Aquinas held that no object can continue its local motion unless some mover is continuously conjoined to it is something of an urban legend. To be sure, this was the view of Averroes and of some Scholastics, but not of Aristotle himself or of St. Thomas. On the contrary, their view was that a body will of itself tend to move toward its natural place by virtue of its form. That which generates the object and thus imparts its form to it can be said thereby to impart motion to it, but neither this generator nor anything else need remain conjoined to the object as a mover after this generation occurs. Aquinas comments:

> [Aristotle] says, therefore, that what has been said is manifested by the fact that natural bodies are not borne upward and downward as though moved by some external agent.
>
> By this is to be understood that he rejects an external mover which would move these bodies *per se* after they obtained their specific form. For light things are indeed moved upward, and heavy bodies downward, by the generator inasmuch as it gives them the form upon which such motion follows ... However, some have claimed that after bodies of this kind have received their form, they need to be moved per se by something extrinsic. It is this claim that the Philosopher rejects here.[10]

Even Aquinas's understanding of projectile motion is more complicated than modern readers often suppose:

> An instrument is understood to be moved by the principal agent so long as it retains the power communicated to it by the principal agent; thus the arrow is moved by the archer as long as it retains the force wherewith it was shot by him. Thus in heavy and light things that which is generated is moved by the generator

---

10   *Sententia de caelo et mundo* I.175, as translated in Aquinas 1964.

as long as it retains the form transmitted thereby ... And the mover and the thing moved must be together at the commencement of but not throughout the whole movement, as is evident in the case of projectiles.[11]

To be sure, even though that which initiated a projectile's motion need not remain conjoined to it for the motion to continue, Aquinas still thought projectiles required other, conjoined movers given that a projectile's motion is not motion toward its *natural* place but is rather imposed on it contrary to its natural tendency. But as Thomas McLaughlin points out, the motions of projectiles require such conjoined movers in Aquinas's view

> because of the *kinds* of motions that they are and *not* because of a general conception of the nature of motion itself. In this respect, projectile ... motions resemble accelerated motions in Newtonian physics, for accelerated motions require a force to act on a body throughout the time that it is accelerating. (2004, p. 243. Emphasis added.)

And insofar as *natural* motions require no such conjoined mover, the Aristotelian-Thomistic view sounds to that extent quite Newtonian indeed: "Thus, the Law of Inertia in the sense of absence of forces is similar to Aristotle's concept of natural gravitation, which is very remarkable" (Moreno 1974, p. 323).

Obviously, the Aristotelian notion of an object having some specific place toward which it tends naturally to move is obsolete, as is Aquinas's view that projectile motions require a continuously conjoined mover.[12] There are also questions to be raised about Aquinas's view that the generator of a natural object moves that object instrumentally by virtue of having imparted to it its form. For how can the generator move the object as an instrument if by Aquinas's own admission it is no longer conjoined to it?

---

11 *Quaestiones disputatae de potentia Dei* 3.11 ad 5, as translated in Aquinas 1952.
12 Though modern writers should not be too quick to ridicule the latter notion. As Ashley (2006) comments: "Aristotle ... suppos[ed] that when the ball is struck some force is communicated to the medium through which it moves, which then keeps it moving after it has left the bat that put it in motion. This seems to us absurd, but we should recall that today science still relies on the notion of 'field,' that is, a medium, to explain the motion of bodies through that field" (p. 99). Cf. Sachs 1995, p. 230.

We will return to this question. The point for now is just to emphasize yet again that when one examines the principles of motion and inertia more carefully, the assumption that they are *necessarily* in conflict can readily be seen to be unfounded.

II.5. Natural science versus philosophy of nature: That certain key aspects of Aristotelian physics have been falsified is not in dispute. However, as contemporary Aristotelians often complain, the moderns have been too quick to throw the Aristotelian metaphysical baby out with the physical bathwater. Though Aristotle and pre-modern Aristotelians did not clearly distinguish the metaphysical aspects of their analysis of nature from the physical ones (in the modern sense of "physical"), these aspects *can* in fact be clearly distinguished. In particular, questions about what the natural world *must* be like in order for any natural science at all to be possible must be distinguished from questions about what, as a matter of *contingent* fact, are the laws that govern that world. The latter questions are the proper study of physics, chemistry, biology, and the like. The former are the proper study of that branch of metaphysics known as the philosophy of nature.[13] Geocentrism, the ancient theory of the elements, and the notion that objects have specific places to which they naturally move, are examples of Aristotelian ideas in physics that have been decisively superseded. But the theory of act and potency, the doctrine of the four causes, and the hylemorphic analysis of material objects as composites of form and matter are examples of notions which have (so the contemporary Aristotelian argues) abiding value as elements of a sound philosophy of nature.

Now the principle of motion is, the Aristotelian will insist, another thesis whose import is *metaphysical*, a corollary of the distinction between act and potency which is the foundation of the Aristotelian philosophy of nature. The principle of inertia, by contrast, is a claim of natural science. Since the domains they are addressing are different, there can be no question of any conflict between them, certainly no direct or obvious conflict.

Physics, as that discipline is understood in modern times, abstracts from concrete material reality and describes the natural world exclusively in terms of its mathematical structure. Though philosophers and scientists beholden

---

13   The term "philosophy of nature" is perhaps not widely used these days outside the circles of Thomists and other modern Scholastics. But that it is not completely unknown to contemporary analytic philosophers, or at least to those with neo-Aristotelian sympathies, is indicated by the title of Ellis 2002.

to scientism suppose that it thereby gives us an exhaustive picture of reality, in fact what it gives us is very nearly the opposite. As Bertrand Russell once wrote:

> It is not always realised how exceedingly abstract is the information that theoretical physics has to give. It lays down certain fundamental equations which enable it to deal with the logical structure of events, while leaving it completely unknown what is the intrinsic character of the events that have the structure. We only know the intrinsic character of events when they happen to us. Nothing whatever in theoretical physics enables us to say anything about the intrinsic character of events elsewhere. They may be just like the events that happen to us, or they may be totally different in strictly unimaginable ways. All that physics gives us is certain equations giving abstract properties of their changes. But as to what it is that changes, and what it changes from and to—as to this, physics is silent. (1985, p. 13)

Newton's laws of motion reflect this tendency, insofar as they provide a mathematical description of motion suitable for predictive purposes without bothering about the origins of motion or the intrinsic nature of that which moves. Indeed, that is arguably the whole point of the principle of inertia. As Weisheipl writes:

> Rather than proving the principle, the mechanical and mathematical science of nature *assumes* it ... [and] the mathematical sciences must assume it, if they are to remain mathematical ...
>
> The basis for the principle of inertia lies ... in the nature of mathematical abstraction. The mathematician must equate: a single quantity is of no use to him. In order to equate quantities he must assume the basic irrelevance or nullity of other factors, otherwise there can be no certainty in his equation. The factors which the mathematician considers irrelevant are ... motion, rest, constancy, and unaltered directivity; it is only the *change* of these factors which has quantitative value. Thus for the physicist it is not motion and its continuation which need to be explained but change and cessation of motion—for only these have equational value ...

In the early part of the seventeenth century physicists tried to find a physical cause to explain the movement [of the heavenly bodies]; Newton merely disregarded the question and looked for two quantities which could be equated. In Newtonian physics there is no question of a cause, but only of differential equations which are consistent and useful in describing phenomena …

[T]he nature of mathematical abstraction … must leave out of consideration the qualitative and causal content of nature … [S]ince mathematical physics abstracts from all these factors, it can say nothing about them; it can neither affirm nor deny their reality … (1985, pp. 42 and 47-48)[14]

The philosophy of nature, however, and in particular the principle of motion and the other components of the Aristotelian metaphysical apparatus, are concerned precisely to give an account of the intrinsic nature of material phenomena and their causes, of which modern physics gives us only the abstract mathematical structure.

III. Is inertia real?

Now, some Aristotelians have gone so far as to insinuate that the principle of inertia really has only an instrumental import, with the Aristotelian philosophy of nature alone providing a description of the reality of motion. Hence Joyce writes that "the mathematician may for practical purposes regard motion as a *state*. Philosophically the concepts of movement and of a state are mutually exclusive" (1924, p. 95). And Garrigou-Lagrange claims: "[T]hat the motion once imparted to a body continues indefinitely, is a *convenient* fiction for *representing* certain mathematical or mechanical relations of the astronomical order" (1939, p. 275, note 24; emphasis in the original).

Certainly a realist construal of inertia is at least open to challenge, not least because the principle is not directly susceptible of experimental test. As William Wallace writes:

It is never found in ordinary experience that a body in uniform motion continues in such motion indefinitely. All the bodies met with in ordinary experience encounter resistive forces in their travel, and sooner or later come to rest. Nor does refined

14   Cf. Wallace 1956, pp. 163–64.

experimentation and research supply any instances where such resistive forces are absent. (1956, p. 178)

And as N. R. Hanson emphasizes, the problem is not merely that we *have* not observed bodies that are force-free and thus operate in accordance with the principle of inertia, but that we *could* not observe them, given Newton's own Law of Universal Gravitation. The law of inertia thus "refers to entities which are unobservable as a matter of physical principle" (Hanson 1963, p. 112; cf. Hanson 1965a).

To be sure (and as Wallace and Hanson acknowledge) the principle can be argued for by extrapolating from observational data to the limiting case, and Galileo and Newton argued in precisely that way. But no such argument can provide a true demonstration. Wallace's remarks are worth quoting at length:

> The observational data are certainly true, but the only way in which it may be maintained that the limiting case is also true would be by maintaining that what is verified in the approach to a limit is also verified at the limit itself. The latter statement, however, cannot be maintained, because it is not universally true. There are many instances in mathematics where it is known to be violated. One illustration is the approach of polygon to circle as the number of sides is increased indefinitely. All through the approach to the limit, assuming the simple case where all figures are inscribed in the limiting circle, every figure constructed that has a finite number of sides is a polygon. The limiting case is a figure of a different species, it is no longer a polygon, but a circle. It is not true to say that a polygon is a circle; the difference is as basic and irreducible as that between the discrete and the continuous. In this case, what is verified in the approach to the limit (polygon), is not verified at the limit itself (circle).
>
> Now if it is not *always* true that what is verified during the approach is necessarily verified at the limit … then the fact that the observational base for the principle of inertia is true cannot be used to prove, or demonstrate, that the limiting case stated in the principle is also true. (1956, pp. 179-80)[15]

15   Cf. Weisheipl 1985, pp. 36–37.

Nor need one be an Aristotelian to wonder about the epistemic credentials of Newton's principle. Einstein wrote:

> The weakness of the principle of inertia lies in this, that it involves an argument in a circle: a mass moves without acceleration if it is sufficiently far from other bodies; we know that it is sufficiently far from other bodies only by the fact that it moves without acceleration. (1988, p. 58)

Eddington is even more pithy, and sarcastic to boot: "Every body continues in its state of rest or uniform motion in a straight line, except in so far as it doesn't" (1963, p. 124). Isaac Asimov makes the same point and at least insinuates an instrumentalist conclusion:

> The Newtonian principle of inertia ... holds exactly only in an imaginary ideal world in which no interfering forces exist: no friction, no air resistance ...
>
> It would therefore seem that the principle of inertia depends upon a circular argument. We begin by stating that a body will behave in a certain way unless a force is acting on it. Then, whenever it turns out that a body does not behave in that way, we invent a force to account for it.
>
> Such circular argumentation would be bad indeed if we set about trying to prove Newton's first law, but we do not do this. Newton's laws of motion represent assumptions and definitions and are not subject to proof... The principle of inertia has proved extremely useful in the study of physics for nearly three centuries now and has involved physicists in no contradictions. For this reason (and not out of any considerations of "truth") physicists hold on to the laws of motion and will continue to do so. (1993, pp. 25–26)[16]

Yet while the difficulty of proving the principle of inertia should certainly give further pause to anyone who claims that modern physics has refuted the Aristotelian principle of motion, that difficulty hardly *forces* a non-realist interpretation on us. Still, it might seem that the Aristotelian's commitment to natural teleology, and in particular to the idea that a potency

---

16   Cf. Ellis 1965 and Hanson 1965b.

or potential is always a potential *for* some definite actuality or range of actualities, would require a non-realist construal of inertia. Andrew van Melsen writes:

> If the law of inertia, that a local motion never stops of its own account, is true, then the conclusion seems obvious that a motion does not have an "end" in the Aristotelian sense of this term ... [I]t seems that the analysis of motion in terms of potency and act assumes the existence of a definite end of each motion as the natural achievement or perfection of that motion ... [But in] such [inertial] motions there seem to be eternal potency but no act. (1954, p. 174)

And as van Melsen indicates, this might lead some Aristotelians to argue that

> such motions as the law of inertia describes do not exist. The law of inertia is not supposed to speak of real motions, for it assumes the absence of physical forces, which, as a matter of fact, are never absent in reality. Since Aristotle's analysis deals with real motions, the difficulty [of reconciling Aristotle with Newton] does not exist. (Ibid.)

But van Melsen immediately goes on to reject such a non-realist interpretation of inertia, as have other Aristotelians. In van Melsen's view, it is an error to assume in the first place that the Aristotelian's commitment to teleology must lead him to conclude that what moves must come to rest:

> Aristotle himself ... would have referred to the eternal circular movement of heavenly bodies as an instance of ceaseless motion. So it must be possible to apply analysis in terms of potency and act to motions which are endless ...
>
> There may be ... no *final* act which gives the motion its unity, but such a final act is not necessary for motion to possess unity. The process of gradual actualization in a definite direction is sufficient. (1954, p. 175)[17]

---

17 While Aquinas thought the ceaseless motion of the heavenly bodies was due to something external to them, other medieval philosophers regarded it as the result of a natural inclination. See Weisheipl 1985, pp. 43–44.

To be sure, there are other questions that an Aristotelian might raise about the idea of ceaseless motion, as we shall see presently. But in any event, an alternative position is suggested by John Keck, who, while like van Melsen affirming a realist interpretation of inertia, also argues that all natural motion does in fact tend toward a definite state of rest, namely the unity of the thing moving with the larger material world. (2011; cf. Keck 2007). That there is no conflict between these claims can in his view be seen when we recognize that inertia is a *passive* and *incomplete* aspect of an object's motion, which cannot by itself account for the object's actual determinate movement but needs completion by an external agent. (Compare the Aristotelian conception of matter as something which, though a real constituent of things, is essentially passive and incomplete until actualized by form.)

So, an Aristotelian need not deny the reality of inertia, and I think most Aristotelians would not. A mathematical description of nature is not an exhaustive description, but it can capture real features of the world. And that the principle of inertia has been especially fruitful in physics is reason to think that it does capture them. As Thomas McLaughlin writes:

> Because inertia is common to so many different kinds of bodies, the proper principles of many different natures can be neglected for various purposes and nature can be analyzed at a minimal level. That a given inertial body is a pumpkin is irrelevant for some purposes, and this is not only a consequence of the mathematization of nature. Inertia is undoubtedly a thin treatment of nature, but that is not the same as treating a body as if it had no nature nor need it exclude a fuller treatment of a body's nature. Failure to recognize this point may mislead a thinker into maintaining that the principle of inertia denies inherent principles of nature. (2008, p. 259)

In short, just as acceptance of the Newtonian principle of inertia does not entail rejection of the Aristotelian principle of motion, neither need the Aristotelian take an instrumentalist or otherwise anti-realist approach to the Newtonian principle. They can be regarded as describing nature at different but equally real levels.[18]

---

18   For a debate over realism about inertia and related matters conducted from a non-Aristotelian point of view, see Earman and Friedman 1973 and the response in Sklar 1985.

IV. How the principles are in fact related

But what, specifically, does this claim amount to? If the principle of motion and the principle of inertia are not at odds, how exactly are they related?

Whatever else we say in answer to these questions, the Aristotelian will insist that real change of any sort is possible only if the things that change are composites of act and potency. And since no potency can actualize itself, whatever changes is changed by another. In this way the principle of motion, as a basic thesis of the philosophy of nature, is necessarily more fundamental than the principle of inertia—at least if we allow that the latter principle does indeed apply to a world of real change. (More on this caveat presently.) Determining how the principle of motion and the principle of inertia are related, then, has less to do with how we interpret the former principle than with how we interpret the latter. And here there are several possibilities:

IV.1. Inertial motion as change: We have noted that writers like Garrigou-Lagrange object to the idea that inertial motion is a kind of "state." Suppose then that we took that to be merely a loose way of speaking and regarded inertial motion as involving real change, the actualization of potency. As van Melsen describes it:

> The moving body goes continuously from one place to another, say from A towards B, from B towards C, etc. If this body is actually in place A, then it is *not* in place B, but is moving towards B. Therefore, there is a definite potency of being at B. The arrival at B means the actualization of that potency … However, the arrival at B includes the potency of going on to C, etc. In other words, each moment of the motion has a definite tendency towards some further actualization, and it is this which gives the motion its unity. (1954, p. 175)

The question, then, is what actualizes these potencies. Now the very point of the principle of inertia is to deny that the continued uniform rectilinear local motion of an object requires a continuously operative external force of the sort that first accelerated the object; so such forces cannot be what actualize the potencies in question. But could we say that the force which first accelerated the object is itself what actualizes these potencies? For example, suppose a thrown baseball were not acted upon by gravitational or other forces and thus continued its uniform rectilinear motion indefinitely, with the actualization of its potency for being at place B followed by the actualization of its potency for being at place C, followed by the actualization of its potency for being at place D, and so on *ad infinitum*. Could we say that the thrower of the baseball is, in effect, himself the actualizer of all of these potencies?

It might seem that Aquinas could sympathize with such a view, since as we have seen, he regarded the motion of an object to its natural place as having been caused by whatever generated the object. The notion of a natural place is obsolete, but if we substitute for it the notion of *inertial* motion as what is natural to an object, then—again, so it might seem—we could simply reformulate Aquinas's basic idea in terms of inertia. That is, we could say that the inertial motion of an object, which involves an infinite series of actualized potencies with respect to location, is caused by whatever force first accelerated the object (or, to preserve a greater parallelism with Aquinas's view, perhaps by whatever generated the object *together with* whatever accelerated it).

But there is a potential problem with this proposal. Natural motions, as Aquinas understood them, are finite; they end when an object reaches its natural place. Inertial motion is not finite. And while there is no essential difficulty in the notion of a finite cause imparting a finite motion to an object, there does seem to be something fishy about the idea of a finite cause (such as the thrower of a baseball) imparting an *infinite* motion to an object.[19] Furthermore, as noted above, Aquinas also regarded the motion of an object toward its natural place as being caused *instrumentally* by the generator of the object, even though the generator does not remain conjoined to the object. And this seems problematic even when modified in light of the principle of inertia. For how could the inertial motion of the baseball in our example be regarded as caused *instrumentally* by the thrower of the baseball, especially if the ball's motion continues long after the thrower is dead?[20]

So, it is difficult to see how inertial motion, when interpreted as involving real change, could have a *physical* cause. But as we implied above, even if it lacks a physical cause, there is nothing in the principle of inertia that rules out a *metaphysical* cause. Indeed, if inertial motion involves real change, then given the principle of motion together with the absence of a physical cause, such a metaphysical cause is necessary.

---

19 Cf. Garrigou-Lagrange 1939, p. 274.
20 Cf. Joyce 1924, p. 98: "What is no longer existing cannot be actually operative."

Of course, that raises the question of what exactly this metaphysical cause is. One suggestion would be that it is something *internal* to the object—an "impetus" imparted to it by whatever initiated its inertial motion, and which continuously actualizes its potencies with respect to spatial location.[21] But as Joyce notes, there are serious problems with the impetus theory (1924, pp. 98–99). For one thing, a finite object (such as the baseball of our example) can only have finite qualities. And yet an impetus, in order to have local motion *ad infinitum* as its effect, would at least in that respect be an infinite quality. In other respects it would be finite (it would, for example, be limited in its efficacy to the object of which it is a quality) but that leads us to a second problem. For an impetus would continually be bringing about new effects and thus (as a finite cause) itself be undergoing change; and in that case we have only pushed the problem back a stage, for we now need to ask what causes these changes in the impetus itself.

If inertial motion involves real change, then, only a metaphysical cause *external* to the moving object could be the ultimate source. Now, we already have a model for such a cause in the Aristotelian tradition. For the motions of celestial bodies were in that tradition regarded as unending, just as inertial motion is (barring interference from outside forces) unending; and while this view was associated with a mistaken astronomy, a metaphysical kernel can arguably be extracted from the obsolete scientific husk. The causes of celestial motion in this earlier Aristotelian tradition were, of course, intelligent or angelic substances. Such substances are regarded as *necessary* beings of a sort, even if their necessity is ultimately derived from God.[22] What makes them necessary is that they have no natural tendency toward corruption the way material things do (even if God could annihilate them if He so willed). Given this necessity, such substances have an unending existence proportioned to the unending character of the celestial motions they were taken to explain. And while it turns out that celestial objects do not as such move in an unending way, *inertial* motion (including that of celestial bodies, but that of all other objects as well) *is* unending. Hence the only possible cause of inertial motion—again, at least *if* it is considered to involve real change—might seem to be a necessarily existing intelligent substance or substances, of the sort the earlier Aristotelian tradition thought moved

---

21 The impetus theory is associated historically with Buridan. Garrigou-Lagrange is one recent advocate.

22 For the reasons why, see Aquinas's Third Way, which I discuss and defend at pp. 90–99 of Feser 2009.

celestial objects. (Unless it is simply God Himself causing it *directly* as Unmoved Mover.[23])

IV.2. Inertial motion as stasis: Needless to say, that would for most contemporary readers seem a pretty exotic metaphysics. But alternatively, of course, we could take seriously the idea that inertial motion is a state, involving no real change and thus no actualization of potency. In this case, the question of how the principle of motion and the principle of inertia relate to one another does not even arise, for there just *is* no motion in the relevant, Aristotelian sense going on in the first place when all an object is doing is "moving" inertially in the Newtonian sense. To be sure, *acceleration* would in this case involve motion in the Aristotelian sense, but as we have seen, since Newtonian physics itself requires a cause for accelerated motion, there isn't even a prima facie conflict with the Aristotelian principle of motion.

Now some defenders of the Aristotelian argument from motion for the existence of God as Unmoved Mover of the world have suggested that precisely for this reason, the principle of inertia really poses no challenge at all to that argument. As long as the Newtonian admits that acceleration involves real change, that will suffice for an argument which, given the principle of motion, leads inexorably to an Unmoved Mover. The other three kinds of change (qualitative, quantitative, and substantial) will also serve well enough for the argument. Newton will have eliminated real change in one area (inertial motion) but not in the others.

But things are a bit more complicated than that. For the tendency of the mechanical picture of the world, of which Newtonian physics is a chief component, has been to try to reduce the other kinds of change to local motion. Qualitative, quantitative, and substantial changes are all, on this view, "really" just a matter of (say) the local motions of basic particles, and any appearance to the contrary is just that—mere appearance, a feature of our subjective, conscious representation of the external world but not of that world as it exists objectively, apart from us. Local motion, in turn, is on this picture then taken to be eternal and thus in no need of any explanation in terms of a first mover—or at least it is so taken by the atheistic successors of Newton (who did not himself go in this atheistic direction[24]).

---

23 Cf. Wallace 1956, p. 184. Though it might be objected that to regard God as the immediate cause of inertial motion goes too far in the direction of occasionalism.

24 Indeed, Newton did not so much reject the argument from motion to the existence

The details of this kind of story have gotten increasingly complicated since the Greek atomists first introduced it, but the basic idea is clear enough. Yet the story is insufficient to eliminate *all* possible starting points for an Aristotelian argument from motion to an Unmoved Mover, as long as local motion is admitted in *some* respect or other to involve real change. As serious students of the argument know, what matters in reasoning to an Unmoved Mover is not whether motion had a beginning in time, but what *keeps motion going* (even if has been going on perpetually).[25] But that brings us at last to another view of motion, inertial and otherwise, associated with modern science.

IV.3. The world as stasis: To some, bothering with the question of how the Aristotelian principle of motion relates to the Newtonian principle of inertia might seem quaint. For it might be thought that the controversy has, for the Newtonian no less than for the Aristotelian, been made moot by Einstein, or at least the construction Hermann Minkowski famously put on relativity theory. As Michael Lockwood sums up a common view:

> To take the space-time view seriously is indeed to regard everything that ever exists, or ever happens, at any time or place, as being just as real as the contents of the here and now. And this rules out any conception of free will that pictures human agents, through their choices, as selectively conferring actuality on what are initially only potentialities. Contrary to this common-sense conception, the world according to Minkowski is, at all times and places, actuality through and through: a four-dimensional *block universe*. (2005, pp. 68–69)

Leave aside the question of free will, with which we are not concerned here. What is relevant is Lockwood's point that on the Minkowskian interpretation of relativity, there is in the natural order no real actualization of potency or potentiality; everything in the world, whether "past," "present," or "future," is all "already" actual, as it were. Thus there is no genuine *change* in the world—not even the sort Newtonian physics would allow occurs with the acceleration of an object. As Hermann Weyl put it:

of God as transform it in light of his new conception of motion. For a comparison of Aristotelian, Newtonian, and other conceptions of the relationship between motion and God, see Buckley 1971.

25   I discuss and defend the argument from motion for God's existence at pp. 65–81 of Feser 2009.

> The objective world simply *is*, it does not *happen*. Only to the gaze of my consciousness … does a section of this world come to life as a fleeting image in space which continuously changes in time. (1949, p. 116)

Thus, as Karl Popper (1998) noted, does Einstein recapitulate Parmenides.

Now, I don't myself believe for a moment that modern physics really *has* shown that there is no genuine change in the physical world. But supposing for the sake of argument that it has, even that would not show that the Aristotelian principle of motion has no application, for two reasons. First, what we have in this case is another instance of the strategy we saw Smolin describe earlier, wherein science attempts to unify phenomena by relativizing the apparent differences between them to the observer. But the observer himself—the "the gaze of [his] consciousness," as Weyl would put it—remains. And as Popper pointed out, there is no getting around the fact that change really occurs *at least within consciousness itself*. Nor could we appeal to the Minkowskian view to justify an eliminativist line on consciousness, since it is conscious experience which provides the empirical evidential basis of the theory in whose name we would be denying it![26]

Hence if Einstein is Parmenides *redevivus*, his position faces the same incoherence the Eleatic philosophers did, at least *if* the Minkowskian interpretation is correct and *if* we want to say that the conscious subject is a *part* of a natural world that is purportedly free of change. Alternatively, we could adopt a dualist view according to which the conscious subject is *not* a part of that world. That will save the Minkowskian view from incoherence, but at the cost of merely relocating change rather than eliminating it. (And also, of course, at the cost of leaving us with the problem of explaining how the conscious subject *is* related to the natural world if it is not part of it.)

A second point is that unlike Parmenides' own block universe, the block universe of Minkowski is supposed to be governed by laws that are

---

26 As Erwin Schrödinger emphasized, there is a paradoxical tendency in modern science in general to leave out of its picture of the world the very sense perceptions that led to that picture. See Schrödinger 1956 and chapter 6 of Schrödinger 1992. This removal of sensory qualities from the material world and relocation of them into the mind—which was a key part of the anti-Aristotelian revolution inaugurated by Galileo, Descartes, Newton, and Co.—is the origin of the "qualia problem" that has so bedeviled contemporary materialists, who generally seem unaware that the problem derives, not from some irrational urge to resist materialist reductionism and the advances of science, but rather from the very conception of matter and of scientific method to which they are committed.

contingent. [27] And if they are contingent, then, the Aristotelian will argue, they are merely potential until actualized. That means that even if there were no real change or actualization of potency *within* an Einsteinian four-dimensional block universe, the sheer existence of that universe as a whole *would* involve the actualization of potency and thus (given the principle of motion) an actualizer or "mover" distinct from the world itself.

V. The mythology of inertia

It seems, then, that we simply cannot avoid the existence of change, and thus the actualization of potency, and thus the principle of motion. The most we can do is move them around like the pea in a shell game, producing thereby the *illusion* that we have eliminated them. The notion that they have been largely or completely abolished by modern physics is therefore a myth—part of what we might call "the mythology of inertia," to borrow a phrase from David Braine (1988, p. 14).[28]

That the world is inherently "inert" or changeless is only part of the myth, however. The other part of the myth is the idea that "physical laws," such as the law of inertia, suffice all by themselves to explain what philosophers traditionally took to be in need of a *metaphysical* explanation. Braine cites some remarks from Wittgenstein in the *Tractatus*:

> The whole modern conception of the world is founded on the illusion that the so-called laws of nature are the explanations of natural phenomena.
>
> Thus people today stop at the laws of nature, treating them as something inviolable, just as God and Fate were treated in past ages. (Wittgenstein 1961, sec. 6.371 and 6.372)

The supposition that "the so-called laws of nature are the explanations of natural phenomena" is, for the Aristotelian, an "illusion" for two reasons (which do not necessarily correspond to Wittgenstein's reasons). First, "laws of nature" are mere abstractions and thus cannot by themselves explain

---

27 But see the qualification in note 29.

28 Alfred North Whitehead attributes to the principle of inertia a quasi-religious status, characterizing it as "the first article of the creed of science; and like the Church's creeds it is more than a mere statement of belief: it is a paean of triumph over defeated heretics. It should be set to music and chanted in the halls of Universities" (1948, p. 171).

anything. What exist in the natural order are concrete material substances with certain essences, and talk of "laws of nature" is merely shorthand for the patterns of behavior they tend to exhibit given those essences. As David Oderberg puts it, *"the laws of nature are the laws of natures,"* i.e., of the natures or essences of the things that behave in accordance with the laws (2007, p. 144).[29] This is as true of the law of inertia as it is of any other law.[30]

Second, that some fundamental material substances (basic particles, say) exist and behave in accordance with such laws can also never be the ultimate explanation of anything, because we need to know, not only how such substances came into existence, but what keeps them in existence. For as compounds of act and potency, they cannot possibly account for themselves, but require something outside them to actualize them at every moment. Or so the Thomist will argue.[31]

So, neither the Newtonian principle of inertia, nor the existence of material substances which behave in accordance with that principle, nor the Minkowskian interpretation of Einstein either undermine the Aristotelian principle of motion or obviate the need to explain the existence and operation of material substances in accordance with the latter principle. Physics provides genuine explanations, but not complete or ultimate explanations. Only metaphysics can do that.[32]

References

Aristotle. 1930. *Physics*, trans. R. P. Hardie and R. K. Gaye. (Oxford: Clarendon Press).

Aquinas, Thomas. 1952. *On the Power of God*, trans. English Dominican Fathers (Westminster, MD: The Newman Press).

29 For this reason, laws of nature are, as Oderberg explains, *not* contingent—they describe the ways things *necessarily* behave or at least tend to behave, given their natures—but they can be said to be contingent in a loose sense insofar as the *existence* of the things that behave in accordance with the laws is contingent.

30 See McLaughlin 2008 for a useful analysis of the law of inertia as a description of how material bodies will tend to behave given their natures, in the Aristotelian sense of "natures."

31 For a defense of this claim, and of the further claim that what actualizes them can only be God, see Feser 2011.

32 For comments on an earlier version of this paper, I thank Michael Rota and audience members at the Society for Medieval Logic and Metaphysics session at the 2011 American Catholic Philosophical Association meeting in St. Louis, Missouri.

Aquinas, Thomas. 1964. *Exposition of Aristotle's Treatise On the Heavens*, trans. Fabian R. Larcher and Pierre H. Conway (Columbus: College of St. Mary of the Springs).

Ashley, Benedict. 2006. *The Way toward Wisdom* (Notre Dame, IN: University of Notre Dame Press).

Asimov, Isaac. 1993. *Understanding Physics: 3 Volumes in 1* (New York: Barnes and Noble Books).

Augros, Michael. 2007. "Ten Objections to the *Prima Via*," *Peripatetikos* 6: 59–101.

Braine, David. 1988. *The Reality of Time and the Existence of God* (Oxford: Clarendon Press).

Buckley, Michael J. 1971. *Motion and Motion's God* (Princeton: Princeton University Press).

DeWitt, Richard. 2004. *Worldviews: An Introduction to the History and Philosophy of Science* (Oxford: Blackwell).

Earman, J. and M. Friedman. 1973. "The Meaning and Status of Newton's Law of Inertia and the Nature of Gravitational Forces," *Philosophy of Science* 40: 329–59.

Eddington, Arthur. 1963. *The Nature of the Physical World* (Ann Arbor: The University of Michigan Press).

Einstein, Albert. 1988. *The Meaning of Relativity*, Fifth edition (Princeton, NJ: Princeton University Press).

Ellis, Brian. 1965. "The Origin and Nature of Newton's Laws of Motion." In Robert G. Colodny, ed., *Beyond the Edge of Certainty: Essays in Contemporary Science and Philosophy* (Englewood Cliffs, NJ: Prentice-Hall).

Ellis, Brian. 2002. *The Philosophy of Nature: A Guide to the New Essentialism* (Chesham: Acumen).

Feser, Edward. 2009. *Aquinas* (Oxford: Oneworld Publications).

Feser, Edward. 2011. "Existential Inertia and the Five Ways," *American Catholic Philosophical Quarterly*, Vol. 85, No. 2.

Garrigou-Lagrange, Reginald. 1939. *God: His Existence and His Nature*, Volume I (London: B. Herder).

Hanson, Norwood Russell. 1963. "The Law of Inertia: A Philosopher's Touchstone," *Philosophy of Science* 30: 107–21.

Hanson, Norwood Russell. 1965a. "Newton's First Law: A Philosopher's Door into Natural Philosophy." In Robert G. Colodny, ed., *Beyond the Edge of Certainty: Essays in Contemporary Science and Philosophy* (Englewood Cliffs, NJ: Prentice-Hall).

Hanson, Norwood Russell. 1965b. "A Response to Ellis's Conception of Newton's First Law." In Robert G. Colodny, ed., *Beyond the Edge of Certainty: Essays in Contemporary Science and Philosophy* (Englewood Cliffs, NJ: Prentice-Hall).

Joyce, George Hayward. 1924. *Principles of Natural Theology*, Second edition (London: Longmans, Green and Co.).

Keck, John W. 2007. "The Natural Motion of Matter in Newtonian and Post-Newtonian Physics," *The Thomist* 71: 529–54.

Keck, John W. 2011. "The Messiness of Matter and the Problem of Inertia." Paper presented at the Society for Aristotelian Studies Meeting, June 17, 2011, Santa Paula, California.

Kenny, Anthony. 1969. *The Five Ways: St. Thomas Aquinas' Proofs of God's Existence* (London: Routledge and Kegan Paul).

Koren, Henry J. 1962. *An Introduction to the Philosophy of Nature* (Pittsburgh: Duquesne University Press).

Lockwood, Michael. 2005. *The Labyrinth of Time* (Oxford: Oxford University Press).

McLaughlin, Thomas. 2004. "Local Motion and the Principle of Inertia: Aquinas, Newtonian Physics, and Relativity," *International Philosophical Quarterly*, Vo. 44, No. 1.

McLaughlin, Thomas J. 2008. "Nature and Inertia," *Review of Metaphysics*, Vol. 62, No. 2.

Moreno, Antonio. 1974. "The Law of Inertia and the Principle '*Quidquid movetur ab alio movetur*,'" *The Thomist*, Vol. 38.

Oderberg, David S. 2007. *Real Essentialism* (London: Routledge).

Popper, Karl. 1998. "Beyond the Search for Invariants." In Karl Popper, *The World of Parmenides* (London: Routledge).

Russell, Bertrand. 1985. *My Philosophical Development* (London: Unwin Paperbacks).

Sachs, Joe. 1995. *Aristotle's* Physics: *A Guided Study* (New Brunswick: Rutgers University Press).

Schrödinger, Erwin. 1956. "On the Peculiarity of the Scientific World-View." In Erwin Schrödinger, *What is Life? and Other Scientific Essays* (New York: Doubleday).

Schrödinger, Erwin. 1992. "Mind and Matter." In Erwin Schrödinger, *What is Life? with Mind and Matter and Autobiographical Sketches* (Cambridge: Cambridge University Press).

Simon, Yves R. 2001. *The Great Dialogue of Nature and Space* (South Bend, Indiana: St. Augustine's Press).

Sklar, Lawrence. 1985. "Inertia, Gravitation, and Metaphysics." In Lawrence Sklar, *Philosophy and Spacetime Physics* (Berkeley and Los Angles: University of California Press).

Smolin, Lee. 2007. *The Trouble with Physics* (New York: Mariner Books).

Van Melsen, Andrew G. 1954. *The Philosophy of Nature*, Second edition (Pittsburgh: Duquesne University).

Wallace, W. A. 1956. "Newtonian Antinomies Against the *Prima Via*," *The Thomist* 19: 151–92.

Wallace, William A. 1983. "Cosmological Arguments and Scientific Concepts." In William A. Wallace, *From a Realist Point of View: Essays on the Philosophy of Science*, Second edition (Lanham, MD: University Press of America).

Weisheipl, James A. 1985. *Nature and Motion in the Middle Ages*, ed. William E. Carroll (Washington, D.C.: Catholic University of America Press).

Weyl, Hermann. 1949. *Philosophy of Mathematics and Natural Science* (Princeton: Princeton University Press).

Whitehead, Alfred North. 1948. *Essays in Science and Philosophy* (New York: Philosophical Library).

Wippel, John F. 2000. *The Metaphysical Thought of Thomas Aquinas* (Washington, D.C.: Catholic University of America Press).

Wittgenstein, Ludwig. 1961. *Tractatus Logico-Philosophicus,* trans. D. F. Pears and B. F. McGuinness (London: Routledge and Kegan Paul).

2
Teleology: A Shopper's Guide

I. Introduction

The *telos* of a thing or process is the end or goal toward which it points. Teleological notions feature prominently in current debates in philosophy of biology, philosophy of action, philosophy of mind, and philosophy of religion. Naturalists generally hold that teleological descriptions of natural phenomena are either false or, if true, are reducible to descriptions cast in non-teleological terms. Non-naturalists generally hold that at least some natural phenomena exhibit irreducible teleology. For example, Intelligent Design (ID) theorists hold that certain biological phenomena cannot properly be understood except as the products of an intelligence which designed them to carry out certain functions.

Teleology's controversial status in modern philosophy stems from the mechanistic conception of the natural world, which early modern thinkers like Bacon, Galileo, Descartes, Hobbes, Boyle, and Locke put in place of the Aristotelian philosophy of nature that featured in medieval Scholasticism. Following Aristotle, the Scholastics took the view that a complete understanding of a material substance required identifying each of its "four causes." Every such substance is, first of all, an irreducible composite of *substantial form* and *prime matter* (irreducible because on the Scholastic view, substantial form and prime matter cannot themselves be understood apart from the substances they compose, making the analysis holistic rather than reductionist). The substantial form of a thing is its nature or essence, the underlying metaphysical basis of its properties and causal powers; it constitutes a thing's *formal cause*. Prime matter is the otherwise formless stuff that takes on a substantial form so as to instantiate it in a concrete object, and apart from which the form would be a mere abstraction; it constitutes a thing's *material cause*. That which brings a thing into existence constitutes its *efficient cause.* And the end or goal towards which a thing naturally points is its *final cause.*[1]

As the last sentence indicates, the notion of a final cause is closely tied to that of a *telos* and thus to the notion of teleology. But the adverb "naturally" is meant to indicate how the Aristotelian notion of final cause differs from other conceptions of teleology. For Aristotle and for the Scholastics, the end or goal of a material substance is *inherent* to it, something it has precisely because of the kind of thing it is by *nature*. It is therefore not to be understood on the model of a human artifact like a watch, whose parts have no inherent tendency to perform the function of telling time, specifically, and must be forced to do so by an outside designer. For example, that a heart has the function of pumping blood is something true of it simply by virtue of being the kind of material substance it is, and would remain true of it whether or not it has God as its ultimate cause.

The thinkers who founded modern philosophy and modern science rejected this picture of nature. In particular, they rejected the notions of substantial form, of matter as that which takes on such a form, and of a final cause as an *inherent* end or *telos* of a thing. Of Aristotle's four causes, only efficient cause was left in anything like a recognizable form (and even then the notion was significantly altered, since, as we shall see, efficient causes were regarded by the Scholastics as correlated with final causes).[2] Material objects were reconceived as comprised entirely of microscopic particles (understood along either atomistic, corpuscularian, or plenum-theoretic lines) devoid of any inherent goal-directedness and interacting in terms of "push-pull" contact causation alone. This "mechanical philosophy" underwent various transformations as modern philosophy and modern science developed. The philosophical inadequacy of the contact model of causal interaction soon became evident in light of the critiques of occasionalists, Humeans, and others; and in any event, the model could not survive the empirical

---

1   For a brief exposition and defense of Aristotelian-Scholastic metaphysics and philosophy of nature, see chapter 2 of my *Aquinas* (Oxford: Oneworld Publications, 2009). For a more detailed exposition and defense, see my *The Last Superstition: A Refutation of the New Atheism* (South Bend: St. Augustine's Press, 2008). The most thorough recent defense of Aristotelian-Scholastic metaphysics is David S. Oderberg, *Real Essentialism* (London: Routledge, 2007).

2   See Kenneth Clatterbaugh, *The Causation Debate in Modern Philosophy 1637–1739* (London: Routledge, 1999) for a useful overview of the history of the early moderns' gradual transformation of the notion of efficient cause.

difficulties posed for it by Newtonian gravitation, electromagnetism, and quantum mechanics. But what has clearly survived the anti-Aristotelian "mechanistic" revolution to the present day is the rejection of teleology as an inherent feature of the natural order. As philosopher of science David Hull has written:

> Mechanism in its extreme form is clearly false because numer- ous physical phenomena of the most ordinary sort cannot be ex- plained entirely in terms of masses in motion. Mechanics is only one small part of physics. Historically, explanations were des- ignated as mechanistic to indicate that they included no refer- ence to final causes or vital forces. In this weak sense, all present-day scientific explanations are mechanistic.[3]

Modern philosophers have almost universally embraced this concep- tion of scientific explanation. They have disagreed about whether an ap- peal to irreducible teleology conceived of as something *extrinsic* to the material world ought to supplement the mechanistic explanations of em- pirical science. Contemporary naturalists deny that any such appeal can be justified. By contrast, early modern thinkers like Boyle and Newton regarded an appeal to extrinsic teleology—in particular, to God's inten- tions and activity as artificer of the natural world—as an essential cap- stone to the edifice of science.[4] William Paley's design argument gave this line of thought its most fully developed and influential articulation. As we will see in a later section, the arguments of contemporary ID theorists like William Dembski, though differing from the arguments of Boyle, Newton, and Paley in various particulars, carry on their appeal to teleology as something extrinsic to the material world, and allow that at least much of the natural order is in principle non-teleological. Where these thinkers all agree with each other and with their naturalistic opponents is in rejecting

---

3   *The Cambridge Dictionary of Philosophy*, s.v. "mechanistic explanation." Cf. William Hasker, *The Emergent Self* (Ithaca: Cornell University Press, 1999), pp. 59–64.

4   For an account of the transition from an intrinsic to an extrinsic conception of tele- ology among such early modern thinkers and its effect on natural theology, see Mar- garet J. Osler, "From Immanent Natures to Nature as Artifice: The Reinterpretation of Final Causes in Seventeenth-Century Natural Philosophy," *The Monist* 79 (1996): 388–407. Cf. William B. Ashworth, Jr., "Christianity and the Mechanistic Uni- verse," in David C. Lindberg and Ronald L. Numbers, eds., *When Science and Christianity Meet* (Chicago: University of Chicago Press, 2003).

the Aristotelian-Scholastic conception of final causes as *inherent* in material substances.

Among contemporary writers, it is primarily Thomists, and especially those who regard Thomism as essentially building on Aristotelianism, who reject mechanism as defined above and endorse a return to something like the Scholastics' philosophy of nature, its application suitably modified in light of the empirical findings of modern science. Aristotelico-Thomistic (A-T) arguments for irreducible teleology, and for the existence of God as the ultimate explanation of the reality of such teleology (such as Aquinas's Fifth Way), thus differ significantly from Paleyan design arguments and the arguments of contemporary ID theory.

Unfortunately, this history and the conceptual nuances reflected in it (only some of which we have touched on so far) seem to have been forgotten in many contemporary philosophical discussions of teleology. Consequently, partisans on either side of various debates within philosophy of biology, philosophy of mind, philosophy of religion, and other philosophical sub-disciplines often talk past one another, or either affirm or reject the existence of irreducible teleology on the basis of arguments that may in fact be relevant only to some conceptions of teleology and not to others.

In the sections that follow, I aim to provide a "shopper's guide" of sorts for philosophers interested in questions about teleology, in the course of which I will expand upon some of the historical and conceptual themes already alluded to. Specifically, I will show in section II that the question of whether teleology exists in nature is not susceptible of a simple "yes or no" answer, but that there are in fact five main positions that can and have been taken on the issue. In section III I will show that there are also at least five levels of nature at which irreducible teleology might be claimed to exist, so that to establish that it exists or does not exist at one of them does not suffice to determine whether it exists at the others. With at least five levels of nature at which teleology might be said to exist, and five possible ways in which to conceive of teleology at any of these levels, the conceptual lay of the land can be seen to be complex indeed. Finally, in part IV I will address the implications of these conceptual distinctions for the debate over teleological arguments for the existence of God. In particular, I will explain how the approach taken by philosophers committed to A-T metaphysics differs radically from that taken by ID theorists and defenders of Paley-style design arguments. In the process I hope to shed light on a phenomenon that many ID theorists seem to find puzzling, viz. that Thomists, who would seem to be their natural allies in the dispute with naturalism, are typically very critical of ID. As we will see, this state of affairs has less to do with disagreements about the merits of Darwinian evolutionary biology (though it does sometimes have something to do with that) than it has to do with disagreements over basic metaphysics—disagreements which, for the A-T metaphysician, show that the ID theorist is (surprising as this might seem) philosophically closer to the Darwinian naturalist than to A-T.

In the interests of full disclosure, I should note that my own sympathies are with the A-T position. But the point of what follows is not to defend that position, but only to provide a roadmap to the debate over teleology in the various branches of philosophy I've mentioned. There is nothing in the classification that I will propose that could not in principle be accepted by any philosopher, whichever position he happens to take on these issues.

II. Five approaches to teleology

As happens, the five main approaches to teleology parallel the five main approaches that have, historically, been taken to the problem of universals—nominalism, conceptualism, and three varieties of realism. Indeed, as we will see, there are several ways in which the problem of universals and the problem of teleology are intertwined. So it will be useful briefly to summarize the main approaches to the former problem before discussing the latter.

They are as follows: *Realism* affirms that universals—triangularity, "catness," humanness, etc.—are irreducible to their particular instances and exist in a way that is in some sense independent of the human mind. *Nominalism* denies that there are any true universals and insists that only particulars are real—there is this triangle and that one, this cat and that one, but no such thing as "triangularity" or "catness" over and above them. *Conceptualism* can be thought of as a kind of middle-ground position, and holds that universals exist, but only in the mind—"triangularity," "catness," and the like are the products of abstraction, and correspond to nothing in the world of external objects, all of which are particular.

Realism in turn takes three different forms. *Platonic realism* (sometimes called "extreme realism") holds that universals exist in a "third realm" distinct from the world of particular things and distinct from the human mind. *Aristotelian realism* (sometimes called "moderate realism") rejects the "third realm" approach, and regards universals as existing only in the particular things that instantiate them and in the intellect that abstracts them from the particulars. It differs from nominalism in regarding universals as irreducible to their instances, and from conceptualism in regarding the products of abstraction as grounded in the particulars themselves and not a sheer invention of the mind—triangularity corresponds to something really there in actual triangles (waiting to be abstracted, as it were). Finally, *Scholastic realism*—the position developed by medieval writers like Aquinas as a way of harmonizing Aristotelian realism with Augustine's brand of Platonism—holds that while universals do indeed exist only in either their particular instances or in intellects, they nevertheless do not depend entirely on particulars or on *finite* intellects for their being insofar as they exist eternally in the infinite *divine* intellect, as the archetypes according to which God creates the world.[5]

Now let us turn to the five corresponding approaches to teleology. *Teleological realism* affirms that teleology is a real and irreducible feature of the natural world, paralleling the realist view that universals are real and irreducible to particulars. Parallel to nominalism is what (following Christopher Shields) we might call *teleological eliminativism*, the view that there is no genuine teleology at all in the natural world. Shields cites ancient atomists like Democritus and Leucippus as representatives of this view, and it seems to be held by at least many contemporary adherents to the modern anti-teleological mechanistic conception of nature described in part I above.[6] Many, but not all. For other contemporary writers whose views are broadly mechanistic would seem more appropriately described as committed to *teleological reductionism*, the view that there is a sense in which teleology exists in nature, but that it is entirely reducible to non-teleological phenomena. For example, philosophers of biology who hold that the function of a biological structure can be analyzed in terms of the reasons why that structure

---

5   For a useful recent introduction to the problem of universals, see J. P. Moreland, *Universals* (Montreal and Kingston: McGill-Queen's University Press, 2001). Unfortunately, contemporary discussions of the issue tend to pay little or no attention to the position I've labeled "Scholastic realism." For a recent exposition and defense, see John Peterson, *Introduction to Scholastic Realism* (New York: Peter Lang, 1999). Cf. pp. 39–49 and 90–91 of *The Last Superstition*.

6   Christopher Shields, *Aristotle* (London: Routledge, 2007), p. 90. Andre Ariew labels this view "materialism," but Shields's label seems more appropriate given that it is (as we will see presently) possible to be a materialist while being a reductionist rather than an eliminativist about teleology. See Ariew's articles "Platonic and Aristotelian Roots of Teleological Arguments," in Andre Ariew, Robert Cummins, and Mark Perlman, eds., *Functions: New Essays in the Philosophy of Psychology and Biology* (Oxford: Oxford University Press, 2002) and "Teleology," in David L. Hull and Michael Ruse, eds., *The Cambridge Companion to the Philosophy of Biology* (New York: Cambridge University Press, 2007).

was favored by natural selection would seem to be taking a reductionist rather than eliminativist position.[7] Since conceptualism can be thought of as a reductionist view—universals are real, but contrary to the realist they are really "nothing but" ideas abstracted by the mind—we can regard teleological reductionism as the approach to teleology that parallels the conceptualist view of universals.[8]

Kant's approach to teleology in the *Critique of Judgment* is an interesting case. It might be interpreted as another possible kind of teleological reductionism, and one with even more obvious parallels to conceptualism insofar as Kant regarded teleological analysis as a regulative principle the mind brings to bear on its explanation of biological phenomena. On the other hand, if it is merely a regulative principle, with no objective validity, Kant's position might instead be interpreted as a kind of eliminativism.[9] But since what Kant denied was not that the notion of teleology has objective validity but rather that we can *know* that it does, it might be best to interpret him as taking the agnostic position that some version of teleological realism, reductionism, or eliminativism is true, but we can never know which.

Of greater interest for our purposes, though, is the fact that teleological realism might be spelled out in ways that correspond to each of the three varieties of realism about universals. Christopher Shields and Andre Ariew have recently emphasized the distinction between the first two of these ways.[10] *Platonic teleological realism* holds that the irreducible teleology manifest in nature is extrinsic, entirely derivative from an outside source.[11] Natural phenomena *as such* are not teleological, but they have been ordered to certain ends by (say) a divine mind. Shields cites Anaxagoras as an

7   For the debate over "naturalistic" analyses of biological functions, see David J. Buller, ed., *Function, Selection, and Design* (Albany: State University of New York Press, 1999).

8   Strictly speaking, then, conceptualism would be a species of a more general approach to universals we might call *reductionism*, where other possible varieties of reductionism would include (for example) the view that universals are reducible to the totality of their instances. But since the standard classification of approaches to the problem of universals as "realism, nominalism, and conceptualism" is so well established, I have opted to follow tradition rather than introduce a novel (but arguably more precise) "realism, nominalism, and reductionism" classification.

9   Such a reading might also be called "instrumentalist," but since a useful fiction is still a fiction, such an instrumentalism would still seem nothing more than a riff on eliminativism rather than a separate view.

10   See Shields, *Aristotle*, pp. 68–90 and the two articles by Ariew cited above.

11   Shields labels this view "teleological intentionalism," and Ariew calls it "Platonic teleologism."

ancient representative of this view; Ariew cites Plato (given the demiurge of the *Timaeus*), Newton, and William Paley. *Aristotelian teleological realism* holds that teleology or final causality is intrinsic to natural substances, and does not derive from any divine source. Aristotle did of course believe in a divine Unmoved Mover. But he thought that the existence of the Unmoved Mover followed from the fact of motion or change, not from the existence of final causes, which he regarded instead as simply a basic fact about the world. The acorn points beyond itself to the oak—not because it was *made* that way, but because it just *is* that way by nature, simply by virtue of being an acorn.[12] It does not do this consciously, of course, since acorns are totally unconscious. The whole point of the Aristotelian view is to insist that goal-directedness does not require a mind which consciously intends the goal. Hence, *pace* many adherents of the Platonic approach to teleology, there is on the Aristotelian view no necessary connection between teleology and theism.

What Shields and Ariew overlook is that there is a middle-ground position between the Platonic and Aristotelian views, which we might call *Scholastic teleological realism*; and it corresponds quite neatly to the Scholastic middle ground position between Platonic and Aristotelian approaches to the problem of universals. On this view, represented most prominently by Aquinas's Fifth Way, final causes are indeed immanent within or intrinsic to natural substances, just as the Aristotelian claims they are. The acorn can be known to be "directed at" the oak entirely independently of the question of God's existence, and theism can in practice be "bracketed off" from the study of final causes as such. All the same, for the Scholastic teleological realist, the existence of final causes must *ultimately* be explained in terms of the divine intellect. The difference from the Platonic approach is that the Scholastic view does not take the existence of a divine ordering intelligence to follow *directly* from the existence of teleology in nature. An intermediate step in argumentation is required, for the link between teleology and an ordering intelligence is (with a nod to Aristotle) not taken to be *obvious*. This is one reason why (as we shall see) the Fifth Way differs from the strategy taken by Paley and by contemporary ID theorists.

Note the parallels with the three versions of realism about the problem of universals. For Platonic realism about universals, the universal essence *acorn*

---

12 See Monte Ransome Johnson, *Aristotle on Teleology* (Oxford: Oxford University Press, 2005), for a recent book-length treatment of Aristotelian teleological realism.

exists entirely apart from particular acorns and from the finite minds that grasp this universal, in a "third realm"; for Platonic teleological realism, the end or goal of an acorn exists entirely apart from it, in (say) a divine mind which orders it to its end. For Aristotelian realism about universals, the universal essence *acorn* exists only in particular acorns themselves and in the finite minds that abstract it; for Aristotelian teleological realism, the end or goal of an acorn exists only intrinsic to the acorn itself. For Scholastic realism about universals, the universal essence *acorn* exists in the particular acorns themselves and in the finite minds that abstract it, but it also pre-exists in the divine intellect as the archetype according to which God creates acorns; for Scholastic teleological realism, the end or goal of an acorn exists intrinsic to the acorn itself, but only because God created it according to the pre-existing essence in question, which includes having the generation of an oak as an end or goal.

To summarize the five main approaches to teleology: *Teleological eliminativism* denies that there is any teleology at all in the natural world. *Teleological reductionism* allows that there is, but holds that it can be reduced to non-teleological phenomena. *Platonic teleological realism* holds that there is irreducible teleology in the natural world but only in the sense that an external ordering intellect orders things to certain ends. *Aristotelian teleological realism* holds that there is irreducible teleology in the natural world and that it is immanent, existing in things simply by virtue of their natures and in no way dependent on an ordering intelligence. *Scholastic teleological realism* holds that there is irreducible teleology in the natural world and that it is immanent to things given their natures, but also that the fact that they exist with natures directing them to those ends cannot itself ultimately be made sense of apart from a divine ordering intelligence.

III. Levels of teleology

We will have more to say about what motivates the Scholastic position. But before doing so, it will be useful to identify the five levels of the natural world at which teleology might be held to exist. In philosophical discussions of teleology, biological examples have tended to dominate, certainly in modern philosophy and to some extent even in Aristotle. Indeed, it is often assumed that to attribute teleology to some natural phenomenon is to attribute to it a function of the kind a biological organ serves, or perhaps of the kind a human artifact serves. But this is a mistake. For many teleological realists—in particular, for the Scholastic teleological realist—biological function is merely one kind of teleology among others.

Biological teleology paradigmatically involves a part serving to realize the good of some whole, in the way the stomach functions to digest food so that the organism as a whole can survive, or the way sexual organs function to enable an organism to reproduce so that the species as a whole will carry on beyond its death. For Scholastic writers, a capacity for this sort of "immanent causation" (to use the Scholastic jargon) *just is* what makes something a living thing. Inanimate phenomena are capable only of "transeunt causation," causation which terminates in an effect outside the cause itself and therefore does not promote the cause's own good. (Living things exhibit transeunt causation as well; the point is that, unlike inanimate things, they are also capable of immanent causation.)[13]

But inanimate phenomena are nevertheless capable of exhibiting a more basic kind of teleology. Indeed, for the Scholastics, even the simplest causal regularity in the order of efficient causes presupposes final causality. If some cause A regularly generates some effect or range of effects B—rather than C, D, or no effect at all—then that can only be because A of its nature is "directed at" or "points to" the generation of B specifically as its inherent end or goal. To oversimplify somewhat, we might say that if A is an efficient cause of B, then B is the final cause of A.[14] If we deny this—in particular, if we deny that a thing by virtue of its nature or essence has causal powers that are directed toward certain specific outcomes as to an end or goal—then (the Scholastic holds) efficient causality becomes unintelligible. Causes and effects become inherently "loose and separate," and there is no reason in principle why any cause might not be followed by any effect whatsoever or none at all. From an A-T point of view, it is precisely the early moderns' rejection of final causes, substantial forms (or inherent essences), and the like that opened the way to Humean puzzles about causation and induction.[15] (Interestingly, there has been a trend in recent analytic

---

13   For discussion, see Feser, *Aquinas*, pp. 132–37 and Oderberg, *Real Essentialism*, pp. 177–183.

14   As Aquinas puts it, "every agent acts for an end: otherwise one thing would not follow more than another from the action of the agent, unless it were by chance" (*Summa Theologiae* I.44.4). By "agent" he means not just thinking beings like us, but anything that brings about an effect.

15   But not only from an A-T point of view. Alfred North Whitehead makes a similar point in *Science and the Modern World* (New York: The Free Press, 1967), arguing that the problem of induction is generated by a mechanistic conception of matter on which for any material particular, "there is no inherent reference to any other times, past or future." (p. 51) Hence, "if the cause in itself discloses no information as to the effect, so that the first invention of it must be *entirely* arbitrary, it follows

metaphysics back toward the idea that material substances have inherent causal powers by virtue of which they exhibit what George Molnar calls a kind of unconscious "physical intentionality," and what David Armstrong calls a "proto-intentionality" or "pointing beyond themselves" to certain outcomes.[16] What such writers do not seem to realize is that they have essentially returned to a Scholastic position.[17])

More complex inanimate causal patterns might also arguably exhibit teleology. A-T philosopher David Oderberg holds that natural cycles like the water cycle and the rock cycle provide clear examples.[18] Consider the water cycle: condensation leads to precipitation, which leads to collection, which leads to evaporation, which leads to condensation, and the cycle begins again. Scientists who study such processes identify each of their stages as playing a certain specific role relative to the others. In particular, each stage has the production of a certain outcome or range of outcomes as the "end" or "goal" toward which it points—the role of condensation is to bring about precipitation, for example. Nor, Oderberg argues, will it do to suggest that the cycle could be adequately described by speaking of each stage as being the efficient cause of certain others, with no reference to its playing a "role" of generating some effect as an "end" or "goal." For each stage has many other effects that are not part of the cycle. Condensation in some area might for all we know cause someone to have arthritic pain in his big toe. But causing arthritic pain is no part of the water cycle. Some causal chains are relevant to the cycle and some are not. Nor is it correct to say that the student of the water cycle just happens to be interested in how water in one form brings about water in another form, and is not interested in arthritis, so that he pays attention to some elements in the overall causal situation rather than others. For the patterns described by scientists studying such

at once that science is impossible, except in the sense of establishing *entirely arbitrary* connections which are not warranted by anything intrinsic to the natures either of causes or effects." (p. 4)

16   See George Molnar, *Powers: A Study in Metaphysics* (Oxford: Oxford University Press, 2003, and D. M. Armstrong, *The Mind-Body Problem* (Boulder, CO: Westview Press, 1999), pp. 138–40.

17   On the other hand, this implicit vindication of Aristotelianism is acknowledged in Nancy Cartwright, "Aristotelian Natures and the Modern Experimental Method," in John Earman, ed., *Inference, Explanation, and Other Frustrations: Essays in the Philosophy of Science* (Berkeley and Los Angeles: University of California Press, 1992).

18   David S. Oderberg, "Teleology: Inorganic and Organic," in Ana Marta Gonzalez, ed., *Contemporary Perspectives on Natural Law* (Aldershot: Ashgate, 2008).

cycles are *objective* patterns in nature, not mere projections of human interests. But the only way to account for this is to recognize that each stage in the process, while it might have various sorts of effects, has only the generation of certain *specific* effects among them as its "end" or "goal" *in the cycle*. In short, it is to recognize such cycles as teleological.

Obviously, many questions might be raised about such arguments, but the point is merely to note that both basic causal regularities and complex inorganic processes provide further examples of arguably teleological natural phenomena, additional to the standard example of biological phenomena. Within biological phenomena too, though, we might distinguish two further possible examples of natural teleology. The "immanent causation" spoken of above is common to all living things, whether plants or animals. But unlike plants, animals are capable of sensation, appetite, and locomotion, viz. movement prompted by appetite in response to what sensation has detected in an animal's environment. All of this entails a kind of goal-seeking—the kind manifest in conscious desires—that goes beyond the mere coordination of parts to the good of the whole that plants also possess. This plausibly indicates a further level of biological teleology, beyond the basic level represented by plants. Furthermore, in human beings, desire is informed by reason; our actions are guided by *thought*, which has a conceptual structure foreign to other animals. Here we have intentionality, and purpose in the fullest sense—and, it seems, yet another level of teleology. And that human action is *irreducibly* teleological is a thesis that has had a long history in philosophy.[19]

Again, whether there really is teleology at these or any other levels of nature—and if so, whether it ought to be interpreted in a reductionist, Platonic, Aristotelian, or Scholastic fashion—is not something we can settle here. The point is that there are at least these five levels at which irreducible teleology *might* be said to exist: in *basic causal regularities*; in *complex*

19 The irreducibly teleological character of human action has been defended most recently in G. F. Schueler, *Reasons and Purposes* (Oxford: Oxford University Press, 2003) and Scott Sehon, *Teleological Realism* (Cambridge, MA: MIT Press, 2005).

20 There are further distinctions that could be made within this level. For example, as Ariew has emphasized in the articles cited above, the adaptation of an organism to its environment is only one apparent instance of biological teleology, and one that is commonly claimed to have been explained away by Darwin. Developmental processes, and in particular the fact that some growth patterns are normal and others aberrant, provide another example, and one that Darwinism has *not* explained away. [Cf. Marjorie Grene, "Biology and Teleology," in her *The Understanding of Nature: Essays in the Philosophy of Biology* (Dordrecht: D. Reidel, 1974), and J. Scott

inorganic processes; in *basic biological phenomena*[20]; in distinctively *animal life*; and in *human thought and action*.[21]

IV. Teleological arguments in Paley, ID theory, and Thomism

It is generally assumed in contemporary philosophy that if irreducible teleology really does exist in nature, then it necessarily follows that there must be an ordering intelligence (presumably a divine one) responsible for this. Naturalists deny that such irreducible teleology exists and defenders of Paley-style design arguments and/or of ID theory affirm that it does, but they share this assumption about what the existence of irreducible teleology would entail if it were real. But as we have seen, Aristotelian teleological realism denies this assumption, and holds instead that teleology is both immanent to the natural world and in need of no further explanation, divine or otherwise. One of the differences between Paley and ID defenders on the one hand, and A-T defenders of Aquinas's Fifth Way on the other, is that the latter acknowledge the Aristotelian challenge and take it seriously. The reason is that they reject the mechanistic conception of nature held in common by naturalists on the one hand and Paley and ID defenders on the other—a conception which, by definition, rules out from the start the Aristotelian view that teleology is immanent to natural substances.

Now, defenders of ID theory do sometimes deny that their position is

Turner, *The Tinkerer's Accomplice: How Design Emerges from Life Itself* (Cambridge, MA: Harvard University Press, 2007).] Then there is the way in which genetic information seems to "point beyond itself" to a phenotypic expression—a circumstance physicist Paul Davies has noted appears to evince precisely the sort of purpose mechanism rules out, and which biophysicist Max Delbrück characterized as a vindication of Aristotle. [See Paul Davies, *The Fifth Miracle* (New York: Simon and Schuster, 1999), pp. 121–22 and Max Delbrück, "Aristotle-totle-totle," in Jacques Monod and Ernest Borek, eds., *Of Microbes and Life* (New York: Columbia University Press, 1971). For a recent debate, see Sahotra Sarkar, "Genes Encode Information for Phenotypic Traits" and Peter Godfrey-Smith, "Genes do not Encode Information for Phenotypic Traits," in Christopher Hitchcock, ed., *Contemporary Debates in Philosophy of Science* (Oxford: Blackwell, 2004).]

21   These last three correspond, of course, to the traditional Aristotelian distinction between vegetative, animal, and rational forms of life. Whether one thinks these really are irreducible, it is (*pace* the glib assumption to the contrary made by most contemporary philosophers and scientists) at least *debatable* whether they are. See Oderberg, *Real Essentialism*, chapters 8–10 for a recent defense of the traditional Aristotelian distinction.

mechanistic. For example, William Dembski does so several times in his book *The Design Revolution*.[22] But elsewhere in the same book, and in other writings, Dembski makes assertions that clearly presuppose the truth of a mechanistic conception of nature, at least as A-T writers understand "mechanism." For example, in discussing Aristotle in *The Design Revolution*, Dembski identifies "design" with what Aristotle called *techne* or "art."[23] As Dembski correctly says, "the essential idea behind these terms is that information is conferred on an object from outside the object and that the material constituting the object, apart from that outside information, does not have the power to assume the form it does. For instance, raw pieces of wood do not by themselves have the power to form a ship." This contrasts with what Aristotle called "nature," which (to quote Dembski quoting Aristotle) "is a principle in the thing itself." For example (again to quote Dembski's own exposition of Aristotle), "the acorn assumes the shape it does through powers internal to it: the acorn is a seed programmed to produce an oak tree"—in contrast to the way the "ship assumes the shape it does through powers external to it," via a "designing intelligence" which "imposes" this form on it from outside.

Having made this distinction, Dembski goes on explicitly to acknowledge that just as "the art of shipbuilding is not in the wood that constitutes the ship" and "the art of making statues is not in the stone out of which statues are made," "so too, *the theory of intelligent design contends that the art of building life is not in the physical stuff that constitutes life but requires a designer*" (emphasis added). In other words, living things are for ID theory (at least as Dembski understands it) to be modeled on ships and statues, the products of *techne* or "art," whose characteristic "information" is not "internal" to them but must be "imposed" from "outside." And that *just is* what A-T philosophers mean by a "mechanistic" conception of life. As Dembski says elsewhere, in putting forward ID theory, "I don't want to give the impression that I'm advocating a return to Aristotle's theory of causation. There are problems with Aristotle's theory, and *it needed to be replaced*."[24] So, for

---

22 William Dembski, *The Design Revolution* (Downers Grove, IL: InterVarsity Press, 2004), pp. 25 and 151.

23 Ibid., pp. 132–33.

24 William Dembski, *Intelligent Design* (Downers Grove: InterVarsity Press, 1999), p. 124, emphasis added. Cf. Dembski's *No Free Lunch* (New York: Rowman and Littlefield, 2002), p. 5. The context of the discussion in both cases is the early modern philosophers' rejection of Aristotelian formal and final causes, and Dembski makes it clear that his problem is not with the rejection of Aristotle's position, but only with how "what replaced it" ended up "excluding design" of *any* sort.

ID theory as for Paley, it is (contrary to the A-T position) at least *possible* that natural substances have no end, goal, or purpose; they just think this is *improbable*. The reason is that their essentially mechanistic conception of nature leads them to model the world on the analogy of a human artifact. The bits of metal that make up a watch have no *inherent* tendency toward functioning as a timepiece; it is at least *theoretically* possible, even if improbable, that a watch-like arrangement might come about by chance. And natural objects are like this too; there is nothing *inherent* in any natural object or system—no essences, natures, substantial forms or anything else corresponding to such Aristotelian-Scholastic categories—by which we might read off final cause or teleology. The world *might* be like a collection of bits of metal that have by sheer accident come together in the form of something resembling a watch. It's just that this is so highly improbable that the "best explanation" is that some intelligence arranged the bits that make up the world into their present purposive configuration, much as a watchmaker arranges bits of otherwise purposeless bits of metal into a watch. This approach is what led Paley to focus on complex biological phenomena, and it has led ID theorists to do the same. It's only because the eye or the bacterial flagellum exhibits "specified complexity" (as William Dembski holds) or "irreducible complexity" (as Michael Behe claims) that they stand out as candidates for design. The implication is that fingernails or eyelids (say)—not to mention inanimate substances and processes—wouldn't provide nearly as powerful a case, or even any case at all.

The A-T approach couldn't be more different.[25] For the Aristotelico-Thomist, there is simply a fundamental metaphysical difference between

25 For a critique of Paley's design argument from an A-T perspective, see Christopher F. J. Martin, *Thomas Aquinas: God and Explanations* (Edinburgh: University of Edinburgh Press, 1997), chapter 13. For a critique of ID theory written from a broadly A-T point of view, see Ric Machuga, *In Defense of the Soul* (Grand Rapids: Brazos Press, 2002), pp. 161–66, though there are significant inaccuracies in Machuga's exposition of A-T metaphysics. Benjamin Wiker, "Review of Ric Machuga, *In Defense of the Soul*," *ISCID Archive* (October 18, 2003), is a response to Machuga that corrects the errors in his exposition and sets out a more detailed account of the differences between A-T and ID. See also Oderberg, *Real Essentialism*, p. 287; Francis J. Beckwith, "How to Be an Anti-Intelligent Design Advocate," *University of St. Thomas Journal of Law and Public Policy* 4:1 (2009–2010); Michael Tkacz, "Aquinas vs. Intelligent Design," *This Rock* (November 2008); and the more-or-less A-T inspired critique of ID presented by Edward T. Oakes in his review of Phillip E. Johnson's *The Wedge of Truth* in *First Things* (January 2001), and the debate this generated in "Edward T. Oakes and His Critics: An Exchange," *First Things* (April 2001).

natural substances and human artifacts. The parts of a living thing, for example, are oriented *inherently* and *by nature* toward functioning together for the good of the whole. The parts of an artifact, by contrast, have no inherent or natural tendency to function together in this way, and must be made to do so by something outside them. Their natural orientation is toward other ends—those inherent in their being whatever natural substances they happen to be—even if an artificer might be able to organize them in such a way that these natural tendencies do not frustrate the artificial end he wants them to serve. To take an example from Aristotle, if a wooden bed could be planted (while the wood was still fresh from the original tree, say) what would grow from it, if anything, would be a tree and not a bed.[26] The *natural* orientation of the fresh wood is to be "treelike" rather than bedlike, even if a skilled craftsman can arrange it so as to function as a bed all the same. In general, for A-T, artifacts and the ends they are *made* to serve presuppose natural substances and the tendencies they *naturally* exhibit, so that it is incoherent to model natural substances on artifacts. That doesn't mean that natural objects are not created by God. But it does entail that God does not create them *in the way* a craftsman arranges parts so as to produce an artifact.

Similarly, the reason A-T philosophers affirm the existence of irreducible teleology in nature has nothing at all to do with complexity or the weighing of probabilities, nor with any analogy to human designers, nor with biological phenomena more than any other natural phenomena. As we saw in section III, A-T affirms the existence of irreducible teleology at all five of the levels of nature there distinguished, including the simplest causal regularities.[27] *Qua teleological*, the functions served by fingernails or eyelids, or the tendency of an ice cube to cause room temperature water to grow colder, are no more or less significant than the eye or the bacterial flagellum. A-T holds that teleology must exist of *metaphysical necessity* in the natural objects that have it, otherwise they simply wouldn't *be* the objects they by nature are—it is not a matter of probability, high or low. For that very reason, A-T philosophers follow Aristotle in holding that *detecting* teleology has nothing whatsoever to do with reasoning on the basis of an analogy between some natural substance or process and the products of human design, or indeed even with supposing that there is a designer in the first place. If a thing is *naturally* directed toward a certain end, that is (naturally) because it is in

---

26 Aristotle, *Physics* Book II, Chapter 1.
27 Contrast Dembski, *The Design Revolution*, p. 140, which allows that such regularities are "as readily deemed brute facts of nature as artifacts of design."

its *nature* to be, and we can know the natures of things without knowing where they came from.

Explaining (as opposed to detecting) the existence of irreducible natural teleology is a different story, at least for Scholastic teleological realism if not for Aristotle himself. But even here the question has nothing to do with drawing analogies with human designers, weighing probabilities, or the like. This brings us to Aquinas's Fifth Way. The argument starts out as follows:

> We see that things which lack intelligence, such as natural bod-
> ies, act for an end, and this is evident from their acting always,
> or nearly always, in the same way, so as to obtain the best result.
> Hence it is plain that not fortuitously, but designedly, do they
> achieve their end.[28]

This essentially sums up what has been said already. Aquinas is not saying here that certain exceptional natural objects—those which exhibit "specified complexity" or "irreducible complexity," say—are so difficult to account for in purely naturalistic terms that it is probable that they were made by an intelligent designer. He is saying that *any natural body at all*—even a very simple one—which regularly behaves in a certain way must have that way of behaving as its natural end. It is not a matter of "high probability," but a matter of the way a thing *has* to act given its nature.[29] It is in this sense that such unintelligent objects act "designedly" rather than "fortuitously." Aquinas is not referring here to an intelligent designer; he doesn't get to God until the second half of the argument. He is instead simply making the Aristotelian point that regularity points to teleology, that if A is an efficient cause of B then generating B must be the final cause of A. Other translations have "by purpose" or "by intention" rather than "designedly," and all of these expressions must be read in an Aristotelian way, as connoting final

---

28 *Summa Theologiae* I.2.3, as translated by the Fathers of the English Dominican Province.

29 Why, then, does Aquinas speak of things acting "always, or *nearly* always" in a certain way? Because a natural tendency can be frustrated. An acorn will always grow into an oak under the right circumstances—rather than into an elm, or a spider, or a dog—because that is its natural tendency. But of course, the right circumstances do not always obtain. The acorn may be damaged, or put into a desk drawer, or eaten. When A-T philosophers talk about the way things have to behave by nature, they don't mean that they will always succeed in behaving that way, but rather that that is the way they naturally *tend* to behave, the way they will behave *unless prevented* from doing so.

causality or immanent end-directedness as opposed to chance or fortuitousness.

At this stage in the argument, then, Aquinas is not saying anything that wouldn't also be said by the Aristotelian teleological realist. Where he goes beyond the latter to a distinctively Scholastic teleological realist position is in the second half of the argument:

> Now whatever lacks intelligence cannot move towards an end, unless it be directed by some being endowed with knowledge and intelligence; as the arrow is shot to its mark by the archer. Therefore some intelligent being exists by whom all natural things are directed to their end; and this being we call God.

Here Aquinas *does* claim that the teleology or end-directedness in nature affirmed in the first half of the argument must ultimately be explained in terms of a divine ordering intelligence. Notice that here too, though, he makes no reference to probabilities—he says that unintelligent natural objects *cannot* move towards an end unless directed by an intelligence, not that it is highly improbable that they will do so. That is one reason why Aquinas's reference to the archer cannot be interpreted along the lines of a Paley-style appeal to watchmakers and the like. Another is that arrows and their behavior when shot are very simple phenomena, unlike watches and other machines of the sort Paley and his heirs use to construct an argument from analogy. Aquinas is not saying "Arrows are complex objects made by intelligent beings, and certain natural objects are also complex; so, by analogy, we can infer that they were made by an intelligent being too." Nor is he even saying "Arrows reach their mark because an intelligent being makes them do so; therefore, by analogy, we can infer that anything that aims at a certain end must be made to do so by an intelligent being"—as if the argument were an extremely feeble inductive generalization based on a single instance! It is not an inductive generalization at all, nor an argument from analogy, nor an argument to the best explanation. Again, Aquinas's claim is a very strong one; he is saying that an unintelligent object *cannot* move toward an end—*cannot* have a certain outcome as its final cause—unless directed by an intelligence. This is a *metaphysical* assertion, not an exercise in empirical hypothesis formation.

What Aquinas *is* doing here is something I have discussed at length elsewhere.[30] For our purposes here, it will suffice to note that Thomists have interpreted the argument along the following lines. One of the common objections to the very idea of final causation is that it seems to entail that a thing can produce an effect even before that thing exists. Hence to say that an oak tree is the final cause of an acorn seems to entail that the oak tree— which doesn't exist yet—in some sense causes the acorn to pass through every stage it must reach on the way to becoming an oak, since the oak is the "goal" or natural end of the acorn. But how can this be? Where goal-directedness is associated with consciousness, as it is in us, there is no mystery. A builder builds a house, and he is able to do so because the *form* of the house exists in his intellect before it is instantiated in a concrete particular object. And of course, the materials that will take on that form also exist already, waiting to take it on. So there is no question of something having a cause that does not yet exist: the materials already exist in the natural world; the form exists in the builder's intellect; and the builder himself already exists, ready to arrange the materials so that they take on the form of a house. Together these already existing factors suffice to account for the coming into being of the house.

So, final causation is perfectly intelligible when associated with an intelligence, because in that case the "end" or "goal" *does* exist already as a form in the intellect. Is there any other way the end or goal might exist already? There would seem to be only four possibilities: It might exist in the natural object itself; it might exist in a Platonic "third realm"; it might exist in some human intellect, or in another intellect within the natural world; or it might exist in an intellect outside the natural world altogether. But it obviously doesn't exist in the natural object itself; if the form of an oak were already in the acorn itself, it would be an oak, and it's not. It cannot exist in a Platonic "third realm" either, at least not if one endorses (as the Scholastic teleological realist does) the Aristotelian realist critique of Platonic realism about universals. Nor can it exist in some human or other intellect within the natural order, at least not without a vicious regress. Humans obviously are not the ones directing acorns and other natural objects (including human beings themselves) to their natural ends; and if we supposed that some other non-human but still natural intellects were doing so, this would just raise

---

30 See Feser, *Aquinas*, pp. 110–20 and *The Last Superstition*, pp. 110–19. Cf. Reginald Garrigou-Lagrange, *God: His Existence and His Nature* (St. Louis: B. Herder, 1939), Volume 1, pp. 345–72; Maurice Holloway, *An Introduction to Natural Theology* (New York: Appleton-Century-Crofts, 1959), pp. 134–53; and Martin, *Thomas Aquinas: God and Explanations*, Chapter 13.

the question of what directs *those* intellects (since they too would be natural objects with final causes of their own) to *their* ends. The only possibility remaining, then, is the last one: Final causation in the natural world is intelligible because there is an intelligence altogether outside the natural order that directs natural objects to their ends.

To the "How can something non-existent be a cause?" objection to final causation, then, the Thomist's reply is to say "It can't. That's why the final cause of a natural object must exist already as an idea or form in an intellect existing altogether outside the natural order." Notice that, though the exposition of the argument made reference to the example of a house builder, it is *not* an "argument from analogy" in the sense that design arguments are thought to be. The reasoning is not "Houses are made by intelligent beings, and natural objects are analogous to houses, so they too are probably made by intelligent beings." The point of the builder example is rather to illustrate one of several possible ways the form of a thing might be efficacious even though the thing itself doesn't yet exist. The argument then goes on to try to show that all the other possibilities can be ruled out, and thus that there is no other way to make sense of the efficacy of final causes. Its structure is that of an attempted metaphysical demonstration, not that of an appeal to analogy, inductive generalization, argument to the best explanation, or any other exercise in empirical hypothesis formation.

In summary, then, the thrust of the Fifth Way is this: (1) Irreducible teleology is immanent to the natural order; (2) But such teleology is unintelligible unless there is an intellect outside the natural order; so (3) There is an intellect outside the natural order. The argument differs from Paley-style design arguments and the arguments of ID theorists in ways other than those already mentioned. For example, since the entities comprising the natural world have the final causes they have as long as they exist, the intellect in question has to exist as long as the natural world itself does, so as continually to direct things to their ends. The deistic notion that God might have "designed" the world and then left it to run independently is ruled out. Here, as in the other main Thomistic arguments for God's existence, the aim is to show that God is a *sustaining or conserving* cause of the world rather than that He got the world started at some point in the past. But why assume that the ordering intellect in question has all the divine attributes in the first place? Here appeal would have to be made to broader themes of A-T metaphysics. For example, an ordering intelligence which sustains a thing's having the *natural* ends it has would thereby be that which gives it its *nature* or *essence*. From an A-T perspective, this in turn entails conjoining an essence with an "act of existence," and only that in which essence and existence are identical—that which is *ipsum esse subsistens* or Subsistent Being Itself—can possibly do that. When this notion is itself unpacked, all the divine attributes follow. Hence the suggestion that the ordering intellect might be a very powerful but still finite designer (often raised against the "design argument") or even an extraterrestrial (as ID theorists sometimes allow) is also ruled out. The Fifth Way, when worked out, is intended to get us all the way to the God of classical theism.

Whether it succeeds in doing so is not something that can be settled here. The point is just to explain how the A-T approach to these questions differs from those that have gotten the bulk of the attention in the contemporary debate over the teleological argument. With at least five main approaches that could be taken to the question of whether teleology exists in the natural world, at least five levels of nature at which it could be said to exist, and at least two main approaches one could take to constructing a teleological argument for God's existence, the issue of teleology is far more complex than many contemporary philosophers may realize.[31]

---

31 The blogosphere has recently seen some fairly intense debate between ID theorists and A-T philosophers. Some readers might find of interest an exchange on the subject between me, Vincent Torley, and William Dembski that occurred in early 2010 at my personal blog and at the blog Uncommon Descent. In the course of the exchange I address several issues that are beyond the scope of the present paper but relevant to understanding the larger dispute between ID and A-T. Here are the relevant web addresses: Feser, "'Intelligent Design' Theory and Mechanism," http://edwardfeser.blogspot.com/2010/04/intelligent-design-theory-and-mechanism.html; Torley, "A Response to Professor Feser," http://www.uncommondescent.com/intelligent-design/a-response-to-professor-feser/; Feser, "ID Theory, Aquinas, and the Origin of Life," http://edwardfeser.blogspot.com/2010/04/id-theory-aquinas-and-origin-of-life.html; Dembski, "Does ID Presuppose a Mechanistic View of Nature?" http://www.uncommondescent.com/intelligent-design/does-id-presuppose-a-mechanistic-view-of-nature/; Feser, "Dembski Rolls Snake Eyes," http://edwardfeser.blogspot.com/2010/04/dembski-rolls-snake-eyes.html; Torley, "In Praise of Subtlety," http://www.uncommondescent.com/intelligent-design/in-praise-of-subtlety/; "ID, A-T, and Duns Scotus: A Further Reply to Torley," http://edwardfeser.blogspot.com/2010/04/id-t-and-duns-scotus-further-reply-to.html

3

On Aristotle, Aquinas, and Paley: A Reply to Marie George

In a note recently published in *Philosophia Christi*, Marie George takes issue with the account of the relationship between the Aristotelian-Thomistic (A-T) tradition and Paley's design argument that I presented in my article "Teleology: A Shopper's Guide."[1] She alleges that I "misconstrue," "misread," "misapply" and "fail to accurately convey" the A-T tradition in various ways, and that I get Paley wrong too. In fact it is her own article which misrepresents both Paley and the standard A-T attitude toward his design argument; and into the bargain, her case rests on several egregious distortions of my own position. By my count she presents eight criticisms, which I will address in the order in which they appear in her note.

First criticism: George takes issue with my statement that for Aristotle, "the end or goal of a material substance is *inherent* to it."[2] To this she replies that "it is not the end itself which is inherent to the natural thing, but rather the inclination or tendency to the end."[3] This is an odd bit of nitpicking. Naturally, I agree with George; *being down* (to use one of her examples) is not in the stone itself, but is rather the end toward which the stone tends. Indeed, on the very same page as the sentence she complains about I explain that the Aristotelian notion of final causes concerns "inherent goal-*directedness*," "inherent *tendency*," and "the end or goal towards which a thing naturally *points*." Strictly speaking, what is inherent is only the pointing, tendency, or directedness itself, and (obviously) not the end that is pointed to. Hence when I wrote that "the end or goal of a material substance is inherent to it," I would have thought it obvious that I was merely speaking

---

1   Marie George, "An Aristotelian-Thomist Responds to Edward Feser's 'Teleology,'" *Philosophia Christi* 12 (2010): 441–49. My article appeared in *Philosophia Christi* 12 (2010): 142–59.

2   Feser, "Teleology," p.

3   George, "An Aristotelian-Thomist Responds," p. 441.

}49{

elliptically. Certainly this minimally charitable reading might at least have been considered by George before putting fingers to keypad. In any event, though she makes much of this "criticism," it plays no role in her subsequent discussion.

Second criticism: I noted in my article that while Aristotle argues from the existence of motion or change in the world to the existence of God as an Unmoved Mover, he does not regard the existence of final causes as providing a separate basis for arguing for God's existence, as Aquinas does in the Fifth Way. George acknowledges that this is "a standard view among Aristotelian scholars" but suggests that a passage from Aristotle's *On Generation and Corruption* implies a different view.[4] In particular, Aristotle says that "nature ... always and in all things strives after the better" and "God, therefore ... perfected the universe by making coming-to-be a perpetual process."[5]

But the passage doesn't show what George thinks it does. What it shows is at most only that Aristotle regards God as the cause of things moving in such a way that they realize their ends; it doesn't show that He is the cause of things *having* those ends in the first place. And the latter thesis is the one that Aristotle scholars typically decline to attribute to Aristotle. Moreover, there are passages in Aristotle that clearly tell against George's preferred interpretation. For example, Aristotle says in the *Eudemian Ethics* that "the divine is not an ordering ruler, since he needs nothing, but rather is that for the sake of which wisdom gives orders."[6] Of course, Aristotle does take God Himself to *be* the ultimate end of things, but that is different from saying that He "orders them" to their end in the sense of *putting the inclination towards their end into them* in the first place. That it is there is, for Aristotle, just a basic fact about them given their natures.

Third criticism: George takes exception to my assertion that the difference between organic and inorganic processes is that the latter tend toward "an effect outside the cause itself and therefore [do] not promote the cause's

---

4   Ibid., p. 442.
5   Aristotle, *On Coming-to-Be and Passing Away*, trans. E. S. Forster, in *On Sophistical Refutations, On Coming-to-Be and Passing Away, On the Cosmos* (Cambridge, MA: Harvard University Press, 1955), pp. 336b25–37a2.
6   *Eudemian Ethics*, 1249b13–15, as translated by Monte Ransome Johnson in *Aristotle on Teleology* (Oxford: Clarendon Press, 2005), p. 262. Cf. Johnson's discussion of the passage at pp. 72–74.

own good."[7] In response she claims that Aquinas "explicitly rejects" this view, citing a passage from the *Summa Contra Gentiles* in which Aquinas says that "all things [and not just organic things] … act for the sake of the good."[8]

But there is no conflict between what I wrote and what Aquinas says. There would be a conflict only if I had said that inorganic processes do not act for the sake of *any* good at all. But I said no such thing; I said only that they "do not promote the cause's *own* good." And what I meant by this is obvious from the context of the remark George quotes, a discussion of the Scholastic distinction between *immanent* and *transeunt* causation, which is central to the A-T analysis of what differentiates living from non-living things. To cite some typical definitions, what is "immanent" in the sense in question is what "begin[s] within and remain[s] within the agent as a perfection of the agent; living"; whereas what is "transeunt" is what "proceed[s] from one being or cause to another being."[9] The "perfection" or "good" in question here has to do with the *flourishing* that living things are capable of and non-living things are not. What I was saying, then (as is, again, clear from the context), is that inorganic causal processes, being merely transeunt and not immanent, do not promote the good of some whole of which they are a part in the sense of promoting the *perfection* or *flourishing* of that whole, but rather terminate in something external to any whole from which they might proceed—a standard part of the A-T understanding of what distinguishes the non-living from the living.

Fourth criticism: George also makes a more general complaint to the effect that I do not say enough in my article about the relationship in A-T philosophy between the notion of final causality and the notion of the good, though she acknowledges that even Aristotle and Aquinas themselves do not always bring the latter into their discussions of the former.[10] She gives the impression that this is a major defect of my article, but it is never made clear how it is. The point of the article was to compare various approaches to teleology, not to present a thorough account of the A-T view specifically. Nor does she show how my treatment of the issues I do address in the article is in any way impaired by my not having said more about this particular issue. George's

7   Feser, "Teleology," p. 150.
8   *Summa Contra Gentiles* III.3, George's own translation.
9   Bernard Wuellner, *Dictionary of Scholastic Philosophy* (Milwaukee: Bruce Publishing Company, 1956), pp. 57 and 125.
10   George, "An Aristotelian-Thomist Responds," pp. 444–45.

"criticism" seems to amount to little more than the expression of her personal desire that I had said more about a topic she (rightly) considers important.

Fifth criticism: George states that the A-T understanding of the differences between natural substances and artifacts "does not mean without qualification that it is 'incoherent to model natural substances on artifacts'" and that "Feser speaks as if human action in no way serves as a model for understanding action for an end in nature."[11] But she is attacking a straw man. I never said or implied either that natural substances are *without qualification* unlike human artifacts, or that action for an end in nature is *in no way* like human action. The question is whether there are similarities *of a sort* that would justify treating Paley's design argument as if it were merely a variation on reasoning of essentially the same sort that Aquinas is engaged in in his Fifth Way. George says nothing to show that there are. On the contrary, what she does say only reinforces the conclusion that there are not, which brings us to her next criticism.

Sixth criticism: George objects to my dissociating Aquinas's Fifth Way from Paley's design argument. But it is not clear why. George concedes that any A-T philosopher must insist on a distinction between natural substances and artifacts insofar as "the parts of natural things are inherently ordered to their ends, whereas the parts of artificial things are ordered by us (and by certain other animals) to ends that they have no tendency to realize."[12] Indeed, she acknowledges that "it would be incoherent to model natural substances on artifacts in a way that would ignore this difference."[13] She also allows that there is a crucial difference between a mere craftsman and God insofar as "the craftsman does not give an artifact its nature, but harnesses the natural tendencies of natural things to his end, whereas God ... gives things their natures in virtue of which they tend to their ends."[14] And she grants that "it may well be that Paley had mechanistic tendencies."[15] In other words, George more or less concedes that Aquinas's argument and Paley's differ in just the ways I said they do.

So what exactly is her problem with what I have said? The closest we get to an answer is George's bizarre suggestion that on my view, the way

11   Ibid., pp. 445 and 441.
12   Ibid., p. 445.
13   Ibid., pp. 445–46.
14   Ibid., p. 446.
15   Ibid., p. 447.

God makes natural things "must be other than [by] employing intelligence."[16] But I have never said or implied such a thing. On the contrary, in my article I summed up the Fifth Way as holding that "final causation in the natural world is intelligible because there is an intelligence altogether outside the natural order that directs natural objects to their ends."[17] No one denies that both Aquinas and Paley argue for an intelligent cause of the order in the world. What A-T philosophers (other than George) object to is the *way* Paley argues for this conclusion (a way which is incompatible with a metaphysics of immanent finality) and his implicitly *anthropomorphic construal* of divine "intelligence" (which is incompatible with the Thomist position that attributes like intelligence are to be predicated of God and of human designers in an analogous rather than univocal way).

Seventh criticism: As we have seen, several of George's criticisms rest on a failure to give what I wrote even a minimally charitable reading, and in particular on a tendency to ignore context. Perhaps the strangest example of these foibles is her statement that "Feser claims that 'it is at least theoretically possible, even if improbable, that a watch-like arrangement come about by chance,'" which is followed by her remark that "Aristotle, Aquinas, and Paley would all regard such a proposition as absurd."[18] As any fair-minded reader of my article can see, the line George has ripped from context was not an expression of my *own* view, but rather a description of what I take to follow from the views of Paley and of Intelligent Design theorists.[19]

Moreover, while I agree that Aristotle and Aquinas would regard the proposition in question as absurd (and *I* certainly regard it as absurd), George is mistaken to claim that Paley would so regard it.[20] Paley argues that, just as we would judge a watch found upon a heath to have been the product of intelligence rather than of unintelligent causes, so too should we judge natural phenomena to be the product of intelligence. "[F]or every indication of contrivance, every manifestation of design, which existed in the watch, exists in the works of nature; with the difference, on the side of nature, of being greater and more, and that in a degree which exceeds all

16   Ibid. p. 446.
17   Feser, "Teleology," p. 158.
18   George, "An Aristotelian-Thomist Responds," p. 447, note 33.
19   Feser, "Teleology," p. 154.
20   It is telling that while George provides citations from both Aristotle and Aquinas to back up her claim that they would find the proposition in question absurd, she provides no such citation from Paley's works.

computation."[21] In other words, the inference to a designer of the natural order is in Paley's view even *more* certain than the inference to a designer of the watch. But as is well known, Paley still regarded the former inference as a matter of *probability*—very high probability, to be sure, but still probability rather than demonstrative reasoning of the sort Aquinas was interested in.[22] That is why he devotes so many pages to describing minute details of the natural order, so as to construct as powerful a cumulative case as possible; if the inference from a single complex natural object sufficed for a strict demonstration of a designer, he needn't have bothered with such details.[23] But if even what Paley regards as the *stronger* inference to a designer of the universe is only a matter of probability, then what he regards as the *weaker* inference to a designer of the watch can also only be in his view a matter of probability, even if high probability.[24] Which is, of course, what I meant when I said that for Paley, "it is at least theoretically possible, even if improbable, that a watch-like arrangement come about by chance."

Eighth criticism: George's final and perhaps oddest objection comes at the end of her article, where she claims that:

> Ultimately, [Feser] proposes that the inherency in the ordering to an end present in natural things is reason to reject the Fifth Way—although he is unaware that he has done so—insofar as he maintains that such inherent ordering differs from the ordering to an end found in artificial things, and therefore one cannot conclude that God creates natural things in the same manner that a craftsman makes an artifact.[25]

21 William Paley, *Natural Theology* (Oxford: Oxford University Press, 2006), p. 16.

22 Paley appeals to what is "probable" or to "probability" or "improbability" several times in the course of his argument for a designer of the natural world, e.g. at pp. 108, 135, 162, 167, 179, and 201.

23 See Matthew Eddy and David Knight's "Introduction" to the edition of Paley's *Natural Theology* cited above for a useful brief discussion of the rise of interest in probabilistic arguments in Paley's day.

24 Note also that when considering for the sake of argument the hypothesis of a watch that generates other watches, Paley allows that for someone finding such a watch on the heath "it be now no longer *probable*, that the individual watch which our observer had found, was made immediately by the hand of an artificer" though the observer would still judge that an artificer had been indirectly responsible for it (*Natural Theology*, p. 12, emphasis added). This implies that the original inference from the watch to a designer was in Paley's view a matter of probability.

25 George, "An Aristotelian-Thomist Responds," p. 449.

Here we have an assertion that is simply bizarre, especially given that I have *defended* the Fifth Way at length.[26] It is, in any event, not clear *why* George thinks my position unwittingly undermines the Fifth Way. It *seems* that she is reasoning that, if we regard finality as inherent to natural substances in a way it is not inherent in artifacts, then we have blocked any means of inferring from the finality of natural substances to a divine intelligence. But if so, then she is simply begging the question against my position. For I have argued that the Fifth Way constitutes a middle-ground position between Aristotle's view (as most Aristotle scholars interpret him) that the teleology that is immanent to the natural order is completely divorced from intelligence, and Paley's view that any teleology that derives from intelligence must not be immanent in natural order, but imposed from outside after the fashion of human artifice. George appears to assume that since Aquinas, in the Fifth Way, obviously rejects Aristotle's view, he must be committed to something like Paley's. I have argued that this is a false choice, and George hasn't *shown* otherwise but merely *asserted* otherwise.

Furthermore, while it is true that there is a *sense* in which I would deny that "God creates natural things *in the same manner* that a craftsman makes an artifact," it is not the sense George apparently supposes. I do not deny that God is, ultimately, the source of the finality in things. What I do deny is that creation involves anything comparable to the taking of pre-existing materials with their own natures and fashioning them into a kind of artifact that serves a function not inherent in the materials, in the manner of a human inventor. (The question of temporal order is irrelevant here; it does not change the point at all if we supposed that the designer somehow conjured the raw materials into existence while *simultaneously* imposing some function on them not already inherent in the materials.) Rather, God creates by conjoining an essence to an act of existence, where the finality of the thing created is inherent in the essence itself rather than "tacked on" in a separate creative act. Since George is an Aristotelian-Thomist, I take it that she agrees with this understanding of creation. In that case, though, it is even harder to see what her problem is with my reading of the Fifth Way.

The uninitiated reader might nevertheless wonder whether a Paley-like view of creation is suggested by a passage from Aquinas cited by George, in which he says that "just as artifacts are compared to human art, so also

---

26 See my books *Aquinas* (Oxford: Oneworld Publications, 2009), at pp. 110–20, and *The Last Superstition: A Refutation of the New Atheism* (South Bend, IN: St. Augustine's Press, 2008), at pp. 110–19.

all natural things are compared to divine art," and gives arrows and clocks as examples of artifacts.[27] In fact the passage suggests just the opposite. For the distinction between "natural things" and "artifacts" that Aquinas takes for granted here is the very distinction Aristotle draws in Book II of the *Physics* between those things which have the principle of their activity inherent in them (what Aquinas calls "natural things") and things which do not (which includes what Aquinas calls "artifacts," and also objects resulting from chance). Indeed, Aquinas explicitly cites Book II of the *Physics* in the passage from the *Summa* quoted by George; and in his commentary on Book II of the *Physics* he *contrasts* animals, plants, and their parts with artifacts like knives, beds, clothing, and the like, precisely because there is no principle of "knife-like" or "bed-like" or "clothing-like" activity *inherent* in the artifacts in question, while there *is* a principle of "animal-like," "plant-like," "eye-like," etc. activity inherent in animals, plants, and their parts. A bed, for instance, is something whose parts already have some other inherent principle—to function in a "tree-like" way, say, if the wood from which the bed is made is still fresh. The "bed-like" function has to be imposed on it from outside by an artisan, in a way that the "tree-like" function does not.

So, even though natural things are like artifacts in being made by an intelligence (God in the former case, human designers in the latter), the *way* they are made is not the same, and cannot be the same. In particular, God does not make natural things (animals, plants, etc.) the way artifacts are made by a craftsman, viz. by combining parts which already have some other inherent principle, the way the wood making up a bed has. They wouldn't *be* natural things in that case. Rather (as I have said) he makes them by conjoining an essence to an act of existence. And anything less than this wouldn't be true *creation* at all, which for Aquinas is always creation *out of nothing*—something which, needless to say, human craftsman are incapable of in principle.

The uninitiated reader might also get the impression from George's article that my views on Paley and design arguments more generally are somehow eccentric, and that hers represent the "mainstream" Aristotelian-Thomistic position. This is the reverse of the truth; in fact my own views are nothing more than a reiteration of what one finds in a great many A-T writers. For example, Maurice Holloway insists that:

> We should be careful not to confuse the fifth way of St. Thomas
> Aquinas, which argues from the existence of order in the

---

27   Aquinas, *Summa Theologiae*, IaIIae, q. 13, a. 2, ad 3, George's own translation.

universe to the existence of an infinite intelligence, with Paley's argument from design. In the latter's argument the universe is seen as a complicated and intricate machine ... [and he] reasons, by way of analogy, to the existence of a divine watchmaker, or supreme architect of the universe. This argument from design, as given by Paley and unfortunately repeated in many books on Christian apologetics, does not prove the existence of God. An architect of the universe would have to be a very clever being, but he would not have to be God ... Many of the objections directed against what some writers believe is the fifth way of St. Thomas are really directed against the watchmaker of Paley. St. Thomas's proof is entirely different. It is grounded in the metaphysics of finality ...[28]

Similar views are expressed by John F. McCormick,[29] Cardinal Mercier,[30] Joseph Owens,[31] R. P. Phillips,[32] Henri Renard,[33] and John Wippel.[34] Benedict Ashley objects to the "philosophical naiveté" of authors like Paley "in confusing extrinsic and intrinsic finality."[35] Etienne Gilson complains of the "anthropomorphic God" of "simple-minded metaphysicians [who] have unwillingly led agnostics to believe that the God of natural theology was the 'watchmaker' of Voltaire, or the 'carpenter' of cheap apologetics."[36]

---

28 Maurice Holloway, S.J., *An Introduction to Natural Theology* (New York: Appleton-Century-Crofts, 1959), p. 146–47.

29 John F. McCormick, S.J., *Scholastic Metaphysics, Part II: Natural Theology* (Chicago: Loyola University Press, 1943), p. 75.

30 Cardinal Mercier, "Natural Theology or Theodicy" in Cardinal Mercier, et al., *A Manual of Modern Scholastic Philosophy*, Volume II (St. Louis: B. Herder, 1933), pp. 53–54.

31 Joseph Owens, *An Elementary Christian Metaphysics* (Houston: Center for Thomistic Studies, 1985), p. 349 and "Aquinas and the Five Ways," in *St. Thomas Aquinas on the Existence of God: The Collected Papers of Joseph Owens*, edited by John R. Catan (Albany: State University of New York Press, 1980), pp. 136–37.

32 R. P. Phillips, *Modern Thomistic Philosophy*, Volume II (Westminster, Maryland: The Newman Press, 1950), p. 290.

33 Henri Renard, S.J., *The Philosophy of God* (Milwaukee: Bruce Publishing Company, 1951), p. 48.

34 John Wippel, *The Metaphysical Thought of Thomas Aquinas* (Washington, D.C.: Catholic University of America Press, 2000), p. 480.

35 Benedict M. Ashley, *The Way toward Wisdom* (Notre Dame, IN: University of Notre Dame Press, 2006), p. 512, n. 11.

36 Etienne Gilson, *God and Philosophy* (New Haven: Yale University Press, 1941), p. 142.

Herman Reith says that the trouble with the design argument is that "the examples used and the interpretation given them prevents the argument from rising to the metaphysical level ... above the order of the physical universe," so that "it cannot conclude to anything more than the existence of some kind of intelligence and power" within that universe.[37] Ronald Knox characterizes Paley's design argument as "feeble," and does not regard it as even a "modification" of any of Aquinas's Five Ways.[38] Christopher F. J. Martin, in the course of defending the Fifth Way, dismisses Paley's design inference as "really a rather poor argument," and avers that "the Being whose existence is revealed to us by the argument from design is not God but the Great Architect of the Deists and Freemasons, an impostor disguised as God."[39]

The themes that I have emphasized recur in these Thomistic writers: that design arguments like Paley's are arguments from analogy, while Aquinas's Fifth Way is not; that they are probabilistic, while Aquinas's argument is a metaphysical demonstration; that they are not grounded in a metaphysics of immanent final causality, as Aquinas's argument is; and that they cannot in principle get us outside the natural order to a divine intelligence of pure actuality but at most to an anthropomorphic demiurge. All of these points are rooted in considerations about the radical differences between A-T metaphysics and the metaphysical assumptions underlying the design arguments of Paley and other modern writers. Clearly the burden of proof is on George to show that Aquinas's argument and Paley's can be assimilated in a way that I and so many A-T writers say they cannot be. It is a burden she has not met.[40]

37   Herman Reith, *The Metaphysics of St. Thomas Aquinas* (Milwaukee: Bruce Publishing Company, 1958), p. 198.

38   Ronald Knox, *Broadcast Minds* (New York: Sheed and Ward, 1933), pp. 52 and 222.

39   Christopher F. J. Martin, *Thomas Aquinas: God and Explanations* (Edinburgh: Edinburgh University Press, 1997), pp. 180–82.

40   I thank Lydia McGrew for comments on an earlier version of this paper.

Natural theology

4

Natural Theology Must Be Grounded in the Philosophy of Nature, Not in Natural Science

I. Introduction

Natural theology, I maintain, can only properly be grounded in the philosophy of nature, and not in natural science. I need immediately to qualify this opening statement in several ways. First, I am speaking, specifically, of arguments in natural theology that purport to arrive at the existence and nature of God *a posteriori*. The ontological argument attempts to do so *a priori*. I am, of course, not claiming that *that* argument should be grounded in the philosophy of nature (a suggestion which would be unintelligible given the nature of the argument). I am saying that any argument that successfully reasons *from the world* to God must be grounded in premises derived from the philosophy of nature rather than from natural science.

Second, I do not mean to deny that natural theology is itself a kind of science. On the contrary, I think theology is the highest science, in the Aristotelian sense of "science." For that matter, in the Aristotelian sense, philosophy of nature itself constitutes a science. But neither natural theology nor philosophy of nature is a science in the *modern* sense of the term—the sense in which physics, chemistry, and biology are regarded as sciences. So, I am claiming that natural theology cannot properly be grounded in sciences like physics, chemistry, or biology, as those are typically understood today. Rather, it must be grounded in that more fundamental discipline which studies the metaphysical preconditions of any possible physics, chemistry, or biology—and that is precisely what the philosophy of nature is concerned with.

Third, when I say that natural theology must be grounded in the philosophy of nature, what I mean, then, is that we are not going to be able successfully to reason from the world to God unless we deal with the most basic philosophical questions about the nature of change, causation, material substance, and the like. But I will also be arguing that we need to defend the specific *answers* to those questions developed within the broadly Aristotelian-Scholastic tradition—a tradition often falsely supposed to have been overthrown by modern science, but which, I maintain, in fact best accounts for the very possibility of there being an empirical world for natural science to study in the first place.

Fourth, when I say that we cannot get from the world to God except via premises derived from philosophy of nature, I have a quite specific conception of God in mind. I do not deny that conclusions of a sort that might in *some* sense of the term be called "theological" might be derived from natural science. But I do deny that arguments grounded in natural science alone can get you to *classical* theism—the conception of God defended by Athanasius and Augustine, Avicenna and Maimonides, Anselm and Aquinas, and enshrined in orthodox Catholic theology as expressed by the fourth Lateran Council and the first Vatican Council. If anything, they have a tendency to lead you *away* from the God of classical theism. You might get to a demiurge, to a being of superhuman intelligence and power, with arguments grounded in physics, chemistry, or biology. What you cannot get to is that which is *ipsum esse subsistens* rather than merely a being among other beings; to a sustaining cause on whom the very being of the world depends at every instant; or to that which is absolutely simple or in no way composed of parts, whether physical or metaphysical. One implication of this is that "design arguments" of the sort associated with William Paley and contemporary "Intelligent Design" theory are at best irrelevant to natural theology (as that discipline is understood in the classical theist tradition), and at worst threaten seriously to distort our understanding of God and His relationship to the world (again, at least from the point of view of classical theism).

Having made these qualifications, I doubt I've made my opening statement much less controversial. I've also no doubt raised as many questions as I've answered. Further to explain my meaning and to justify my claims, it will be best to begin at the beginning—at the beginning of the history of natural theology, the beginning of natural science, and the beginning of the philosophy of nature. As it happens, they all have the *same* beginning, in ancient Greece, with the Pre-Socratics.

II. Classical philosophy of nature and classical theism

The Pre-Socratic philosophers were famously concerned to discover a principle that might account for the unity and permanence they took to underlie the change and multiplicity in the world of our experience. Some thought they found it in a purely material principle—for Thales, water; for Anaximenes, air; for Leucippus and Democritus, atoms. Heraclitus came as close as one can get to denying that there really is any unity or permanence to the world in the first place; for him all is flux, and the conflict between the ever-shifting elements of the world of our experience is itself the only unchanging reality. Parmenides and Zeno went to the opposite extreme of denying the reality of change and multiplicity. For these Eleatic thinkers there is and can be no becoming but only Being, static and undifferentiated. Change, Parmenides argued, would have to involve being arising from non-being, something coming from nothing. But from nothing, nothing can come. Hence there can be no change.

Aristotle identified the error in Parmenides' reasoning. When an ice cream cone melts in the sun, what we have is not a transition to being from sheer non-being or nothingness. What we have is rather the *actualization of a potential* that was already present in the ice cream. For in addition to the ways the ice cream cone actually is (cold, solid, sweet, and so forth) and the ways it absolutely is not (it is not made of granite, it is not an octopus) there are the ways it potentially could be (melted, for example, or digested). For Aristotle, potentialities are real features of things alongside the ways in which they are actual, and that is why things are capable of changing. Potentialities constitute a middle ground between the two options Parmenides affords us in his false dichotomy between fully actualized being and sheer non-being or nothingness.

Now the distinction between actuality and potentiality (or act and potency, to use the more traditional jargon) is the foundation of Aristotelian-Scholastic philosophy of nature. It is implicit in the hylemorphic analysis of natural substances as composites of substantial form and prime matter. For matter is on the Aristotelian analysis just the potency or potential to take on form and make of it something individual and concrete rather than a mere abstraction; and form is that which actualizes otherwise indeterminate matter and thereby makes of it a substance. The theory of act and potency is also closely tied to the Aristotelian understanding of final causes as immanent to the natural order. For a potency or potential is always a potential *for* being actualized in some way. Potencies are thereby *directed toward* or *point to* their actualizations, as to an end or goal. (For example, the ice cream "points to" being melted as one possible future state.)

In this way efficient causation is for the Aristotelian-Scholastic tradition unintelligible without final causation. An efficient cause (a match, say) generates its typical effect or effects (such as flame and heat) precisely because by virtue of its potencies it is directed toward the generation of those effects as toward an end or goal. The phosphorus in the match head is "directed at" or "points to" the generation of flame and heat, specifically, rather than to the generation of frost or the smell of lilacs. It is flame and heat that the match *will* generate if struck (unless prevented from doing so, by water damage, say), and it is flame and heat that it *would have* generated even if it is never in fact struck but kept in a drawer until it turns to dust. And the phosphorus has those specific potencies precisely because of its substantial form. Act and potency, efficient cause, final cause, substantial form, prime matter—all of these concepts are tightly interconnected, and all are in the Aristotelian-Scholastic view necessary for making sense of the very possibility of a world of changing and causally interrelated natural substances.

To this Aristotelian picture the Thomistic tradition added the distinction between essence and existence, which is also rooted in the distinction between act and potency. For a thing to be real is for its nature or essence to be conjoined with an act of existence. Hence the tree in my back yard is real because to the essence or nature of being a tree there is conjoined an act of existence; while phoenixes are not real because to the nature or essence of being a phoenix (if there is such a nature or essence) there is conjoined no act of existence. But for a thing's essence to be conjoined to an act of existence is for it to go from potentiality to actuality; for an essence or nature is merely potential until an act of existence actualizes it. This is true even of immaterial finite substances, such as angels.

Now, that they are composites of actuality and potentiality entails, in the mature Aristotelian-Scholastic tradition, that no finite substance, whether material or immaterial, can in principle exist even for an instant on its own, without a divine sustaining cause. That is to say, no finite substance has what has sometimes been called "existential inertia," the inherent tendency to remain in being. This is a theme I have elaborated upon at length elsewhere, but the basic idea can be briefly stated.[1] Confining ourselves for present purposes to the case of material substances, an argument for the claim that no such substance can have existential inertia begins with a familiar principle of Scholastic metaphysics:

1. A cause cannot give what it does not have to give.
2. A material substance is a composite of prime matter and substantial form.

---

1   For a more detailed treatment, see Edward Feser, "Existential Inertia and the Five Ways," *American Catholic Philosophical Quarterly*, Vol. 85, No. 2 (2011).

3. Something has existential inertia if and only if it has of itself a tendency to persist in existence once it exists.
4. But prime matter by itself and apart from substantial form is pure potency, and thus has of itself no tendency to persist in existence.
5. And the substantial form of a material thing by itself and apart from prime matter is a mere abstraction, and thus of itself also has no tendency to persist in existence.
6. So neither prime matter as the material cause of a material substance, nor substantial form as its formal cause, can impart to the material substance they compose a tendency to persist in existence.
7. But there are no other internal principles from which such a substance might derive such a tendency.
8. So no material substance has a tendency of itself to persist in existence once it exists.
9. So no material substance has existential inertia.

The transition from these key themes in Aristotelian-Scholastic philosophy of nature to natural theology should be obvious. For the inherent impossibility of any natural substance's maintaining itself in being even for an instant leads inexorably to the existence of God as its sustaining cause. As I have argued at length elsewhere, this is the overall thrust of each the families of theistic arguments represented by Aquinas's famous Five Ways, as they have been developed within the Thomistic tradition.[2] The argument from motion to an Unmoved Mover is at bottom an argument to the effect that whatever is a composite of act and potency must be actualized by that which just is pure actuality, with no admixture of potentiality. The argument for an Uncaused Cause is at bottom an argument to the effect that whatever is a composite of essence and existence must be caused to exist by something whose essence and existence are identical, something which just is subsistent being itself. More generally, whatever is composite in any respect must have its source in that which is absolutely simple or non-composite. And so forth.

Now these arguments lead precisely to the conception of God and His relationship to the world that is enshrined in classical theism. For example, they entail the doctrine of divine conservation, according to which the world could not continue in existence for an instant apart from God's conserving action—a doctrine that is clearly taught in Scripture, that has been affirmed

2   Ibid. See also Edward Feser, *Aquinas* (Oxford: Oneworld, 2009), chapter 3, for a detailed exposition and defense of the Five Ways.

by such Doctors of the Church as Augustine, Gregory the Great, and Aquinas, that is taught by the Roman Catechism and is arguably implicit in the teaching of the first Vatican Council.[3] They entail the doctrine of divine simplicity, which was explicitly taught by Vatican I and by the fourth Lateran Council and is the common teaching of the great theologians not only of the Catholic tradition but also within Judaism and Islam. They entail the doctrines of divine immutability and eternity, which like the doctrine of divine simplicity are *de fide* doctrines of the Catholic Church and the common teaching of the classical theologians. These doctrines follow from God's being pure actuality rather than a mixture of actuality and potentiality. What is composed of parts of any sort is a mixture of potentiality and actuality insofar as the whole is only potentially in the parts and needs to be actualized; hence God, as pure actuality, cannot be composed of parts. What is changeable or temporal passes from potentiality to actuality; hence God, as pure actuality, cannot be changeable or temporal.

In short, the theory of act and potency, which is the core of the Aristotelian-Scholastic philosophy of nature, when fully developed leads us to a conception of the world as utterly dependent on God at every instant but also to a conception of God as utterly distinct from the world (since, unlike the world, He is simple, immutable, and eternal). It thereby not only refutes atheism, but rules out both deism and pantheism, views which Christian orthodoxy require us to condemn in any event. It gives us the foundation, then, for a sound natural theology, certainly from the point of view of classical theism.

Now, am I insinuating that to abandon the Aristotelian-Scholastic philosophy of nature, and in particular the theory of act and potency, would be to undermine natural theology, at least if we understand natural theology to be in the business of arguing from the world to the God of classical theism? Am I insinuating that abandoning it would threaten to open the door to pantheism, deism, or even atheism? That is exactly what I am insinuating. And here's one reason to think that I am right: These dire consequences are exactly what followed when the Aristotelian-Scholastic tradition lost its hegemony in Western thought.

---

3 It is classified as *de fide* in Ludwig Ott's *Fundamentals of Catholic Dogma* (Cork: Mercier Press, 1955), p. 87. The relevant text from Vatican I is the declaration that "God protects and governs by His providence all things which He created" (Denzinger, *Sources of Catholic Dogma*, sec. 1784), which theologians typically interpret as teaching that God keeps created things from lapsing into nonexistence.

III. The mechanistic revolution

This brings us to natural science. If the philosophy of nature and natural theology reached their high point with Thomas Aquinas, this third of the disciplines we are concerned with had to wait until the scientific revolution. And of course, the scientific revolution had something to do with the Aristotelian-Scholastic tradition losing its hold over the Western mind. But not in the way commonly supposed. Modern science has indeed falsified certain empirical scientific theses that had been associated with the Aristotelian-Scholastic tradition—geocentrism, the ancient theory of the elements, the idea that material objects have specific places to which they naturally move, and so forth. Aristotelian-Scholastic arguments in the philosophy of nature and natural theology had often been stated in terms of these now superseded scientific ideas. But the metaphysical and theological claims can be disentangled from the false scientific claims, and were so disentangled by later Scholastic thinkers. Thus, that the scientific revolution put paid to Aristotelian-Scholastic *physics* does not entail that it put paid to Aristotelian-Scholastic philosophy of nature and natural theology, and in fact it did not do so.

The reason many suppose otherwise is that they fail to keep in mind that the scientific revolution was not merely a revolution in science. It was also a *philosophical* revolution, and the latter revolution has inherited the prestige of the former. As Hilary Putnam has written:

> For the last three centuries a certain metaphysical picture suggested by Newtonian or Galilean physics has been repeatedly confused with physics itself ... Philosophers who love that picture do not have very much incentive to point out the confusion—if a philosophical picture is taken to be the picture endorsed by science, then attacks on the picture will seem to be attacks on science, and few philosophers will wish to be seen as enemies of science.[4]

What this revolutionary metaphysical picture involved was, of course, an overthrow of the Aristotelian-Scholastic philosophy of nature. The theory of act and potency, immanent final causes or teleology, substantial form and

---

4   Hilary Putnam, *Renewing Philosophy* (Cambridge, MA: Harvard University Press, 1992), p. 19.

prime matter, were all tossed out. In their place was put a new description of the natural world in essentially mathematical and non-teleological terms. No longer were material things to be understood as possessed of potentialities or potencies by virtue of which they were inherently directed toward the generation of certain effects. Rather, they were to be understood as inherently inert but related by mathematically expressible laws. Why does a cause A generate its typical effect B? A Scholastic would say that A does so because given its nature or substantial form, A inherently points to the generation of B specifically, as to a final cause. The new philosophy of nature of the moderns denies this. It says that there is no *inherent* link between A and B at all, that neither A nor anything else in the natural world points to anything beyond itself. Rather, it is just a "law of nature" that As tend to be followed by Bs, where this law is, as it were, imposed from outside. A and B could in theory have been related by a very different law, or by no law at all. For A, B, and every other element of the world are, as Hume would put it, entirely "loose and separate."

Hence, whereas natural phenomena were modeled on organic substances in the Aristotelian-Scholastic tradition, the moderns modeled them instead on machines or artifacts. The parts of a plant (say) have an *inherent* or *built-in* tendency to function together for the sake of the whole. Roots have an *inherent* tendency to sink into the ground and to draw water and nutrients into the body of the plant; leaves have an *inherent* tendency toward photosynthesis; and so forth. Moreover, the parts only count as the kinds of things they are relative to the whole. A root *just is* that part of a plant that anchors it the ground and takes in water and nutrients, and a leaf *just is* that part of a plant which carries out photosynthesis and thereby produces food for the plant. They just would not be the kinds of things they are apart from their relations to the plant of which they are parts. By contrast, the parts of a watch have no inherent tendency to function together so as to measure time. That function is imposed on them from outside. Accordingly, the parts could in principle have been related instead for the realization of some other end. Now, all natural substances, including inorganic ones, are for the Aristotelian-Thomistic tradition like the plant in having inherent or built-in teleology and causal tendencies. For the moderns, however, all natural substances (including plants) are to be thought of on the model of the watch. They are machine-like in having no inherent tendency toward an end. Such an end might be imposed from outside by a divine machinist, but there is no *immanent* or *intrinsic* tendency towards it.

For this reason the moderns' new anti-Aristotelian philosophy of nature has been called "mechanistic." Of course, there were aspects of the original "mechanical philosophy" (as it was known in the seventeenth century) that have not survived—corpuscularianism, a crude push-pull model of causation, and so forth. But what has survived is the idea that there is no teleology or final causality *immanent* or *inherent* to the natural order, and an insistence on pushing an exclusively mathematical description of nature as far as it can go. Needless to say, this method has had dramatic predictive and technological successes—precisely, I would say, because it deliberately focuses exclusively on those aspects of nature which can be predicted and controlled. And conceived of *merely* as a method, it is unobjectionable. But from the time of the scientific revolution onward, boosters of science have tended to regard it as a *metaphysics* no less than a method—as a description, indeed an exhaustive description, of the *real nature* of natural phenomena. And they have insinuated, quite fallaciously, that the successes of modern science have vindicated it as a metaphysics.

There are many problems with this position, but the one I am concerned with here is theological. And that is that from the essentially mathematical and non-teleological description of the material world you get from natural science, you are not going to reason your way one inch closer to the God of classical theism. Indeed, if you treat this description, even if only for the sake of argument, as if it were a *complete* metaphysical description of nature, then you are if anything going to get *away* from the God of classical theism. It is no accident that that's exactly what happened in the history of Western thought after the scientific revolution. The theological pendulum swung away from classical theism, first toward the occasionalism of Descartes and Malebranche and the pantheism of Spinoza, and then in the direction of deism, until deism finally gave way to atheism.

IV. Berkeley's insight

Berkeley was one early modern philosopher who clearly perceived the theological dangers in the new conception of matter. He warns us in the *Three Dialogues*:

> *Matter*, or *material substance*, are terms introduced by philosophers; and as used by them, imply a sort of independency, or a subsistence distinct from being perceived by a mind ... [T]here

is not perhaps any one thing that hath more favoured and strengthened the depraved bent of the mind toward *atheism*, than the use of that general confused term.[5]

And again:

> But allowing matter to exist, and the notion of absolute existence to be as clear as light; yet was this ever known to make the Creation more credible? Nay hath it not furnished the *atheists* and *infidels* of all ages, with the most plausible argument against a Creation? That a corporeal substance, which hath an absolute existence without the minds of spirits, should be produced out of nothing by the mere will of a spirit, hath been looked upon as a thing so contrary to all reason, so impossible and absurd, that not only the most celebrated among the ancients, but even divers modern and Christian philosophers have thought matter coeternal with the Deity.[6]

Now of course, Berkeley was an idealist, and he objected to the notion of matter as such, not merely the modern conception of matter. Nevertheless, his immediate target was the notion of matter as he found it in Locke and Newton. And there is a *sense* in which even the staunchest Aristotelian-Scholastic realist must agree that Berkeley was correct to object to the suggestion that matter might exist apart from *all* minds, including the divine intellect. For as I have emphasized, for the Scholastic, the material world could not persist for an instant were God not continually causing it to exist. And on the doctrine of divine simplicity, God's causing the world and God's knowing the world are really one and the same thing considered from different points of view. Hence to say that matter might in principle exist apart from God's thinking about it would implicitly be to say that matter might in principle exist without God continually causing it to exist. As the analytical Thomist John Haldane has put the point:

> As Aquinas reminds us, rather than God's knowing being logically posterior to its objects, it is the creative cause of them. God

5   *Three Dialogues*, in George Berkeley, *Principles of Human Knowledge* and *Three Dialogues*, ed. Howard Robinson (Oxford: Oxford University Press, 2009), p. 207.
6   Ibid., p. 201.

knows reality as a writer knows his narrative: not by being an
attentive reader but by being a deliberative author.[7]

In *that* sense, Haldane says, "Berkeley was correct: to be is to be known—
by God."[8]

But does the modern mechanistic conception of matter really imply that
matter could exist even apart from God's conserving action? It does indeed;
or at least, it's hard to see how it can avoid that implication if mechanism is
interpreted as a metaphysics rather than merely as a method. Berkeley was
clear that what he objected to was not the suggestion that matter might exist
apart from some mind or other, but that matter had what he called an "*absolute* subsistence" or "*absolute* existence" apart even from the divine intellect.[9] And you don't have to be a Berkeleyan idealist to see that the
modern conception of matter entails that it has such an "absolute subsistence." For recall what I said earlier about the reason why material things
do not, on the Aristotelian-Scholastic view, possess existential inertia, do
not have the capacity to remain in being on their own. The reason is that
they are mixtures of act and potency. Matter all by itself is just pure potentiality, with no actuality at all; while the substantial forms of material things
are mere abstractions apart from matter, with no concrete existence. More
generally, an essence is purely potential and not at all actual apart from an
act of existence; while an act of existence is a mere abstraction apart from
a nature or essence. Matter and form, essence and existence in a concrete
material thing are thus interdependent. To avoid vicious ontological circularity, then, there must be something outside a material thing that combines
and keeps combined its metaphysical components if it is to exist even for
an instant.

But what happens when we deny, as the moderns did, that material
things have any immanent or built-in final causality? What happens when
we deny that they are mixtures of act and potency—something we have to
deny if we deny that they have immanent final causality, since (as we noted
earlier), potency or potentiality goes hand in hand with immanent finality?
What happens is that we return to something like Parmenides' position. Or
rather, we return to what the Greek atomists made of Parmenides' position.

---

7   John Haldane, "Common Sense, Metaphysics, and the Existence of God," *American
    Catholic Philosophical Quarterly*, Vol. 77, No. 3 (2003), p. 394.
8   Ibid.
9   Berkeley, *Three Dialogues*, pp. 152 and 177. Emphasis added.

For the ancient atomists held that the atoms corresponded to Parmenides' notion of Being, and thus never come into existence or go out of existence. But it also follows that they not only have no beginning but exist absolutely and independently of anything else here and now. For that is what one *has* to say of a thing if one denies that it is a mixture of act and potency. If there is no Aristotelian middle ground of potency or potentiality between Parmenides' dichotomy between full actuality and sheer non-being or nothingness, then the only way for matter at the most *fundamental* level to exist if it exists at all is in *a fully actual way*, without the need to be *made* actual by anything else. That's essentially what the ancient atomists said about the atoms, and it is what the moderns implicitly committed themselves to when they rejected the Aristotelian distinction between act and potency. As the historian of philosophy Dennis Des Chene has written of Descartes' version of mechanism:

> The directedness of natural change, and with it the contrast between potential and actual, are ... banished in the Cartesian restriction of natural properties to figure, size, and motion ... Cartesian matter ... is, from an Aristotelian standpoint, at every instant entirely actual.[10]

Hence, while the everyday material objects of our experience may come and go, the basic material stuff of which they are made implicitly becomes, on the modern picture, something which has what Berkeley called an "absolute subsistence"—even apart from God.

One can avoid this result only if one denies that the modern conception of matter really does give us the whole, metaphysical truth about matter after all. And some who have no theological ax to grind would admit that it does not. As Bertrand Russell once wrote:

> It is not always realised how exceedingly abstract is the information that theoretical physics has to give. It lays down certain fundamental equations which enable it to deal with the logical structure of events, while leaving it completely unknown what is the intrinsic character of the events that have the structure. We only know the intrinsic character of events when they happen to

10   Dennis Des Chene, *Physiologia: Natural Philosophy in Late Aristotelian and Cartesian Thought* (Ithaca: Cornell University Press, 1996), pp.5–6.

us. Nothing whatever in theoretical physics enables us to say anything about the intrinsic character of events elsewhere. They may be just like the events that happen to us, or they may be totally different in strictly unimaginable ways. All that physics gives us is certain equations giving abstract properties of their changes. But as to what it is that changes, and what it changes from and to—as to this, physics is silent.[11]

This, I would say, is essentially correct. But *merely* acknowledging that physics gives us only the mathematical structure of the material world rather than its intrinsic nature doesn't really solve the problem raised by Berkeley—the problem that modern science gives us a conception of matter which at least *allows* for the possibility that it might exist apart from God. As James Collins glosses Berkeley's concern, in his book *God in Modern Philosophy*:

> Since the nature of this material substance remains unknowable, we have no way of showing that it has a real relation of causal dependence on God, any more than that it has a noetic relation of accessibility to our mind. Grant the reality of matter so defined, and there is no way to overcome skeptical doubt or to offer demonstrative proof of the causal dependence of the sensible world on a first cause.[12]

Now as Collins goes on to point out, avoiding this problem hardly necessitates following Berkeley in the direction of idealism:

> Alternative ways were open for Berkeley to deal with this issue. He might have challenged the accepted definition of matter and proposed one that would allow jointly for the reality of matter, its knowability by the human mind, and its causal dependence upon God. To follow this route, however, he would have had to repudiate the Cartesian and Lockean assumption about the immediate object of the understanding, and this he was not prepared to do.[13]

---

11   Bertrand Russell, *My Philosophical Development* (London: Unwin Paperbacks, 1985), p. 13.

12   James Collins, *God in Modern Philosophy* (Chicago: Henry Regnery Company, 1959), p. 108.

13   Ibid., pp. 108–09.

Though he saw the theological dangers inherent in the modern conception of matter, then, Berkeley was still himself committed to the modern philosophical project, and had no intention of returning to the Scholasticism that would have given him just the conception of matter Collins describes, but which he followed Descartes and Locke in repudiating. He chose, then, to propose a novel, idealist account of God's relationship to the world.

Unless we are willing to follow Berkeley's idealism, then—a route that few would take, and which is certainly philosophically and theologically problematic—we need to find some realist solution to the problem he raises, a solution that both affirms the existence of matter and makes it intelligible how the material world must depend on God for its continuance in existence from moment to moment. I submit that there is no way to accomplish this without going beyond the purely mathematical description of the material world physics gives us, and addressing the questions in the philosophy of nature that it leaves unanswered, questions about the "intrinsic character" of the material world (as Russell put it). And I submit also that there is no way to accomplish it without acknowledging that that intrinsic character includes potency or potentiality as a real constituent, just as the Aristotelian-Scholastic tradition has always claimed.

V. The dead ends of Paley and Leibniz

If there is any doubt about this, let me try to dispel it by examining the two main alternative approaches to arguing from the world to the existence of God developed by the moderns—the broadly empiricist approach most prominently represented by William Paley, and the rationalist approach most prominently represented by Leibniz. Both are seriously deficient from the point of view of classical theism, and their deficiencies arise precisely from their eschewal of the Aristotelian-Scholastic philosophy of nature.

Consider first Paley's famous "design argument" for the existence of God as a kind of cosmic machinist, who imposes purposes or teleology on the world from outside, the way a watchmaker imposes a time-telling function on parts that in no way have it intrinsically.[14] Now it is often acknowledged that Paley's argument gets us at best to a designer who is extremely powerful and intelligent, but who for all we know may yet be finite and thus

---

14   I discuss the crucial differences between Paley's argument and Aquinas's Fifth Way in *Aquinas*, and also in my article "Teleology: A Shopper's Guide," *Philosophia Christi*, Vol. 12, No. 1 (2010).

non-divine. But the problem is not just that Paley's designer *may* be something other than God as classical theism understands Him. There is reason to think that Paley's designer *could not* be God as classical theism understands Him. Consider first that for classical theists like Aquinas, when we predicate attributes of God, we necessarily do so *analogously* rather than *univocally*. But Paley is evidently predicating attributes to his designer and to us in a univocal way, which (for the Thomist at least) entails a radically deficient conception of God.

A simple example will illustrate the difference between the two kinds of predication. When I say that this is a good cheeseburger and that is good pizza, I am using "good" univocally. I am predicating the very same thing to both the cheeseburger and the pizza. And I will still be doing so if I say that the cheeseburger is *better* than the pizza. I will be saying that the pizza and the cheeseburger both have the very same attribute, but that the cheeseburger has it to a higher degree than the pizza. But when I say that this is a good cheeseburger and that Aquinas was a good man, I am *not* using "good" univocally and I am not predicating exactly the same thing both to the cheeseburger and to Aquinas. I am saying instead that there is something in Aquinas that is *analogous* to what we call "good" in the cheeseburger, though of course it is not precisely the same thing, since the moral qualities that lead us to attribute goodness to a human being are not the same as the gustatory and nutritive qualities that lead us to attribute goodness to food.

Similarly, when we speak of Aquinas's intelligence and my intelligence, we are using "intelligence" univocally. Hence to say that Aquinas was more intelligent than I am is to say that Aquinas had the same thing I have, but to a greater degree. But in Aquinas's view, when we speak of our intelligence and *God's* intelligence, we are *not* using "intelligence" univocally. We are not saying that God has the same thing we have, but to a higher degree. Rather, we are saying that there is in God something *analogous* to what we call "intelligence" in us. The reason is that God, as pure actuality, does not merely *participate* in being, goodness, intelligence, and the like, as we and other created things do. For Aquinas, God doesn't "have" being; he *is* being itself. He doesn't "have" goodness; He *is* goodness itself. He doesn't "have" intelligence; He *is* intelligence itself. And so forth. Moreover, He is, given the doctrine of divine simplicity, *identical to* His attributes. What we call God's being, God's goodness, God's intelligence, and so forth are really just the same thing—God Himself—considered from different points of view. It follows that God is radically unlike anything in the created order. He is not "a being" alongside others, not even a very grand and remote being among other beings, but rather *ipsum esse subsistens*, that on which all mere beings depend for their being. By contrast, Paley's procedure is to model his designer on human designers. By implication, his designer exercises the same faculty human designers do—he works out design problems, performs calculations, and so forth—but does so with massively greater facility. He is an *essentially anthropomorphic* designer. And as such it is hard to see how he could be as classical theism says God is — absolutely simple, immutable, eternal, and so forth.

So, the anthropomorphism implicit in Paley's conception of God is one reason many classical theists are bound to object to Paley's style of argument. To be sure, there are some classical theists (Scotists, for example) who don't subscribe to Aquinas's doctrine of analogy, and they may be willing to cut Paley some slack on this particular issue. But there are other problems with Paley's argument. In particular, Paley's implied conception of God's *relationship to the world* is another potential source of incompatibility with classical theism. To see how, consider the three main approaches in the history of theology to understanding God's causal relationship to the world, as Alfred Freddoso has usefully classified them.[15] *Occasionalism* holds that God alone is the cause of everything that happens, so that there are no true secondary causes in nature. For example, on this view, one billiard ball which makes contact with another during a game of pool does not in any way cause the other to move. Rather, God causes the second ball to move on the occasion when the first makes contact with it. *Mere conservationism* holds that while God maintains natural objects and their causal powers in existence at every moment, they alone are the immediate causes of their effects. On this view, the one billiard ball really does cause the other one to move, and God has nothing to do with it other than keeping the ball and its causal powers in being. He is not in any direct way the cause of the second ball's motion. Finally, *concurrentism* is a middle ground position which holds on the one hand (and contrary to occasionalism) that natural objects are true causes, but on the other hand (and contrary to mere conservationism) that God not only maintains natural objects and their causal powers in being, but also cooperates with them in immediately causing their effects. On this view, the one billiard ball really does cause the other ball to move, but only *together with* God, Who acts as a concurrent cause.

15 See Alfred J. Freddoso, "God's General Concurrence With Secondary Causes: Pitfalls and Prospects," *American Catholic Philosophical Quarterly* 67 (1994): 131–56.

Concurrentism became the standard view within the Scholastic tradition, because the other views are philosophically and theologically problematic.[16] For example, occasionalism veers in the direction of pantheism, while mere conservationism veers in the direction of deism. We can understand how if we recall the Scholastic dictum that "a thing *operates* according as it *is*."[17] If, as occasionalism holds, only God alone ever operates or brings about effects, and natural objects operate not at all, then it is difficult to see how they *exist* at all, at least in any robust way. God alone would seem to be real; natural objects would be like mere fictional characters in the mind of a divine Author. By contrast, if, as mere conservationism holds, natural objects can at least operate or bring about effects apart from God's immediate causal action, then it seems that they could also *exist* apart from his immediate causal action. The world would in that case not depend for its continued existence on God's conserving action. (This is not to say flatly that *occasionalism entails pantheism* or that *mere conservationism entails deism*. The issues are complex, and careful analysis is required in order to determine precisely what these views do or do not entail, either by themselves or on conjunction with other assumptions. The point is just to indicate some of the reasons they have been considered at least problematic.)

Now I have noted that the Aristotelian-Scholastic tradition regards efficient causality as intelligible only in light of final causality. If the phosphorus in a match head regularly generates flame and heat rather than frost and cold, or the smell of lilacs, or no effect at all, that can only be because the phosphorus is inherently *directed toward* or *points beyond itself to* the generation of those specific effects as to an end or goal. The clear implication would seem to be that if natural objects are to be true causes, they must possess immanent or built-in finality, and not merely the extrinsic or externally imposed final causality affirmed by Paley. To deny them immanent finality—to hold that whatever finality they have exists only in the divine intellect (in the way that the time-telling function exists in the mind of the

---

16 For discussion of occasionalism, see Freddoso's article "Medieval Aristotelianism and the Case against Secondary Causation in Nature," in Thomas V. Morris, ed., *Divine and Human Action: Essays in the Metaphysics of Theism* (Ithaca, NY: Cornell University Press, 1988). For discussion of mere conservationism, see his article "God's General Concurrence with Secondary Causes: Why Conservation is Not Enough," *Philosophical Perspectives* 5 (1991): 553-585.

17 Thomas Aquinas, *Summa theologiae* I.75.2, as translated in St. Thomas Aquinas, *Summa Theologica*, trans. Fathers of the English Dominican Province (New York: Benziger Brothers, 1948). Emphasis added.

designer of a watch), and in no way in the natural objects themselves—would therefore seem to entail denying natural objects genuine causal power, and to attribute all causal power to God alone. And that would be to embrace occasionalism.

Insofar as Paley's position presupposes a rejection of immanent finality, then, it arguably threatens to collapse into occasionalism. Of course, Paley and other defenders of the design argument would no doubt find this charge surprising. Certainly they do not typically deny that natural objects are true efficient causes. But the point is that their position at least arguably *entails* such a denial, whether they realize it or not. If digestion, oxidation, gravitation, and other natural causal processes are as extrinsic to natural phenomena as time-telling is extrinsic to the parts of a watch, then natural phenomena have no more power to carry out these activities than metal gears have the power to convey the time of day. After all, that a particular bit of physical activity means that *it is now 11:27* is entirely observer-relative, and does not follow from anything in the watch parts themselves. It is *we*, the designers and users of the watch, who cause the marks on its face of to mean what they do. Similarly, if something counts as digestion, oxidation, gravitation, or the like also entirely extrinsically, only relative to God's activity as designer, then these things too are really *God's* activities rather than those of natural objects themselves.

To be sure, some of Paley's other commitments would seem to lead in the opposite direction. In particular, that he regards it as at best highly *probable* that complex natural phenomena were designed by God seems to entail that they could at least *in principle* exist and operate apart from Him. But this leads him out of the frying pan of occasionalism only to fall into the fire of deism—bypassing not only concurrentism, but even mere conservationism, altogether. And of course, Paley's position is indeed sometimes characterized as reflective of the eighteenth-century trend toward deism.

That trend was inevitable. The elements comprising the material world—no longer regarded as united organically into substances via substantial forms and immanent final causes—came to seem essentially "loose and separate," having no more *inherent* unity than the parts of a machine do. Hence the regularities they did exhibit were reconceived on the model of the regularities a watch or some other mechanical artifact exhibits when its parts are arranged by an artificer. The "laws of nature"—as these regularities came to be described, displacing talk of the natures or substantial forms of things—were just the patterns the divine artificer had put into the bits of clockwork that make up the world. As a machine can operate in the absence of its maker, though, so too did the world come to seem as something that could operate in the absence of the artificer. Thus did the doctrine of divine conservation give way to deism. And the sequel, naturally, was atheism, once it occurred to mechanists that if the "machine" of the world could operate here and now without a machinist, maybe it always has so operated—maybe the "machine" and the "laws" governing it are all that has ever existed. That the mechanistic, anti-Aristotelian view of matter insinuated the ancient atomist view that matter was fully actual (and thus without need of a sustaining cause) could only serve to grease the skids.

From a classical theistic point of view, then, Paley's position is bound to appear metaphysically unstable, ambiguous between unacceptable extremes vis-à-vis the question of God's causal relationship to the world. And it wavers between these extremes precisely because of its rejection of the Aristotelian-Scholastic philosophy of nature, and in particular its rejection of immanent, rather than merely extrinsically imposed, final causes. That, together with its tendency toward anthropomorphism, makes it doubly objectionable from a theological point of view. It is no surprise, then, that Thomists have often distanced Aquinas's Fifth Way from the design argument of Paley and other modern writers, sometimes in harsh terms.

Now Leibniz's rationalist approach to natural theology is less problematic in terms of its theological content. But it *is* nevertheless problematic *methodologically*. For the notions of contingency and necessity are, in rationalist cosmological arguments, no longer grounded, as they are in the Aristotelian-Scholastic tradition, in the natures of things. In particular, contingency is no longer grounded in the real composition of actuality and potentiality and of essence and existence in contingent things; and necessity is no longer grounded in the pure actuality and identity of essence and existence in God. Instead, a thing's contingency is reduced to the *logical* possibility of its non-existence, and necessity is reduced to *logical* necessity. A "principle of sufficient reason" is deployed in place of the Aristotelian-Scholastic principle of causality that features in arguments like the Five Ways. Whereas the principle of causality—that is to say, the principle that whatever is contingent has a cause and that nothing that changes can change itself—is grounded in the objective impossibility of a mere potentiality actualizing itself, the "principle of sufficient reason" is put forward instead as a would-be "law of thought." No longer grounded in aspects of the natural world itself, the rationalist cosmological argument thus comes to seem little more than a demand that the world meet certain explanatory criteria which may (or may not) be built into the structure of the human mind, but which do not necessarily reflect any aspect of objective, extra-mental reality. The door is thereby opened to the refutations of Hume and Kant.

Yet what of the contemporary *kalām* cosmological argument, which in some versions appeals to evidence derived from modern cosmology? Doesn't it show that natural theology of a classical theistic sort can be grounded in natural science rather than the philosophy of nature (and Aristotelian-Scholastic philosophy of nature in particular)? It does not. For to get from the world to the God of classical theism, it is not enough to get from the world to a cause of the world. One must get to a cause that has the attributes distinctive of the God of classical theism—such as simplicity, immutability, and eternity—and one must get to a God who is not only the temporal cause of the world, but apart from whose sustaining causal activity the world could not exist even for an instant. And I submit that neither condition can be met without recourse to the distinction between actuality and potentiality that is at the core of Aristotelian-Scholastic philosophy of nature. The reasons are implicit in what was said earlier: Unless the world is a mixture of potentiality and actuality, it cannot be dependent for its continued existence on something outside it; and unless God is pure actuality, He cannot be simple, immutable, or eternal.

To be sure, this is not to deny that considerations from modern cosmology—or from other natural sciences, for that matter—can be useful to the natural theologian; the *kalām* cosmological argument, I concede, shows that much. But I maintain that such considerations can never be *sufficient*, and that recourse to the philosophy of nature is necessary to get from the world to the God of classical theism.

VI. Return to Scholasticism

Now, suppose I am correct to maintain that natural theology needs to be grounded in Aristotelian-Scholastic philosophy of nature, specifically. Is a revival of anything close to this philosophy of nature realistic or even possible at this point in the history of philosophy?

Not only is it possible, it is actual. Recent decades have seen, within mainstream academic philosophy, a renewed interest in traditional Aristotelian metaphysical notions like substance, essence, causal power, act versus potency (these days referred to as the distinction between "categorical" and "dispositional" properties), and finality (these days referred to as "physical intentionality" or the "directedness" of dispositions toward their manifestations). Moreover, this revival has taken place among secular metaphysicians and philosophers of science with no Thomistic or theological ax to grind.[18]

Among metaphysicians, the revival has largely been motivated by dissatisfaction with the standard modern philosophical accounts of causation, which take Hume as their point of departure. For example, regularity theories of causation hold that for *A* to cause *B* is just for *A* and *B* to be instances of a general pattern according to which events like *A* are succeeded by events like *B*. Counterfactual theories of causation hold that the claim that *A* caused *B* is to be analyzed as the claim that had *A* not occurred, *B* would not have occurred either. Various technical objections have been raised against such accounts, but for those attracted to a neo-Aristotelian approach to causation, the fundamental difficulty is that these theories do not capture causation itself, but only phenomena that presuppose causation. That is to say, to the extent that the regularities in question hold and to the extent the counterfactuals in question are true, that is only because they are grounded in the causal powers of things. They don't *explain* causation but *presuppose* causation.

The term "disposition" is sometimes preferred to "power," but some of the theorists in question go on to argue that we can only make sense of these powers or dispositions if we think of them as "pointing" to or being "directed" at their characteristic manifestations or effects. George Molnar characterizes this as "physical intentionality," since it is like the intentionality of mental states in that it involves directedness onto an object that may or may not exist, but unlike it in being unconscious.[19] John Heil calls it "natural intentionality" for similar reasons.[20] Whatever the label, in substance it is a return to something like the Scholastic view that efficient causality presupposes final causality, and the similarity has not gone unnoticed by historians of philosophy.[21]

Within the philosophy of science, a movement toward neo-Aristotelianism has been motivated by dissatisfaction with the idea that scientific

---

18 For a brief history of this development and a useful overview of its central themes, see Stephen Mumford, "Causal Powers and Capacities," in Helen Beebee, Christopher Hitchcock, and Peter Menzies, eds., *The Oxford Handbook of Causation* (Oxford: Oxford University Press, 2009). Cf. Ellis, *The Philosophy of Nature: A Guide to the New Essentialism.*

19 George Molnar, *Powers: A Study in Metaphysics* (Oxford: Oxford University Press, 2003).

20 John Heil, *From an Ontological Point of View* (Oxford: Clarendon Press, 2003).

21 See Walter Ott, *Causation and Laws of Nature in Early Modern Philosophy* (Oxford: Oxford University Press, 2009), who (at pp. 29–30) compares Scholastic views of causation to those of contemporary writers like Ellis and Molnar.

explanation is a matter of discovering "laws of nature." As Nancy Cartwright has emphasized, a serious problem with the Humean notion that science is in the business of establishing regularities on the basis of observation is that the sorts of regularities that the hard sciences tend to uncover are rarely observed, and in fact are in ordinary circumstances impossible to observe.[22] Beginning students of physics quickly become acquainted with idealizations like the notion of a frictionless surface, and with the fact that laws like Newton's law of gravitation strictly speaking describe the behavior of bodies only in circumstances where no interfering forces are acting on them (a circumstance which never actually holds). Moreover, physicists do not in fact embrace a regularity as a law of nature only after many trials, after the fashion of popular presentations of inductive reasoning. Instead, they draw their conclusions from a few highly specialized experiments conducted under artificial conditions. None of this is consistent with the idea that science is concerned with cataloguing observed regularities. But it is consistent, in Cartwright's view, with the Aristotelian picture of science as in the business of uncovering the hidden natures of things. Experimental practice indicates that what physicists are really looking for are the inherent powers a thing will manifest when interfering conditions are removed, and the fact that a few experiments, or even a single controlled experiment, are taken to establish the results in question indicates that these powers are taken to reflect a nature that is universal to things of that type.

The notion of "regularities" or "laws of nature" is therefore misleading, in Cartwright's view, given that science actually uncovers few laws or regularities outside highly artificial conditions. Strictly speaking, what science discovers are the universal natures and inherent powers of things, and talk of "laws of nature" can only be shorthand for this. As Cartwright concludes, "the empiricists of the scientific revolution wanted to oust Aristotle entirely from the new learning," but "they did no such thing."[23]

While references to "substantial form," "final causes," and other traditional Scholastic concepts do not exactly pepper the contemporary academic philosophy journals, then, the *substance* of these ideas is getting a renewed

---

22 Nancy Cartwright, "Aristotelian Natures and the Modern Experimental Method," in John Earman, ed., *Inference, Explanation, and Other Frustrations: Essays in the Philosophy of Science* (University of California Press, 1992), and *Nature's Capacities and Their Measurement* (Oxford University Press, 1989).

23 Cartwright, "Aristotelian Natures and the Modern Experimental Method," p. 70. See Feser, "Teleology: A Shopper's Guide" for references to some Aristotelian tendencies in contemporary philosophy of biology.

hearing in at least some influential quarters. There has also been renewed interest in aspects of Aristotelian metaphysics other than those which have been our central concern here.[24] Then there are those contemporary analytic philosophers who have shown sympathy toward a specifically Aristotelian-*Thomistic* approach to metaphysics.[25] If renewed interest in Aristotelian-Scholastic natural theology waits upon renewed interest in its Aristotelian metaphysical underpinnings, then, it will not have to wait as long as many might suppose. Indeed, the latter revival is already underway.

24   See, e.g., Tuomas Tahko, ed., *Contemporary Aristotelian Metaphysics* (Cambridge: Cambridge University Press, forthcoming).
25   See, e.g., John J. Haldane, "A Thomist Metaphysics," in Richard Gale, ed., *The Blackwell Guide to Metaphysics* (Oxford: Blackwell, 2002); Gyula Klima, "Contemporary 'Essentialism' vs. Aristotelian Essentialism," in John Haldane, ed., *Mind, Metaphysics, and Value in the Thomistic and Analytical Traditions* (Notre Dame: University of Notre Dame Press, 2002); David Oderberg, *Real Essentialism* (London: Routledge, 2007); David Oderberg, "Teleology: Inorganic and Organic," in Ana Marta Gonzalez, ed., *Contemporary Perspectives on Natural Law* (Aldershot: Ashgate, 2008); and James Ross, *Thought and World: The Hidden Necessities* (Notre Dame: University of Notre Dame Press, 2008).

5
Existential Inertia and the Five Ways

I. Introduction

The Doctrine of Divine Conservation (DDC) holds that the things that God has created could not continue in existence for an instant if He were not actively preserving them in being. DDC is a standard component of classical philosophical theology. St. Thomas Aquinas holds that:

> Now, from the fact that God rules things by His providence it follows that He preserves them in being ... [T]o be is not the nature or essence of any created thing, but only of God ... Therefore, no thing can remain in being if divine operation cease.[1]
>
> Both reason and faith bind us to say that creatures are kept in being by God ... [T]he being of every creature depends on God, so that not for a moment could it subsist, but would fall into nothingness were it not kept in being by the operation of the Divine power, as Gregory says.[2]

The Gregory referred to is Pope St. Gregory the Great, like Aquinas a Doctor of the Church. A third such Doctor to advocate DDC was St. Augustine, who writes:

> Wisdom, when It governs created things graciously, gives them a motion beyond our powers to comprehend or describe ... And

---

1 *Summa Contra Gentiles* 3:65, as translated by Vernon J. Bourke in Saint Thomas Aquinas, *Summa Contra Gentiles, Book Three: Providence, Part I* (Notre Dame: University of Notre Dame Press, 1975).
2 *Summa Theologiae* I.104.1. All quotes from the *Summa Theologiae* (ST) are taken from St. Thomas Aquinas, *Summa Theologica*, translated by the Fathers of the English Dominican Province (New York: Benziger Brothers, 1948).

if this motion is withdrawn and Wisdom ceases from this work, creatures will immediately perish.[3]

Let us, therefore, believe and, if possible, also understand that God is working even now, so that if His action should be withdrawn from His creatures, they would perish.[4]

That "faith binds us" to affirm DDC (as Aquinas puts it) is indicated by various biblical passages. Wisdom 11:25 asks: "How would anything have endured if thou hadst not willed it?"[5] Hebrews 1:3 speaks of Christ "upholding the universe by his word of power" and Colossians 1:17 says that "in him all things hold together." Especially within the Catholic tradition, DDC is regarded as essential to Christian orthodoxy.[6] The *Catechism of the Council of Trent* (or Roman Catechism) teaches that:

> [A]s all things derive existence from the Creator's supreme power, wisdom, and goodness, so unless preserved continually by His Providence, and by the same power which produced them, they would instantly return into their nothingness.[7]

The first Vatican Council declares that "God protects and governs by His providence all things which He created,"[8] which theologians typically interpret as teaching that God keeps created things from lapsing into nonexistence. (Cf. the passage from the *Summa Contra Gentiles* quoted above, wherein Aquinas links conservation to divine providence.)

These citations should suffice to establish the theological importance of DDC, and thus the significance of any challenge to the doctrine, such as that posed by what Mortimer Adler called the "principle of inertia in being"[9] and what, following John Beaudoin's more elegant formulation, we will call the Doctrine of Existential Inertia (DEI).[10] According to DEI, the world of

---

3   *De Genesi ad litteram* 4:12, as translated by John Hammond Taylor in St. Augustine, *The Literal Meaning of Genesis* (New York: Paulist Press, 1982), Volume I, p. 118.

4   *De Genesi ad litteram* 5:20.

5   Revised Standard Version throughout.

6   It is classified as *de fide* in Ludwig Ott's *Fundamentals of Catholic Dogma* (Cork: Mercier Press, 1955), p. 87.

7   Part I, Article I.

8   Denzinger, *Sources of Catholic Dogma* 1784.

9   Mortimer Adler, *How to Think About God: A Guide for the 20th-Century Pagan* (New York: Collier/Macmillan, 1980), pp. 125, 132.

10   John Beaudoin, "The world's continuance: divine conservation or existential iner-

contingent things, once it exists, will tend to continue in existence on its own at least until something positively acts to destroy it. It thus has no need to be conserved in being by God.

Beaudoin asserts that "despite its centrality to the orthodox view about God's relationship to his creation ... attempts to *prove* that the world could not endure but for God's conserving activity are scarce."[11] Similarly, Robert Pasnau and Christopher Shields claim that Aquinas, when defending DDC, "does not offer anything like a decisive refutation" of DEI.[12] If accurate, such claims would be surprising given that, as we have seen, Aquinas holds that *reason* as well as faith "binds us" to affirm DDC. But such claims are not accurate. For one thing, the very passages from Aquinas quoted above, wherein he affirms DDC, occur in contexts in which he presents arguments for that doctrine and against DEI. But more importantly, the main arguments for God's existence within classical philosophical theology are, when properly understood, themselves arguments for DDC and against DEI. In particular, this is precisely how Aquinas's famous Five Ways (which are really just summaries of traditional arguments Aquinas did not claim to have invented himself) should be understood, or so I will argue. DDC is not regarded by Aquinas and other defenders of the arguments in question as some additional thesis that must be established separately, after God's existence has first been demonstrated via the theistic proofs. Rather, the proofs are intended to establish God's existence precisely by showing that the world could not exist even for an instant, or at least could not exist in the specific ways it actually does exist, were it not for the continual conserving action of God. And if the proofs succeed (as Aquinas obviously thinks they do), then DEI would by implication be thereby "decisively refuted" (as Pasnau and Shields put it).

In the next section, I will develop and defend the suggestion that the traditional theistic proofs represented by the Five Ways are best read as

---

tia?" *International Journal for Philosophy of Religion* 61 (2007): 83–98. The expression "existential inertia" is used by other writers too. See, e.g., Norman Kretzmann, *The Metaphysics of Theism* (Oxford: Clarendon Press, 1997), p. 98. Cf. Robert Pasnau and Christopher Shields, *The Philosophy of Aquinas* (Boulder, CO: Westview Press, 2004), pp. 144–45, which speaks of "the principle of inertia for existence." Jonathan Kvanvig and Hugh McCann characterize the rival to DDC as the doctrine of the world's "self-sustenance," and regard talk of existential inertia as one possible construal of self-sustenance. See their article "Divine Conservation and the Persistence of the World," in Thomas V. Morris, ed., *Divine and Human Action: Essays in the Metaphysics of Theism* (Ithaca: Cornell University Press, 1988).

11   Ibid., p. 84.

12   Pasnau and Shields, *Philosophy of Aquinas*, p. 144.

defenses of DDC and, consequently, as implicit critiques of DEI. That they are challenging critiques, deserving the attention of contemporary philosophers, is something I hope will be evident from the discussion, as well as from section III, where I will explore how the traditional proofs so interpreted might form the basis of a response to recent defenses of DEI. The fourth and final section will attempt to make explicit the core metaphysical disagreements which, as the preceding discussion will have indicated, underlie the dispute over DDC and DEI. It will be argued that a proper understanding and resolution of the latter dispute is impossible without a proper understanding and resolution of the former, more fundamental metaphysical disagreements. While the paper does not pretend to resolve either of these disputes, I hope it will contribute to the understanding of both.

II. DDC, DEI, and the Five Ways

How to interpret the Five Ways, and whether and how they might be defended against the standard objections, are, of course, large questions that I cannot address in any detail here. I have done so elsewhere.[13] Here I will ignore exegetical questions, borrowing freely from the history of Thomistic interpretation of the proofs rather than sticking closely to Aquinas's texts. I will focus on what I take to be the nerve of each of the arguments, treating them (somewhat anachronistically) as representative of the five main traditional Thomistic approaches to arguing from the world to the existence of a divine conserver of the world (some of the details of which are not explicit in Aquinas but suggested in the work of later Thomists).[14] These approaches can be summarized as follows: The first argues that the existence, even for an instant, of composites of act and potency presupposes the simultaneous existence of that which is pure act; the second argues that the existence, even for an instant, of composites of essence and existence presupposes the simultaneous existence of that

13   See Edward Feser, *Aquinas* (Oxford: Oneworld, 2009), especially chapter 3.
14   I am in this regard merely treating the Five Ways as the Thomistic tradition has always treated them, as living arguments rather than museum pieces. What matters ultimately is not whether Aquinas himself explicitly said such-and-such in the course of stating the proofs, but rather whether such-and-such in fact follows from what he did say, or at least whether it is the sort of thing one could or should say if one is committed to the same principles Aquinas was. Hence the arguments to be examined here are certainly *Thomistic* arguments, whether or not they are in every respect *Aquinas's* arguments.

which is being or existence itself; the third argues that the existence, even for an instant, of composites of form and matter presupposes the simultaneous existence of an absolutely necessary being; the fourth argues that the existence, even for an instant, of things which are many and come in degrees of perfection presupposes the simultaneous existence of something one and absolutely perfect; and the fifth argues that the existence, even for an instant, of finality or directedness toward an end presupposes the simultaneous existence of a supreme ordering intellect. Let us examine each of these in turn.

II.1 The First Way

The First Way is otherwise known as the argument from motion to an Unmoved Mover, where by "motion" Aquinas means change of any sort and where by "change" he means the reduction of potency to act (or potentiality to actuality). Given the details of Aquinas's presentation of the argument in the *Summa Theologiae* and elsewhere, contemporary discussions of it tend, understandably, to focus on a myriad of questions about whether its treatment of local motion is vitiated by Newton's law of inertia, whether the cause of something's actually having some feature F must itself actually be F, and so forth. But I would suggest that the heart of the argument is actually much more straightforward than it might at first appear, or at least that the argument suggests a more straightforward argument that can be expressed exclusively in the language of act and potency, leaving to one side questions about local motion and the like. Moreover, while it is natural and useful to introduce the notion of the reduction of potency to act using events as examples—like Aquinas's example of wood being heated by fire—I would suggest also that the thrust of the argument is best understood in terms of substances rather than events. For the occurrence of an event ultimately presupposes (for an Aristotelian like Aquinas, certainly) the existence of a substance or substances[15]; and the existence of a natural substance involves, no less than the events it enters into does, the reduction of potency to act. Accordingly, we might present a "streamlined" reconstruction of the argument as follows:

---

15   "It is evident that anything whatever operates so far as it is a being" (*Quaestiones disputatae de anima*, article 19, as translated by John Patrick Rowan in St. Thomas Aquinas, *The Soul* (St. Louis: B. Herder, 1949)). See Feser, *Aquinas*, pp. 74–76 for discussion and defense of the suggestion that the argument from motion is ultimately concerned to explain the existence of the things which move no less than the fact of their motion.

1. That the actualization of potency is a real feature of the world follows from the occurrence of the events we know of via sensory experience.
2. The occurrence of any event E presupposes the operation of a sub stance.
3. The existence of any natural substance S at any given moment presup poses the concurrent actualization of a potency.
4. No mere potency can actualize a potency; only something actual can do so.
5. So any actualizer A of S's current existence must itself be actual.
6. A's own existence at the moment it actualizes S itself presupposes either (a) the concurrent actualization of a further potency or (b) A's being purely actual.
7. If A's existence at the moment it actualizes S presupposes the concurrent actualization of a further potency, then there exists a regress of concur rent actualizers that is either infinite or terminates in a purely actual ac tualizer.
8. But such a regress of concurrent actualizers would constitute a causal series ordered *per se*, and such a series cannot regress infinitely.
9. So either A itself is purely actual or there is a purely actual actualizer which terminates the regress of concurrent actualizers.
10. So the occurrence of E and thus the existence of S at any given moment presupposes the existence of a purely actual actualizer.

The argument is, admittedly, highly abstract compared to Aquinas's own presentation. Again, I am not putting forward textual exegesis here, but something more like "rational reconstruction" (if such positivist jargon can be forgiven in this context) in light of the history of Thomistic interpretation of the argument. But the reduction of potency to act—the explanation of which, as I have indicated, is Aquinas's ultimate concern in the argument— is itself a highly abstract notion in any event. And the point of focusing on it is to make as evident as possible the relevance of the argument from mo tion to the dispute between DDC and DEI.

All the same, the reader might reasonably ask what sort of potency it is the actualization of which premise (3) tells us is presupposed by the existence at any moment of a natural substance S. The answer is that there are several possible answers. In an Aristotelian vein, one might hold that any natural sub stance S must be a composite of prime matter and substantial form, and that since prime matter is of itself purely potential, S cannot exist unless some ac tualizer A conjoins (and keeps conjoined) to its prime matter the substantial form of *S*. Or, in a more distinctively Thomistic vein, one might hold that any natural substance *S* must be a composite of an essence and an act of existence, and that since an essence is of itself purely potential, *S* cannot exist unless some actualizer *A* conjoins (and keeps conjoined) to its essence *S*'s act of existence. Or, in a more Neo-Platonic vein, one might hold that any natural substance *S* will be in some respect or other composite so that its parts only potentially constitute the whole unless conjoined (and kept conjoined) by some actualizer *A* which is incomposite or One. Indeed, among the rest of the Five Ways are arguments which deploy precisely these sorts of analyses of · natural substances. The argument from motion to an Unmoved Mover—or what we might more fittingly (if less elegantly) call the argument from the actualization of potency to that which is *Actus Purus*—can be understood, then, as holding that whatever the metaphysical details turn out to be vis-à-vis the structure of events and substances, they will involve the actualization of potency, and that this presupposes the operation of that which is pure act.[16]

The rest of the argument will be familiar to those acquainted with the literature on the Five Ways. For example, the notion of a causal series ordered *per se*, to which (8) appeals, is the notion of a series all but one of whose members have no independent causal power, but derive their efficacy from an uncaused cause to whom they are related as instruments. (Recall Aquinas's example of the stick which can move the stone only insofar as it

16   An anonymous referee objects that in the First Way Aquinas is concerned only with explaining motion and not with explaining the existence of things. But whether this is so is a matter of dispute among Thomists; and in any event (and as I have emphasized already) I am not putting forward exegesis of Aquinas's own texts here, but rather considering the Five Ways as they have been developed within the Thomistic tradition as a whole. For the view that the argument from motion *is* implicitly concerned with existence (or that it can at least plausibly be developed in that direction), see: Etienne Gilson, *The Christian Philosophy of St. Thomas Aquinas* (South Bend, IN: University of Notre Dame Press, 1994), pp. 77–83; Norman Kretzmann, *The Metaphysics of Theism* (Oxford: Oxford University Press, 1997), pp. 111–12; D. Q. McInerny, *Natural Theology* (Elmhurst, PA: Priestly Fraternity of St. Peter, 2005), pp. 89–91; Joseph Owens, *An Elementary Christian Metaphysics* (Houston: Center for Thomistic Studies, 1985), pp. 343–46; Henri Renard, *The Philosophy of God* (Milwaukee: Bruce Publishing Company, 1951), p. 31; and Stephen Weber, "Concerning the Impossibility of A Posteriori Arguments for the Existence of God," *Journal of Religion* 53 (1973): 83–98. A critical discussion of the views of Gilson, Owens, and Weber can be found in William Lane Craig, *The Cosmological Argument from Plato to Leibniz* (New York: Harper and Row, 1980), pp. 162–72. Again, I have defended the idea that the argument from motion is ultimately concerned with the existence of things that move no less than their motion in my *Aquinas*, pp. 74–76.

is being used by the hand to move it.) That Aquinas has this sort of series in mind (rather than a series ordered *per accidens*, of the sort which might trace back infinitely into the past) is well known to serious students of the argument, even if not to some of its popular critics and defenders. And the idea (at least as some commentators would interpret or extend Aquinas's argument) is that if *A*'s existence depends on the concurrent existence and actualizing activity of some further actualizer *B*, and *B*'s existence depends on the concurrent existence and actualizing activity of some further actualizer *C*, then we clearly have a series ordered *per se* which can terminate only in that which can actualize without itself requiring actualization— something that just is, already, purely actual.

As I have said, a more detailed discussion and defense of the argument is not something I can get into here, though I have done so elsewhere and I will make some general remarks in the final section of the present paper. The point for now is to note that the argument clearly constitutes a defense of DDC and a critique of DEI. For if successful, it would show that no natural substance could exist at any given moment without a purely actual actualizer either directly or indirectly maintaining it in existence. And the notion of *Actus Purus* or pure act is the philosophical core of at least the Aristotelian-Thomistic conception of God.

II.2 The Second Way

The Second Way is also known as the argument from efficient causality to an Uncaused Cause. As is often noted, the argument can seem at first glance to differ from the First Way only verbally. But several commentators have suggested (correctly, in my view) that there is a substantive difference between them insofar as the Second Way takes as its *explanandum* the existence or being of things, whereas the First Way seeks to explain their motion or change (even if it, too, as I have suggested, must account for their existence in the course of explaining their motion). In this respect, the Second Way is reminiscent of what is sometimes called the "existential proof" of Aquinas's *De ente et essentia*, and since the point of the Five Ways is to survey what Aquinas takes to be the main arguments for God's existence, it is natural to wonder whether the former argument was intended as a summary of the latter. The suggestion is controversial but, I think, correct, and I will take it for granted in my discussion here.[17]

17 William Lane Craig, who agrees that the Second Way is concerned to explain the existence or being of things, nevertheless resists any assimilation of it to the argu-

Now, the existential proof presupposes Aquinas's famous doctrine (alluded to above) of the real distinction between essence and existence in everything other than God. The proof seeks to show that nothing in which essence and existence are distinct could exist even for an instant unless there is something in which essence and existence are identical—something which just is *ipsum esse subsistens*, Subsistent Being Itself—conjoining its essence to an act of existence and thereby maintaining it in being. Reading the Second Way in light of this approach suggests the following reconstruction:

1. That efficient causation is a real feature of the world is evident from sensory experience.
2. Nothing can be the efficient cause of itself.
3. The existence of any natural substance S at any given moment presup poses that its essence is concurrently being conjoined to an act of exis tence.
4. If S itself were somehow conjoining its own essence to an act of exis tence, it would be the efficient cause of itself.
5. So there must be some concurrent efficient cause C distinct from S which is conjoining S's essence to an act of existence.
6. C's own existence at the moment it conjoins S's essence to an act of ex istence presupposes either (a) that C's essence is concurrently being conjoined to an act of existence, or (b) that in C essence and existence are identical.
7. If C's existence at the moment it conjoins S's essence to an act of exis tence presupposes that C's own essence is concurrently being conjoined to an act of existence, then there exists a regress of concurrent conjoin ers of essences and acts of existence that is either infinite or terminates in something whose essence and existence are identical.
8. But such a regress of concurrent conjoiners of essence and existence would constitute a causal series ordered *per se*, and such a series cannot regress infinitely.
9. So either C's own essence and existence are identical, or there is some thing else whose essence and existence are identical which terminates the regress of concurrent conjoiners of essences with acts of existence.
10. So the existence of S at any given moment presupposes the existence of something in which essence and existence are identical.

ment of *De ente et essentia*. See his *The Cosmological Argument from Plato to Leibniz*, p. 177. I defend the assimilation and reply to Craig in my *Aquinas*, pp. 84–87.

There are obvious parallels between this argument and the argument for a purely actual actualizer. The notion of a causal series ordered *per se* plays a similar role in both, and that which initiates the potential regress is similar too. In the first argument, the idea was that the existence of any natural substance S at any given moment presupposes the actualization at that moment of a potency, and that whatever does the actualizing must itself already be actual. We saw that this actualizing might be conceived of more concretely in terms of S's prime matter having conjoined to it the substantial form of S, or in terms of S's essence being conjoined to an act of existence. The argument for an Uncaused Cause, as I have interpreted it, essentially makes a separate argument of this second more concrete conceptualization of the actualizing of S. It holds that S's essence, and thus S itself, is merely potential until that essence is conjoined with an act of existence. But if S or S's essence did this conjoining, then S would be the cause of itself, which is impossible. Hence the conjoining must be done by some cause C distinct from S. But the distinction between S's essence and existence that this presupposes is as real after S first comes into existence as it was before; and for S or S's essence to conjoin S's essence to an act of existence even after S first comes into existence would be for S to cause itself, which is no less impossible after S already exists than before.[18] Hence the conjoining of S's essence and existence by a cause distinct from S must be maintained at any moment S exists.

As with the argument for a purely actual actualizer, there is much more to be said about the argument, and as with the former argument, a completely general treatment is beyond the scope of this paper while some of the specific issues germane to the theme of the paper will be addressed in the later sections. The point to emphasize for the moment is that here too we have an argument for DDC and against DEI. For if S cannot cause its own continuance in existence any more than its coming into being, then DEI is false. And if what does cause its continuance in existence must ultimately be something in which essence and existence are identical, then since this just is the core of the Thomistic conception of God, DDC is true.

II.3 The Third Way
The Third Way is otherwise known as the argument from the contingency of the world to the existence of an absolutely Necessary Being. It would be

---

18 Obviously the temporal language here ("until," "after," "before") is to be understood metaphorically, as implying relations of *ontological* rather than temporal priority or posteriority.

a serious mistake to read into the argument themes of the sort familiar from contemporary discussions of contingency and necessity, such as appeals to the "conceivability" of this or that, or to possible worlds, or the assimilation of metaphysical necessity to logical necessity. For Aquinas, as for Aristotelians generally, possibility and necessity are grounded in what is actual. We do not determine the essence of a thing by first considering what it would be like in various possible worlds; rather, we determine what it would be like in various possible worlds only after first determining its essence, which means determining what it is like in the actual world. Hence, when in the Third Way Aquinas says that the things our senses reveal to us are "possible not to be," he doesn't mean that we can "conceive" of them going out of existence or that there is at least one possible world in which they do so. He means that there is something in their nature that makes them inherently incapable of persisting indefinitely. And when he goes on to say that "that which is possible not to be at some time is not," he is not fallaciously arguing that if some event is possible in some completely abstract way—in the sense that we can conceive of it without contradiction, say, or that there is a possible world where it occurs—then it will happen in the actual world. He is saying rather that if a thing has an inherent tendency to go out of existence, then eventually that tendency will be manifested in its actually going out of existence.

The basis of this tendency in the things of our experience is their form/matter composition, for "a possibility of non-being is in the nature of those things ... whose matter is subject to contrariety of forms."[19] But even if one concedes that material things have and will realize such a tendency, and even if one concedes too Aquinas's further claim that if everything is "possible not to be" then at one time there would have been nothing, might one not argue that the underlying matter out of which the things of our experience are made is itself not "possible not to be," that it is a kind of necessary being? Indeed, some critics of the Third Way make precisely this suggestion.[20] Where they go wrong is in assuming that Aquinas would disagree with them. For in fact, Aquinas himself holds that while individual material things are generated and corrupted, matter and form themselves

---

19   *Quaestiones disputatae de potentia Dei* 5.3, as translated by Lawrence Shapcote in Thomas Aquinas, *On the Power of God* (Westminster, MD: The Newman Press, 1932).

20   See, e.g., J. L. Mackie, *The Miracle of Theism* (Oxford: Clarendon Press, 1982), p. 91; and Bede Rundle, *Why there is Something rather than Nothing* (Oxford: Clarendon Press, 2004), pp. 96–97.

are (apart from special divine creation, to which he would not appeal for the purposes of the argument at hand lest he argue in a circle) not susceptible of generation and corruption.[21] So, Aquinas is happy to concede, at least for the sake of argument, that matter might be a kind of necessary being. Moreover, he recognizes the existence of other non-divine necessary beings as well, such as angels and even heavenly bodies (which, given the astronomical knowledge then available, the medievals mistakenly regarded as not undergoing corruption). This should not be surprising when we keep in mind that getting to the existence of a necessary being is only the first half of the Third Way. The second half is devoted to showing that any necessary being that does not have its necessity of itself must ultimately derive it from a necessary being which does have its necessity of itself. In particular, it is Aquinas's view that even if matter and form, angels and heavenly bodies count as necessary beings of a sort, they do not have their necessity of themselves but must derive it from an absolutely necessary being, namely God.[22]

That the matter which persists throughout the generations and corruptions of particular material objects cannot have its necessity of itself should be obvious when we consider that for Aquinas such matter is just prime matter or pure potentiality, which by itself and apart from the forms it takes on has no actuality nor indeed any reality at all, necessary or otherwise. And for Aquinas the forms in question have (apart from the postmortem souls of human beings) no existence apart from matter, so that they cannot be said to have their necessity of themselves either. Nor will it do to suggest that any particular form/matter composite might have its necessity of itself, even apart from the fact that such composites have an inherent tendency to go out of existence. For since in purely material substances matter depends on form and form depends on matter, we would have a vicious explanatory circle unless there was something outside the form/matter composite which accounts for its existence.[23] Then there is the fact that material objects are composites of essence and existence as well, as are disembodied human souls and angels; and for reasons already stated, such composites must be

21 *De principiis naturae* 2.15
22 That angels and the like are "necessary" in this derivative sense does not entail for Aquinas that they cannot go out of existence, only that they cannot do so in the way material things do, i.e., via corruption. Such a derivatively necessary being could go out of existence via annihilation, if God ceased conjoining its essence to an act of existence.
23 Cf. Christopher F. J. Martin, *Thomas Aquinas: God and Explanations* (Edinburgh: Edinburgh University Press, 1997), pp. 166–67.

sustained in being by something in which essence and existence are identical. In this way, then, necessary beings other than God must derive their necessity from God.[24]

With this interpretive background in place, we can propose the following reconstruction of the basic thrust of the argument from contingency:

1. That the particular substances revealed to us in sensory experience are contingent is evident from the fact that they are generated and corrupted.

2. Their generation and corruption presuppose matter and form, which are neither generated nor corrupted and are thus necessary.

3. But matter of itself is pure potency and material forms of themselves are mere abstractions, so that neither can exist apart from the other; and even when existing together they cannot depend on each other alone on pain of vicious circularity.

4. So matter and form do not have their necessity of themselves but must derive it from something else.

5. Material substances are also composites of essence and existence, as are non-divine necessary beings like angels, and any such composite must have its essence and existence conjoined by something distinct from it.

6. So these other necessary beings too must derive their necessity from something else.

7. But a regress of necessary beings deriving their necessity from another would constitute a causal series ordered *per se*, which of its nature cannot regress infinitely.

8. So there must be something which is necessary in an absolute way, not deriving its necessity from another and (therefore) not a composite of form and matter or essence and existence.

Note that prime matter cannot at any moment exist without form and a material form cannot at any moment exist without prime matter; they depend on each other at every moment in which they are conjoined together in a material substance. Hence the circularity inherent in explaining the existence of a material substance's form in terms of its matter and the existence of its matter in terms of its form holds at any moment at which the substance exists, so that they require an external cause of their conjunction at any

---

24 For a detailed defense of this reading of the Third Way, see Feser, *Aquinas*, pp. 90–99.

moment it exists. Something similar holds of any composite of essence and existence, for reasons already explained. So, we have in the present argument too an argument against DEI and, since the ultimate explanation arrived at is an absolutely necessary being which is not a compound of essence and existence but that in which essence and existence are identical, an argument for DDC as well.

II.4 The Fourth Way

The Fourth Way is sometimes described as an argument from grades of perfection to a divine Exemplar, and sometimes as a henological argument from the multiplicity of things to a divine Unity. Like the Five Ways in general, it is very widely misunderstood, perhaps even more so than the other arguments. For example, it is often assumed that Aquinas is arguing that every attribute that comes in degrees must have its fullest exemplar in God; and it is then objected that this entails such absurdities as that God must be the supreme exemplar of smelliness. But in fact Aquinas is concerned only with what the Scholastics called the *transcendentals*—being, one, good, true, and the like—which, unlike smelliness, sweetness, heat, cold, red, green, etc., are predicable of everything without exception. And it is because the transcendentals are (as the Scholastics held) "convertible" with one another that Aquinas takes what is most true, most good, and so forth to be one and the same thing, and to be identical in turn with what is "uttermost being." The argument is also often read in Platonic terms, and while this is not an egregious misunderstanding, it is also not quite right. Aquinas is indeed committed to a doctrine of "participation," but he does not understand participation in terms of purely formal causation, and he does not regard the being, goodness, unity, and truth in which things participate as abstract objects *à la* Plato's Forms. Rather, he takes the transcendentals participated in to be the *efficient* causes of things' being good, true, one, etc. to the extent that they are, where what this ultimately entails is that the Subsistent Being Itself with which all the transcendentals are identical is the one efficient cause of their being, goodness, truth, unity, etc. at any given moment.[25]

In short, we can think of the Fourth Way as a kind of extension, via the doctrine of the transcendentals, of the basic thrust of the earlier argument

---

25 This is not to deny that there is also a sense in which they are formal causes. As an anonymous referee notes, "Aquinas also takes them to be *formal causes* as *exemplars*" and thereby "proves that God is both the formal exemplar cause of the being (*esse*) of all beings as well as their efficient cause."

for an Uncaused Cause whose essence and existence are identical. That in which essence and existence are distinct, and which is thus limited in being, depends upon that which just is pure existence or being. But being is convertible with goodness, unity, truth, etc. Hence that which is good only in some limited way must depend on that which is pure goodness, that which has unity only in some limited way must depend in on that which is absolutely one, and so forth.[26] This suggests the following reconstruction of the argument from grades of perfection:

1. The things of our experience exhibit goodness, unity, and the other transcendentals only to some limited degree.
2. But they can do so only insofar as they participate in that which is good, one, etc. without limitation.
3. Moreover, the transcendentals are convertible with one another, and ultimately with Being Itself.
4. So there is some one thing which is being itself, goodness itself, unity itself, and so forth, in which the things of our experience participate to the degrees they do.
5. But that in which things participate is their efficient cause.
6. So the one thing which is being itself, goodness itself, unity itself, etc. is the efficient cause of the things of our experience.

Keep in mind that for Platonism, things participate in the Forms at every moment in which they exist at all, and otherwise would not exist at all. For instance, a dog is a dog only insofar as it participates in the Form of Dog, and if it were to cease participating in that Form even for an instant, it would cease to exist qua dog. And though Aquinas's notion of participation is not identical to Plato's, it has that much in common with it. Just as that in which essence and existence are distinct—that is to say, that which has being only in a limited way—could not in Aquinas's view exist for an instant if it were not sustained in being by that which just is Being Itself, so too he thinks that that which has goodness, unity, etc. only in a limited way could not exist (or at least not exist *qua* good, one, and so forth) even for an instant if it were not sustained by that which just is supreme goodness, unity, etc. So, once again we have an implicit argument against DEI and (given that that which is being itself, goodness itself, unity itself, etc. is God) an implicit argument for DDC.

---

26   Once again, see my *Aquinas* for a detailed defense of my proposed reading of the Fourth Way, especially pp. 99–109.

II.5 The Fifth Way

The Fifth Way is also known as the argument from finality to a supreme ordering intelligence. It might also be described as a teleological argument,
but it has nothing to do with the "design argument" of William Paley. Paley
and other defenders of the latter sort of argument take for granted a mechanistic conception of the natural order on which it is devoid of anything like
Aristotelian substantial forms or final causes. While they argue that certain
natural phenomena are teleological, the teleology in question is understood
to be extrinsic or imposed from outside rather than immanent or "built in,"
as Aristotelian natures and final causes are. The basis for a Paleyan inference
to design is a judgment to the effect that certain natural phenomena are too
complex plausibly to have arisen through natural processes and are thus
probably the artifacts of a superior intelligence. Aquinas's argument is nothing like this. He regards teleology as immanent to the natural order, as manifest in even the simplest causal processes rather than only in complex
phenomena, and as something that leads us conclusively to the existence of
a supreme intellect rather than merely as a matter of probability.

Take a simple causal regularity, such as a match's tendency to generate
flame and heat when struck, or ice's tendency to cool the air or liquid surrounding it, or some even more basic causal regularity at the micro level.[27]
Why is it that it is flame and heat specifically that a match will tend to generate when struck? It will not always actually generate it, of course, for it
might be impeded in some way from doing so—oxygen might be absent,
or it might have been water damaged, or it might have simply gotten so old
that the chemicals in the match head have lost their potency. But unless impeded in such ways, it will produce its characteristic effects, and only those
effects, rather than generating frost and cold, say, or the smell of lilacs, or a
thunderclap. Again, why? Aquinas's answer is that "every agent acts for an
end: otherwise one thing would not follow more than another from the action of the agent, unless it were by chance."[28] By "agent" he means an efficient cause, and by "acting for an end" he means that such a cause is as it
were "directed toward" the production of its characteristic effect or effects
as to an end or goal. In this way, efficient causality presupposes final causality: If we do not suppose that some cause A of its nature "points to" or is

27 Nothing hinges on the specific examples. If a reductionist insists that the causal
    properties of matches, or ice, or any macro-level object can be reduced without re-
    mainder to the causal properties of some micro-level entities, the defender of the
    Fifth Way can simply re-state the point in terms of those more basic regularities.
28 *Summa Theologiae* I.44.4.

"directed at" the generation of some effect or range of effects B, specifically—rather than to C, D, or no effect at all—then we have no way of making intelligible why it does in fact regularly generate B rather than these other effects. Notice that this does not involve attributing anything like a biological function to such causes—biological functions are, contrary to a common misconception, only one, relatively rare kind of finality in nature, and do not exhaust final causality—and that it has nothing to do with complexity. Furthermore, the end-directedness in question is inherent to causes, something they have by virtue of their natures or essences. At least in the case of natural causes (such as ice's tendency to cool surrounding water or air) we can determine from the regularity of their behavior alone what their causal tendencies and thus "final causes" are, and do not need to advert to the intentions of a designer. (Indeed, Aristotle, who believed both in final causes and in God, did not think that the former needed to be explained in terms of the latter.)

This essentially Aristotelian, anti-mechanistic conception of the world as immanently teleological is what Aquinas means to affirm in the first half of the Fifth Way, when he writes:

> We see that things which lack intelligence, such as natural bodies, act for an end, and this is evident from their acting always, or nearly always, in the same way, so as to obtain the best result. Hence it is plain that not fortuitously, but designedly, do they achieve their end.

By "designedly" (*ex intentione*), he does not mean "because of a designer," *à la* Paley. Rather, he means, as Aristotle would, "because of the teleology or end-directedness inherent in things, rather than by chance."[29] Whether

---

29 Christopher F. J. Martin translates *ex intentione* as "in virtue of some tendency" (*Thomas Aquinas: God and Explanations*, p. 179), which is, I think, to be preferred both to the widely used Fathers of the English Dominican Province translation quoted above and to the common alternative translation "by intention." "Designedly" and "by intention," while not incorrect, can be misleading given the way "design" and "intention" are typically used in contemporary philosophical discussion of these issues, which differs from the way they are used in Scholastic philosophy. As Bernard Wuellner explains in his *Dictionary of Scholastic Philosophy* (Milwaukee: Bruce Publishing Company, 1956), in Scholastic metaphysics "intention" can mean "the direction or application of causal power to an effect; the influence of the primary cause on the instrument" (p. 63). (For the first "of," Wuellner's text actually reads "or," but this is evidently a typo.) Wuellner adds: "This may be

this teleology must itself be explained in terms of intelligence is a further question, one Aquinas gets to only in the next sentence, when he writes that "whatever lacks intelligence cannot move towards an end, unless it be directed by some being endowed with knowledge and intelligence." The claim is peremptory; there is no question here of "weighing probabilities" or the like. Why?

The basic idea is this. A cause cannot be efficacious unless it exists in some way. But in the case of the final cause of some unintelligent causal process, the cause in question does not exist in the natural order. For instance, the oak is the end or final cause of the acorn, and yet until the acorn develops into the oak, the oak does not actually exist in the natural world. Now with artifacts, the final cause can be efficacious because it exists (or rather its form exists) in the mind of the artificer. For example, a building is the final cause of the actions of a builder, and it serves as a genuine cause despite its not yet existing in the natural order by existing at least as an idea in the builder's intellect. Now unless there is some third alternative, this is how the final causes operative in the order of unintelligent natural things must exist, for they have to exist somehow in order to be efficacious. But there is no third alternative, given Aquinas's rejection of Platonism. If the oak does not exist in a Platonic third realm and it does not yet exist either in the natural world, the only place left for it to exist, as it must if it is to have any efficacy vis-à-vis the acorn, is as a form or idea in an intellect. And the same thing is true of all the other final causes operative in the order of unintelligent natural processes, which means it is true of the entire order of efficient causes making up the natural world, since all efficient causality presupposes final causality.

So, there must be an intellect outside the natural order directing things to their ends, where these ends pre-exist as ideas in said intellect. And notice that this must be the case at any moment at which natural substances exist at all, for they retain their inherent causal powers and thus their immanent finality or end-directedness at every moment at which they exist. Notice too that precisely since this finality or end-directedness is immanent, "built into" things given their natures or essences, that which directs natural things to their ends must be what gives them their natures or essences, and thus

---

the primary meaning of intention as it best shows the notion of directing or tending on the part of a being or power." Again, what is in view is the Aristotelian notion of *immanent* teleology, rather than the *extrinsic* teleology in terms of which Paley and his contemporary successors frame their "design argument."

what conjoins their essences to an act of existence. Since for reasons already stated this must ultimately be something in which essence and existence are identical, we are led by yet another route to the existence of God, and not merely to a finite designer (which Paley-style arguments cannot rule out).[30]

We are led, then, to the following reconstruction of the overall thrust of the argument from finality:

1. That unintelligent natural causes regularly generate certain specific effects or ranges of effects is evident from sensory experience.
2. Such regularities are intelligible only on the assumption that these efficient causes inherently "point to" or are "directed at" their effects as to an end or final cause.
3. So there are final causes or ends immanent to the natural order.
4. But unintelligent natural causes can "point to" or be "directed at" such ends only if guided by an intelligence.
5. So there is such an intelligence.
6. But since the ends or final causes in question are inherent in things by virtue of their natures or essence, the intelligence in question must be the cause also of natural things having the natures or essences they do.
7. This entails its being that which conjoins their essences to an act of existence, and only that in which essence and existence are identical can ultimately accomplish this.
8. So the intelligence in question is something in which essence and existence are identical.

---

30 An anonymous referee objects that this goes beyond what Aquinas himself says in his statement of the Fifth Way. But again, what we are concerned with here is how the Five Ways have been interpreted and developed in the Thomistic tradition, not with exegesis of Aquinas's own texts. For one statement of the view that the Fifth Way leads to a supreme intellect which not only orders things to their ends but is also their creator, see Maurice Holloway, *An Introduction to Natural Theology* (New York: Appleton-Century-Crofts, 1959), p. 142. For the view that the Fifth Way leads to a supreme intellect in which essence and existence are identical, see Reginald Garrigou-Lagrange, *God: His Existence and His Nature* (St. Louis: B. Herder, 1939), Volume I, p. 370, and Renard, *The Philosophy of God*, pp. 45–48. (Cf. also the works by Gilson and Owens cited earlier, which regard all of the Five Ways as ultimately concerned with explaining the existence of that in which existence and essence are distinct in terms of that in which essence and existence are identical.) For my own more detailed defense of the reading of the Fifth Way proposed in the text, see Feser, *Aquinas*, pp. 110–20. For further discussion of the differences between a Paleyan conception of teleology and an Aristotelian one, see Edward Feser, "Teleology: A Shopper's Guide," *Philosophia Christi*, Vol. 12, No. 1 (2010).

Once again we have an implicit argument against DEI, since the claim is that a natural substance could not have the final cause or end it has even for an instant without some intelligence distinct from it ordering it to that end, which (it is argued) entails in turn that this intelligence must be keeping its essence conjoined to an act of existence at every such instant. And since that intelligence would have to be something in which essence and existence are identical, we also have an implicit argument for DDC.

The reference, yet again, to the essence/existence distinction is likely to raise in many readers' minds a thought that has no doubt occurred to them already, viz. that the Five Ways as I (and other Thomists historically) have interpreted them overlap significantly. That impression is not entirely misleading. The Aristotelian-Thomistic metaphysical framework upon which the arguments rest—comprising the act/potency, form/matter, and essence/existence distinctions, the notions of the transcendentals, of causal powers, finality, causal series ordered *per se*, and so on and so forth—constitutes a tightly integrated structure which offers several avenues of approach to what is ultimately one and the same summit. Still, the avenues *are* different, at least at their beginning points. And even where they overlap, there is value in considering the proofs individually. If we might borrow Wittgenstein's description of his own (admittedly very different!) method, in order fully to grasp the theological implications of the Aristotelian-Thomistic system, "the very nature of the investigation ... compels us to travel over a wide field of thought criss-cross in every direction," making "a number of sketches of landscapes ... in the course of these long and involved journeyings," and with "the same or almost the same points ... always being approached afresh from different directions, and new sketches made."[31]

III. Recent debate over DDC and DEI

If I am right, then, each of the traditional theistic arguments represented by the Five Ways embodies, or at least suggests, an argument for DDC and against DEI. Let us turn now to some recent defenses of DEI and critiques of DDC and consider how a defender of the Five Ways as I have interpreted them might respond.

---

31   As translated by G. E. M. Anscombe in Ludwig Wittgenstein, *Philosophical Investigations*, Third edition (New York: Macmillan, 1968), p. v.

III.1 Radical versus superficial contingency: One of the more noteworthy defenses of DEI comes, somewhat surprisingly, from Mortimer Adler, who was himself something of a Thomist.[32] Adler presents two arguments, a negative argument intended to undermine what he takes to be the main grounds for rejecting DEI, and a positive argument from Ockham's razor for preferring DEI to its rejection. I will address the positive argument in a later subsection. Let's consider for the moment the negative argument, which appeals to a distinction between radical and superficial contingency. The reason the opponent of DEI maintains that a natural substance will go out of existence without a divine sustaining cause, Adler says, is because such substances are contingent in the sense of being generated and corrupted, and thus have no tendency of their own to continue in existence. But the contingency in question, objects Adler, is only superficial. When natural substances go out of existence, they are merely broken down into their material components, which persist in another form. They are not *radically* contingent in the sense of being utterly annihilated. If they were, we would have grounds for saying that they have no inherent tendency to remain in existence, but since their contingency is only superficial—they don't really go out of existence, but merely change form—such an inference is blocked. And with the inference to the falsity of DEI blocked, so too is the inference to DDC.

Adler attributes to Etienne Gilson an acknowledgment that generation and corruption are not the same thing as exnihilation (coming into being out of nothing) and annihilation, but says that he cannot find an explicit acknowledgment of this distinction in Aquinas.[33] This is odd, given that (as I noted above when discussing the Third Way) Aquinas explicitly affirms in *De principiis naturae* that it is only particular individual material substances that are generated and corrupted, while matter and form themselves are not. It is also odd that Adler does not take account of the fact that Aquinas explicitly acknowledges in the Third Way that there can be non-divine beings which are necessary—that is to say, beings which have no inherent tendency to go out of existence—while maintaining that such beings nevertheless require a divine sustaining cause insofar as they do not have their necessity of themselves. Had he taken account of it, he might have seen that the fact that something has no tendency to go out of existence *by itself* does nothing to show that it possesses existential inertia. For everything depends on *why* it lacks such a tendency. If there is something in a thing's own nature that

32 Adler, *How to Think About God*, especially chapter 13.
33 Ibid., p. 127.

explains why it lacks that tendency, then DEI would indeed be vindicated. But if there is nothing in its nature that could account for the lack of such a tendency, then DEI is false and we have to appeal to something external to the thing to account for it.

Unfortunately, Adler never addresses the question of what there might be in a thing's nature that could either give it, or prevent it from possessing, existential inertia. But that question is at the heart of the dispute between Aquinas and the defender of DEI. Adler mistakenly assumes that Aquinas's position has to do fundamentally with contingency *as such*, that Aquinas is saying something like:

If *S* is contingent, then *S* lacks existential inertia.

and Adler's objection is that at least in the case where the contingency in question is superficial rather than radical, then the conditional is false. But Aquinas is not saying that, or rather not *merely* saying that. He is saying instead something like:

If *S* has feature *F*, then *S* lacks existential inertia *whether S is contingent or necessary*.

And what *F* is, specifically, is *being metaphysically composite*—being, that is to say, a compound of form and matter, or of essence and existence, or, more generally, of act and potency. This is explicitly what is at issue in the first three Ways as I have proposed interpreting them, and it is implicit in the Fourth and Fifth Ways as well insofar as they too ultimately infer to something which maintains its effect in existence by conjoining an essence to an act of existence.[34]

Adler's failure to see that it is compositeness rather than contingency that lies at the heart of Aquinas's objection to DEI is related to a muddle in

---

34 That it is being composite that ultimately makes a thing dependent for its continued existence upon a sustaining cause is emphasized in David Braine, *The Reality of Time and the Existence of God: The Project of Proving God's Existence* (Oxford: Clarendon Press, 1988). See especially pp. 177–96 and 342–45. That whatever is composite must ultimately be explained in terms of that which just is existence itself is also more or less the thrust of the arguments of Barry Miller, *From Existence to God* (London: Routledge, 1992) and William F. Vallicella, *A Paradigm Theory of Existence: Onto-Theology Vindicated* (Dordrecht: Kluwer Academic Publishers, 2002).

his distinction between radical and superficial contingency. Adler holds that a cat, say, is only superficially rather than radically contingent because its parts remain after the cat dies; and this is meant to support the claim that the cat possesses existential inertia. This at least gives the impression that the cat is no more than the sum of its parts—that something *of the cat* in fact remains after its death insofar as its parts persist, which is at least a natural way to read the claim that its contingency is only "superficial." Alternatively, D. Q. McInerny suggests that Adler thinks of a radically contingent being as one which depends on something else for its very existence, but of a superficially contingent being as one which depends on something else only for a "mode of being."[35] And if so, then (now to go beyond what McInerny himself says) it would seem to follow that for Adler, being a cat—or being a tree, or a stone, or a car, or any other of the ordinary objects of our experience—is really only a mode of the material world itself, which persists as a substance throughout the acquisition and loss of these modes. Whichever of these readings we adopt, from the point of view of the Aristotelian hylemorphism informing Aquinas's position, Adler simply misunderstands the nature of material substances, or at least begs the question against Aquinas. For the hylemorphist, a cat is neither an aggregate of material parts nor a mode of some material substance, but rather is itself a substance composed of prime matter and substantial form. Its going out of existence consists in its prime matter losing the substantial form of a cat and taking on some other substantial form or forms, such as the forms of the chemical elements that existed in the cat virtually while it was still alive. And because the substantial form of the cat is lost, there is absolutely nothing of the cat left after its death. The "parts" which carry on are not really *cat* parts in the strict sense—they cannot be, since there is no substantial form of a cat left to inform them—but rather new substances which came into being when the prime matter acquired new substantial forms. (A dead cat is not a kind of cat, but rather, as Monty Python might put it, an "ex-cat.")[36]

Even if Adler insisted that a cat or any other natural object was really just an aggregate of material parts or a mode of a substance constituted

---

35 McInerny, *Natural Theology*, p. 137.
36 Accordingly, McInerny says that in the relevant sense, and contrary to what Adler claims, a material substance qua substance *is* "annihilated" when it goes out of existence; for the *substance* really is completely gone even if its prime matter persists under another substantial form. (Ibid., p. 138.) But it seems to me less misleading to reserve the description "annihilation" for the case where neither the substance nor its prime matter persists in any way.

by the material world as a whole, the hylemorphist could respond that the fundamental material parts themselves—basic particles, or whatever—or the world considered as one gigantic substance, would still be composed of prime matter and substantial form. And *if* the material world is susceptible of a hylemorphic analysis at *some* level of description (a question we'll return to in the last section of the paper), we have an argument from the nature of material substances against DEI. That argument is already implicit in what was said in the previous section about the Third Way, but it will be worthwhile to make it explicit at this point, adding as a first premise a familiar principle of Scholastic metaphysics:

1. A cause cannot give what it does not have to give.
2. A material substance is a composite of prime matter and substantial form.
3. Something has existential inertia if and only if it has of itself a tendency to persist in existence once it exists.
4. But prime matter by itself and apart from substantial form is pure potency, and thus has of itself no tendency to persist in existence.
5. And substantial form by itself and apart from prime matter is a mere abstraction, and thus of itself also has no tendency to persist in existence.[37]
6. So neither prime matter as the material cause of a material substance, nor substantial form as its formal cause, can impart to the material substance they compose a tendency to persist in existence.
7. But there are no other internal principles from which such a substance might derive such a tendency.[38]
8. So no material substance has a tendency of itself to persist in existence once it exists.
9. So no material substance has existential inertia.

37 I ignore for present purposes the special case of the rational soul.
38 This premise reflects the Aristotelian thesis that among the four causes of a thing, its formal and material causes are intrinsic to it while its final and efficient causes are extrinsic. See Aquinas, *De principiis naturae* III.20. To be sure, that a natural substance *has* such-and-such a final cause is something intrinsic to it, but that is true by virtue of its *formal* cause. To take an example from earlier, the tendency of ice to cool what surrounds it is intrinsic to it, something determined by the substantial form of the water that it is composed of. It is part of its nature to have the generation of this outcome as an "end." But the end *itself*—coolness in the surrounding environment—is obviously something extrinsic to the ice.

III.2 Nothing to explain?: This argument, as well as the readings of the Five Ways I've proposed, also constitute an obvious response to an objection sometimes raised against DDC to the effect that it is an answer to a question that we shouldn't bother asking in the first place. For instance, Bede Rundle holds that "no form of causation, divine or otherwise, is in general required to ensure persistence in being ... [M]any things in the universe, as indeed the universe itself, do not have to fight for their survival, but, in the absence of forces which would bring them to an end, their continuation from moment to moment is in no need of explanation."[39] But if the composite act/potency or form /matter or essence/existence structure of natural substances entails that they cannot persist in existence on their own, then the fact of their persistence *does* require explanation, and the arguments in question purport to show that DDC is that explanation.

Other critics of DDC do not deny that the persistence of natural substances requires explanation, but claim that DEI suffices to explain it. Adler takes this approach himself, as does Beaudoin. The trouble is that for this strategy to work, the defender of DEI has to provide some account of natural substances that is both consistent with what we know about them and does not entail rejecting DEI, and no such account has been offered. For instance, as Beaudoin acknowledges, a plausible version of DEI will have to acknowledge that natural substances are contingent. But *why* are they contingent? As we saw when discussing Adler, Aquinas's answer is that they are composite in various ways, and it is this compositeness that entails that they cannot enjoy existential inertia. Only something non-composite, and thus something necessary (indeed something divine) can in his view have that. So, to defend his proposal Beaudoin would have to provide some account of natural substances on which their contingency does not derive from their being composite, or on which it does but where this compositeness somehow does not entail a rejection of DEI. Yet he gives no such account.

What he does tell us is merely that DEI is committed to the minimal claim that there exist some fundamental constituents of the natural world— whether they are conceived of as particles, or superstrings, or some continuous ever-morphing kind of stuff is irrelevant, he says—which are contingent but which nevertheless given their nature have no inherent tendency to go out of existence.[40] He acknowledges that it will not do to suggest

39   Rundle, *Why there is Something rather than Nothing*, p. 93.
40   Beaudoin, "The world's continuance: divine conservation or existential inertia?" pp. 86–87. Beaudoin says that a stronger version of DEI would assert that the every-

that it is simply a "brute fact" that things have existential inertia, and that it would be a "metaphysical muddle" to think of existential inertia as an active power a thing exerts on itself.[41] At the same time, he never explains *how it is* that the basic constituents he speaks of would have existential inertia despite being contingent. He merely puts forward the suggestion that they could have it as a claim that is not obviously incoherent, and suggests also that "it is far from clear that the proponent of DDC will fare better" in explaining why God's existence is not a brute fact.[42]

But it is obvious from the foregoing that the DDC proponent *does* fare better, for he can say that the reason God's existence is necessary is that He is Pure Act, Subsistent Being Itself, something absolutely One. The DDC proponent has—in the Aristotelian-Thomistic theories of act and potency, form and matter, essence and existence, final causality, the transcendentals, and so forth—a worked-out general metaphysics that *both* explains why natural substances lack existential inertia *and* provides an account of the divine nature. And as we will see in the final section of the paper, this general metaphysics is independently motivated, put forward as a way of accounting for basic features of the natural world and of our scientific knowledge of it that are acknowledged by the theist and the atheist alike. By contrast, Beaudoin offers little more than the bare assertion that at least at some, fundamental level, the natural world of contingent things enjoys existential inertia, where the assertion seems to have no theoretical motivation other than as a means of blocking an inference to DDC. It would be tempting to accuse Beaudoin of putting forward a "dormitive power" explanation of why things have existential inertia, except that this would be unfair to "dormitive power" explanations. For to say that opium puts people to sleep because of its dormitive power is (contrary to the stock dismissal of such explanations as tautologous) at least minimally informative: It tells us that the fact that opium puts people to sleep is no accident, but is rooted in some active power opium has by nature. But Beaudoin explicitly eschews the suggestion that

day objects comprised of arrangements of these fundamental constituents also enjoy existential inertia, but that this is not essential to countering DDC and that such a stronger thesis is in any event implausible in light of "radioactive decay and some other quantum-level events."

41   Ibid., pp. 88 and 93. Beaudoin agrees with Kvanvig and McCann that it would be incoherent to suggest that the continued existence of a thing can be explained in terms of an "active power" of self-sustenance, since the operation of such a power would itself *presuppose* the thing's continued existence.

42   Ibid., p. 89.

existential inertia involves the operation of an active power, and offers no other explanation of why a thing might have it.

For this reason, it will not do to suggest, as both Adler and Beaudoin appear to, that an appeal to Ockham's razor or the principle of parsimony favors DEI over DDC. For this would be so only if both views offered equally good explanations of the relevant facts—such as the contingency of the natural world—where DEI did so without postulating as many entities as DDC. But DEI does not offer any *explanation* at all. It simply amounts to the denial of the DDC explanation. DEI proponents do not say: "Yes, given an Aristotelian-Thomistic analysis of natural substances in terms of act and potency, form and matter, essence and existence, and so forth, no such substances can have existential inertia; but here is an alternative analysis of the nature of such substances on which they do have it." Rather, they offer no analysis at all. True, they do not affirm the Aristotelian-Thomistic conceptual apparatus, but neither do they put anything in its place. And merely to refrain from describing a phenomenon in some particular way is not to provide an alternative description of it.

III.3 The mythology of inertia: To reason from the premise that material substances are governed by Newton's law of inertia with respect to motion to the conclusion that they therefore enjoy existential inertia as well would be a gross non sequitur, and Beaudoin explicitly rejects any such argument.[43] He also follows Jonathan Kvanvig and Hugh McCann in rejecting the suggestion that the principle of the conservation of mass-energy entails DEI.[44] Still, both principles hover like specters over the debate about DEI and DDC, and defenders of DEI clearly believe that these findings of modern science at least lend plausibility to DEI and to that extent pose a difficulty for DDC. The idea seems to be that since the principles in question "explain" the phenomena of motion, mass, and energy, so too might a further inertial principle plausibly "explain" the continuance of the world. David Braine characterizes this sort of thinking as beholden to what he aptly labels "the mythology of inertia," and he quotes the following lines from Wittgenstein to indicate what is wrong with it:

> The whole modern conception of the world is founded on the illusion that the so-called laws of nature are the explanations of natural phenomena.

43   Ibid.
44   Ibid., pp. 90–91 and Kvanvig and McCann, "Divine Conservation and the Persistence of the World," pp. 31–34.

> Thus people today stop at the laws of nature, treating them as something inviolable, just as God and Fate were treated in past ages.
>
> And in fact both are right and both wrong: though the view of the ancients is clearer in so far as they have a clear and acknowledged terminus, while the modern system tries to make it look as if everything were explained.[45]

Of course, Wittgenstein was not endorsing the Thomistic arguments for God's existence, or any other such arguments. But those arguments are indeed "clearer" than is the scientism Wittgenstein is criticizing, not only about what their proposed terminus is but also (and contrary to what Wittgenstein implies) about *how* that proposed terminus really does "explain everything." For if there really is something that just is Pure Act, Subsistent Being Itself, absolute simplicity, and so forth, then there is no mystery about why this something requires no further explanation. But the same cannot be said for "laws of nature," inertial or otherwise. As Kvanvig and McCann emphasize, "laws, after all, are descriptive in import. They do not *operate* at all, despite our figures of speech, and they do not do anything in or to the world. If they are true, it is because things themselves have features the laws describe."[46] But neither will it do to appeal to these "things themselves," to some basic material entities which by their nature operate in accordance with the laws, as if they would constitute a plausible explanatory terminus. For we need to know why these entities exist—not merely how they got here in the first place, but why they persist in existence. And as Braine emphasizes, it would be incoherent to suggest that their natures *explain* their persistence in being, since their having natures in the first place *presupposes* that they persist in being.[47]

It is worth reemphasizing that the DEI proponent has no *tu quoque* escape available here, no way of stalemating the defender of DDC by accusing him of a similar failure of explanation. For, to repeat, the difficulty arises from the *composite* nature of any explanans posited by DEI, and the whole

---

45 Braine, *The Reality of Time and the Existence of God*, pp. 14–15. The Wittgenstein passage is from the D. F. Pears and B. F. McGuinness translation of *Tractatus Logico-Philosophicus* (London: Routledge and Kegan Paul, 1961), at 6.371 and 6.372.

46 Kvanvig and McCann, "Divine Conservation and the Persistence of the World," p. 34.

47 Braine, *The Reality of Time and the Existence of God*, p. 10.

point of DDC, at least as understood by thinkers like Aquinas, is to end the explanatory regress by concluding to something *non*-composite.[48]

IV. Metaphysical issues underlying the debate

Obviously, whether the Aristotelian-Thomistic critique of DEI and defense of DDC that I have been developing here succeeds is a question that cannot be settled apart from a more detailed evaluation of the family of theistic arguments represented by the Five Ways. (As I have said, I have presented such an evaluation elsewhere, in my *Aquinas*.) Equally obviously, there are more fundamental metaphysical considerations to be evaluated as well. In particular, as my discussion has made clear, the dispute between the proponent of DEI on the one hand and at least Thomistic defenders of DDC on the other crucially hinges on whether something like a general Aristotelian-Thomistic metaphysics and philosophy of nature is correct. If the correct analysis of natural substances entails recognizing something like the traditional distinctions between act and potency, form and matter, essence and existence, and so forth, then as we have seen, this would entail at the very least a powerful case against DEI and in favor of DDC. But if such an analysis is fundamentally in error, then the basis for the Thomistic position on these issues would seem to collapse.

There can be no question that the prevailing attitude among modern philosophers has been that the Aristotelian-Thomistic metaphysics and philosophy of nature *is* in error. Indeed, this attitude can plausibly be seen as *definitive* of modern philosophy. When Galileo, Descartes, Boyle, Locke, and the other early moderns replaced the Scholastics' conception of nature with a "mechanistic" one, what this entailed, essentially, was a rejection of substantial forms and final causes. Other elements too were part of the original mechanistic project (corpuscularianism, a push-pull model of causation, and so forth) but while these were all eventually either radically modified or dropped altogether, the negative, anti-Aristotelian element of the program—the resolve to avoid any appeal to *immanent teleology*, to the notion of an *end* to which a natural substance or process is directed given its *nature*

---

48   Though Beaudoin eschews an active power construal of DEI, he does regard existential inertia as part of the essence or nature of whatever fundamental material elements turn out to have it (p. 94). But here as elsewhere, he never considers, much less answers, the question of how something composed of act and potency, or form and matter, or essence and existence could possibly have existential inertia, despite the Thomist's claim to have shown that it cannot have it.

or essence[49]—has remained, and remained definitive of a mechanistic approach to nature, down to the present day.[50]

From an Aristotelian-Thomistic point of view, it was this move to mechanism that effectively undermined the possibility of arguing from the world to God, especially to God as a conserving cause. For the various elements of the Aristotelico-Thomistic metaphysical system are tightly integrated; remove one and the rest could not fail to go with it. In particular, if things have no substantial forms or immanent final causes, then they cannot coherently be said to be compounds of act and potency either. A substantial form just is what actualizes a potency inherent in matter. A potency is a potency *for* some actuality, *toward which* it is directed as towards an end. Hence, if there are no substantial forms, there is no actualizing of potencies, and if there are no ends or final causes, there are no potencies either. The notion of substances as compounds of essence and existence goes out the window too, since from a Thomistic point of view an essence is in potency relative to an act of existence, which actualizes it.

With this conceptual apparatus abandoned, the foundations of the traditional theistic arguments summarized in the Five Ways were undermined. The elements comprising the material world—no longer united organically

49   As noted earlier when discussing the Fifth Way, the Aristotelian conception of teleology as immanent to the natural order must be distinguished from the view of Newton, Boyle, Paley, and other proponents of the "design argument" to the effect that God imposes order on the world in the way an artificer re-works natural materials to serve an end they wouldn't otherwise have. Though committed to teleology, the latter sort of view is mechanistic precisely because it holds that final causes are not *immanent*, not in things by virtue of their *substantial forms*. For useful discussion of the differences between these two conceptions of teleology, see Margaret J. Osler, "From Immanent Natures to Nature as Artifice: The Reinterpretation of Final Causes in Seventeenth-Century Natural Philosophy," *The Monist* Vol. 79., No. 3 (1996), and André Ariew, "Platonic and Aristotelian Roots of Teleological Arguments," in André Ariew, Robert Cummins, and Mark Perlman, eds., *Functions: New Essays in the Philosophy of Psychology and Biology* (Oxford: Oxford University Press, 2002). See also my "Teleology: A Shopper's Guide."

50   That what is essential to a "mechanistic" conception of nature is the eschewal of immanent teleology seems fairly widely recognized. For example, such an understanding of mechanism is expressed by the philosopher of science David Hull (in his entry on "Mechanistic explanation" in Robert Audi, ed., *The Cambridge Dictionary of Philosophy* (Cambridge: Cambridge University Press, 1995), by philosopher of mind Tim Crane (in his book *The Mechanical Mind*, Second edition (London: Routledge, 2003), pp. 2–4) and by philosopher of religion William Hasker (in his book *The Emergent Self* (Ithaca: Cornell University Press, 1999), pp. 62–64).

into substances via immanent formal and final causes—came to seem essentially "loose and separate," having no more *inherent* unity than the parts of a machine do. Hence the regularities they did exhibit were reconceived on the model of the regularities a watch or some other mechanical artifact exhibits when its parts are arranged by an artificer. The "laws of nature"— as these regularities came to be described, displacing talk of the natures or substantial forms of things—were just the patterns the divine artificer had put into the bits of clockwork that make up the world. As a machine can operate in the absence of its maker, though, so too did the world come to seem something that could operate in the absence of the artificer. Thus did the doctrine of divine conservation give way to deism. And the sequel, naturally, was atheism, once it occurred to mechanists that if the "machine" of the world could operate here and now without a machinist, maybe it always has so operated—maybe the "machine" and the "laws" governing it are all that has ever existed.

Rationalist cosmological arguments of the sort associated with Leibniz were intended to counter this atheistic trend. But the notions of contingency and necessity they employ are no longer grounded in the natures of things— in the real composition of act and potency and essence and existence in contingent things, and in the pure actuality and identity of essence and existence in God. Instead, a thing's contingency is reduced to the logical possibility of its non-existence, and necessity is reduced to logical necessity. A "principle of sufficient reason" is deployed in place of the Scholastics' principle of causality, and where the latter is grounded in the objective impossibility of a mere potency actualizing itself, the former is put forward as a would-be "law of thought." The cosmological argument comes to seem little more than a demand that the world meet certain explanatory criteria which may (or may not) be built into the structure of the human mind, but which do not necessarily reflect any aspect of objective, extra-mental reality, and the door is thereby opened to the refutations of Hume and Kant.[51]

Whatever its consequences for philosophical theology have been, the anti-Aristotelian mechanistic revolution is often claimed to have been vindicated by the successes of modern science. But though it features

---

51 Though defending DEI with respect to the objects of our ordinary experience, Adler does in *How to Think About God* endorse a version of the cosmological argument that appeals to the contingency of the universe as a whole. But Adler's reason for judging the universe to be contingent is that it is one possible universe among others, which makes his argument more Leibnizian and rationalist in spirit than Aristotelian or Thomistic.

prominently in the rhetoric of contemporary scientism, the inference is confused. Mechanism was not and never has been a "result" or "finding" of empirical science, but rather a methodological preference, a stipulation about what would be allowed to *count* as science. This seems to have been widely recognized by earlier generations of intellectuals, and not just those sympathetic to Aristotelianism or Thomism. According to Basil Willey, what the mechanistic revolution reflected was "a *transference of interests* rather than ... the mere 'exantlation' [drawing out] of new truth or the mere rejection of error," and in particular a "wish for a new life-orientation" which required "a hitherto unthought-of degree of control over 'things.'"[52] "Galileo typifies the direction of modern interests," Willey says, "in this instance, not in refuting St. Thomas, but in taking no notice of him."[53] According to W. T. Stace, final causes were abandoned "on the ground that inquiry into purposes is useless for what science aims at: namely, the prediction and control of events."[54] What Willey and Stace are alluding to is, of course, the express desire of early modern thinkers to enhance "human utility and power" through the "mechanical arts" or technology (as Bacon put it) and to make us "masters and possessors of nature" (in the words of Descartes).[55] And the preference for a reductively mathematical theoretical description of the natural world that this entailed led in the view of E. A. Burtt to a "metaphysical barbarism" which only "wishful thinking" or "uncritical confidence" could support in face of the various difficulties afflicting it.[56]

Not the least of these difficulties is the Humean challenge to the intelligibility of efficient causality that followed in the wake of the early moderns' rejection of immanent final causality, together with the related problem of induction. For as we noted when discussing the Fifth Way, for Aquinas and other Scholastics, there is no way to make sense of the fact that some cause A regularly generates a specific effect or range of effects B unless we suppose that the generation of B is the "end" or "goal" toward which A is directed, as toward a final cause. The link between the anti-Scholastic

52 Basil Willey, *The Seventeenth Century Background* (New York: Doubleday, 1965), p. 23, emphasis in original.
53 Ibid., p. 25.
54 W. T. Stace, "Man against Darkness," *The Atlantic* (September, 1948).
55 See Bacon's *The Great Instauration*, in *The New Organon and Related Writings*, edited by Fulton H. Anderson (Liberal Arts Press, 1960), pp. 8 and 16, and Descartes's *Discourse on Method*, translated by Donald A. Cress (Hackett, 1980), p. 33.
56 E. A. Burtt, *The Metaphysical Foundations of Modern Physical Science* (Atlantic Highlands, NJ: Humanities Press, 1952), pp. 305–06.

revolution and Hume's puzzles was noted by Alfred North Whitehead, who judged that:

> If the cause in itself discloses no information as to the effect, so that the first invention of it must be *entirely* arbitrary, it follows at once that science is impossible, except in the sense of establishing *entirely arbitrary* connections which are not warranted by anything intrinsic to the natures either of causes or effects. Some variant of Hume's philosophy has generally prevailed among men of science. But scientific faith has risen to the occasion, and has tacitly removed the philosophic mountain.[57]

The ironic consequence is that "the clergy were in principle rationalists, whereas the men of science were content with a simple faith in the order of nature."[58]

From an Aristotelian-Thomistic point of view, then, not only does science not vindicate the move away from an Aristotelian philosophy of nature; the intelligibility of science in fact presupposes such a philosophy of nature. To focus only on those aspects of the world which can be quantified, predicted, and controlled is indeed methodologically useful if all one cares about are those particular aspects. But it simply does not follow from the success of this purely methodological decision that no other aspects exist, that one ought in Burtt's words to "make a metaphysics out of [one's] method."[59] And the quantifiable aspects are in any event abstracted from substances, a complete characterization of which must include reference to essences and causal powers—and thus to something like substantial forms and final causes—if one is to account for the truth of the laws stated in quantificational terms.

Needless to say, this is a very large subject. Suffice it for now to point out that it is not only Thomists or those with a theological ax to grind who

---

57   Alfred North Whitehead, *Science and the Modern World* (New York: The Free Press, 1967), p. 4.
58   Ibid., p. 51. For two useful accounts of the gradual transformation of the Scholastics' conception of causation in early modern philosophy, and of the philosophical problems this occasioned, see Kenneth Clatterbaugh, *The Causation Debate in Modern Philosophy 1637–1739* (London: Routledge, 1999) and Walter Ott, *Causation and Laws of Nature in Early Modern Philosophy* (Oxford: Oxford University Press, 2009).
59   Burtt, *The Metaphysical Foundations of Modern Physical Science*, p. 229.

would defend a return to something like an Aristotelian conception of nature. Analytic metaphysicians like John Heil, C. B. Martin, and George Molnar have argued that to make sense of efficient causality we need to recognize the existence of dispositional properties inherently directed towards their manifestations—essentially a return to Aquinas's thesis that "every agent acts for an end."[60] "New essentialist" philosophers of science like Brian Ellis and Nancy Cartwright have proposed a neo-Aristotelian essentialist interpretation of the results of physics and chemistry.[61] The biologist J. Scott Turner and philosophers of biology like Marjorie Grene and André Ariew propose that something like Aristotelian teleology must be acknowledged if we are to make sense of developmental processes.[62] Examples could be multiplied of work in recent philosophy from outside the Thomistic orbit which is sympathetic to a reconsideration of various Aristotelian metaphysical themes. And then there is of course the work of writers like David Oderberg, James Ross, and other so-called "analytical Thomists," which defends a more thoroughgoing return to a specifically Aristotelian-*Thomistic* metaphysics and philosophy of nature.[63]

So, the dispute between Aristotelianism and mechanism is very much a *live* one. That entails that the Thomistic critique of DEI and associated defense of DDC remains a live position as well. And as I have tried to show, it is a position that proponents of DEI and critics of DDC have yet seriously to deal with.[64]

60   John Heil, *From an Ontological Point of View* (Oxford: Clarendon Press, 2003); C. B. Martin, *The Mind in Nature* (Oxford: Clarendon Press, 2008); George Molnar, *Powers: A Study in Metaphysics* (Oxford: Oxford University Press, 2003).

61   Brian Ellis, *The Philosophy of Nature: A Guide to the New Essentialism* (Chesham: Acumen, 2002); Nancy Cartwright, "Aristotelian Natures and the Modern Experimental Method," in John Earman, ed., *Inference, Explanation, and Other Frustrations: Essays in the Philosophy of Science* (Berkeley and Los Angeles: University of California Press, 1992).

62   J. Scott Turner, *The Tinkerer's Accomplice: How Design Emerges from Life Itself* (Cambridge, MA: Harvard University Press, 2007); Marjorie Grene, "Biology and Teleology," in *The Understanding of Nature: Essays in the Philosophy of Biology* (Dordrecht: Reidel, 1974); Ariew, op. cit.

63   See David S. Oderberg, *Real Essentialism* (London: Routledge, 2007) and James Ross, *Thought and World: The Hidden Necessities* (Notre Dame: University of Notre Dame Press, 2008). I have defended such a return in *Aquinas* and also, in a more polemical and semi-popular fashion, in *The Last Superstition: A Refutation of the New Atheism* (South Bend, IN: Saint Augustine's Press, 2008).

64   For comments on earlier versions of this paper, I thank Mark Anderson, David Clemenson, David Oderberg, Bill Vallicella, an anonymous referee, and audience members at a conference on *Metaphysics: Aristotelian, Scholastic, Analytic* in Prague in July 2010.

6

The New Atheists and the
Cosmological Argument

Cosmological arguments for the existence of God purport to show that the world exists only because it is caused to exist by a First Uncaused Cause. They have, in the history of Western philosophy and theology, been the central sort of philosophical argument for God's existence. The basic idea was developed in various ways by Plato, Aristotle, and the Neoplatonic tradition; Muslim thinkers like Al-Ghazali, Avicenna, and Averroes; Jewish philosophers like Maimonides; Christian Scholastic thinkers such as Bonaventure, Aquinas, Scotus, and Suarez; rationalist metaphysicians like Leibniz and Clarke; and empiricists like Locke and Berkeley. Even Anselm, better known for the ontological argument for the existence of God, also defended a version of the cosmological argument. Twentieth-century Thomist writers such as Reginald Garrigou-Lagrange, Jacques Maritain, Etienne Gilson, and Mortimer Adler defended it. In recent philosophy versions of the argument have been defended by Bruce Reichenbach, Richard Taylor, Richard Swinburne, Robert Koons, Richard Gale and Alexander Pruss, John Haldane, Christopher Martin, David Oderberg, Brian Davies, William Lane Craig, and others.[1]

---

1   For this recent work, see, e.g., Bruce Reichenbach, *The Cosmological Argument: A Reassessment* (Springfield: Charles Thomas, 1972); Richard Taylor, *Metaphysics*, Fourth edition (Englewood Cliffs: Prentice-Hall, 1992); Richard Swinburne, *The Existence of God* (Oxford: Clarendon Press, 1979); Robert C. Koons, "A New Look at the Cosmological Argument," *American Philosophical Quarterly*, 34 (1997): 193–211; Richard M. Gale and Alexander R. Pruss, "A New Cosmological Argument," in Gale and Pruss, eds., *The Existence of God* (Burlington, VT: Ashgate, 2003); J. J. C. Smart and J. J. Haldane, *Atheism and Theism* (Oxford: Blackwell, 1996); Christopher F. J. Martin, *Thomas Aquinas: God and Explanations* (Edinburgh; Edinburgh University Press, 1997); David S. Oderberg, "Traversal of the Infinite, the 'Big Bang' and the Kalām Cosmological Argument," *Philosophia Christi* 4 (2002): 305–34; Brian Davies, *The Reality of God and the Problem of Evil* (London: Continuum, 2006); and William Lane Craig, *The kalām Cosmological Argument* (New York: Barnes and Noble, 1979).

The writers whose best-sellers inaugurated the "New Atheist" movement include, most famously, Richard Dawkins, Christopher Hitchens, Sam Harris, and Daniel C. Dennett.[2] Other writers who have contributed to the New Atheist literature include Victor J. Stenger, Lawrence M. Krauss, and Alex Rosenberg.[3] Some recent works of popular science from Peter Atkins and Stephen Hawking and Leonard Mlodinow also evince something like a New Atheist attitude toward religion.[4] Among the elements which make the atheism of these writers "new" is the easy confidence with which they suppose that the traditional arguments for God's existence can, at least at this point in history, be dismissed out of hand as unworthy of any further serious consideration. Hitchens avers that "we [will] never again have to confront the impressive faith of an Aquinas or a Maimonides" insofar as "[r]eligion comes from the period of human prehistory where nobody ... had the smallest idea what was going on" whereas "[t]oday the least educated of my children knows much more about the natural order than any of the founders of religion."[5] Science, in short, has put religion, including philosophy of religion, out of business for good. Dawkins assures his readers that Aquinas's Five Ways (which include several versions of the cosmological argument) are "easily ... exposed as vacuous."[6] Rosenberg thinks such exposure is not even worth the effort, telling his own book's readers that:

> [W]e won't treat theism as a serious alternative that stills [sic] needs to be refuted. This book's intended readers have moved past that point. We know the truth.[7]

---

2   See Richard Dawkins, *The God Delusion* (New York: Houghton Mifflin, 2006); Christopher Hitchens, *God is not Great* (New York: Twelve, 2007); Sam Harris, *The End of Faith* (New York: Norton, 2004); Sam Harris, *Letter to a Christian Nation* (New York: Alfred A. Knopf, 2006); and Daniel C. Dennett, *Breaking the Spell: Religion as a Natural Phenomenon* (New York: Viking, 2006).

3   See, e.g., Victor J. Stenger, *God: The Failed Hypothesis* (Amherst, NY: Prometheus Books, 2008); Victor J. Stenger, *God and the Folly of Faith* (Amherst, NY: Prometheus Books, 2012); Lawrence M. Krauss, *A Universe from Nothing* (New York: Free Press, 2012); and Alex Rosenberg, *The Atheist's Guide to Reality* (New York: W. W. Norton and Co., 2011).

4   Peter Atkins, *On Being* (Oxford: Oxford University Press, 2011); Stephen Hawking and Leonard Mlodinow, *The Grand Design* (New York: Bantam Books, 2010).

5   Hitchens, *God is not Great*, pp. 63–64.

6   Dawkins, *The God Delusion*, p. 77.

7   Rosenberg, *The Atheist's Guide to Reality*, p. xii.

That the self-confidence of the New Atheists is massively out of proportion to their knowledge and understanding of the actual arguments of theologians and philosophers of religion has by now been established by their critics many times over.[8] My aim in what follows is to show in a more systematic way than has perhaps been done before how, in the particular case of the cosmological argument—which has, again, historically been the central argument for the existence of God—the objections raised by the New Atheists draw no blood. There are two reasons why these objections are worth answering, despite their philosophical shallowness. The first is that the New Atheists have many readers who are philosophically unsophisticated, and who will for that reason falsely suppose that their objections carry weight. The second is that—as is evidenced by the fact that Dennett and Rosenberg are to be numbered among the New Atheists—even many professional philosophers who are not experts in the philosophy of religion are prone to endorse some of the same superficial objections. To debunk New Atheist criticisms of the cosmological argument is, sad to say, to debunk much of what passes for the conventional wisdom on the subject in academic philosophy (again, at least outside the circles of professional philosophers of religion).

Much of the superficiality that surrounds criticism of the argument derives from the fact that the criticism is commonly directed at a nearly omnipresent straw man—an argument that is widely regarded as representing the basic thrust of the cosmological argument, but which in fact bears no interesting relationship to what any of the defenders of the argument referred to above have ever actually said. In the next section of this paper, I will identify this straw man in the hope that the otherwise unwary reader will be

---

8   I have criticized the four original New Atheists at length in *The Last Superstition: A Refutation of the New Atheism* (South Bend, IN: St. Augustine's Press, 2008). I reviewed Rosenberg's and Krauss's books in *First Things* magazine, in the November 2011 and June/July 2012 issues, respectively. I reviewed Hawking and Mlodinow's book in the November 29, 2010 issue of *National Review*, and Atkins's book in the Winter 2011/2012 issue of *The Claremont Review of Books*. Among the great many other critiques of the New Atheists are David Berlinksi, *The Devil's Delusion: Atheism and Its Scientific Pretensions* (New York: Crown Forum, 2008); Terry Eagleton, *Reason, Faith, and Revolution: Reflections on the God Debate* (New Haven: Yale University Press, 2009); David Bentley Hart, *Atheist Delusions: The Christian Revolution and Its Fashionable Enemies* (New Haven: Yale University Press, 2009); Alvin Plantinga, *Where the Conflict Really Lies: Science, Religion, and Naturalism* (Oxford: Oxford University Press, 2011); and Keith Ward, *Why There Almost Certainly Is a God: Doubting Dawkins* (Oxford: Lion UK, 2008).

forewarned not to presuppose either that defenders of the cosmological argument are committed to it, or that objections to the straw man have any tendency to cast doubt on what defenders of the cosmological argument actually do say. In the subsequent section I will summarize four representative approaches that actually have been taken historically to spelling out a cosmological argument, which I call the *act/potency approach*, the *simplicity/composition approach*, the *necessity/contingency approach*, and the *kalām approach*. In the final section, I will survey the objections against the cosmological argument raised by New Atheist writers, and show that whether or not they have force against the straw man version of the argument, they completely fail as refutations of any of the approaches actually taken by the argument's defenders.

I hasten to emphasize that I do not pretend that what I have to say in this paper suffices to show, all by itself, that the cosmological argument ultimately succeeds (though my own view is that at least some versions of it do succeed). To make that case would require a book. What I do claim to show is that the criticisms raised by the New Atheists are intellectually unserious.

I. What the cosmological argument does not say

Dennett begins the single paragraph he devotes to the cosmological argument as follows:

> The Cosmological Argument … in its simplest form states that since everything must have a cause the universe must have a cause—namely, God …[9]

The assumption that this is the basic thrust of the cosmological argument is, as I say, by no means confined to New Atheist polemical literature. It can be found not only in purportedly neutral works of pop philosophy but even in at least one book by someone who specializes in the philosophy of religion. Robin Le Poidevin summarizes what he calls "the basic cosmological argument," of which at least some other versions are "modifications," this way:

1. Anything that exists has a cause of its existence.
2. Nothing can be the cause of its own existence.
3. The universe exists.

9   Dennett, *Breaking the Spell*, p. 242.

Therefore: The universe has a cause of its existence which lies outside the universe.[10]

Examples of similar summaries of the argument could easily be multiplied.[11] The standard next move of those presenting these summaries is, of course, to suggest that the argument founders on the obvious retort: If everything has a cause, then what caused God? If the response is that nothing caused God, then, the critic maintains, we might as well say that nothing caused the universe. The critics also sometimes suggest that the argument gratuitously assumes that the universe had a beginning, whereas if we suppose instead that it did not, the pressure to look for a first cause of any sort disappears. More complex versions of the cosmological argument are then sometimes treated as if they were desperate and doomed attempts to patch up the glaring holes in this "basic cosmological argument."

The problem is this: *Not one of the many prominent defenders of the cosmological argument referred to above ever actually put forward anything like this so-called "basic cosmological argument."* In particular—and to hammer the point home—you will not find such an argument in Plato, Aristotle, Plotinus, Al-Ghazali, Avicenna, Averroes, Maimonides, Anselm, Bonaventure, Aquinas, Scotus, Suarez, Leibniz, Clarke, Locke, Berkeley, Garrigou-Lagrange, Maritain, Gilson, Adler, Reichenbach, Taylor, Swinburne, Koons, Gale, Pruss, Haldane, Martin, Oderberg, Davies, Craig, or, as far as I know, in any other philosopher who has defended the cosmological argument. Indeed, Le Poidevin (who, as a philosopher of religion, is better informed about the subject than the other critics quoted above) admits as much, writing that "no-one has defended a cosmological argument of precisely this form."[12] He just thinks it "provides a useful stepping-stone to the other, more sophisticated, versions" of the argument.

10 Robin Le Poidevin, *Arguing for Atheism: An Introduction to the Philosophy of Religion* (London: Routledge, 1996), p. 4.

11 Further examples taken mostly just from books lying around my study would be Michael Martin, *Atheism: A Philosophical Justification* (Philadelphia: Temple University Press, 1990), at p. 96; Graham Priest, *Logic: A Very Short Introduction* (Oxford: Oxford University Press, 2000), at pp. 21–22; Bertrand Russell, *Why I Am Not a Christian* (New York: Simon and Schuster, 1957), at p. 6; Jenny Teichman and Katherine C. Evans, *Philosophy: A Beginner's Guide*, Second edition (Blackwell, 1995), at p. 22; Nigel Warburton, *Philosophy: The Basics*, Fourth edition (London: Routledge, 2004), at p. 17; and Rebecca Newberger Goldstein's philosophical novel *36 Arguments for the Existence of God: A Work of Fiction* (New York: Pantheon, 2010), at p. 348.

12 Le Poidevin, *Arguing for Atheism*, p. 4.

This is, when you think about it, extremely odd. Suppose "Intelligent Design" theorists routinely characterized "the basic Darwinian thesis" as the claim that at some point in the distant past a monkey gave birth to a human baby. Suppose they never cited any sources for this claim (which, of course, they couldn't do, since no Darwinian has ever said such a thing) and even admitted that no one has ever defended it. But suppose that they nevertheless suggested that it "provides a useful stepping-stone to the other, more sophisticated, versions" of Darwinism. Darwinians would rightly be outraged, objecting that such a procedure gets the whole discussion off on the wrong foot, and in particular conveys the false impression that anything Darwinians have to say about human origins is really just a desperate exercise in patching up a manifestly absurd position. Yet it is precisely that sort of false impression that is conveyed by the insinuation that the thinkers cited above, however complex their arguments, are all ultimately in the business of trying to salvage or "modify" something that at bottom amounts to what Le Poidevin characterizes as "the basic cosmological argument."

Nor could it honestly be suggested by anyone familiar with the work of defenders of the cosmological argument that they are at least *implicitly* committed to the so-called "basic cosmological argument." For one thing, none of the thinkers in question actually appeals to the premise that "everything has a cause." Indeed, some of them either explicitly or implicitly *deny* that everything has a cause! For another thing, none of the defenders of the argument cited above *assumes* that the universe had a beginning, and only one version of the argument (the *kalām* approach) is even concerned to try to *show* that it did. Indeed, many versions do not even require as a premise any claim about the universe *as a whole* in the first place.

But if defenders of the cosmological argument not only do not assume, but in fact often deny, that everything has a cause; if most of them not only do not assume that the universe had a beginning but are not even interested in the question of whether it did; and if many of them are not even arguing in the first place from any premise about the universe considered as a whole; then it is, to say the very least, highly misleading to begin a discussion of the cosmological argument the way Dennett and so many others do.

II. What the cosmological argument does say

So, as we turn to an exposition of the main approaches to developing a cosmological argument, readers who are used to looking at the argument through the lens of what Le Poidevin calls the "basic" argument are asked to put that straw man out of their minds and to try to see the issue with fresh eyes. Let's consider each approach in turn.

II.1. The act/potency approach: Aristotle's argument for an Unmoved Mover of the world was grounded in his theory of act and potency, which was developed in response to the claim of Parmenides and other Eleatic philosophers that change is an illusion. Parmenides had argued that change would have to involve *being* arising from *non-being*, which is impossible given that non-being is just nothing, and from nothing nothing can arise. What Parmenides failed to see, in Aristotle's view, is that between complete being or *actuality* on the one hand and non-being or sheer nothingness on the other, there is a middle ground of *potency* or potential being. For example, we might say of a certain rubber ball that it is actually red in color, solid, spherical, and sitting motionless in a drawer; and we might note as well that it is in no way a stone, a squirrel, or a Buick Skylark. But while it is actually solid and spherical while not being even potentially a squirrel, it *is* at least potentially flat and squishy (if you melt it, say). Its potency or potential for being flat and squishy is real—it is not nothing or non-being, even though the flatness and squishiness are not actual. And change, for Aristotle, does not involve being, full stop, arising from non-being, but rather "being in act" or *actual* being arising from "being in potency" or *potential* being. Change is the actualization of a potency, where the potency is something real even before it is actualized.

While the jargon of act and potency might seem archaic to many contemporary philosophers, the notions to which they refer are by no means outdated. On the contrary, the debate in contemporary metaphysics over causal powers, capacities, and categorical versus dispositional properties is essentially a revival of concerns that would have been familiar to any Aristotelian Scholastic philosopher—"powers," "dispositions," and "capacities" being more or less what the Aristotelian would call "potencies," and "categorical properties" being more or less what the Aristotelian would call "actualities." Indeed, that realism about causal powers and/or dispositions amounts to a revival of Aristotelian and Scholastic notions is now fairly widely recognized by those involved in the debate.[13]

13 For a useful brief survey of the recent debate, see Stephen Mumford, "Causal Powers and Capacities," in Helen Beebee, Christopher Hitchcock, and Peter Menzies, eds., *The Oxford Handbook of Causation* (Oxford: Oxford University Press, 2009). For a book-length survey, see Brian Ellis, *The Philosophy of Nature: A Guide to the New Essentialism* (Chesham: Acumen, 2002). For a collection of articles, see

When the theory of causation of which the theory of act and potency is the core is worked out, the Aristotelian arrives at two further notions relevant to the argument for the Unmoved Mover. The first is that *a potential can be actualized only by something already actual.* This is a version of what Scholastic writers called the "principle of causality," and it is important to take note of what it does and does not imply. It *does* imply that the actualization of a potential always has a cause; when, for instance, the rubber ball becomes flat and squishy, that is only because something already actual (the heat of a microwave oven, say) caused that to happen. For the potential flatness and squishiness, precisely because it is *merely* potential, cannot have actualized itself. The principle does *not* imply, however, that *everything* has a cause. Indeed, the Aristotelian would *deny* that everything requires a cause. A potency or potential cannot actualize itself because it is, again, merely potential and not actual, and only what is actual can do anything. That is why it needs a cause. But what is already actual does not need a cause, precisely because it is already actual. Now in general things are mixtures of actuality and potentiality—actual in some respects, potential in others— and thus while they do not require causes in some respects, they do require them in others. But suppose there were something that was *pure actuality*, with no potentials in need of actualization. Then it would be something that not only does not in any respect have a cause, but could not in principle have had one or needed one.

The other relevant further notion is the distinction between *accidentally ordered* series of causes on the one hand, and *essentially ordered* series on the other. The stock example of the former is a series consisting of a father who begets a son, who in turn begets another, who in turn begets another. The stock example of the latter is a hand which pushes a stick which in turn pushes a stone. The key difference is that in the former case each member of the series has *independent* causal power, while in the latter the members have *derivative* causal power. Once begotten, a son has the power to beget further sons of his own even in the absence of his father. This power is "built in," as it were. But the stick has no power on its own to move the stone. It derives its causal power to push the stone from the hand that uses it to push the stone. The hand's continual action is essential to the existence of the causal series in a way that a father's continued action is not essential to the existence of the series of begetters.

John Greco and Ruth Groff, eds., *Powers and Capacities in Philosophy: The New Aristotelianism* (London: Routledge, 2012).

Now on analysis, the Aristotelian holds, it turns out that any essentially ordered series of causes must terminate in a first member. But it is absolutely crucial to understand that "first" here does not mean "first in a temporal sequence," and it doesn't even mean "first in the sense of coming before the second, third, fourth, etc. members of a finitely long series." Rather, what is meant by a "first cause" in this context is "a cause which can impart causal power without having to derive it." The stone's potential for movement is actualized by the stick, but the stick can *actualize* that potential only insofar its own potential for movement is in turn *being actualized* by the hand. Unless this series terminated in something that can actualize without being actualized in the same respect—as I can move the stick without someone in turn picking me up and moving me as I do so—then we would have a vicious regress, a series of causes that have *derivative* causal power without anything *from which to derive it*. The situation would be comparable to a mirror which reflects the image of a face present in another mirror, which in turn reflects the image of a face present in another, and so on *ad infinitum*, with only mirror images and never any actual face. Notice that the *length* of the series is not what is at issue here. Even if there could be an infinitely long series of mirrors each reflecting the image of a face present in the next mirror in the series, there would still have to be something outside this infinite series—the face itself—which could impart the content of the image without having to derive it. Similarly, even if the stick that moves the stone was being moved by another stick, which was in turn moved by another, and so on *ad infinitum*, there would have to be something outside the series of sticks which imparted to them the power to move things, since sticks by themselves have no such power, however many of them you add together.

Now though in examples like the one in question a thing might be a "first cause" in one respect—as I can move the stick without anyone moving me in turn—there are other respects in which it will not be "first," but depend on other things. Most crucially, any material thing will depend on other things for its *existence* at any moment. There are different ways in which this dependence might be understood. For the Aristotelian, natural substances like stones, plants, and animals are to be understood as composites of *prime matter* and *substantial form*, where prime matter is purely potential until informed by a substantial form, and substantial form is a mere abstraction apart from its instantiation in prime matter. This hylemorphic analysis of substances opens the door to an argument to the effect that no material substance can continue in existence even for an instant "under its own steam." For since the prime matter of a material substance depends for its concrete existence on the substance's substantial form, and the substantial form depends for its concrete existence on being realized in prime matter, we would have an explanatory vicious circle unless there were something outside the form-matter composite which actualizes it or keeps it in being.

Alternatively, we could hold (contrary to the standard Aristotelian story) that material substances like stones, plants, and animals are really just aggregates of simpler substances—that they are, say, "nothing but" molecules arranged in such-and-such a way. In that case too a material thing will depend for its existence at any moment on something other than it. It will depend, say, on its molecules being arranged in just such-and-such a way; these molecules will in turn depend for their existence at any moment on their atoms being arranged in just such-and-such a way; and so forth.

What we will have either way is a kind of *essentially* ordered causal series, with the potential existence of one level of reality actualized by the potential existence of another, which can in turn do this actualizing only insofar as *its* potential existence is actualized by yet another level. For instance, the water in a certain cup will exist at any moment only insofar as a certain potential of its atoms—to constitute water, specifically, rather than (say) separate quantities of oxygen and hydrogen—is actualized; this will in turn depend on the subatomic particles being combined in one specific way rather than another, at that very same moment, which also involves a certain potential being actualized; and so on.

Now since what is being caused in this case is the *existence* of a thing, the only way to end the regress of causes is with something which can impart existence without having to derive it from anything else. That will have to be something whose existence does not in any respect have to be actualized, but just is, already, fully actual—a *purely actual actualizer*, which is, given the analysis of change as the actualization of potency, essentially what Aristotle meant by an unmovable mover ("motion" being understood by Aristotle as synonymous with change).

To be sure, Aristotle himself, as commonly interpreted, was concerned only to explain the change that things exhibit, rather than the existence of the things that change. But some later Aristotelians (and in particular, some Thomistic philosophers) have argued that the basic thrust of the Aristotelian argument can and ought to be extended to an account of the existence of things, as I have done. This, together with the other elements of the Aristotelian position I've sketched out, suggests the following possible summary of a broadly Aristotelian cosmological argument:

1. That the actualization of potency is a real feature of the world follows from the occurrence of the events we know of via sensory experience.
2. The occurrence of any event E presupposes the operation of a substance.
3. The existence of any natural substance S at any given moment presupposes the concurrent actualization of a potency.
4. No mere potency can actualize a potency; only something actual can do so.
5. So any actualizer A of S's current existence must itself be actual.
6. A's own existence at the moment it actualizes S itself presupposes either (a) the concurrent actualization of a further potency or (b) A's being purely actual.
7. If A's existence at the moment it actualizes S presupposes the concurrent actualization of a further potency, then there exists a regress of concurrent actualizers that is either infinite or terminates in a purely actual actualizer.
8. But such a regress of concurrent actualizers would constitute an essentially ordered causal series, and such a series cannot regress infinitely.
9. So either A itself is purely actual or there is a purely actual actualizer which terminates the regress of concurrent actualizers.
10. So the occurrence of E and thus the existence of S at any given moment presupposes the existence of a purely actual actualizer.

Notice a few things about this argument. First, as I have already emphasized, it does not rest on the premise that "everything has a cause"; what it says is that what actualizes a potency must itself be actual (which leaves it open that there is something whose action or existence does not involve the actualization of a potency, and thus does not require a cause). Second, it does not involve tracing a series of accidentally ordered causes backward in time to a cause which is first in a temporal sense, but rather tracing a series of essentially ordered causes existing here and now to a cause which is first in the sense of having its causal power in a non-derivative way. Indeed, most Aristotelians hold that the former sort of series, precisely because it is accidentally ordered, cannot be demonstrated to have a first member, and so they don't bother arguing for a first temporal cause when giving a cosmological argument. Third, the argument does not rest on any premise about the universe as a whole. The conclusion can be arrived at from premises that make reference only to *some natural substance or other*, the hand which moves the stick or whatever. To be sure, any defender of such an argument would go on to say that the purely actual actualizer would in fact be the cause of every other natural substance, and thus of the universe as a whole. But that would be a *consequence* of the argument rather than part of the argument itself.

The reason it would be a consequence of the argument is that there can be only one purely actual actualizer, or so proponents of this sort of argument typically argue. For there is, so the argument goes, no way to make sense of there being more than one instance of a kind of thing other than by attributing to each instance some potency or potentiality. For example, two trees differ because they are made up of different parcels of matter, occupy different regions of space, may also differ in height or color, and so forth. All of that involves potency in various ways; for instance, being material involves potency insofar as matter is always capable of taking on various forms, being at one point in space involves having the potency for being at another, and so on. But what is purely actual has no potency or potentiality. So there is no way to make sense of there being more than one thing that is purely actual. Thus, it is to one and the same purely actual actualizer that we have to trace the existence of everything whose existence needs to be actualized.

Defenders of this sort of argument typically argue that the purely actual actualizer can be shown to have many other attributes as well. Aquinas, for example, who in the first of his Five Ways puts forward a version of the Aristotelian approach to the cosmological argument, goes on later in the *Summa Theologiae* (and in several other works) to argue that a purely actual cause of things would have to be immaterial, immutable, eternal, perfect, omnipotent, omniscient, and so forth. Some of the arguments for these attributes appeal to further theses in general Aristotelian-Thomistic metaphysics. Naturally, that metaphysical system would itself need to be defended, and various possible objections answered, for a successful defense of what I am calling the Aristotelian approach to developing a cosmological argument. But what has been said suffices for the purposes of the present paper, which is to examine the specific objections raised by the New Atheists, to which we will turn after looking at the other main approaches to the cosmological argument.[14]

---

14 I have defended the Aristotelian approach, and Aquinas's First Way in particular, in several places. See *The Last Superstition* for a polemical and semi-popular treatment, and my book *Aquinas* (Oxford: Oneworld Publications, 2009) for a more detailed and academic treatment. I have defended specific aspects of the argument in

II.2. The simplicity/composition approach: Whereas the Aristotelian tradition in natural theology emphasizes that whatever is a mixture of act and potency must ultimately be explained by reference to that which is pure actuality, the Neoplatonic tradition emphasizes that whatever is in any way composite or made up of parts (whether physical or metaphysical parts) must ultimately be explained by reference to that which is utterly non-composite or metaphysically simple. The idea is that whatever has parts is metaphysically less fundamental than the parts themselves and whatever principle accounts for their combination. The *ultimate* explanation of anything would therefore have to be without parts, otherwise it would not be ultimate but would require a cause of its own.

Lloyd Gerson argues that something like a cosmological argument developing this basic theme is at least implicit in Plotinus.[15] My own outline of Gerson's reconstruction is as follows:

1. There must be a first principle of all if there is to be an explanation of the orderly existing world, or why anything at all exists rather than nothing.
2. If the first principle of all were composed of parts, then those parts would be ontologically prior to it.
3. But in that case it would not be the first principle of all.
4. So the first principle is not composed of parts, but is absolutely simple.
5. If there were a distinction between *what* the first principle is and the fact *that* it is, then there could be more than one first principle.
6. But in order for there to be more than one, there would have to be some attribute that distinguished them.

"Existential Inertia and the Five Ways," *American Catholic Philosophical Quarterly* 85 (2011): 237–67, and "Motion in Aristotle, Newton, and Einstein," in Edward Feser, ed., *Aristotle on Method and Metaphysics* (Basingstoke: Palgrave Macmillan, 2013). For other recent defenses of the Aristotelian approach to the cosmological argument, see chapter 9 of Martin, *Thomas Aquinas: God and Explanations*; chapter 2 of Smart and Haldane, *Atheism and Theism*; chapter 2 of David Conway, *The Rediscovery of Wisdom* (Basingstoke: Macmillan, 2000); and David S. Oderberg, "'Whatever is Changing is Being Changed by Something Else': A Reappraisal of Premise One of the First Way," in J. Cottingham and P. Hacker, eds., *Mind, Method and Morality: Essays in Honour of Anthony Kenny* (Oxford: Oxford University Press, 2010).

15 See chapter 1 of Lloyd P. Gerson, *Plotinus* (London: Routledge, 1994) and Gerson's paper "Neoplatonism," in Christopher Shields, ed., *The Blackwell Guide to Ancient Philosophy* (Oxford: Blackwell, 2003).

7. But since a first principle is absolutely simple, there can be no such attribute.
8. So there cannot be more than one first principle.
9. So there is no distinction in the first principle between *what* it is and the fact *that* it is.
10. So the first principle is not only absolutely simple but utterly unique, what Plotinus called "the One."

Let's walk through the argument step by step. (The comments that follow to some extent go beyond what Gerson himself says.) What is meant by a "first principle" in step (1) is, essentially, a bottom-level explanation of things, something that explains everything else without needing an explanation itself. One could reasonably take this premise to be at least implicitly accepted by many atheists no less than by the theist, at least insofar as the atheist regards scientific explanations as terminating in a most fundamental level of physical laws that determine all the rest—whether this takes the form of a "Theory of everything" or instead a conjunction of several physical theories left unreduced to some such single theory. The dispute between Plotinus and such atheists, then, would not be over the *existence* of a "first principle," but rather over its *character*.

Of course, when the attributes of Plotinus's first principle are unpacked—and he goes on to argue that the One must have necessity, infinity, power, omnipresence, goodness, life, and so forth—the atheist might decide to reject premise (1) if that is where it will lead him. He might suggest that the existence of composite things is ultimately inexplicable, a brute fact. But as Gerson notes, this will not do:

> The possibility that the existence of a composite depends on nothing or that it is inexplicable is not considered as a serious one by Plotinus. If this possibility amounts to the claim that it is impossible that there should be an explanation of the existence of a composite, it is difficult not to share Plotinus's diffidence. How could such a thing be shown? If, however, the claim merely amounts to the assertion that, though it is possible that there should be an explanation, there is in fact none, then Plotinus' obvious reply is that he has an explanation at hand and its adequacy needs to be addressed, not by saying that there is no explanation but by showing why his explanation is not satisfactory.[16]

16 Gerson, *Plotinus*, p. 13.

The "parts" referred to in step (2) of the argument are, as I have indicated, parts of any sort, whether material or metaphysical. Again, the idea here is that if a thing is composed of parts, then the parts are more fundamental than it is. Moreover, those parts would need to be combined in order for the thing to exist. (This is true even if the thing has always existed—for there would in that case still have to be something that accounts for why the parts have always been conjoined.) A purported "first principle" with parts just wouldn't be a bottom-level explanation or first principle at all, then— it would in that case need explanation itself, as step (3) says. With step (4), then, we arrive at the simplicity of the first principle of all. But when Plotinus refers to this principle as "the One," he does not mean merely that it has no parts but also that it is utterly unique—that the sort of theism his argument leads us to is necessarily a *mono*theism. That is part of what the next stage of the argument seeks to establish.

It also seeks to establish a thesis that is usually thought to be distinctive of later, Scholastic philosophical theology. The distinction in step (5) between *what* a thing is and *that* it is is, as Gerson says, an anticipation of the famous medieval distinction between a thing's *essence* and its *existence*. In things whose essence and existence are distinct—which, for a Scholastic like Aquinas, is everything other than God—the essence entails a general category under which distinct instances might fall. There is, for example, the essence *human being*, under which Socrates and Plotinus both fall as particular instances, each with its own "act of existing." Similarly, if the essence of the first principle of all were distinct from its existence, there might be *this* "first principle of all" with its act of existing, *that* "first principle of all" with its own act of existing, and so forth.

But for that to be possible, there would, step (6) tells us, have to be some attribute that one "first principle of all" had that the other lacked. And that, Plotinus holds, makes no sense. For then it would be what they did *not* differ with respect to—what they had in *common*—that would be the true first principle of all, since it would be that which ultimately makes each of them the kind of thing it is. That is to say, one "first principle of all" and a second "first principle of all" would each be what it is only because each instantiates the same essence; and in that case it would be the common essence itself, and neither of the individual instances, which (as the explanation of these instances) would be the true first principle. Moreover, we would have in this case a distinction between a first principle and its attributes, which conflicts with the simplicity arrived at in (4). Hence there can be no such attribute (step (7)), and thus no way in principle to distinguish one first principle of all from another (step (8)), and thus no difference between the essence of a first principle and its existence (step (9)). The first principle of all is thus "simple" or without any parts in the strongest possible sense.

Once again we have an argument which raises many questions, but for present purposes I want to emphasize the following points. First, notice that this argument does not rest on the premise that "everything has a cause." What it says is that *what is composite* must have a cause, but of course it also goes on to say that there is something that is *not* composite. Second, the argument is also not concerned to argue for a *temporally* first principle but rather for a principle that is "first" in the sense of being ontologically absolutely fundamental. Third, though Gerson takes Plotinus to be offering an explanation of the universe, it seems that the argument doesn't *need* to start with the universe as its *explanandum*. It could start with *any* composite thing, and argue that *its* ultimate explanation would have to be the One. Naturally, given what Plotinus says, the One would be the explanation of everything other than itself, and thus his position entails that the One is the explanation of the entire universe. But that is an *implication* of the completed argument. The argument need not appeal to any *premise* about the universe as a whole.

II.3. The necessity/contingency approach: A third kind of cosmological argument holds that only a necessary being can be the ultimate cause of the contingent things of our experience. Avicenna defended this sort of argument, as did Aquinas in the Third Way. In modern philosophy, however, it is best known from the versions defended by rationalist metaphysicians like Leibniz and Clarke. One way to understand their approach is as an attempt to show how we can get to the sort of conclusion Aristotelians, Neoplatonists, and Thomists arrived at, but without having to commit to their metaphysical premises. In place of the Aristotelian principle that *the actualization of any potential requires a cause* and the Neoplatonic principle that *anything composite requires a cause*—both of which are variations on what is sometimes called "the principle of causality"—the modern rationalist puts the Principle of Sufficient Reason (PSR), according to which there must be a sufficient reason (i.e., an adequate explanation) for why anything exists, any event occurs, or any truth obtains.

There are three key, related differences between the two principles. First, causality is a metaphysical notion, whereas PSR makes reference instead to explanation, which is a logical and epistemological notion. Second, for that reason, whereas the principle of causality is a statement about mind-independent reality as such, PSR is more along the lines of a "law of thought," a statement about how we have to think about mind-independent reality. Of course, for the rationalist, since the structure of reality can be read off from the structure of thought, PSR purports to tell us something about mind-independent reality as well. But it does so less directly, as it were, than the principle of causality does. Third, whereas proponents of the principle of causality typically hold that nothing can cause itself, proponents of PSR typically hold that something can explain itself. (Of course, some philosophers have held that there can be such a thing as a causa sui or self-causing being, but it is not clear that this is or coherently could be anything more than a colorful way of talking about a self-explanatory being.)

David Blumenfeld reconstructs Leibniz's PSR-based version of the cosmological argument as follows[17]:

1. If anything exists, there must be a sufficient reason why it exists.
2. But this world exists and it is a series of contingent beings.
3. Therefore, there must be a sufficient reason why this series of contingent beings exists.
4. But nothing contingent—and, in particular, neither the existing series as a whole nor any of its members—can contain a sufficient reason why this series exists.
5. A sufficient reason for any existing thing can only be in an existing thing, which is itself either necessary or contingent.
6. Therefore, a sufficient reason why this series exists must be in a necessary being that lies outside the world.
7. Therefore, there is a necessary being that lies outside the world.

The idea behind step (4) of this argument is that since anything contingent could have failed to exist, there is nothing in its nature that can explain why it exists, so that it requires an explanation outside itself. This is as true of a collection of contingent things as it is of a given individual contingent thing, since there is no good reason to suppose that a collection of two contingent things is any less contingent than one of them is taken individually, or that three are any less contingent than two, four any less contingent than three, and so on. It might be suggested that this inference commits a fallacy

---

17   David Blumenfeld, "Leibniz's ontological and cosmological arguments," in Nicholas Jolley, ed., *The Cambridge Companion to Leibniz* (Cambridge: Cambridge University Press, 1995), at p. 367.

of composition, but on reflection it is hard to see how. Part-to-whole reasoning is, after all, not per se fallacious. It all depends on what property we are attributing to the whole on the basis of the parts. If I infer from the fact that each individual component of a computer weighs less than a pound that the computer as a whole weighs less than a pound, then I commit a fallacy of composition. But if I infer from the fact that every Lego block that has gone into constructing a certain wall is red to the conclusion that the wall itself is red, then I have committed no fallacy. And it seems at the very least highly plausible to say that contingency is in this respect more like redness than it is like weight.

Like Aristotle, Plotinus, and Aquinas, Leibniz argues that this ultimate cause of things that he's arrived at can on analysis be shown to have various other attributes—which include, Leibniz argues, understanding, will, power, infinity, and unity.

As before, there are various questions and objections that might be raised, some of which we will turn to in a moment, but for now let us note the following. First, yet again we see no commitment to the premise that "everything has a cause." We *do* see a commitment to the claim that everything has an *explanation*, but as we have noted, the notion of an explanation (an epistemological and logical notion) is not the same thing as the notion of a cause (which is a metaphysical notion). Furthermore, there is no exception here to the claim that everything has an explanation. In particular, the rationalist does not say that everything has an explanation except God—which might invite the retort that maybe the world lacks an explanation as well. Rather, the rationalist says that God too has an explanation. The difference between God and the world is that God, qua necessary being, is self-explanatory, whereas the world, qua contingent, is not. This entails that the *world* has a cause insofar as it requires an explanation external to it, but it does not entail that God has a cause, and indeed entails that he could not have had one. For as a necessary being, he could not have failed to exist in the first place, so that there would be nothing for a would-be cause to do. If the rationalist cosmological argument is committed to a version of the principle of causality, then, we might formulate it as the claim that *whatever is contingent requires a cause*.

A second point to note is that, once again, we do not have an argument that either assumes or argues that the world had a beginning. The rationalist view is that even if the universe of contingent things had no beginning in time, it would qua contingent still require a cause outside itself.

II.5. The kalām approach: The *kalām* cosmological argument, named for the *kalām* tradition in medieval Islamic thought that championed it and in recent years famously defended by William Lane Craig, is, among the main versions of the cosmological argument, the only one concerned to show that the universe had a beginning. In this connection Craig has made use of arguments from modern scientific cosmology, but his metaphysically-oriented arguments, which are the ones that most clearly echo the *kalām* tradition, are intended to be decisive whatever the empirical facts turn out to be. Their aim is to show that the notion of an actually infinitely large collection (as opposed to a merely potentially infinite collection, i.e., a finite collection to which we could always add another member) reduces to absurdity, and that since a beginningless series of events in time would constitute such a collection, we should conclude that such a series is not possible. To this end Craig deploys paradoxes like Hilbert's Infinite Hotel paradox. We might summarize the *kalām* approach as follows:

1. There cannot be an actually infinitely large collection (as paradoxes like Hilbert's Infinite Hotel paradox show).
2. But a universe without a beginning would constitute an actually infinitely large collection (of moments of time).
3. So the universe must have had a beginning.
4. But whatever begins to exist has a cause.
5. So the universe has a cause.

As with the other approaches to the cosmological argument, defenders of the *kalām* approach go on to argue that the cause of the world whose existence they claim to have established must have various divine attributes. Craig argues that the cause must be timeless, spaceless, changeless, beginningless, immaterial, uncaused, powerful, unique, and personal.[18] Obviously, all this raises questions, but we can note for present purposes, first, that while we have in this case an argument that does make a claim about the universe as a whole, and a claim to the effect that it must have had a beginning, it does indeed *argue* for this claim rather than merely assuming it. Second, we nevertheless have here yet another argument that does not rest on the premise that "everything has a cause." The claim instead is that *that which begins to exist* must have a cause.

---

18 Craig's views about God's relationship to time are more complicated than this indicates, but the complications are irrelevant for present purposes.

III. New Atheist objections to the cosmological argument

With these summaries of the main versions of the cosmological argument in hand, we can turn to the New Atheist criticisms of the argument. We will see that the objections are not merely weak, but for the most part miss the entire point of the cosmological argument. Let's consider them in turn:

III.1. If everything has a cause, then what caused God?: This objection is raised in various ways by Dawkins, Dennett, Harris, Hawking and Mlodinow, Hitchens, Krauss, and Stenger.[19] As I have indicated, it is, even outside New Atheist literature, perhaps the most common objection to the cosmological argument. But it is also the least intellectually serious. For one thing, as has already been emphasized, *not a single* prominent proponent of the cosmological argument actually appeals to the premise that "everything has a cause," and some of them explicitly deny that everything has a cause. For that reason alone, the suggestion that the proponent of the cosmological argument is contradicting himself or making an arbitrary exception to his own rule is simply directed at a straw man.

But rhetorically to ask "What caused God?" is a bad objection even apart from the fact that the cosmological argument does not rest on the premise in question. For it is not as if the defender of the argument has given no reason why God does not need a cause even if other things do. On the contrary, part of the point of the argument is to establish that there must be something that not only lacks a cause but could not even in principle have had one, precisely because it lacks the very feature that makes other things in need of a cause.

The Aristotelian argument holds that other things require a cause because they are mixtures of actual and potential, and any potential, precisely because it is merely potential, cannot actualize itself. By contrast, what is purely actual, precisely because it lacks any potentiality, not only need not have a cause but could not have had one. The Neoplatonist argument holds that composite things require a cause because there must be some principle outside them that accounts for the composition of their parts. But what is utterly simple or non-composite has no parts to be put together in the first place, not even an act of existence distinct from its essence. Hence it not

---

19 Dawkins, *The God Delusion*, p. 77; Dennett, *Breaking the Spell*, p. 242; Harris, *Letter to a Christian Nation*, pp. 72–73; Hawking and Mlodinow, *The Grand Design*, p. 172; Hitchens, *God is Not Great*, p. 71; Krauss, *A Universe from Nothing*, p. xii; Stenger, *God and the Folly of Faith*, pp. 215 and 323–24.

only need not have been caused but could not have been caused. The Leibnizian argument entails that contingent things require a cause precisely because they are contingent and could have been otherwise, but what is necessary, and thus could not have been otherwise, neither need have nor could have had a cause. The *kalām* argument, since it appeals only to the notion that what has a temporal beginning requires a cause, is in no way arbitrary in denying that what has no such beginning requires a cause.

So, to ask "What caused God?", far from being the devastating retort the New Atheist supposes it to be, is in fact painfully inept. When interpreted in light of what the various approaches to the cosmological argument actually *mean* by "cause" and "God," it really amounts to asking "What caused the thing that cannot in principle have had a cause?" In particular, it amounts to asking "What actualized the potentials in that thing which is pure actuality and thus never had any potentials of any sort needing to be actualized in the first place?"; or "What principle accounts for the composition of the parts in that which has no parts but is absolutely simple or non-composite?"; or "What imparted a sufficient reason for existence to that thing which has its sufficient reason for existence within itself and did not derive it from something else?"; or "What gave a temporal beginning to that which has no temporal beginning?" And none of these questions makes any sense.

Of course, a New Atheist might say that he isn't convinced that any version of the cosmological argument succeeds in showing that there really is something that could not in principle have had a cause—something that is purely actual, or absolutely simple, or which has a sufficient reason for its existence within itself, or which lacks a temporal beginning. He might even try to argue that there is some sort of hidden incoherence in these notions. But *merely* to ask "What caused God?"—as if the defender of the cosmological argument had overlooked the most obvious of objections—simply misses the whole point. A serious critic has to grapple with the details of the arguments. He cannot short-circuit them with a single smarmy question.

III.2. Maybe the universe itself (or the Big Bang, or the multiverse, or indeterministic quantum events, or the laws of physics) is the uncaused, self-explanatory, or necessary being: This objection, often concomitant with the first, is raised in various forms by Dawkins, Dennett, Krauss, Rosenberg, and Stenger.[20]

---

20 Dawkins, *The God Delusion*, p. 78; Dennett, *Breaking the Spell*, p. 242; Krauss, *A Universe from Nothing*, p. xii; Rosenberg, *The Atheist's Guide to Reality*, pp. 36–39; Stenger, *God and the Folly of Faith*, p. 215.

And like the first objection, it completely misses the point of each of the versions of the cosmological argument we've considered. As we have seen, whatever one thinks of those arguments, there is no arbitrariness or special pleading in their denying that God requires a cause while insisting that everything other than God does. The difference is in each case a principled one. And the principle in each case gives an answer to the question why the universe, the Big Bang, etc. cannot be the terminus of explanation.

For the Aristotelian, any actualization of a potency requires a cause, while what is pure actuality, and only what is pure actuality, does not. But the universe is a mixture of actuality and potentiality, and the Big Bang involved the actualization of a potential, as would each stage in the evolution of a multiverse and each quantum event (indeterminism being irrelevant). The laws of physics are also by themselves merely potential insofar as they could have been other than they are. Hence none of these could be self-explanatory, necessary, or "uncaused" in the relevant sense of being the sort of thing that need not and could not have a cause.

Similarly, for the Neoplatonist neither the universe nor a multiverse could be uncaused, necessary, or self-explanatory, precisely because they are composite. Quantum events and laws of physics also lack the metaphysical simplicity that the Neoplatonist argues we must attribute to the first principle of all. Their contingency is one indication of this, insofar as the fact that they could have been other than they are entails a distinction between essence and existence. Leibniz, of course, would point out that the universe, Big Bang, quantum events, and laws of nature are all contingent rather than necessary and thus could not provide an ultimate explanation; while the defender of the *kalām* argument would point out that since his claim is precisely that the Big Bang and everything that came into being with it—the universe along with the laws of physics, including the laws of quantum mechanics, that govern it—require a cause, it simply begs the question against him to claim that any of these things might be the terminus of explanation.

Much more could be said. In particular, the metaphysical status of laws of nature is itself so vexed an issue that it is amazing that anyone could think a glib reference to the laws of physics might settle anything in this context. What is a law of nature? How does it have any efficacy? Is a law of nature merely a statement to the effect that such-and-such a regularity exists? In that case it isn't an *explanation* of anything but merely a *description* of the very thing that needs to be explained. Is a law of nature a kind of Platonic entity? In that case we need an account of how the world comes to participate in such a law, and why it participates in the specific laws it does rather than others. And in that case too, laws cannot be *ultimate* explanations. Is a law of nature a shorthand description of the way a natural substance will tend to behave given its nature or essence? In that case the existence of laws is parasitic on the existence of the substances themselves, and again cannot then be an ultimate explanation.[21]

Naturally the New Atheist might reject any of these views of laws of nature, along with the Aristotelian, Neoplatonic, Leibnizian, or *kalām* accounts of why the universe cannot be an uncaused cause or self-explanatory or necessary being. The point, however, is that the New Atheist has given *no reason* whatsoever to reject any of this. *Merely* to suggest that the universe, Big bang, etc. might be the terminus of explanation is simply to *ignore* the cosmological argument, not to *answer* it.

III.3. It is false to suppose in the first place that everything has a cause or an explanation: In putting forward this objection, Stenger cites Hume's famous views on causality, and attributes some events to "chance" rather than causation.[22] Dennett and Rosenberg suggest that quantum mechanics shows that events can occur without a cause.[23]

Leave aside the point that no version of the argument actually rests on the premise that everything has a cause. None of these objections has force even against the causal principles to which the various approaches to the cosmological argument *are* committed. Take Stenger's objection, which is directed at a straw man. Naturally, no proponent of the cosmological argument denies that chance events occur. But there is simply nothing about chance that rules out causality. On the contrary, chance *presupposes* non-chance causal regularities. To take a stock example, when a farmer plowing a field comes across buried treasure, that is a chance event. But it occurs only because of the convergence of two non-chance lines of causality: the farmer's decision to plow in a certain direction that day, and someone else's decision to bury treasure at precisely that spot. Similarly, that following an

---

21 For a useful account of recent debate over this issue, see Stephen Mumford, *Laws in Nature* (London: Routledge, 2004). For an Aristotelian-Thomistic defense of the view that laws of nature are summaries of the ways natural substances tend to operate given their natures, see David S. Oderberg, *Real Essentialism* (London: Routledge, 2007), pp. 143–51.

22 Stenger, *God and the Folly of Faith*, p. 97.

23 Dennett, *Breaking the Spell*, p. 242; Rosenberg, *The Atheist's Guide to Reality*, pp. 38–39.

earthquake, tumbling boulder A shattered boulder B, specifically, is a chance event. But it occurs only because of causal regularities like the ones involved in plate tectonics, gravitational attraction, the solidity of boulders, etc.

Quantum physics shows at most that some events do not have a *deterministic* cause or explanation, but there is nothing in either the principle of causality or PSR per se that requires that *sort* of cause or explanation, specifically. Furthermore, quantum events occur even in a non-deterministic way only *given* the laws of quantum mechanics, which (the proponent of the cosmological argument would say) are contingent and by themselves merely potential until a universe that follows them is actualized. So it either misses the point or begs the question to appeal to quantum mechanics, since that is itself part of what the cosmological argument claims stands in need of explanation.

Hoary though the Humean argument is, there are three reasons why it simply will not do to pretend, as Stenger does, that the mere mention of it constitutes a devastating response to theistic arguments. First, no working physicist, chemist, biologist, or neuroscientist would for a moment take seriously the suggestion that perhaps there simply is no cause or explanation when investigating some specific physical, chemical, biological, or neurological phenomenon. The critic of the cosmological argument thus owes us an explanation of how *his* appeal to such a suggestion in the current context is anything less than special pleading. And as Gerson points out, the fact that the cosmological argument is *itself* a proposed explanation suffices to show that it is no good to say "Maybe there's no explanation in this case." The cosmological argument has just *given* one. Therefore if the critic wants to avoid accepting it, he has to find some reason other than the bare suggestion that there might not be an explanation.

A second problem with the Humean move is that it is simply fallacious to infer from the premise that we can conceive of effects independently of causes to the conclusion that some event might in fact not have a cause. We can conceive of what it is to be a triangle without conceiving what it is to be a trilateral, but it doesn't follow that there could be a triangle which is not a trilateral. We can conceive of a man without conceiving of how tall he is, but it doesn't follow that any man could exist without having some specific height or other. And so forth.

A third problem is one identified by Elizabeth Anscombe.[24] Hume

---

24   G. E. M. Anscombe, "'Whatever Has a Beginning of Existence Must Have a Cause': Hume's Argument Exposed," in G. E. M. Anscombe, *Collected Philosoph-*

claims that it is conceivable that something could come into being without a cause, and he evidently has in mind something like conceiving of an object suddenly appearing, out of the blue as it were, where nothing had been a moment before. But what is it about this exercise in conception that makes it a case of conceiving something coming into being *without a cause*—as opposed, say, to coming into being with an *unseen* cause, or being *transported* from somewhere else in an unknown or unusual manner (by teleportation, perhaps)? The trouble is that the Humean scenario is underdescribed. We need to add something to our exercise in conception in order to make it what Hume needs it to be in order to make his point. Yet it is hard to see what we can add to it that wouldn't involve bringing causation back into the picture and therefore undermining the whole point of the example. For instance, it is hard to see how to distinguish something's coming into being as opposed to being transported unless it is by reference to its having a generating rather than a transporting cause.

Of course, perhaps the atheist can respond to these various objections. The point, however, is that the appeal to Hume is at most something which might, with considerable work, be *turned into* a serious criticism of the cosmological argument. By itself it is very far from being a serious criticism, much less the decisive one Stenger and others suppose it to be.

III.4. Why assume that the universe had a beginning or that a regress of causes must terminate?: Rosenberg and Krauss put forward something like this sort of objection when they propose that the multiverse hypothesis—according to which the Big Bang that gave rise to our universe involved a branching off from a preexisting universe, which in turn is part of a beginningless series of universes—eliminates the need for a divine cause. Krauss, citing Richard Feynman, also suggests that for all we know there might always be deeper and deeper layers of laws of physics which we can probe until we get bored.[25]

One problem with this is that as we have seen, most versions of the cosmological argument are not concerned in the first place with the question of whether the universe had a beginning. They are concerned instead to argue that even if the universe (or multiverse for that matter) had no

ical Papers, Volume I (Oxford: Blackwell, 1981). Cf. the discussion in Brian Davies, *An Introduction to the Philosophy of Religion,* Third edition (Oxford: Oxford University Press, 2004), pp. 50–51.

25   Krauss, *A Universe from Nothing,* p. 177.

beginning, it would require a divine cause to sustain it in existence perpetually and/or to explain why it exists at all, even beginninglessly. And the one approach that is concerned with the question of whether the universe had a beginning, the *kalām* approach, offers a metaphysical argument purporting to show that there could not in principle be a beginningless universe, or multiverse, if there is one. Craig has also raised scientific criticisms of the multiverse hypothesis. Hence, appealing to the multiverse hypothesis as if it undermined the cosmological argument either misses the point or begs the question.

I have already explained why it is no good glibly to appeal to laws of nature as if they could be the ultimate explanation of things, and the point holds true however many layers of laws of nature there are. Note also that level upon level of laws of nature would constitute an essentially ordered series—laws at one level would hold only as a special case of laws at a deeper level, which would in turn hold only as a special case of yet deeper laws—and we have seen why Aristotelians would hold that such a series cannot fail to have a first member in the sense of something which can impart causal power without deriving it. Nothing Krauss or any other of the New Atheists have to say even addresses this argument, much less undermines it.

III.5. Even if there were a first cause, there is no reason to think it would be omnipotent, omniscient, perfectly good, etc.: Like "What caused God?", this is commonly put forward as a devastating objection to the cosmological argument. And like "What caused God?", it is in fact embarrassingly inept. Dawkins assures his readers that there is "absolutely no reason" to attribute omnipotence, omniscience, etc. to a first cause.[26] Krauss makes a similar claim.[27]

In fact, as I've already indicated, the proponents of each version of the cosmological argument put forward a series of arguments claiming to show that the cause of the world whose existence they've argued for must have the key divine attributes. Aquinas devotes around a hundred double-column pages of dense argumentation in Part I of the *Summa Theologiae* alone—just after presenting the Five Ways—to showing that to the cause of the world we must attribute simplicity, goodness, infinity, immutability, unity, knowledge, life, will, power, and the like. About two hundred pages of

26   Dawkins, *The God Delusion*, p. 77.
27   Krauss, *A Universe from Nothing*, p. 173.

argumentation in Book I of the *Summa Contra Gentiles* are devoted to this topic. Much argumentation along these lines can also be found in Aquinas's other works, such as *De potentia* and *De veritate*. Much of Samuel Clarke's book *A Demonstration of the Being and Attributes of God* is, as anyone who has read just the title will discover, devoted to arguing for various divine attributes—infinity, omnipresence, unity, intelligence, free choice, power, wisdom, and goodness. I have already indicated that Plotinus, Leibniz, and Craig argue for various divine attributes. Further examples could easily be given.

Dawkins, Krauss, and the other New Atheist writers offer no response at all to these arguments. In fact it seems that they are entirely unaware that the arguments even exist.

III.6. The cosmological argument proposes a "god of the gaps" in order to explain something which in fact either is, or eventually will be, better explained via a naturalistic scientific theory: This is, I think it is fair to say, the central conceit of the entire New Atheist project. In the view of the New Atheists, if something is going to be explained at all, it is going to be explained via the methods of science. Therefore (so the argument goes) the appeal to God can at best be a kind of quasi-scientific hypothesis, and the problem is that it is not a good one. For Hitchens, it violates Ockham's razor.[28] Similarly, Dawkins suggests that "it is more parsimonious to conjure up, say, a 'big bang singularity', or some other physical concept as yet unknown."[29] Harris thinks that at least at the moment we can't say much more than this, opining that "[t]he truth is that no one knows how or why the universe came into being."[30] Krauss, Hawking and Mlodinow, by contrast, think that science has already given us a complete non-theistic explanation of the existence of the world, or near enough. "Because there is a law like gravity," Hawking and Mlodinow write, "the universe can and will create itself from nothing."[31] Krauss's *A Universe from Nothing* is a book-length attempt to make this sort of view plausible.

There are two basic problems with all of this. The first is that the characterization of the question of how to explain the existence of the universe as a matter for empirical science rather than philosophical theology to settle either completely misses the point or simply begs the question. For one thing, whether or not one thinks any of them ultimately succeeds, the

28 Hitchens, *God is Not Great*, pp. 70–71.
29 Dawkins, *The God Delusion*, p. 78.
30 Harris, *Letter to a Christian Nation*, p. 73.
31 Hawking and Mlodinow, *The Grand Design*, p. 180.

versions of the cosmological argument sketched above are simply *not* "god of the gaps" explanations. A "god of the gaps" explanation is one on which it is at least possible in principle that some non-divine explanation might be correct, and the claim is at most that the theistic explanation is more probable than these alternatives. The versions of the cosmological argument we've looked at, by contrast, are all attempts at *strict metaphysical demonstration*. They claim that there is no way *in principle* to account for what they set out to explain other than a purely actual cause, or an absolutely simple or non-composite cause, or a necessary being, or a cause that is timeless and spaceless. Whether or not these claims are correct, the arguments do not stand or fall by the standards by which empirical hypotheses are evaluated—parsimony, fit with existing well-confirmed empirical theories, etc.

For another thing, the starting points of these attempts at metaphysical demonstration are not matters about which empirical scientific theory has anything to say in the first place. Rather, they have to do with what any possible empirical theory must itself take for granted. That is to say, their starting points are *metaphysical* rather than physical. Whatever the empirical facts turn out to be, they will at some level involve the actualization of potency, or so the Aristotelian will argue; they will involve composite beings, or so the Neoplatonist will argue; they will all be contingent, or so the defender of the contingency approach will argue; and they will all exist within a universe (or perhaps multiverse) that will itself require a temporal beginning, or so the defender of the *kalām* approach will argue.

Simply to assert that any explanation worth taking seriously will have to be an empirical scientific theory rather than an exercise in philosophical theology is merely to *assume* that all of this is mistaken. It is not to *show* that it is mistaken.

The second problem is that the non-theistic scientific explanation of the existence of the universe proposed by Krauss, Hawking and Mlodinow is manifestly a non-starter. "A law like gravity" is not *nothing*; hence an explanation of the existence of the universe that makes reference to such a law is rather obviously *not*, contrary to what Hawking and Mlodinow suggest, an account of how the universe might arise from nothing. Krauss's book is notoriously shameless in committing the same basic fallacy.[32] In 185 pages

---

32   I say "notoriously" because Krauss's position has been widely and harshly criticized even by philosophers with no theological ax to grind. Probably the best-known critique is that of philosopher of physics David Albert, who reviewed Krauss's book in the March 23, 2012 *New York Times* book review section.

purporting boldly to show how the universe can arise from nothing, Krauss spends the first 152 arguing that the universe arose from empty space endowed with energy and governed by physical laws, all of which he admits does not count as "nothing." By page 170 be tries to take all of this down to just the laws of quantum gravity, but admits that this does not really count as "nothing" either. At page 177 he finally resorts to suggesting that perhaps there is just layer upon layer of laws.

What is never explained is how any of this counts as explaining how the universe arose from *nothing*. There is some obfuscatory chin-pulling about "possible candidates for nothingness," and "what 'nothing' might actually comprise," along with an insistence that any "definition" of nothingness must ultimately be "based on empirical evidence" and that "'nothing' is every bit as physical as 'something'"—as if "nothingness" were a highly unusual kind of stuff that is more difficult to observe or measure than other things are. But of course "nothing" is not a kind of stuff (physical or otherwise), nor anything that is terribly difficult to define (empirically or otherwise), nor something that "comprises" anything, nor anything particularly mysterious or worth pulling one's chin over. It is just the absence of anything. Moreover, Krauss himself seems well aware of this insofar as he ends up acknowledging that his main "candidates for nothingness" are not really *nothing* after all. And what he's left with—a basic level of physical laws or layers of laws—is not only not nothing, but cannot be the ultimate explanation of the world, for the reasons given earlier.

* * *

In the history of Western thought, the cosmological argument has not only been the central argument for the existence of God, but the fundamental approach to the question of ultimate explanation. New Atheist writers have claimed to be able to refute the argument "easily." They also purport to offer a superior approach to questions of ultimate explanation. They have, manifestly for those who know the relevant subject matter, failed miserably on both counts. The intrinsic value (or lack thereof) of their arguments does not merit them even the critical attention they have received. But the acclaim they have received in some quarters makes such attention necessary. They also offer an object lesson in intellectual hubris that all philosophers ought to heed.[33]

---

33   For helpful comments on an earlier draft of this paper, I thank Howard Wettstein and an anonymous referee.

7

Between Aristotle and William Paley:
Aquinas's Fifth Way

I. Introduction

In the *Summa Theologiae*, Aquinas puts forward Five Ways of demonstrating the existence of God. The Fifth Way is stated as follows:

> The fifth way is taken from the governance of the world. We see that things which lack intelligence, such as natural bodies, act for an end, and this is evident from their acting always, or nearly always, in the same way, so as to obtain the best result. Hence it is plain that not fortuitously, but designedly, do they achieve their end. Now whatever lacks intelligence cannot move towards an end, unless it be directed by some being endowed with knowledge and intelligence; as the arrow is shot to its mark by the archer. Therefore some intelligent being exists by whom all natural things are directed to their end; and this being we call God.[1]

Insofar as this argument affirms that final causality or teleology is inherent to the natural order, it is Aristotelian in spirit. Insofar as it explains this teleology in terms of a divine intelligence, the argument may seem reminiscent of "design arguments" of the sort associated with William Paley. But while the Fifth Way does indeed proceed from Aristotelian premises, it takes them in a theological direction Aristotle himself refrained from going in. At the same time, Aquinas's essentially Aristotelian conception of teleology, however modified, radically differentiates the proof from the non-Aristotelian "design arguments" of Paley and other modern philosophers. The Fifth Way's

---

1   *Summa Theologiae* I.2.3. All quotes from the *Summa Theologiae* are taken from St. Thomas Aquinas, *Summa Theologica*, trans. Fathers of the English Dominican Province (New York: Benziger Brothers, 1948).

account of natural teleology constitutes a middle position between what we might call the radically immanent teleology of Aristotle and the radically extrinsic teleology of Paley. Moreover, while it is paid less attention by contemporary philosophers than is Paley's argument, Aquinas's proof is more philosophically formidable and theologically sound, or so I would argue.

The next section will spell out the conception of natural teleology that Aquinas shares with Aristotle and which underlies the Fifth Way. In section III we will see that though Aristotle believed that the motion we observe in the world must be sustained by an Unmoved Mover, such a divine source was *not* in his view necessary to account for teleology. Section IV will show how Paley's argument for a divine "watchmaker" presupposes a modern "mechanistic" conception of nature that is fundamentally at odds with the Aristotelian one that informs Aquinas's argument. In sections V and VI we will see how the Fifth Way contends that even given an Aristotelian conception of teleology as immanent to the natural world, a divine intelligence is, contrary to what Aristotle thought, necessary to account for its existence—though for reasons (and with consequences) that are very different from the sort we find in Paley. In section VII we will look more carefully at the differences between Aquinas and Paley with a view to their theological implications. Finally, in section VIII we will see that, even outside the orbit of Thomists, many contemporary metaphysicians and philosophers of science are returning to a broadly Aristotelian conception of nature, so that to differentiate Aquinas from Paley is by no means to make him less relevant to the contemporary discussion.

II. Nature versus art

For a thing to exhibit teleology or final causality is for it to be oriented toward some end or goal, as an acorn is oriented toward becoming an oak or a watch is oriented toward telling time. Acorns and watches differ, though, in that the former are natural objects while the latter are artifacts—products of human "art" or ingenuity. And understanding how Aristotle and Aquinas regard teleology as immanent rather than extrinsic to the natural order requires understanding the Aristotelian distinction between natural objects or substances on the one hand, and everyday artifacts and other accidental arrangements on the other hand.[2] Aristotle sets the theme in the *Physics*:

2   For a more detailed discussion of the Aristotelian-Thomistic understanding of teleology than I can offer here, see my books *Aquinas* (Oxford: Oneworld Publications,

Some things exist by nature, others are due to other causes. Natural objects include animals and their parts, plants and simple bodies like earth, fire, air and water ... The obvious difference between all these things and things which are not natural is that each of the natural ones contains within itself a source of change and of stability, in respect of either movement or increase and decrease or alteration. On the other hand, something like a bed or a cloak has no intrinsic impulse for change—at least, they do not under that particular description and to the extent that they are a result of human skill, but they do in so far as and to the extent that they are coincidentally made out of stone or earth or some combination of the two.

The nature of a thing, then, is a certain principle and cause of change and stability in the thing, and it is *directly* present in it—which is to say that it is present in its own right and not coincidentally.[3]

The basic idea, then, is that a natural object is one whose characteristic behavior—the ways in which it manifests either stability or changes of various sorts—derives from something intrinsic to it. A non-natural object is one which does not have such an intrinsic principle of its characteristic behavior; only the natural objects out of which it is made have such a principle. We can illustrate the distinction with a simple example. A *liana vine*—the kind of vine Tarzan likes to swing on—is a natural object. A *hammock* that Tarzan might construct from living liana vines is a kind of artifact, and not a natural object. The parts of the liana vine have an inherent tendency to function together to allow the liana to exhibit the growth patterns it does, to take in water and nutrients, and so forth. By contrast, the parts of the hammock—the liana vines themselves—have no inherent tendency to function together as a hammock. Rather, they must be arranged by Tarzan to do so, and left to their own devices—that is to say, without pruning, occasional rearrangement, and the like—they will tend to grow the way they otherwise would have had Tarzan not interfered with them, including in ways that will

2009), especially pp. 16–19, 36–51, 112–20, and 177–82, and *The Last Superstition: A Refutation of the New Atheism* (South Bend, IN: St. Augustine's Press, 2008), especially pp. 62–72 and 235–65; and my article "Teleology: A Shopper's Guide," *Philosophia Christi* Vol. 12, No. 1 (2010).

3   *Physics*, Book II, Part 1, in Aristotle, *Physics*, trans. Robin Waterfield (Oxford: Oxford University Press, 1996), p. 33.

impede their performance as a hammock. Their natural tendency is to be liana-like and not hammock-like; the hammock-like function they perform after Tarzan ties them together is extrinsic or imposed from outside, while the liana-like functions are intrinsic or immanent to them.[4]

To put the point in terms of traditional Scholastic jargon, a liana vine is a compound of *substantial form* and *prime matter* (that is, matter devoid of any form at all—something which for the Aristotelian is only an abstraction, since matter in the actual world always has *some* substantial form or other). The hammock qua hammock is *not* such a compound. Its existence involves instead the imposition of an *accidental form* on components each of which already has a substantial form, namely the substantial form of a liana vine. A liana vine is, accordingly, a true *substance*. The hammock is not a true substance, precisely because it does not qua hammock have a substantial form but only an accidental form. In general, true substances are typically natural objects, whereas (Aquinas tells us, commenting on Aristotle) "some things are not substances, as is clear especially of artificial things."[5] Again:

> Man and wood and stone are natural bodies, but a house or a saw is artificial. And of these the natural bodies seem to be the more properly called substances, since artificial bodies are made out of them. Art works upon materials furnished by nature, giving these, moreover, a merely accidental form, such as a new shape and so forth ...[6]

Now the liana-like tendencies of the vines are paradigm instances of *immanent* or "built in" final causality or teleology. For these tendencies involve an orientation toward certain *ends*—growth patterns of a certain sort, the taking in of water and nutrients, and so forth—and it is by virtue of its nature or substantial form that a vine has them. By contrast, the hammock-

---

4   Cf. Aristotle's example (borrowed from an earlier thinker, Antiphon): "[I]f you bury a [wooden] bed and, as it rots, it manages to send up a shoot, the result is wood, not a bed" (ibid., p. 34). That is to say, the natural tendency of the material that makes up the bed is to be wood-like, not bed-like.

5   *Sententia super Metaphysicam* VII.17.1680, in St. Thomas Aquinas, *Commentary on Aristotle's* Metaphysics, trans. John P. Rowan (Notre Dame, IN: Dumb Ox Books, 1995), at p. 552.

6   *Sententia super De anima* II.1.218, in St. Thomas Aquinas, *Commentary on Aristotle's* De Anima, trans. Kenelm Foster, O.P. and Silvester Humphries, O.P. (Notre Dame, IN: Dumb Ox Books, 1994), at p. 73.

like tendencies of the vines are paradigm instances of *extrinsic* final causality, or teleology imposed "from outside." For those tendencies are not ones that the vines have given their nature or substantial form. They are there only insofar as an artificer has put them there.

But not all accidental forms are the result of artifice. A group of liana vines which has by chance taken on a hammock-like arrangement does not count as a true substance either, any more than a pattern made by a trail of ants that looks vaguely like the word "No" is really the word "No." For while this arrangement is not an artifact (not having been deliberately constructed, as Tarzan's hammock was), the resulting object still does not have the substantial form of a hammock (if there were such a thing as the "substantial form of a hammock"), but is a mere accidental arrangement of parts, like a heap of stones that has formed at the bottom of a hill over time as a consequence of erosion. So though in one sense it obviously occurred "naturally," it is not a "natural" object *in the sense* in which Aristotle contrasts nature with art, since a tendency to work together in a "hammock-like" way is not *inherent* to the parts.

What's true of a hammock (or a hammock-like chance object) made of living liana vines is no less true of a hammock made of dead liana vines, even though the difference between artifacts and natural objects is in this case less dramatic. For while the dead vines will not exhibit the growth patterns the living vines will (constantly threatening to upset the hammock-like function Tarzan has imposed on them) they still have no *inherent or built in* tendency to function as a hammock. Being dead, they have lost the substantial form of liana vines, but they have not taken on the substantial form of a hammock (if, again, there were such a thing). Rather, they have the very same substantial form that other bits of dead liana lying randomly around the forest have—the substantial form of a kind of wood, say. Perhaps this substantial form gives them enough durability to make them useful to put together into the form of a hammock, but that does not mean that they now have a natural "hammock-like" tendency per se, only that they have a natural tendency toward a certain degree of durability (which might also make them useful for making lots of things other than hammocks).

Now what we have said about hammocks is from an Aristotelian point of view true also of watches, knives, computers, cars, houses, airplanes, telephones, cups, coats, beds, and countless other everyday artifacts. Like the hammock, these objects do not count as natural or as true substances because their specifically watch-like, knife-like, etc. tendencies are extrinsic rather than immanent, the result of externally imposed accidental forms rather than substantial forms. The teleology or final causality of a watch or knife *qua* watch or knife is, accordingly, extrinsic rather than intrinsic. To be sure, the distinctively *metallic* tendencies of the parts of the watch or the blade of the knife *will* be instances of intrinsic or immanent final causality, for these tendencies follow from the nature or substantial form of these components. As Aquinas puts it, "a knife has in itself a principle of downward motion, not insofar as it is a knife, but insofar as it is iron."[7] But functions like time-telling, meat-cutting, and the like do not follow from the substantial form of the metal parts, and thus are not immanent to them.

We have seen that some objects that are not substances, and thus not "natural" in the technical sense Aristotle uses in the *Physics*—a heap of stones which has gradually formed at the bottom of a hill, a group of liana vines which by chance has grown into a hammock-like arrangement—are not artifacts. But the converse is also true; that is to say, it is possible for something to be a product of "art" or human skill and yet to have a substantial form, and thus to be in the relevant sense "natural." Aquinas says:

> Art is not able to confer a substantial form by its own power ... [but] it is nevertheless able to do so by the power of natural agents, as is made clear by the fact that the form of fire is induced in wood through art.[8]

Fire is, after all, something natural, and remains so even if it is generated by human beings rather than (say) lightning. Similarly, water synthesized out of hydrogen and oxygen in a laboratory is in no relevant respect different from water from a river or from the clouds. It has the substantial form of water and is in that sense a true substance. Dog breeds are also man-made, but a dog of any breed is still a natural object, for its parts have an inherent tendency to function together in a dog-like way (by contrast with a watch, whose parts have no inherent tendency to function in a watch-like way). Of course, fire and water already exist in many places no human being has ever trod, and dogs are variations on a kind of animal (the gray wolf) that already occurs in the wild. But even something which in no way exists apart from

7   *Sententia super Physicam* II.1.142, in St. Thomas Aquinas, *Commentary on Aristotle's* Physics, trans. Richard J. Blackwell, Richard J. Spath, and W. Edmund Thirlkel (Notre Dame, IN: Dumb Ox Books, 1999), at p. 75.

8   *Scriptum super Sententiis* 2.7.3.1 ad 5, as translated by Michael Rota in his article "Substance and Artifact in Thomas Aquinas," *History of Philosophy Quarterly* Vol. 21, No. 3 (July 2004), at p. 245.

human intervention could also count as a true substance, and thus as "natural" in the relevant sense. Eleonore Stump suggests Styrofoam as a possible example.[9]

Stump's rationale is that what seems to be essential to true substances, as Aquinas understands them, is that they have properties and causal powers that are irreducible to those of their parts. Hence water has properties and causal powers that hydrogen and oxygen do not have, whereas the properties and causal powers of an axe seem to amount to nothing over and above the sum of the properties and causal powers of the axe's wood and metal parts. When water is synthesized out of hydrogen and oxygen, then, what happens is that the prime matter underlying the hydrogen and oxygen loses the substantial forms of hydrogen and oxygen and takes on a new substantial form, namely that of water. By contrast, when an axe is made out of wood and metal, the prime matter underlying the wood and the prime matter underlying the metal do not lose their substantial forms. Rather, while maintaining their substantial forms, they take on a new accidental form, that of being an axe. Now the making of Styrofoam, Stump suggests, seems to be more like the synthesis of water out of hydrogen and oxygen than it is like the making of an axe. For Styrofoam has properties and causal powers which are irreducible to those of the materials out of which it is made, and which therefore indicate the presence of a substantial form and thus a true substance.

The metaphysical issues here are complex, but we need not pursue them further for present purposes.[10] Suffice it to note that things are more complicated than the traditional "nature versus art" distinction might at first glance indicate. The *fundamental* distinction is actually that between things having substantial forms, and those having merely accidental forms. The former are true substances, the latter are not. Natural objects (in the everyday sense of "natural") like water, iron, animals, or the liana vines of my example are paradigm instances of the former. Artifacts like watches, knives, beds, or the hammock of my example are paradigm instances of the latter. Still, there are objects which are "natural" in the everyday sense, but

9   Eleonore Stump, *Aquinas* (London: Routledge, 2003), p. 44.
10 For useful recent discussions of the Aristotelian-Thomistic metaphysics of substances and artifacts, see Rota, "Substance and Artifact in Thomas Aquinas"; Stump, *Aquinas*, pp. 39–44; Eleonore Stump, "Substance and Artifact in Aquinas's Metaphysics," in Thomas M. Crisp, Matthew Davidson, and David Vanderlaan, eds., *Knowledge and Reality: Essays in Honor of Alvin Plantinga* (Dordrecht: Springer, 2006); and David S. Oderberg, *Real Essentialism* (London: Routledge, 2007), pp. 166–70.

which are nevertheless not true substances—and thus *not* "natural" in Aristotle's *technical* sense—such as the heap of stones that forms by chance at the bottom of a hill. And there are objects that are "artifacts" in the sense of being man-made that *are* nevertheless true substances (and thus "natural" in Aristotle's sense) such as water synthesized in a lab and (perhaps) Styrofoam. But it is not surprising that writers in the Aristotelian tradition have often spoken, more loosely, in terms of a distinction between nature and art. For the *typical* object that is "natural" in the sense of existing apart from human action is also "natural" in the sense of having a substantial rather than accidental form, even if not *all* objects that are "natural" in either one of these senses are also "natural" in the other. And the *typical* object that has only an accidental form rather than a substantial form is also an artifact or something man-made, even if not *all* objects which lack substantial forms are artifacts and not all artifacts lack substantial forms.

In any event, the distinction between immanent and extrinsic teleology that is so vital to understanding the Fifth Way is, then, at bottom a distinction between the teleology or final causality a thing exhibits by virtue of its substantial form, and the teleology a thing exhibits only because of some accidental form. This distinction closely, if imperfectly, tracks the distinction between natural objects and human artifacts, which is why the natural tendencies of acorns and the like are standard examples of immanent teleology and the functions of watches and the like are standard examples of extrinsic teleology. But immanent teleology can also exist in objects that are in some sense man-made, as when human skill produces substances like water or Styrofoam, with their distinctive causal powers.

This brings us to one final, crucial aspect of our account of immanent teleology. It might seem odd to speak of water or Styrofoam as exhibiting teleology or final causality. For the standard examples of teleology—acorns, bodily organs, and other biological phenomena, or watches and other artifacts and their components—typically involve either an arrangement of parts working toward a common end or some sort of goal-directed process. The acorn develops into an oak; eyes, ears, hearts, and lungs function together to allow an organism to survive and flourish; the parts of a watch are arranged so that it can function as a timepiece; and so on. But what is there in water, Styrofoam, and the like that parallels the developmental process of an acorn, or the function of a bodily organ or watch part?

But it is a mistake to think that teleology need always involve a process with stages (as in the development from acorn to oak) or a part functioning for the sake of a whole (as with an eye or a watch gear). Rather, what is essential to teleology is an inclination towards an end, and this can exist at levels of reality simpler than those involving developmental processes or part-to-whole relationships of the sort found in organisms and machines. In particular, for Scholastic writers like Aquinas, it exists even in the simplest instances of efficient causality. Take, for example, the tendency of an ice cube to cause the liquid or air surrounding it to grow cooler, or of a match to generate flame and heat when struck. These, specifically, are the effects the ice cube or match will reliably bring about unless somehow impeded (for instance, by melting the ice cube before it has a chance to cool its surroundings, or by damaging the match by submerging it in water). The ice cube will cool the surrounding air *rather than* heating it, or causing it to become toxic, or having no effect at all; the match will cause flame and heat *rather than* frost and cold, or the smell of lilacs, or no effect at all. That the ice cube and match have just the specific effects they do in fact have rather than some others or none at all—or, counterfactually, that they would have had those specific effects had they not been impeded—is explicable only if we suppose that there is something in them that "points to" precisely those outcomes rather than any others, as to an end or goal. In short, if A is by nature an *efficient* cause of B, then generating B must be the *final* cause of A. As Aquinas says, "every agent [i.e., efficient cause] acts for an end: otherwise one thing would not follow more than another from the action of the agent, unless it were by chance."[11] Later Scholastics would come to refer to this as the *principle of finality*.[12]

We will have reason to return to this theme, since it plays a central role in the Fifth Way. Suffice it for the moment to note that Aquinas takes immanent teleology or final causality to be manifest not only in relatively complex and rare natural phenomena like plants, animals, and their organs, but also in all inorganic entities insofar as they have, by virtue of their substantial forms, distinctive powers of efficient causality. The causal powers of water, Styrofoam, iron, gold, lead, and the like—and indeed the causal

---

11   *Summa Theologiae* I.44.4. Cf. *Summa Theologiae* I-II.1.2, *Summa contra gentiles* III.2, *Sententia super Physicam* II.5.186, and *De principiis naturae* III. In the case of a match—which is, of course, an artifact with certain externally imposed ends (lighting cigars, pilot lights, and the like)—it is only the phosphorus in the match head which, by virtue of its chemistry, has an *inherent* inclination toward the ends in question, and only effects like flame, heat, and the like (rather than lit cigars and pilot lights per se) that are included in those ends.

12   Reginald Garrigou-Lagrange regards the principle, when rightly understood, as *self-evident*. See *God: His Existence and His Nature* (St. Louis: B. Herder, 1939), Volume I, pp. 199–205.

powers of even the most elementary particles—are no less instances of "built in" inclination towards an end than the tendencies of acorns and liana vines are. Thus, since efficient causality exists *everywhere* in the natural world, from top to bottom, so too does final causality.[13]

III. Aristotle contra Anaxagoras and Plato

What explains this? Here is where Aquinas parts ways with Aristotle. The aim of the Fifth Way is to show that the teleology that exists in nature, though immanent rather than extrinsic, nevertheless presupposes the existence of a divine intelligence which orders things to their ends. Aristotle did not take such a view. To be sure, he held that there *is* a divine intelligence, that this intelligence is the Unmoved Mover of the universe, and that the way in which He moves the world is by virtue of being its final cause. God is in that way the explanation of the fact that things *realize* their ends, to the extent that they do. But He is not in Aristotle's view the explanation of the fact that they *have* those ends in the first place. That is just a basic fact about them given their natures. Hence, though there is in Aristotle a precursor to Aquinas's First Way, there is no precursor to the Fifth Way.

Lurking in the background of the view of final causes we have seen Aristotle develop in the *Physics* is a critique of the theories of atomists like Democritus, who favored a materialist explanation of the world which eschews final causes altogether, and the view of Anaxagoras that the order of the world requires an explanation in terms of intelligence. Aristotle regards the latter as no more successful than the former:

> [Earlier thinkers] in the peregrinations often strike good blows, but they do not do so from knowledge, and no more do these thinkers seem to have known what they were saying. For they seem to have made more or less no use of these principles except to a small extent. For Anaxagoras uses the mind as a device for the making of the cosmos, and when he puzzles for what reason it is of necessity, then he drags in mind, but in other matters he ascribes cause to anything else rather than to mind ...[14]

13 For discussion of the various distinct levels at which immanent teleology might be said to exist in the natural world, see Feser, "Teleology: A Shopper's Guide."

14 *Metaphysics*, Book Alpha, Part 4, in Aristotle, *The Metaphysics,* trans. Hugh Lawson-Tancred (London: Penguin, 2004), at p. 17.

Aristotle evidently seeks to defend a middle ground position according to which there is such a thing as final causality in nature, but that it is *entirely* immanent to the natural world rather than in any way derivative from something like the "mind" of Anaxagoras or the demiurge of Plato's *Timaeus*. For Aristotle rejects the view that the natural world requires ordering in the first place: "That which is by nature and natural is never *dis*ordered. For nature is everywhere a *cause* of order."[15] For Aristotle, for a thing to be "natural" is *ipso facto* for it to be ordered in the sense of having an end toward which it is directed. That which requires an outside source to order or direct it towards an end would, for him, by that very fact not be a natural object at all but an artifact.

To those who claim that goal-directedness or purpose requires conscious deliberation or planning of the sort rational beings engage in, Aristotle responds:

> It is ridiculous for people to deny that there is purpose if they cannot see the agent of change doing any planning. After all, skill does not make plans. If ship-building were intrinsic to wood, then wood would naturally produce the same results that ship-building does. If skill is purposive, then, so is nature.[16]

In other words, that goal-directedness does not require conscious deliberation is evident from the fact that a skilled craftsman can largely carry out his work without even thinking about it—"on autopilot" as we might put it today, or without first "making plans," as Aristotle puts it. But if this is possible for someone with such skill, there is in Aristotle's view no reason not to think it also possible for natural objects. This is the force of the ship-building example: If there were something in the very nature of wood that "directed it" toward the end of becoming a ship, then what in the case of human craftsmanship results from deliberate design—a ship—would in that case result "naturally" instead, i.e., without conscious deliberation at all. Indeed, "it looks as though things happen at the plant level too which serve some purpose" in just this way, even though plants do not deliberate—for instance, an oak derives from an acorn without the acorn planning this

---

15   *Physics*, Book VIII, Part 1, as translated by Monte Ransome Johnson in his book *Aristotle on Teleology* (Oxford: Clarendon Press, 2005), at p. 249. Emphasis added.
16   *Physics,* Book II, Part 8, Waterfield translation at p. 53.

result—and there is also of course the example of "non-human animals, whose products are not the result of skill, enquiry, or planning."[17]

Because he took the natures of things to suffice to account for their being directed or ordered towards their ends, Aristotle saw no need to attribute this ordering to God:

> The divine is not an ordering ruler, since he needs nothing, but rather is that for the sake of which wisdom gives orders.[18]

Hence while God Himself *is* the ultimate end toward which things are directed, He does not in Aristotle's view *impart* to things their ends. Indeed, far from paying other things and their ends any mind, God has in Aristotle's view Himself alone as the proper object of His thought. Nor is there any need to explain the *origin* of the world, together with its teleological features, in terms of divine ordering, since Aristotle takes the world *always* to have existed.

This, at any rate, is the usual view of Aristotle's position on the relationship of natural teleology to God.[19] There are some who dissent from it. For example, while acknowledging that what I have described is "a standard view among Aristotelian scholars," Marie George has suggested that a passage from Aristotle's *On Generation and Corruption* implies a different interpretation.[20] In particular, she notes that Aristotle says that "nature ... always and in all things strives after the better" and "God, therefore ... perfected the universe by making coming-to-be a perpetual process."[21] However, this passage doesn't show what George thinks it does. What it shows is at most only that Aristotle regards God as the cause of things' moving in such a way that they realize their ends; it doesn't show that He is the cause of things *having* those ends in the first place. And the latter thesis is the one that Aristotle scholars typically decline to attribute to Aristotle.[22]

---

17 *Physics*, Book II, Part 8, Waterfield translation at pp. 51–52.

18 *Eudemian Ethics*, Book VIII, Part 3, as translated by Johnson in *Aristotle on Teleology*, at p. 262. Cf. Johnson's discussion of the passage at pp. 72–74.

19 For important recent expositions, see Johnson, *Aristotle on Teleology*, and Christopher Shields, *Aristotle* (London: Routledge, 2007), pp. 68–90.

20 Marie George, "An Aristotelian-Thomist Responds to Edward Feser's 'Teleology,'" *Philosophia Christi* 12 (2010), at p. 442.

21 Aristotle, *On Coming-to-Be and Passing Away*, trans. E. S. Forster, in *On Sophistical Refutations, On Coming-to-Be and Passing Away, On the Cosmos* (Cambridge, MA: Harvard University Press, 1955), 336b25–37a2.

22 See Johnson, *Aristotle on Teleology*, pp. 258–63 for discussion and criticism of attempts by scholars of earlier generations to show that Aristotle was committed to a teleological argument for God's existence.

IV. From William of Ockham to William Paley

Unlike Aristotle, and like Aquinas, William Paley regarded God as the source of the teleology that exists in the natural world. But unlike either Aristotle or Aquinas, he did not regard final causes as *immanent* or *intrinsic* to the world, but rather as entirely *extrinsic*. It is not, for Paley, *qua natural* that a natural object manifests teleology. Rather, it is only those specific natural objects whose complexity is so great that they are unlikely to have come about except through the agency of an intelligence like ours that point to the existence of teleology, and even then only as a matter of high probability rather than metaphysical necessity.

The stage was set for Paley's probabilistic and extrinsicist approach long before "design arguments" of the kind he is associated with became fashionable in the eighteenth century, indeed, even before the rise of modern philosophy. We find its Scholastic roots in William of Ockham, who denied that it could be *demonstrated* through natural reason that final causes exist in non-rational natural objects. In Ockham's view, only agents with free will clearly exhibit teleology:

> [S]omeone who is just following natural reason would claim that the question 'For what reason?' is inappropriate in the case of natural actions. For he would maintain that it is no real question to ask for what reason a fire is generated; rather, this question is appropriate only in the case of voluntary actions.[23]

To the argument that without final causes, an agent or efficient cause would act by chance rather than reliably generating its associated effect, Ockham responds:

> I reply that this argument goes through for a free agent, which is no more inclined by its nature toward the one effect than toward the other. However, the argument does not go through for a natural agent, since an agent of this sort is by its nature inclined toward one determinate effect in such a way that it is not able to

---

23 *Quodlibet* 4, q. 1, in William of Ockham, *Quodlibetal Questions*, trans. Alfred J. Freddoso and Francis E. Kelley (New Haven: Yale University Press, 1991), at p. 249.

cause an opposite effect. This is evident in the case of fire with respect to heat.[24]

In general, Ockham held that apart from revelation, we could know very little about teleology:

> If I accepted no authority [i.e., the truths of faith], I would claim that it cannot be proved either from propositions known per se or from experience that every effect has a final cause that is either distinct or not distinct from its efficient cause. For it cannot be sufficiently proved that every effect has a final cause.[25]

The tendency to associate teleology only with rational agents is even more pronounced in the work of John Buridan. As Dennis Des Chene writes:

> Ockham had already argued, following Avicenna, that the final cause acts only by virtue of existing in the intellect of an agent; to which Buridan added that when it acts thus, it acts as an efficient cause, and that where the agent is not such as to conceive the ends by which it acts, there is no final cause at all, only efficient causes. To the argument that if there were no ends in nature, then one thing would follow from another haphazardly, Buridan replies (as we would) that efficient causes suffice.[26]

As Des Chene notes, this tendency continued through the late Scholastic period, though there were also writers who returned to the more traditional Aristotelian view. But the upshot of the trend begun by Ockham and Buridan was "a significant step away from Aristotle and toward Plato"—that is, toward seeing the ends of inanimate natural objects as imposed from outside by a divine intelligence analogous to the demiurge of the *Timaeus*. It also pointed forward to the revolution of the moderns, for "when [these later

---

24   Ibid.
25   Ibid., p. 246. For (somewhat divergent) treatments of the subject of Ockham's understanding of causality, see Harry R. Klocker, *God and the Empiricists* (Milwaukee: Bruce Publishing Company, 1968), Chapter 1, and Marilyn McCord Adams, *William Ockham* (Notre Dame: University of Notre Dame Press, 1987), Volume II, Chapter 18.
26   Dennis Des Chene, *Physiologia: Natural Philosophy in Late Aristotelian and Cartesian Thought* (Ithaca: Cornell University Press, 1996), pp. 186–87.

Scholastics] assimilate the inanimate world to a divine artifact, and final causation to intentional action, they hark back to [Plato] even as they unwittingly prepare the way to the world-machine of Descartes."[27]

Indeed, with Descartes, Aristotle's sharp distinction between natural objects and artifacts (or at least those artifacts which do not have substantial forms) is completely obliterated, with the former assimilated to the latter:

> For I do not recognize any difference between artefacts and natural bodies except that the operations of artefacts are for the most part performed by mechanisms which are large enough to be easily perceivable by the senses ... [I]t is no less natural for a clock constructed with this or that set of wheels to tell the time than it is for a tree which grew from this or that seed to produce the appropriate fruit. Men who are experienced in dealing with machinery can take a particular machine whose function they know and, by looking at some of its parts, easily form a conjecture about the design of the other parts, which they cannot see. In the same way I have attempted to consider the observable effects and parts of natural bodies and track down the imperceptible causes and particles which produce them.[28]

In effect, as Des Chene observes, Descartes reverses Aristotle's dictum about the relationship between art and nature:

> But if art is like nature, then so too nature is like art. Yet artifacts are bereft of any intrinsic principle, active or passive, of movement. If nature were indeed like art, nature too would lack such a principle: it would have, in short, no nature [in Aristotle's technical sense of "nature"].[29]

The result has been the hegemony in modern Western thought of what Brian Ellis has called "the dead world of mechanism" or "passivism," the view of Descartes, Newton, Hume, and their successors that matter is essentially devoid of any "intrinsic impulse for change" of the sort that Aristotle attributed

---

27   Ibid., pp. 187–88.

28   *Principles of Philosophy*, Part 4, sec. 203, in Rene Descartes, *The Philosophical Writings of Descartes*, trans. John Cottingham, Robert Stoothoff, and Dugald Murdoch (Cambridge: Cambridge University Press, 1985), Volume I, pp. 288–89.

29   Des Chene, *Physiologia*, p. 240.

to natural objects in the *Physics*.[30] Rather, it is governed by external "laws of nature" which impose on it an order it could not otherwise have.

We are used today to hearing it asserted matter-of-factly that the "operation" of "laws of nature" suffices to "explain" natural phenomena—a very curious claim, given that, as Jonathan Kvanvig and Hugh McCann have pointed out:

> Laws, after all, are descriptive in import. They do not *operate* at all, despite our figures of speech, and they do not do anything in or to the world. If they are true, it is because things themselves have features the laws describe.[31]

Now the Aristotelian would say that it is precisely "things themselves" that are primary, that it is their natures which explain the operation of the laws rather than the laws which explain how things operate. But the early modern philosophers and scientists who inaugurated the anti-Aristotelian mechanical or "passivist" view of nature would (contra contemporary naturalists) have denied that laws of nature should be regarded as a terminus of explanation in the first place—only God, as the Author of those laws, can be that. Nor in their view should teleology disappear from our account of nature. Rather, as Margaret Osler writes of thinkers like Gassendi, Newton, and Boyle:

> Although most seventeenth-century mechanical philosophers rejected immanent final causes—in the sense of the actualization of forms—they accepted an idea of finality as imposed on nature from without. What is at stake here is not the rejection of final causes *per se*, but their reinterpretation within a new concept of nature. With the mechanical reinterpretation of final causes, the idea of individual natures that possess immanent finality was

30 Brian Ellis, *The Philosophy of Nature: A Guide to the New Essentialism* (Chesham: Acumen, 2002), pp. 1–3, 60–63.

31 Jonathan L. Kvanvig and Hugh J. McCann, "Divine Conservation and the Persistence of the World," in Thomas V. Morris, ed., *Divine and Human Action: Essays in the Metaphysics of Theism* (Ithaca: Cornell University Press, 1988), p. 34. For an account of how the Aristotelian conception of the natures of things gave way in modern philosophy to the notion of "laws of nature," see Walter Ott, *Causation and Laws of Nature in Early Modern Philosophy* (Oxford: Oxford University Press, 2009). For discussion of the philosophical issues and difficulties surrounding the notion of laws of nature, see Stephen Mumford, *Laws in Nature* (London: Routledge, 2004).

replaced with the idea of nature as a whole which is the product of the divine artificer. Nature became a work of art.[32]

In short, these thinkers replaced Scholastic philosophical theology, grounded in an Aristotelian philosophy of nature, with the "design argument."

And that brings us to William Paley, the most famous defender of that argument. The basic thrust of his version is familiar.[33] Though we might reasonably suppose that a stone we had come across upon a heath had possibly lain there forever, we could not reasonably think the same of a watch discovered in the same place. For a watch has parts that are evidently arranged for a purpose; and had the parts been different or arranged differently, they could not have served that purpose. Hence we must conclude that "an artificer or artificers … formed it for the purpose which we find it actually to answer."[34] Nor would we be any less inclined to this conclusion if we found that the watch contained a mechanism which enabled it to make copies of itself; indeed, to deny that the watch was designed would in this case be even more of an "absurdity."[35] Yet the atheist maintains something no less absurd. For "every indication of contrivance, every manifestation of design, which existed in the watch, exists in the works of nature; with the difference, on the side of nature, of being greater and more, and that in a degree which exceeds all computation."[36] This is particularly evident from the anatomical features of living things. Even more than the watch, then, the natural world exhibits "proof of design, and of a designing Creator."[37]

This is, however, just an outline of the argument. Paley devotes the bulk of his book to a detailed description of diverse biological phenomena, from the structure of the eye and the ear to the skeletal system, the muscles, the properties of fish, birds, insects, plants, and so on. His aim is to overwhelm

---

32 Margaret J. Osler, "From Immanent Natures to Nature as Artifice: The Reinterpretation of Final Causes in Seventeenth Century Natural Philosophy," *The Monist* vol. 79, no. 3 (July 1996), pp. 389–90. Later generations of philosophers and scientists would, of course, ban even extrinsic final causes from science. As David Hull writes, "Historically, explanations were designated as mechanistic to indicate that they included no reference to final causes or vital forces. In this weak sense, all present-day scientific explanations are mechanistic." (*The Cambridge Dictionary of Philosophy*, s.v. "mechanistic explanation".)

33 William Paley, *Natural Theology* (Oxford: Oxford University Press, 2006).

34 Ibid., p. 8.

35 Ibid., p. 15.

36 Ibid., p. 16.

37 Ibid., p. 40.

the atheist with an "argument cumulative."[38] The argument concerns probabilities, but Paley thinks the probability of design so high that he speaks confidently of "the *necessity* of an intelligent Creator."[39] He also includes a chapter on astronomy, but says that "it is *not* the best medium through which to prove the agency of an intelligent Creator," for heavenly bodies are simple in their appearance, and "we deduce design from relation, aptitude, and correspondence of *parts*. Some degree therefore of *complexity* is necessary to render a subject fit for this species of argument."[40]

Thus, whereas for Aquinas, the existence of even the simplest efficient-causal regularity establishes the reality of final causality, for Paley only complex phenomena can give us reason to believe in purpose and "design." Moreover, whereas for Aquinas final causes exist in the natural world of metaphysical necessity, for Paley the existence of design (and thus of purpose in nature) is a mere probabilistic hypothesis (even if the probability is in his view so great that the conclusion cannot reasonably be doubted). These differences reflect the radical differences in the two thinkers' basic metaphysical commitments. For Aquinas the Aristotelian, a natural object, however simple or complex, simply wouldn't *be* a natural object at all it is unless it had a substantial form and thus the final causality immanent to something with that form. For Paley the inheritor of the early moderns' anti-Aristotelian mechanical or "passivist" view of nature, nothing in the natural order has any *inherent* purpose or finality, any more than the metal parts that make up a watch have an inherent tendency to function as a timepiece. There cannot be any question of natural things pointing with *necessity* to the reality of final causes or teleology, then, though certain inherently purposeless natural phenomena might be so complex that we can judge with high probability that an *extrinsic* purpose must have been imposed on them.

V. Aquinas's middle position: First stage

Still, like Paley and unlike Aristotle, Aquinas holds that natural teleology points to the existence of God. His is a middle position between the ones

---

38   Ibid., p. 45.
39   Ibid., emphasis added. Paley appeals to what is "probable" or to "probability" or "improbability" several times in the course of his argument, e.g., at pp. 108, 135, 162, 167, 179, and 201. See Matthew D. Eddy and David Knight's "Introduction" to the edition of Paley's *Natural Theology* cited above for a useful brief discussion of the rise of interest in probabilistic arguments in Paley's day.
40   Ibid., p. 199. Emphasis in the original.

staked out by Paley and Aristotle. But how could there be such a thing? Monte Ransome Johnson, Christopher Shields, and Andre Ariew have sharply distinguished the Aristotelian conception of teleology as immanent to the natural world from the view one finds in the Plato of the *Timaeus*, Newton, and Paley to the effect that teleology exists in nature only insofar as a deity has imposed it from outside.[41] Call the former view *Aristotelian teleological realism* and the latter *Platonic teleological realism*.[42] If we reject one, mustn't we embrace the other? Johnson, Shields, and Ariew imply as much. Their view seems to be that to endorse Aristotle's view that teleology is immanent to the natural order (a view each of these writers regards as at least philosophically interesting) entails rejecting the idea that God has anything at all to do with it. Arguing from a different direction but arriving at a similar conclusion, Marie George and Jay Richards suggest that since Aquinas thinks God does have something to do with natural teleology, his view must after all be closer to Paley's than I have allowed.[43]

But this is a false choice. As is well known, Aquinas held that God is the "first cause" of things in the sense that all other efficient causes derive whatever causal power they have from Him. But Aquinas is no occasionalist. He nevertheless insists that "secondary causes" are *true* causes, making a genuine causal contribution to their effects. But what is true in the order of efficient causes is in Aquinas's view no less true in the order of final causes. Just as secondary causes have genuine causal power of their own despite their ultimately deriving it from God, so too do is the teleology of natural objects immanent to them despite their ultimately deriving that too from God.

We might call this position *Scholastic teleological realism*, and its status as a middle ground between Platonic and Aristotelian extremes is analogous to (and might be illuminated by comparison with) the similarly middle-ground position Aquinas and other Scholastics took on the problem of

---

41 See Johnson, *Aristotle on Teleology*; Shields, *Aristotle*, pp. 68–90; and Ariew's articles "Platonic and Aristotelian Roots of Teleological Arguments," in Andre Ariew, Robert Cummins, and Mark Perlman, eds., *Functions: New Essays in the Philosophy of Psychology and Biology* (Oxford: Oxford University Press, 2002) and "Teleology," in David L. Hull and Michael Ruse, eds., *The Cambridge Companion to the Philosophy of Biology* (New York: Cambridge University Press, 2007).

42 Shields calls the latter view "teleological intentionalism," and Ariew calls it "Platonic teleologism."

43 George, "An Aristotelian-Thomist Responds to Edward Feser's 'Teleology,'" and Jay W. Richards, "Separating the Chaff from the Wheat," in Jay W. Richards, ed., *God and Evolution* (Seattle: Discovery Institute Press, 2010).

universals.[44] Plato, Aristotle, and Aquinas are all realists about universals rather than nominalists or conceptualists. But they famously differ about what realism entails. For Platonic realism about universals, the universal essence *acorn* (to take a simple example) exists entirely apart from particular acorns and from the finite minds that grasp this universal, in a "third realm" as the "Form of Acorn." For Aristotelian realism about universals, the universal essence *acorn* exists only in particular acorns themselves and in the finite minds that abstract it. For Scholastic realism about universals, the universal essence *acorn* exists in the particular acorns themselves and in the finite minds that abstract it, but it also *pre*-exists in the *divine* intellect as the archetype according to which God creates acorns. Similarly, for Platonic *teleological* realism, the end or goal of an acorn exists entirely apart from it, in a divine mind which orders it to its end. For Aristotelian teleological realism, the end or goal of an acorn exists only intrinsic to the acorn itself. For Scholastic teleological realism, the end or goal of an acorn exists intrinsic to the acorn itself, but only because God created it according to the pre-existing essence in question, which includes having the generation of an oak as an end or goal. With respect to realism about both universals and teleology, then, the Platonic approach tends to emphasize transcendence to the exclusion of immanence, the Aristotelian approach tends to emphasize immanence to the exclusion of transcendence, and the Scholastic approach seeks to show that each side is partially correct in that the phenomena in question are immanent to the created order in one respect and transcend it in another.

But to understand more deeply the nature of Aquinas's middle ground position, it is best to proceed to an examination of the Fifth Way itself. The argument has two stages, the first of which, as the reader will recall, goes as follows:

> We see that things which lack intelligence, such as natural bodies, act for an end, and this is evident from their acting always, or nearly always, in the same way, so as to obtain the best result. Hence it is plain that not fortuitously, but designedly, do they achieve their end.

By "designedly" (*ex intentione*), Aquinas does not mean "because of a designer," *à la* Paley; the role of divine intelligence enters the argument only

---

44   I develop this analogy at greater length in Feser, "Teleology: A Shopper's Guide."

in its second stage. Rather, he means, as Aristotle would, "because of inherent teleology, rather than by chance." Christopher Martin translates *ex intentione* as "in virtue of some tendency," which is, I think, to be preferred both to the widely used Fathers of the English Dominican Province translation quoted above and to the common alternative translation "by intention."[45] "Designedly" and "by intention," while not incorrect, can be misleading given the way "design" and "intention" are typically used in contemporary philosophical discussion of these issues, which differs from the way they are used in Scholastic philosophy.[46]

What Aquinas is asserting here, then, is what we referred to earlier as the *principle of finality*, which states that every agent or efficient cause acts for an end. And the argument in this case is essentially the same as the argument given earlier for that principle. Unless we suppose that causes inherently or of their nature "point to" their characteristic effects as to an end, we have no way of making intelligible why it is that they "act always, or nearly always, in the same way." It might seem that regarding this regularity as "fortuitous" or attributable to chance would give us an alternative explanation. But for the Aristotelian, chance *presupposes* regularity and thus finality, and so provides no genuine alternative at all. Chance is nothing more than the accidental convergence of non-accidental lines of causation. To take a stock example from Boethius, suppose a farmer discovers treasure buried in the field he is plowing.[47] The discovery was in no way intended by either the farmer or the person who buried the treasure, nor is there any causal regularity in nature connecting plowing and the discovery of treasure. Still, the farmer did intend to plow, someone did intend to bury the treasure, and there are all sorts of natural causal regularities instantiated when the farmer plows the field and discovers the treasure. It would be

45   Christopher F. J. Martin, *Thomas Aquinas: God and Explanations* (Edinburgh: Edinburgh University Press, 1997), p. 179.
46   As Bernard Wuellner explains in his *Dictionary of Scholastic Philosophy* (Milwaukee: Bruce Publishing Company, 1956), in Scholastic metaphysics "intention" can mean "the direction or application of causal power to an effect; the influence of the primary cause on the instrument" (p. 63). (For the first "of," Wuellner's text actually reads "or," but this is evidently a typo.) Wuellner adds: "This may be the primary meaning of intention as it best shows the notion of directing or tending on the part of a being or power." Again, what is in view is the Aristotelian notion of *immanent* teleology, rather than the *extrinsic* teleology in terms of which Paley and his contemporary successors frame their "design argument."
47   Boethius, *Consolations of Philosophy*, Book V, Chapter 1. Cf. Aristotle, *Physics*, Book II, Part 5.

incoherent, then, to suggest that regularity can be accounted for by chance rather than finality, since to make sense of chance we need to appeal to finality and regularity.

But what of the objection raised by Ockham and Buridan to the effect that efficient causes are sufficient to account for regularity in unintelligent natural objects? Des Chene develops this sort of view as follows:

> The [Aristotelian] argument is, on its face, unconvincing. Everyone agrees that efficient causes necessitate their effects ("if the cause is given, so is the effect," writes Eustachius with his usual brevity ...). So people will not emerge from the sea ever if they do not always: one does not need ends to account for that regularity. Given that we have not seen any such occurrence, and that the sea remains constant in composition, there is no reason to expect that the weird event will occur. Likewise, if people have always given birth to people, and birds to birds, and if they remain constant in composition, then there is no reason to expect that people will bear birds or birds people. So if the regularity to be explained is 'people give birth only to people, and no other kind of thing does', then an appeal to the necessity of efficient causes seems to suffice.[48]

But this won't do. For we need to know what it *means* to say that efficient causes necessitate their effects, and we need an *explanation* of this necessitation. Now the necessitation either involves something intrinsic to the causes and effects, or it does not; and either possibility poses grave problems for the view that efficient causation suffices to account for regularity.

Consider first the possibility that necessitation involves something *extrinsic* to the causes and effects themselves. On this view, that an efficient cause A necessitates its effect B has nothing to do with A or B themselves, but with something else. But what is this something else? One option is to hold that *God* ensures that B follows upon A. But that just raises the question of *how* God does so. If we answer that He efficiently causes B merely by necessitating it, then we have simply pushed the problem back a stage rather than solved it. If we answer instead that He causes B by virtue of having it in view as an *end*, then we will have resorted to finality after all and given up the view that efficient causation alone suffices to account for regularity.

---

48   Des Chene, *Physiologia*, p. 178.

Of course, the appeal to God also has obvious drawbacks if one's motivation for challenging this first stage of the Fifth Way is atheistic.[49]

Rather than appeal to God, though, might we not say that it is a "law of nature" that B follows upon A? Yet as we noted earlier, the appeal to "laws of nature" *by itself* hardly suffices to explain anything, for it just raises the question of what "laws of nature" are and why they hold. Now if we say that a law of nature is simply a kind of regularity, then we are led into either a vicious circle or a vicious regress, since the regularity of the connection between A and B is what we're trying to explain in the first place. For to explain regularities in nature in terms of efficient causal necessitation, efficient causal necessitation in terms of laws of nature, and laws of nature in terms of regularities, would be to go around in a circle; while if, to avoid this circularity, we say that the regularity enshrined in a law of nature is of a *higher order* than the sort we started out trying to explain, then we will now need an account of this higher-order regularity, and will thereby merely have pushed the problem back a stage rather than solved it.

To explain "laws of nature," then, we cannot appeal to regularity. And if, to explain them, we appeal instead either to higher-order instances of efficient causal necessitation or higher-order laws of nature, we will once again merely have pushed the problem back a stage rather than solved it. While if we explain laws of nature by reference to God, we will merely have reintroduced at a higher level the very problems the appeal to laws of nature was supposed to help us avoid. The only remaining alternative would seem to be to appeal instead to the Aristotelian idea that "laws of nature" are really a shorthand for a description of how things act given their natures. But this would be to concede that there is, after all, something *intrinsic* to A and B that explains the efficient causal relations holding between them, and thus to abandon the suggestion that the necessitation we've been discussing is *extrinsic* to causes and effects.

So, treating causal necessitation as grounded in something *extrinsic* to causes and effects would seem a hopeless strategy for anyone who wants to defend the view of Ockham, Buridan, and Des Chene that efficient causation suffices to explain regularity. The only realistic option is to treat the necessitation as grounded in something *intrinsic* to the causes and effects.

---

49   But the proposal under consideration has drawbacks for the theist as well. For to hold that A's necessitation of B is entirely attributable to God and has nothing to do with A itself entails occasionalism, at least if we suppose that whatever necessitates an effect is also its sole efficient cause. For reasons we will consider later, occasionalism is philosophically and theologically problematic.

In particular, since an effect B doesn't even exist until generated by its efficient cause A, the necessitation will have to be grounded in something *intrinsic to A*. But what can this intrinsic feature be if it is not the very inclination to an end that Aquinas affirms and that the view in question is trying to avoid? What can it possibly be for A to be such that it *necessitates* the generation of B, other than that there is something in A that *inherently "points" to* the generation of *B specifically*, even before it actually generates B? It seems the only possible alternative intrinsic explanatory feature would be some further instance of efficient causal necessitation internal to A. But this would just raise the same questions all over again—and it would, yet again, thus lead the purported explanation of regularity in terms of efficient causes alone into either vicious regress or vicious circularity.[50]

There seems, then, to be no way to avoid Aquinas's conclusion that to make efficient causal regularities intelligible we need to attribute finality to efficient causes. Every attempt to avoid doing so merely raises further puzzles which cannot be solved except by admitting finality. But it might seem that the defender of the view that efficient causes alone suffice to account for regularity has one more arrow in his quiver. For isn't Aquinas's position open to the same sorts of objection as his opponent's view is? In particular, if Aquinas holds that efficient causal regularities need to be accounted for by reference to final causes, can it not be said with equal plausibility that final causes in turn need to be accounted for, and that accounting for them will also lead to vicious regress or vicious circularity? Aren't the two positions—Aquinas's on the one hand, and that of Ockham, Buridan, Des Chene, and modern philosophers in general on the other hand—therefore at least at a stalemate?

In fact such a comparison would be spurious. The two views would be on a par only if each made use of its favored notion of causation *to the exclusion* of the other. And Aquinas is doing no such thing. His critic holds that efficient causes *suffice* to explain the regularity that exists in the world, so that no appeal to finality is necessary; indeed, naturalist philosophers typically hold that final causes are ultimately not needed to explain *any* aspect of the natural world.[51] But Aquinas does not hold that final causality

---

50 Cf. Garrigou-Lagrange, *God: His Existence and His Nature*, Volume I, pp. 356–58.

51 Of course, many such philosophers regard teleological explanations as legitimate in domains like biology and psychology, but they also typically maintain that such explanations are either to be interpreted in instrumentalist rather than realist terms, or that they can be reduced to explanations that make reference only to efficient causes. See Feser, "Teleology: A Shopper's Guide."

suffices to explain either regularity or natural phenomena in general. He merely holds that it is a *necessary part* of a complete explanation. As an Aristotelian, he is committed to the explanatory indispensability of *all* of the traditional four causes—material, formal, efficient, and final—each of which has its place:

> Matter, indeed, is prior to form in generation and time, inasmuch as that to which something is added is prior to that which is added. But form is prior to matter in substance and in fully constituted being, because matter has complete existence only through form. Similarly, the efficient cause is prior to the end in generation and time, since the motion to the end comes about by the efficient cause; but the end is prior to the efficient cause as such in substance and completeness, since the action of the efficient cause is completed only through the end. Therefore, the material and the efficient causes are prior by way of generation, whereas form and end are prior by way of perfection.[52]

There is no parity between the view of Aquinas and that of his critic, then. The critic has tried to show that efficient causes suffice to explain regularity, and has failed. Aquinas has not tried to show that final causes suffice to explain it, only that efficient causes do not and that reference to finality is needed as well. In failing to make his own case, the critic has only lent plausibility to Aquinas's. Moreover, far from denying that the finality inherent in natural phenomena itself requires an explanation, Aquinas's whole point in presenting (the second stage of) the Fifth Way is to show that it does require one—though for reasons we will see, he does not think such an explanation leads either to a vicious regress or a vicious circle.

Before turning to the second stage, though, a further issue needs to be addressed. The attentive reader will have noticed that in the Fifth Way Aquinas speaks of natural bodies acting for an end insofar as they act "so as to obtain the *best result.*" In the passage just quoted he speaks of them as prior "by way of *perfection.*" What he has in mind seems in part related to the qualified way in which he describes the behavior of natural bodies, insofar as he says that we find them "acting always, or *nearly* always, in the

---

52 *De principiis naturae* IV.25, as translated in "The Principles of Nature," in Thomas Aquinas, *Selected Writings of St. Thomas Aquinas*, trans. Robert P. Goodwin (Upper Saddle River, NJ: Prentice Hall, 1965), at pp. 20–21.

same way." An acorn, for example, grows into an oak if it grows into anything at all, but the oak might be imperfect in various ways if the acorn has been damaged or the growth patterns interfered with. The phosphorus in a match will generate flame and heat if it hasn't lost its potency, but it might do so only weakly or after several strikes if the match has been damaged or aged. Insofar as a cause A "aims" or "points" to the generation of a certain effect B, then, it is the "perfect," "best," or complete realization of that effect to which it points, even when it is somehow impeded from doing so and as a result generates only an imperfect effect.

That Aquinas also takes the notion of finality to be connected to the notion of the good in a broader way is evident from his discussion of providence in *De veritate*, in the course of which he presents an argument that parallels the Fifth Way. In defense of the reality of final causes, one of the considerations he there puts forward is the following:

> Material and efficient causes, as such, cause only the existence of their effects. They are not sufficient to produce goodness in them so that they be aptly disposed in themselves, so that they could continue to exist, and toward others so that they could help them. Heat, for example, of its very nature and of itself can break down other things, but this breaking down is good and helpful only if it happens up to a certain point and in a certain way. Consequently, if we do not admit that there exist in nature causes other than heat and similar agents, we cannot give any reason why things happen in a good and orderly way.[53]

The idea here, then, is that there must be an end toward which things in the natural world work together if we are to explain how they balance each other out in the way they do—for example, to explain how heat, which of its nature tends to break down other things, does so "only to a certain point and in a certain way" rather than completely destroying the rest of the world.

Naturally Aquinas would also find teleology present in biological phenomena. Indeed, it is present in a particularly vivid way. To use some traditional Scholastic jargon, Aristotelians take the key difference between living and non-living things to lie in the distinction between *immanent* and *transe-*

---

53   *De veritate* V.2, in St. Thomas Aquinas, *Truth*, Volume I, trans. Robert W. Mulligan, S.J. (Indianapolis: Hackett, 1994), at pp. 209–10. Cf. *Summa contra gentiles* I.13.35.

unt (or "transient") causation.[54] Immanent causation begins and remains within the cause (though it may also have some external effects), and it typically in some way involves the fulfillment or perfection of the cause. Transeunt causation, by contrast, is directed entirely outwardly, from the cause to an external effect. An animal's digestion of a meal would be an example of immanent causation, since the process begins and remains within the animal and serves to fulfill or perfect it insofar as it enables it to stay alive and to grow. One rock knocking another one off the side of a cliff would be an example of transeunt causation. Living things can serve as transeunt causes, but what is characteristic of them is that they are also capable of immanent causation in a way that non-living things are not. Now since immanent causation, like the transeunt causation that pervades the inorganic realm, concerns causes which "point" to certain characteristic effects as to an end, living things present us with another instance of finality. Since the end in this case is the perfection or flourishing of the organism, we also have an instance in which the link between finality and the *good* is particularly clear. Immanent (as contrasted with transeunt) causation is thus a special and more complex case of the teleology Aquinas regards as immanent to (as opposed to extrinsic to) the natural order in general. (Note that "immanent" has two distinct, though related, senses here.)

It is important to emphasize, though, that the Fifth Way ultimately does not stand or fall with the defensibility either of the traditional Aristotelian view that organic phenomena are irreducible to inorganic phenomena, or the view that natural causes work together toward some larger, cosmic end. Even if one rejected both of these views, the basic Aristotelian claim that even the simplest instances of efficient causality are unintelligible without final causality would remain intact. Indeed, even if it could be shown that *all* natural phenomena without remainder were reducible to those described by physics, the basic Aristotelian claim would remain intact, since the most fundamental physical phenomena are still governed by efficient causality, and thus (given the arguments stated above) by final causality.[55] And that

---

54 See Feser, *Aquinas*, chapter 4 for an overview of the Aristotelian-Thomistic conception of the difference between living and non-living things, and Oderberg, *Real Essentialism*, chapter 8 for a recent defense.

55 That is not to say that it is *plausible* to suggest that all natural phenomena can be reduced to those described by physics. Reductionist claims in social science, psychology, and even biology are notoriously controversial even among philosophers and scientists with no theological ax to grind. Indeed, some have argued that even *chemistry* is irreducible to physics. (For an overview of the relevant literature on

suffices for the purposes of the Fifth Way. To prove the existence of a divine ordering intelligence, we need in Aquinas's view establish only that *some teleology or other* is immanent to the natural order.[56] Controversies about this or that purported *instance* of natural teleology can be bracketed off for purposes of evaluating the argument.

VI. Aquinas's middle position: Second stage

Let us at last turn, then, to Aquinas's reason for holding that even immanent teleology requires a divine ordering intelligence. The second stage of the Fifth Way goes as follows:

> Now whatever lacks intelligence cannot move towards an end, unless it be directed by some being endowed with knowledge and intelligence; as the arrow is shot to its mark by the archer. Therefore some intelligent being exists by whom all natural things are directed to their end; and this being we call God.

Now, the Fathers of the English Dominican Province translation is a bit misleading here as well. The Fifth Way is not concerned to explain how things "move" towards an end in the sense of motion or change that involves the actualization of a potential; explaining that is, of course, the aim of the First Way.[57] For "move" (*tendunt*), other translations have "tend," and that is a preferable rendering. What Aquinas is saying here, then, is that things cannot tend or incline toward a certain end unless some intelligence directs them to it. But *why* not, if the inclination is immanent in the way Aristotelians say it is?

An answer is suggested by the parallel argument in *De veritate*, where Aquinas says that an unintelligent thing tends directly toward an end only

---

that subject, see J. van Brakel, *Philosophy of Chemistry* (Leuven: Leuven University Press, 2000), chapter 5.) See Feser, "Teleology: A Shopper's Guide," for discussion of the different levels of nature at which irreducible teleology might be said to exist.

56 As G. H. Joyce writes: "It is possible to establish that, wherever there is efficient causality, there must also be final causality … If this principle be assured, then an argument from finality may be derived from any substance which is subject to change." (*Principles of Natural Theology*, Second edition (London: Longmans, Green, and Co., 1924), p. 116.) Cf. Garrigou-Lagrange, *God: His Existence and His Nature*, Volume I, p. 364.

57 For discussion of the differences and similarities between the Five Ways, see chapter 3 of my *Aquinas*, and my article "Existential Inertia and the Five Ways," *American Catholic Philosophical Quarterly*, Vol. 85, No. 2 (2011).

where an intellect "has *established* an end for it, and directs it to that end" in a manner comparable to the "foresight" by which a man rules his family or a ruler governs a city or kingdom.[58] Now *part* of what Aquinas has in mind here is, no doubt, the idea that the disparate ends we find in nature need in some way to be harmonized, so that (to return to an earlier example) heat doesn't destroy everything else in the world, and so forth. And (so the argument presumably goes) only intelligent direction of the sort comparable to that of a ruler over his subjects can effect such harmonization.[59] But it seems that that can't be *all* that he has in mind. For it is evidently not merely the *harmony* of diverse ends in nature that Aquinas seeks to explain in the Fifth Way, but the very *existence* of such ends, harmonized or not. He implies that even a *single* unintelligent natural object—like the arrow of his illustration—could not tend toward an end unless directed by an intellect. That is to say, it could not do so even if there were no other, discordant ends with which it had to be reconciled. So, again, why not?

"Foresight" and "established" provide the clues, and foreshadow two lines of argument one finds developed by later Thomists. First, the end toward which a thing naturally points can be efficacious only if it exists beforehand in an intellect, as the plan for a house exists in the mind of a builder before it is realized in the actual house. Second, intelligence is needed to direct a cause to the effect it points to for the same reason that it is needed to establish the means most appropriate for realizing some end.[60] Let's examine these arguments in turn.

A common objection to the very idea of final causality is that it seems to entail that a thing can produce an effect even before that thing exists. Hence to say that an oak tree is the final cause of an acorn seems to entail that the oak tree—which doesn't exist yet—in some sense causes the acorn to pass through every stage it must reach on the way to becoming the oak, since the oak is the "goal" or natural end of the acorn. But how can a nonexistent oak cause anything?

To see how, consider those cases where goal-directedness is associated with intelligence, as it is in us. A builder builds a house, and he is able to

---

58 *De veritate* V.2, Mulligan translation at p. 210. Emphasis added.
59 The brief parallel argument in *Summa contra gentiles* I.13.35 would seem to support this interpretation.
60 Such arguments are presented in Joyce, *Principles of Natural Theology*, pp. 117–18; Garrigou-Lagrange, *God: His Existence and His Nature*, Volume I, pp. 367–68; and Maurice Holloway, *An Introduction to Natural Theology* (New York: Appleton-Century-Crofts, 1959), pp. 138–41.

do so because the effect, the house, "exists" as an idea in his intellect before it exists in reality. Or rather, the *form* of the house exists in the builder's intellect, and *that very same form* comes to exist in the matter that makes up the house. As Scholastic philosophers would put it, there is in this way a "formal identity" between the builder's intellect and the house. In that way the house can serve as the *final* cause of the actions of the builder even as those actions are the *efficient* cause of the house. For strictly speaking, what the builder brings about is a circumstance in which the form of the house exists in a certain parcel of matter. And that form *already exists* in his intellect, and for that reason can be efficacious. There is no mystery here, then, of how a cause which doesn't yet exist can be efficacious, because when we carefully analyze the situation we see that everything which plays a role in bringing about the effect—the materials, the builder and his intellect, and the form as it is grasped by his intellect—*does* already exist before the effect does. But notice that this is only the case precisely because the effect—the form of the house—does already exist *in an intellect*, even if not yet in the material that will make up the house. Nor is there anywhere else for it to exist. For by hypothesis, it doesn't yet exist in the material world; and (at least for an Aristotelian like Aquinas) neither does it exist in a Platonic "third realm" apart from the material world and apart from any mind. That exhausts the alternatives. Hence, not only is it the case that the house *does* in fact serve as a final cause by virtue of its form existing in the builder's intellect. That is the only way it *could* have done so, at least if—as this argument concedes to the critic of final causality—a cause must in some way exist if it is to be efficacious.

Turn now to the vast system of causes that constitutes the physical universe. Each of them is directed towards its characteristic effect or effects as to an end, for the reasons given in the previous section. Yet almost none of them is associated with any consciousness or intellect at all. Even animals and human beings, which are conscious, are comprised in whole or in part of unconscious and unintelligent material components which themselves manifest immanent finality. And neither we nor any other intelligent agents in the natural order are directing those components to their respective ends. For instance, your blood has a tendency to clot, but you are not directing it to do so, and neither is any other human being—it just happens. Even if we supposed, fancifully, that extraterrestrials or beings from another dimension were doing the directing in these cases, these agents would themselves be made up of unintelligent and unconscious material components each with their own tendencies toward certain ends. Now, given what has just been said, it is impossible for anything to be directed towards an end unless that end exists formally in an intellect which directs the thing in question toward it. It follows that the system of ends manifest in the universe of unintelligent material things can only exist at all if there is an intellect *outside* that universe which directs these things towards their ends. Moreover, this intellect must exist *here and now*, and not merely at some beginning point in the past, because causes are *here and now*, and at any point at which they exist at all, directed toward certain ends.

That is one argument, then, for the claim that a tendency toward an end presupposes a directing intelligence. A second argument, alluded to above, appeals to the proportion of means to ends. Aquinas writes:

> [T]hings can be ordered only by knowing their relation and pro-
> portion to one another, and to something higher, which is their
> end; for the order of certain things to one another is for the sake
> of their order to an end. But only a being endowed with intellect
> is capable of knowing the mutual relations and proportions of
> things; and to judge of certain things by the highest cause is the
> prerogative of wisdom. All ordering, therefore, is necessarily ef-
> fected by means of the wisdom of a being endowed with intel-
> ligence.[61]

Now one obvious application of this line of argument would be to explain the harmonization of the discordant ends found in nature—consider once again Aquinas's example of how, though heat tends to destroy, it does not in fact do so always and everywhere. The idea would be that for a stable system of causes to exist, something must ensure that their divergent outcomes are balanced against one another. This can only be something capable of grasp-ing their respective natures in the abstract and determining how they might be related in such a way that harmony is possible. And from an Aristotelian point of view, to be capable of grasping such abstract natures and relations *just is* to have an intellect.

As I have emphasized, though, the Fifth Way is intended to explain *all* natural teleology as such in terms of a divine intellect, not merely the way in which the ends of diverse natural objects might be said to serve an

---

61 *Summa contra gentiles* II.24.4, in Saint Thomas Aquinas, *Summa Contra Gentiles, Book Two: Creation*, trans. James F. Anderson (Notre Dame: University of Notre Dame Press, 1975), at p. 72.

overarching cosmic end; for the finality of causes considered individually would still exist even if it turned out that there is no such common, overarching end. The present argument, then, is also to be understood to apply even to the relationship between a single cause considered in isolation and its characteristic effect or effects. The idea would be that fire, for example, can "point" to heat as its typical effect only if an intellect fits the former to the latter as appropriate means to the latter. For whatever relates them in this law-like way must be capable of grasping their natures and relations in the abstract, and something capable of such abstraction just is something with intellect.

It might be objected, though, that an Aristotelian conception of natural objects would seem to make this sort of explanation otiose. For isn't it just in the *nature* of fire, given its substantial form, that it generates heat? And if so, then what need is there to appeal to a divine intellect in order to account for why fire is related to heat as a means is to an end? The answer is that Aquinas evidently does not take these to be competing explanations in the first place. The act of ordering a natural cause to its typical effect *just is* the imparting to it of a certain nature or substantial form. For "*upon the form* follows an inclination to the end, or to an action, or something of the sort; for everything, in so far as it is in act, acts and tends towards that which is in accordance *with its form.*"[62] Hence, as John Wippel says, to impart to things their forms is for Aquinas thereby to impart to them "a permanent inclination which is part of their very being."[63]

This suggests an answer to the question of whether the Fifth Way leads necessarily to a *divine* intelligence, as opposed to some lesser ordering intelligence (for example, an angelic intelligence). It might appear (and has appeared to many readers) that it does not. Yet from a Thomistic point of view, the ultimate cause of a thing's existing with the particular nature it has is what conjoins its essence to an act of existence. And this (as Aquinas argues in *De ente et essentia*) can only be something whose essence and existence are identical, and thus something divine. Hence, if that which directs a natural thing to its end is also what gives it its very nature, this would lead us, ultimately, to a divine cause of things having the ends they do.

Now this might seem to make the Fifth Way dependent on a separate, cosmological argument if it is to get all the way to God. But in fact there is

---

62   *Summa theologiae* I.5.5, emphasis added.
63   John F. Wippel, *The Metaphysical Thought of Thomas Aquinas* (Washington, D.C.: Catholic University of America Press, 2000), p. 484.

a more direct approach, grounded in considerations about finality of the sort that make the Fifth Way distinctive. As Reginald Garrigou-Lagrange writes:

> [T]he intelligence claimed by this fifth proof must be *pure act*. If it were not so, we should have to say that its essence differed from its existence, that its intelligence was not its intellection, and that in it intellection and the intelligible were not identical. Now, essence cannot be *directed* to existence, nor intelligence to the intelligible object, except by a higher intelligence which is identical with its very being, always in the act of knowing itself.[64]

Garrigou-Lagrange's point is that any ordering intelligence that was other than pure act—the philosophical core of the Aristotelian-Thomistic conception of God—would be composite rather than simple and thus in various respects a mixture of act and potency. In particular, it would have an essence that is merely potential until actualized by an act of existence; it would be distinct from its particular acts of intellection, which acts would therefore also need to be actualized; and it would be distinct from the intelligible objects of its intellection. Now such an intellect would therefore have to be *directed to* its objects; and since any potency is just a potency *for* some actuality, the potencies of this intellect would also have to be *directed towards* their actualization. But that means that a non-divine intelligence would merely be yet another instance of the sort of thing the Fifth Way is intended to explain, namely something exhibiting finality or directedness to an end. Supposing the intelligence which orders natural things to their ends is other than divine thus merely opens the way to a vicious explanatory regress, a regress that can in principle be terminated only by a purely actual, and thus divine, intelligence.

Note that the series of ordering intelligences posited here for the sake of argument would constitute a series of causes ordered *per se* rather than *per accidens*, and would thus necessarily terminate in a first member. For as we noted above, the logic of the argument implies that a thing could not be directed towards an end *even for an instant* apart from an ordering intelligence, and the same would be true of that ordering intelligence itself if it

---

64 Garrigou-Lagrange, *God: His Existence and His Nature*, Volume I, p. 370. Cf. Holloway, *An Introduction to Natural Theology*, pp. 141–42.

was other than purely actual, and of any other non-purely-actual intelligence we suppose might be directing *it*. What we are describing here, then, is not a series of ordering causes extending "backward" in time, but rather extending "upward," simultaneously, at any particular moment at which anything exhibits finality at all. And insofar as the "lower" intelligences direct natural objects to their ends only insofar as they are themselves being so directed by something higher still, we would have a series of *instrumental* causes which require for their efficacy an uncaused cause, something which can direct without being directed. In short, the Fifth Way reaches the same conclusion as Aquinas's other arguments for God's existence, but by beginning with final causes rather than with change, efficient causality, contingency, or degrees of perfection. And like those other arguments, it opens the way to further arguments to the effect that what is pure act must possess the other divine attributes.[65]

To be sure, this goes beyond anything Aquinas himself says explicitly about the Fifth Way. But it is a natural outworking of what he does say, and it is hardly surprising that later Thomists have read the Fifth Way as providing, at least by implication, a proof of a truly divine intelligence rather than a mere demiurge or committee of intelligences. There might still be lingering doubts, however, about whether Aquinas is able to depart from Aristotle in the way he does without falling into Paley's position. For how could teleology be both *immanent to* the natural order and yet *derived from* God?

Some everyday examples may help. A white wall on which ordinary sunlight is shining is white and not at all red. A white wall on which red light is shining is in one sense red, but it derives its redness entirely from the light. A red wall on which ordinary sunlight is shining is in some sense red inherently, but the redness is nevertheless manifest only insofar as the light is shining on it. Now compare God's imparting of teleology to nature to the light's shining on a wall. Natural teleology as Paley understands it can be compared to the redness a white wall has only when the red light is shining on it. But natural teleology as Aquinas understands it is like the redness a red wall has when ordinary sunlight is shining on it. The redness is really there in the wall, yet it cannot in any way manifest itself apart from the light. (I ignore the scientific details as irrelevant to the purpose of the analogy, and I do not claim that the analogy is perfect, only suggestive.)

---

65 See Feser, *Aquinas*, pp. 69–72 and 88–89 for discussion of the distinction between *per se* and *per accidens* series of causes, and pp. 120–30 for discussion of Aquinas's derivation of the various divine attributes.

Or consider signs, linguistic and otherwise. The word "triangle" and the symbol Δ can both be used to represent triangles in general. Now neither one can do so on its own, for each by itself is a mere set of physical marks with no symbolic content. A mind must *impart* such content to them. Moreover, the connection between the word "triangle" and triangles is entirely arbitrary, an accident of the history of the English language. And even Δ hardly resembles all triangles; for example, there are obvious respects in which it does not resemble right triangles, or green ones, or very large ones. All the same, there is obviously something inherent to Δ which makes it a more natural symbol for triangles in general than the word "triangle" is. Though both symbols ultimately depend for their symbolic content on a mind which imparts that content to them, Δ nevertheless has an *inherent* aptness for representing triangles in general that "triangle" does not. Now compare God's imparting of teleology on natural objects to a mind's imparting symbolic content on signs. For Paley, natural objects are like the word "triangle," whereas for Aquinas they are like Δ. As with the word, the symbol Δ refers to triangles in general only insofar as that meaning is imparted to it, but there is still a natural connection between Δ and triangles in general that does not exist between "triangle" and triangles in general. (Again, I do not say that the analogy is perfect, only suggestive.)

A final analogy is taken from linguistic representation specifically. If we consider the words and sentences we speak and write, it is obvious that they get their meaning from the community of language users that produces them, and ultimately from the ideas expressed by those language users in using them. Apart from these users, these linguistic items would be nothing more than meaningless noises or splotches of ink. Still, once produced, they take on a kind of life of their own. Words and sentences printed in books or recorded on tape retain their meaning even when no one is thinking about them; indeed, even if the books or tapes sit in a dusty corner of a library or archive somewhere, ignored for decades and completely forgotten, they still retain their meaning. Moreover, language has a structure that most language users are unaware of, but which can be studied by linguists. Still, if the community of language users were to disappear entirely—every single one of them killed in a worldwide plague, say—then the recorded words that were left behind *would* in that case revert to meaningless sounds or marks. While the community of language users exists, its general background presence is all that is required for meaning to persist in the physical sounds and markings, even if some of those sounds and markings are not the subject of anyone's attention at a particular moment. But if the community goes away altogether, the meaning goes with it.

By analogy (and here too I do not claim that the analogy is exact) we might think of the relationship of the divine intelligence of the Fifth Way to the system of final causes in the world as somewhat like the relationship of language users to language. God directs things to their ends, but the system thereby created has a kind of independence insofar as it can be studied without reference to God Himself, just as linguists can study the structure of language without paying attention to the intentions of this or that language user. The ends are in a sense just "there" in unintelligent causes like the meaning is just "there" in words once they have been written. At the same time, if God were to cease directing things toward their ends, final causes would immediately disappear, just as the meaning of words would disappear if all language users disappeared. In this way, immanent teleology plays a role similar to secondary causes in the order of efficient causes, as I suggested above. Just as secondary causes have real causal power of their own, even if it derives ultimately from God as first cause, so too natural objects have immanent teleology, even if it derives ultimately from God as ordering intelligence.

This last point puts us in a position to understand why Thomists have often been so keen to distance Aquinas's argument from Paley's. For the arguments are not merely different. Given their divergent metaphysical assumptions, they are arguably *fundamentally incompatible*, theologically as well as philosophically.

VII. Thomism versus the "design argument"

Before seeing how, let us note some of the indisputable differences between Aquinas's position and Paley's. As we have emphasized, Paley's argument presupposes that teleology is *extrinsic*; Aquinas follows Aristotle in holding that it is *immanent to* the natural order. Paley therefore focuses on *complex* phenomena, especially biological phenomena, as uniquely indicative of teleology; Aquinas takes *all* natural phenomena, however simple or complex and whether organic or inorganic, to manifest teleology. Paley is presenting a *cumulative and probabilistic* "argument to the best explanation"; Aquinas is putting forward a *metaphysical demonstration*.

Now neither Paley nor Aquinas is refuted by Darwin's account of evolution by natural selection. But Paley is at least seriously threatened by it, while the Fifth Way is not threatened by it at all. For Darwin presents an alternative, non-teleological explanation of the complex biological phenomena on which Paley builds his case. To salvage their design argument, Paley's followers therefore have to argue either that there are some complex biological phenomena that Darwinism cannot plausibly account for, or that even if successful Darwinism only pushes the problem back a stage insofar as it presupposes yet deeper levels of complexity that are best explained by reference to a designer. The argument then turns to a consideration of various cosmological speculations and biological minutiae—the purported "irreducible complexity" of the bacterial flagellum, the "anthropic principle" and the apparent "fine-tuning" of the laws of nature, and so on. Critics of the "design argument" then accuse its defenders of peddling a "god of the gaps" hypothesis which is open to refutation by future scientific discoveries.

For Thomists, none of this wrangling over empirical details is necessary, and it tends to distract attention from the more fundamental and straightforward *metaphysical* issues. As we have seen, for Aquinas even the simplest patterns of efficient causation suffice to demonstrate the reality of immanent teleology, and will do so *whatever* physics, chemistry, and biology end up telling us. Hence while a Thomist may or may not object to this or that evolutionary account of this or that biological phenomenon, *for purposes of the Fifth Way* such issues are irrelevant.

Now we have also seen that the Fifth Way, at least as developed by later Thomists, does indeed plausibly get us to a *divine* intelligence. By contrast, Paley's argument is often acknowledged to get us at best to a designer who is extremely powerful and intelligent, but who for all we know may yet be finite and thus non-divine. But it is not just that Paley's designer *may* be something other than God as Aquinas understands Him. There is reason to think that Paley's designer *could not* be God as Aquinas understands Him. For Aquinas, when we predicate attributes of God, we necessarily do so *analogously* rather than *univocally*. But Paley is evidently predicating attributes to his designer and to us in a univocal way, which (for the Thomist at least) entails a radically deficient conception of God.

A simple example will illustrate the difference between the two kinds of predication. When I say that this is a good cheeseburger and that is good pizza, I am using "good" univocally. I am predicating the very same thing to both the cheeseburger and the pizza. And I will still be doing so if I say that the cheeseburger is *better* than the pizza. I will be saying that the pizza and the cheeseburger both have the very same attribute, but that the cheeseburger has it to a higher degree than the pizza. But when I say that this is a good cheeseburger and that Aquinas was a good man, I am *not* using "good" univocally and I am not predicating exactly the same thing both to the cheeseburger and to Aquinas. I am saying instead that there is something in Aquinas that is *analogous* to what we call "good" in the cheeseburger, though of course it is not precisely the same thing, since the moral qualities that lead us to attribute goodness to a human being are not the same as the gustatory and nutritive qualities that lead us to attribute goodness to food.

Similarly, when we speak of Aquinas's intelligence and my intelligence, we are using "intelligence" univocally. Hence to say that Aquinas was more intelligent than I am is to say that Aquinas had the same thing I have, but to a greater degree. But in Aquinas's view, when we speak of our intelligence and *God's* intelligence, we are *not* using "intelligence" univocally. We are not saying that God has the same thing we have, but to a higher degree. Rather, we are saying that there is in God something *analogous* to what we call "intelligence" in us. The reason is that God, as pure act, does not merely *participate* in being, goodness, intelligence, and the like, as we and other created things do. For Aquinas, God doesn't "have" being; he *is* being itself. He doesn't "have" goodness; He *is* goodness itself. He doesn't "have" intelligence; He *is* intelligence itself. And so forth. Moreover, He is, given the doctrine of divine simplicity, *identical to* His attributes. What we call God's being, God's goodness, God's intelligence, and so forth are really just the same thing—God Himself—considered from different points of view. It follows that God is radically unlike anything in the created order. He is not "a being" alongside others, not even a very grand and remote being among other beings, but rather *ipsum esse subsistens*, that on which all mere beings depend for their being.

By contrast, Paley's procedure is to model his designer on human designers. At least by implication, his designer exercises the same faculty human designers do—he works out design problems, performs calculations, and so forth—but does so with massively greater facility. He is an *essentially anthropomorphic* designer. Understandably, then, Paley's argument is often characterized as an "argument from analogy," but it is crucial to emphasize that "analogy" as it is used in that expression does *not* mean what it does in Aquinas's doctrine of analogy. On the contrary, Paley's procedure implies the opposite of what Aquinas's doctrine of analogy does. For Paley presupposes that natural objects are *like* human artifacts in having only extrinsic teleology, while the Fifth Way insists that they are *not like* human artifacts because they have immanent teleology. The implication is that Paley's designer imparts teleology the way human designers do, by imposing on raw materials a function they have no inherent tendency to serve. But for Aquinas, creation does not involve anything comparable to the taking of preexisting materials and fashioning them into a kind of artifact. It does not involve imposing an accidental form on things already having their own substantial forms. (Hence the question of temporal order is irrelevant here; it does not change the point at all if we supposed that the designer somehow conjured the raw natural materials into existence while *simultaneously* imposing some function on them not already inherent in the materials.) Rather, God creates by conjoining an essence to an act of existence, where the finality of the thing created is inherent in the essence itself rather than "tacked on" in a separate creative act.[66]

Aquinas's argument is thus immune to the sorts of objections Hume pressed upon design arguments, to the effect that the designer would have to work through corporeal organs the way human designers do, and would manifest complexity which itself requires explanation. To be sure, Paley's defenders have developed replies to these objections, but they typically appeal to such considerations as the greater parsimony of postulating a disembodied designer. They do not, and cannot, deny that the designer at least *could in principle* be the sort Hume describes. But the Humean objections do not even get off the ground against Aquinas's divine intelligence, who, being pure act, is *necessarily* absolutely simple and incorporeal.

So, the anthropomorphism implicit in Paley's conception of God is one reason Thomists are bound to object to Paley's argument. But his implied conception of God's *relationship to the world* is another potential source of incompatibility. To see how, consider the three main approaches within traditional theism to understanding God's causal relationship to the world, as Alfred Freddoso has usefully classified them.[67] *Occasionalism* holds that God alone is the cause of everything that happens, so that there are no true secondary causes in nature. For example, on this view, one billiard ball which makes contact with another during a game of pool does not in any

---

66   Aquinas does sometimes find it useful to compare God to an artificer and natural objects to artifacts (*Summa Theologiae* I.27.1, I.44.3, I.65.2, and I–II.13.2; *Summa contra gentiles* III.100.6). But he does not put forward this analogy as a way of arguing for God's existence or explaining how God imparts teleology to natural objects. When he does address those issues—in the Fifth Way, and in the parallel arguments in *De veritate* and *Summa contra gentiles* cited above—his preferred analogies are to the archer who shoots an arrow and the ruler who governs a family, city, or kingdom. His focus is always on *directedness to an end*, not on complexity, skilled craftsmanship, clever engineering, or the like.

67   See Alfred J. Freddoso, "God's General Concurrence With Secondary Causes: Pitfalls and Prospects," *American Catholic Philosophical Quarterly* 67 (1994): 131–56.

way cause the other to move. Rather, God causes the second ball to move on the occasion when the first makes contact with it. *Mere conservationism* holds that while God maintains natural objects and their causal powers in existence at every moment, they alone are the immediate causes of their effects. On this view, the one billiard ball really does cause the other one to move, and God has nothing to do with it other than keeping the ball and its causal powers in being. He is not in any direct way the cause of the second ball's motion. Finally, *concurrentism* is a middle ground position which holds on the one hand (and contrary to occasionalism) that natural objects are true causes, but on the other hand (and contrary to mere conservationism) that God not only maintains natural objects and their causal powers in being, but also cooperates with them in immediately causing their effects. On this view, the one billiard ball really does cause the other ball to move, but only *together with* God, Who acts as a concurrent cause.

Concurrentism became the standard view within the Scholastic tradition, because the other views are philosophically and theologically problematic.[68] For example, occasionalism veers in the direction of pantheism, while mere conservationism veers in the direction of deism. We can understand how if we recall the Scholastic dictum that "a thing *operates* according as it *is*."[69] If, as occasionalism holds, only God alone ever operates or brings about effects, and natural objects operate not at all, then it is difficult to see how they *exist* at all, at least in any robust way. God alone would seem to be real; natural objects would be like mere fictional characters in the mind of a divine Author. By contrast, if, as mere conservationism holds, natural objects can at least operate or bring about effects apart from God's immediate causal action, then it seems that they could also *exist* apart from his immediate causal action. The world would in that case not depend for its continued existence on God's conserving action. (This is not to say flatly that *occasionalism entails pantheism* or that *mere conservationism entails deism*. The issues are complex, and careful analysis is required in order to determine precisely what these views do or do not entail, either by themselves or in conjunction with other assumptions. The

---

68 For discussion of occasionalism, see Freddoso's article "Medieval Aristotelianism and the Case against Secondary Causation in Nature," in Thomas V. Morris, ed., *Divine and Human Action: Essays in the Metaphysics of Theism* (Ithaca, NY: Cornell University Press, 1988). For discussion of mere conservationism, see his article "God's General Concurrence with Secondary Causes: Why Conservation is Not Enough," *Philosophical Perspectives* 5 (1991): 553–85.

69 *Summa theologiae* I.75.2. Emphasis added.

point is just to indicate some of the reasons they have been considered at least problematic.)

Now I have emphasized that Aquinas is committed to the reality of secondary causes. We have also seen that he regards efficient causality as intelligible only in light of final causality. The clear implication would seem to be that if natural objects are to be true causes, they must possess immanent finality. To deny them immanent finality—to hold that whatever finality they have exists only in the divine intellect and in no way in the natural objects themselves—would therefore seem to entail denying them genuine causal power, and to attribute all causal power to God alone. And that would be to embrace occasionalism. Insofar as Paley's position presupposes a rejection of immanent finality, then, it arguably threatens to collapse into occasionalism. Of course, Paley and other defenders of the design argument would no doubt find this charge surprising. Certainly they do not typically deny that natural objects are true efficient causes. But the point is that their position at least arguably *entails* such a denial, whether they realize it or not, given an Aristotelian-Thomistic understanding of causation. If digestion, oxidation, gravitation, and other natural causal processes are as extrinsic to natural phenomena as time-telling is extrinsic to the parts of a watch, then natural phenomena have no more power to carry out these activities than metal gears have the power to convey the time of day. After all, that a particular bit of physical activity means that *it is now 11:27* is entirely observer-relative, and does not follow from anything in the watch parts themselves. It is *we*, the designers and users of the watch, who cause the marks on its face to mean what they do. Similarly, if something counts as digestion, oxidation, gravitation, or the like also entirely extrinsically, only relative to God's activity as designer, then these things too are really *God's* activities rather than those of natural objects themselves.

To be sure, some of Paley's other commitments would seem to lead in the opposite direction. In particular, that he regards it as at best highly *probable* that complex natural phenomena were designed by God seems to entail that they could at least *in principle* exist and operate apart from Him. But this leads him out of the frying pan of occasionalism only to fall into the fire of deism—bypassing not only concurrentism, but even mere conservationism, altogether. And of course, Paley's position is indeed sometimes characterized as reflective of the eighteenth-century trend toward deism.

From a Thomistic point of view, then, Paley's position is bound to appear metaphysically unstable, ambiguous between unacceptable extremes vis-à-vis the question of God's causal relationship to the world. That, together with its tendency toward anthropomorphism, makes it doubly objectionable from a theological point of view.[70] It is no surprise, then, that Thomists have often distanced the Fifth Way from the design argument of Paley and other modern writers, sometimes in harsh terms. For example, Maurice Holloway insists that:

> We should be careful not to confuse the fifth way of St. Thomas Aquinas, which argues from the existence of order in the universe to the existence of an infinite intelligence, with Paley's argument from design. In the latter's argument the universe is seen as a complicated and intricate machine ... [and he] reasons, by way of analogy, to the existence of a divine watchmaker, or supreme architect of the universe. This argument from design, as given by Paley and unfortunately repeated in many books on Christian apologetics, does not prove the existence of God. An architect of the universe would have to be a very clever being, but he would not have to be God ... Many of the objections directed against what some writers believe is the fifth way of St. Thomas are really directed against the watchmaker of Paley. St. Thomas's proof is entirely different. It is grounded in the metaphysics of finality ...[71]

Similar views are expressed by John F. McCormick,[72] Cardinal Mercier,[73] Joseph Owens,[74] R. P. Phillips,[75] Henri Renard,[76] and John Wippel.[77]

---

70 This also explains why Thomists are often critical of "intelligent Design" theory, which inherits these tendencies. See Feser, "Teleology: A Shopper's Guide."

71 Holloway, *An Introduction to Natural Theology*, pp. 146–47.

72 John F. McCormick, S.J., *Scholastic Metaphysics, Part II: Natural Theology* (Chicago: Loyola University Press, 1943), p. 75.

73 Cardinal Mercier, "Natural Theology or Theodicy" in Cardinal Mercier, et al., *A Manual of Modern Scholastic Philosophy*, Volume II (St. Louis: B. Herder, 1933), pp. 53–54.

74 Joseph Owens, *An Elementary Christian Metaphysics* (Houston: Center for Thomistic Studies, 1985), p. 349 and "Aquinas and the Five Ways," in *St. Thomas Aquinas on the Existence of God: The Collected Papers of Joseph Owens*, edited by John R. Catan (Albany: State University of New York Press, 1980), pp. 136–37.

75 R. P. Phillips, *Modern Thomistic Philosophy*, Volume II (Westminster, Maryland: The Newman Press, 1950), p. 290.

76 Henri Renard, S.J., *The Philosophy of God* (Milwaukee: Bruce Publishing Company, 1951), p. 48.

77 Wippel, *The Metaphysical Thought of Thomas Aquinas*, p. 480.

Benedict Ashley objects to the "philosophical naiveté" of authors like Paley "in confusing extrinsic and intrinsic finality."[78] Etienne Gilson complains of the "anthropomorphic God" of "simple-minded metaphysicians [who] have unwillingly led agnostics to believe that the God of natural theology was the 'watchmaker' of Voltaire, or the 'carpenter' of cheap apologetics."[79] Herman Reith says that the trouble with the design argument is that "the examples used and the interpretation given them prevents the argument from rising to the metaphysical level... above the order of the physical universe," so that "it cannot conclude to anything more than the existence of some kind of intelligence and power" within that universe.[80] Ronald Knox characterizes Paley's design argument as "feeble," and does not regard it as even a "modification" of any of Aquinas's Five Ways.[81] Christopher F. J. Martin, in the course of defending the Fifth Way, dismisses Paley's design inference as "really a rather poor argument," and avers that "the Being whose existence is revealed to us by the argument from design is not God but the Great Architect of the Deists and Freemasons, an impostor disguised as God."[82]

Hence, if the design argument is in any case controversial at best within contemporary philosophy, the Thomist may decide that attempts to revive it are worse than a waste of time. But is the Fifth Way in any better shape? In particular, is it possible within the context of contemporary philosophy and science to revive the Aristotelian notion of immanent finality, on which Aquinas's argument rests?

VIII. Immanent teleology in contemporary philosophy

Not only is such a revival possible, it is actual. Recent decades have seen, within mainstream academic philosophy, a renewed interest in traditional Aristotelian metaphysical notions like substance, essence, causal power, act versus potency (these days referred to as the distinction between "categorical" and "dispositional" properties), and finality (these days referred to as

---

78 Benedict M. Ashley, *The Way toward Wisdom* (Notre Dame, IN: University of Notre Dame Press, 2006), p. 512, n. 11.

79 Etienne Gilson, *God and Philosophy* (New Haven: Yale University Press, 1941), p. 142.

80 Herman Reith, *The Metaphysics of St. Thomas Aquinas* (Milwaukee: Bruce Publishing Company, 1958), p. 198.

81 Ronald Knox, *Broadcast Minds* (New York: Sheed and Ward, 1933), pp. 52 and 222.

82 Martin, *Thomas Aquinas: God and Explanations*, pp. 180–82.

"physical intentionality" or the "directedness" of dispositions toward their manifestations). Moreover, this revival has taken place among secular meta-physicians and philosophers of science with no Thomistic or theological ax to grind.[83]

Among metaphysicians, the revival has largely been motivated by dis-satisfaction with the standard modern philosophical accounts of causation, which take Hume as their point of departure. For example, regularity theories of causation hold that for *A* to cause *B* is just for *A* and *B* to be instances of a general pattern according to which events like *A* are succeeded by events like *B*. Counterfactual theories of causation hold that the claim that *A* caused *B* is to be analyzed as the claim that had *A* not occurred, *B* would not have occurred either. Various technical objections have been raised against such accounts, but for those attracted to a neo-Aristotelian approach to causation, the fundamental difficulty is that these theories do not capture causation it-self, but only phenomena that presuppose causation. That is to say, to the ex-tent that the regularities in question hold and to the extent the counterfactuals in question are true, that is only because they are grounded in the causal pow-ers of things. They don't *explain* causation but *presuppose* causation.

The term "disposition" is sometimes preferred to "power," but some of the theorists in question go on to argue that we can only make sense of these powers or dispositions if we think of them as "pointing" to or being "di-rected" at their characteristic manifestations or effects. George Molnar char-acterizes this as "physical intentionality," since it is like the intentionality of mental states in that it involves directedness onto an object that may or may not exist, but unlike it in being unconscious.[84] John Heil calls it "natural intentionality" for similar reasons.[85] Whatever the label, in substance it is a return to something like Aquinas's view that efficient causality presupposes final causality, and the similarity has not gone unnoticed by historians of philosophy.[86]

---

83 For a brief history of this development and a useful overview of its central themes, see Stephen Mumford, "Causal Powers and Capacities," in Helen Beebee, Christo-pher Hitchcock, and Peter Menzies, eds., *The Oxford Handbook of Causation* (Ox-ford: Oxford University Press, 2009). Cf. Ellis, *The Philosophy of Nature: A Guide to the New Essentialism*.

84 George Molnar, *Powers: A Study in Metaphysics* (Oxford: Oxford University Press, 2003).

85 John Heil, *From an Ontological Point of View* (Oxford: Clarendon Press, 2003).

86 See, e.g., Ott, *Causation and Laws of Nature in Early Modern Philosophy,* pp. 29–30, which compares Scholastic views of causation to those of contemporary writers like Ellis and Molnar.

Within the philosophy of science, a movement toward neo-Aristotelianism has been motivated by dissatisfaction with the idea that scientific explanation is a matter of discovering "laws of nature." As Nancy Cartwright has emphasized, a serious problem with the Humean notion that science is in the business of establishing regularities on the basis of observation is that the sorts of regularities that the hard sciences tend to uncover are rarely observed, and in fact are in ordinary circumstances impossible to observe.[87] Beginning students of physics quickly become acquainted with idealizations like the notion of a frictionless surface, and with the fact that laws like Newton's law of gravitation strictly speaking describe the behavior of bodies only in circumstances where no interfering forces are acting on them (a circumstance which never actually holds). Moreover, physicists do not in fact embrace a regularity as a law of nature only after many trials, after the fashion of popular presentations of inductive reasoning. Instead, they draw their conclusions from a few highly specialized experiments conducted under artificial conditions. None of this is consistent with the idea that science is concerned with cataloguing observed regularities. But it is consistent, in Cartwright's view, with the Aristotelian picture of science as in the business of uncovering the hidden natures of things. Experimental practice indicates that what physicists are really looking for are the inherent powers a thing will manifest when interfering conditions are removed, and the fact that a few experiments, or even a single controlled experiment, are taken to establish the results in question indicates that these powers are taken to reflect a nature that is universal to things of that type.

The notion of "regularities" or "laws of nature" is therefore misleading, in Cartwright's view, given that science actually uncovers few laws or regularities outside highly artificial conditions. Strictly speaking, what science discovers are the universal natures and inherent powers of things, and talk of "laws of nature" can only be shorthand for this. As Cartwright concludes, "the empiricists of the scientific revolution wanted to oust Aristotle entirely from the new learning," but "they did no such thing."[88]

---

87   Nancy Cartwright, "Aristotelian Natures and the Modern Experimental Method," in John Earman, ed., *Inference, Explanation, and Other Frustrations: Essays in the Philosophy of Science* (University of California Press, 1992), and *Nature's Capacities and Their Measurement* (Oxford University Press, 1989).

88   Cartwright, "Aristotelian Natures and the Modern Experimental Method," p. 70. See Feser, "Teleology: A Shopper's Guide" for references to some Aristotelian tendencies in contemporary philosophy of biology.

While references to "substantial form," "final causes," and other traditional Scholastic concepts do not exactly pepper the contemporary academic philosophy journals, then, the *substance* of these ideas is getting a renewed hearing in at least some influential quarters. There has also been renewed interest in aspects of Aristotelian metaphysics other than those which have been our central concern here.[89] Then there are those contemporary analytic philosophers who have shown sympathy toward a specifically Aristotelian-*Thomistic* approach to metaphysics.[90] If renewed interest in Aquinas's Fifth Way waits upon renewed interest in its Aristotelian metaphysical underpinnings, then, it will not have to wait as long as many might suppose. Indeed, the latter revival is already underway.

89   See, e.g., Tuomas Tahko, ed., *Contemporary Aristotelian Metaphysics* (Cambridge: Cambridge University Press, 2012).

90   See, e.g., John J. Haldane, "A Thomist Metaphysics," in Richard Gale, ed., *The Blackwell Guide to Metaphysics* (Oxford: Blackwell, 2002); Gyula Klima, "Contemporary 'Essentialism' vs. Aristotelian Essentialism," in John Haldane, ed., *Mind, Metaphysics, and Value in the Thomistic and Analytical Traditions* (Notre Dame: University of Notre Dame Press, 2002); Oderberg, *Real Essentialism*; David Oderberg, "Teleology: Inorganic and Organic," in Ana Marta Gonzalez, ed., *Contemporary Perspectives on Natural Law* (Aldershot: Ashgate, 2008); and James Ross, *Thought and World: The Hidden Necessities* (Notre Dame: University of Notre Dame Press, 2008).

8
Why McGinn is a Pre-Theist

In his essay "Why I am an Atheist" (2012), Colin McGinn tells us that he has so moved beyond theism that his position might be described as not only atheist, but "post-theist." Yet it seems to me that he fundamentally misconceives what the debate between theism and atheism is all about, or at least what it has always been about, historically, in the thinking of the most sophisticated philosophical theists. McGinn evidently supposes that it is a question of whether there exist one or more instances of an unusual class of entities called "gods," understood as "supernatural beings" comparable to werewolves, ghosts, and Santa Claus. And he supposes that the way to answer this question is to consider whether there is "evidence" that any of these "gods" is the most "plausible explanation" of this or that observed phenomenon.

But this way of talking reflects a basic misunderstanding of what Aristotle, Plotinus, Anselm, Maimonides, Avicenna, Aquinas, et al. were all arguing about in the first place. By "God" such thinkers generally do not mean to refer merely to a member of some genus (not even a unique member), one being or cause alongside the others who differs from them only in the degree of his power or the range of his efficacy. Nor is he postulated as the most probable explanation of certain unusual phenomena that have yet to be explained scientifically. God, as understood in the tradition represented by such thinkers, is rather the necessary metaphysical precondition of there being any causality, any existent things, and indeed any genera at all. And the historically central arguments for his existence are not exercises in "god of the gaps"-style probabilistic empirical hypothesis formation, but attempts at strict metaphysical demonstration. A reasonable person might reject such alleged proofs, but to characterize the debate the way McGinn implicitly does is to make a basic category mistake.

In order to see how, it will be useful first to consider a couple of analogies. Suppose someone skeptical about Euclidean geometry said:

Euclideans already agree that the particular triangles we see drawn on chalkboards, in books, in the sand at the beach, and so forth, all have sides that are less than perfectly straight. But I maintain that Euclidean plane triangles *as such* have sides that are less than perfectly straight. Euclideans will object to this as dogmatic or excessively agnostic, but all I am doing is extending the doubt they share with me to their favored triangles too. I find their disbelief in the perfect straightness of the sides of the triangles we see drawn in books, etc. thoroughly sensible; I would merely urge them to push it one stage further, to triangularity itself. I favor total disbelief in the straightness of the sides of triangles; they favor selective disbelief. I have also reached the point that the issue of the straightness of the sides of Euclidean triangles as such no longer strikes me as an interesting issue. I'm not merely anti-Euclidean, but post-Euclidean.

Or suppose a critic of Platonism said:

Platonists already agree with me that the things we come across in everyday experience are all in various ways imperfect or less than fully good instances of their kinds. But I maintain that the Form of the Good is also imperfect or less than a fully good instance of goodness. Platonists will object to this as dogmatic or excessively agnostic, but all I am doing is extending the doubt they share with me to their own favored entity. I find their disbelief in the perfect goodness of the things of our experience thoroughly sensible; I would merely urge them to push it one stage further, to the Form of the Good itself. I favor total disbelief in the idea that things are ever perfect instances of their kinds; they favor selective disbelief. I have also reached the point that the issue of the goodness of the Form of the Good no longer strikes me as an interesting issue. I'm not merely anti-Platonist, but post-Platonist.

Now, obviously such remarks would hardly constitute devastating objections to Euclidean geometry and Platonic metaphysics. Rather, our imagined anti-Euclidean and anti-Platonist would be making serious category mistakes, and demonstrating that they have badly misunderstood the views they are dismissing.

In particular, the anti-Euclidean in question would be supposing that the concept of a triangle as defined in textbooks of Euclidean geometry is merely one triangle alongside all the others that one comes across in traffic signs, dinner bells, and the like, only invisible and better drawn. But of course, that is not what it is at all. What the textbooks describe is not *a* triangle, not even an especially well-drawn one, but rather *(Euclidean) triangularity itself*, and the triangles one comes across in everyday experience are defective precisely because they fail to conform to the standard it represents. Similarly, the anti-Platonist in question supposes that the Form of the Good is merely one more or less perfect or imperfect instance of some class or category alongside the other instances, albeit an especially impressive one. But of course, that is not at all what the Form of the Good is supposed to be. The Form of the Good doesn't *have* goodness in some more or less incomplete way; rather, it just *is* goodness, participation in which determines the degree of goodness had by things which *do* have goodness only in some more or less incomplete way.

Notice that the point has nothing to do with whether either Euclidean geometry or Platonism is true, or with whether there are good arguments for or against either view. Even if the material world actually conforms to some non-Euclidean geometry, on which the sides of triangles are curved rather than straight, the remarks of our hypothetical anti-Euclidean would still be confused. For the Euclidean would even in that case not be making the *kind* of mistake our hypothetical anti-Euclidean supposes. It would not be that there *are* Euclidean triangles but that they too have, after all, sides that are imperfectly straight; *that* claim doesn't even make sense. It would rather be that Euclidean triangles, which of course always have perfectly straight sides, just aren't instantiated after all. Similarly, even if objections to Platonism like the Third Man Argument are correct, the remarks of our hypothetical anti-Platonist would also still be confused. For it would not in that case be that there is a Form of the Good but that it too is, after all, less than perfectly good; that claim also makes no sense. It would rather be that there is no Form of the Good in the first place.

Our hypothetical anti-Euclidean and anti-Platonist, then, haven't earned the right to call themselves "post-Euclidean" or "post-Platonist," because neither has correctly understood what the debate over these views is really about. Accordingly, they would more appropriately be labeled "*pre*-Euclidean" and "*pre*-Platonist."

Now McGinn seems to me open to a similar criticism. In his essay, he compares belief in the God of philosophical theism to belief in the Greek gods, ghosts, werewolves, and Santa Claus, and writes:

> "People believe in the reality of their own God, but they are not similarly credulous when it comes to other people's gods; here their disbelief is patent and powerful ... I am with them on this point, but I extend it to their God too. My point is that they are as 'dogmatic' as I am in their atheism; we are just atheists about different gods. I am an atheist about all gods; typical theists are atheists about the majority of gods believed in over the centuries by human beings of one tribe or another. I find their disbelief thoroughly sensible; I would merely urge them to push it one stage further. I favor total atheism; they favor selective atheism ...
>
> I am beyond [belief in ghosts, Santa, etc.] as I assume you are too. And that is my actual position with respect to God: I am post-theist ...
>
> I have also reached the point (I reached it long ago) that the issue of God's existence no longer strikes me as an interesting issue ..."

The trouble with all this is that it evinces a misunderstanding of theism comparable to the misunderstandings of Euclidean geometry and Platonism evinced by our hypothetical anti-Euclidean and anti-Platonist. Or at least, it misunderstands *classical* theism, viz. the theism of Roman Catholic, Eastern Orthodox, and much Protestant theology, of the Aristotelian, Neo-Platonic, and Thomistic traditions in philosophical theology, and of thinkers like the ones I cited at the beginning of this essay.

For Aristotelians, to change is to go from potential to actual, and that any change occurs in the world at all is intelligible only if there is something which actualizes everything else without the need (or indeed even the possibility) of having to be actualized itself, precisely because it is already "Pure Actuality": an Unchangeable Changer or Unmovable Mover. For Neo-Platonists, whatever is composite or made up of parts of any kind requires explanation by reference to something which combines the parts. Accordingly, the *ultimate* explanation of things must be utterly simple or non-composite, and thus without the need (or, again, even the possibility) of something's bringing it into being: what Plotinus called The One. For Thomists, whatever is composed of an essence together with a distinct "act of existence" must ultimately derive its being from something whose essence *just is* existence:

that which is Subsistent Being Itself. In general, classical philosophical theology argues for the existence of a First Cause of the world which does not merely *happen* not to have a cause of its own, but which (unlike everything else that exists) *cannot even in principle* have required one. Anything less would fail to provide an *ultimate* explanation of the world.

Now, a critic might intelligibly question whether the arguments for such a divine Cause succeed. (I defend some of them at length in Feser 2009 and Feser 2011.) But to suggest that belief in the God of classical theism is relevantly comparable to believing in Zeus, werewolves, ghosts, or Santa Claus is to miss the whole point. Each of these beings would be an instance of a kind: "*a* being" among other beings, "*a* cause" among other causes, and thus (given general Thomistic metaphysics) something with an essence distinct from its act of existence. Each would be composite in some way: made up of parts, whether physical or metaphysical. Each would be a mixture of actuality and potentiality, and thus in various ways in need of being actualized. In short, each is, like the ordinary objects of our experience, the sort of thing that for the Aristotelian, Neo-Platonist, and Thomist would require an explanation outside itself.

The very point of classical theism, as developed within these traditions, is to argue for the necessity of there being something that is not at all like that. God is not an instance of a kind, not even a unique instance; he is not in any way composite; he not only has no need of being actualized or caused, but could not even intelligibly be described as having been actualized or caused. He thus differs from atoms and molecules, stones and trees, animals and human beings (and indeed, from werewolves, ghosts, and the gods of the various pantheons) in a manner analogous to the way Euclidean triangularity differs from individual concrete triangles, or the way the goodness of the Form of the Good differs from that of individual good things. He is not "*a* being" alongside other beings, not even an especially impressive one, but rather Being Itself or Pure Actuality, that from which all mere "beings" (including gods like Zeus, Mercury, and Quetzalcoatl, if they existed) derive the limited actuality or existence they possess. He is not "*a* cause" who is like other causes except for coming before the second, third, and fourth ones. Rather, he is "first" in the sense of being the metaphysical precondition of any possible causality: that which, as "Pure Actuality," can impart the power to actualize without having to receive it.

Nor is any of this a matter of formulating empirical explanatory hypotheses, weighing probabilities, or the like. The arguments for classical theism are grounded in metaphysical premises that are more fundamental than anything empirical science has to tell us, and indeed (as classical theists argue) in premises that any possible empirical science itself has to take for granted. Whatever the laws of physics, chemistry, biology, etc. turn out to be, they will (so the Aristotelian argues) describe a world in which potentials are actualized, which (it is also argued) cannot occur even for an instant without a Purely Actual cause of change. Such laws will also describe a world of things that are composite in various ways, and which in particular are composed of an essence together with an "act of existence," and thus things which must be maintained in being at every instant by that which is utterly One (as the Neo-Platonist would argue), or that in which essence and existence are identical (as the Thomist would argue).

The point has nothing to do with whether or not classical theism is true, or with whether the arguments for it are ultimately any good. Even if the atheist were correct, that would not be because it turned out that the God of classical theism really was the sort of thing that could intelligibly be said to require a cause of his own, or was composed of parts, or was merely one instance of a kind among others. That is to say, it wouldn't be because he turned out to be comparable to werewolves, Santa Claus, ghosts, and Zeus after all. *That* sort of suggestion doesn't even make sense, any more than the suggestions of our hypothetical anti-Euclidean or anti-Platonist make sense. It rests on a basic mistake—the assumption that since the God of classical theism along with Zeus, Thor, ghosts, werewolves, Santa Claus are all said to have unusual powers (with some of them even referred to as "gods") they must all be instances of the same kind. That is like saying that since individual good things and the Form of the Good are all called "good," they must be just different particular instances of the same kind; or that since the triangles one sees on chalkboards and in books and Euclidean tri-angularity as such are all triangular, they must just be different particular instances of the same kind.

McGinn's mistake is a very common one among contemporary atheists. Nor is it entirely his fault. Ever since William Paley presented his feeble "design argument," with its crudely anthropomorphic description of God as a kind of cosmic tinkerer, pop apologetics and pop atheism alike have tended to characterize God as if he were more or less like us, only smarter, stronger, and invisible. By the late twentieth century the tendency had even crept into academic philosophy of religion, leading to the partial displacement of the classical theistic conception of God by what Brian Davies (2004) has called a "theistic personalist" conception. This anthropomorphic conception of God is often read back into the arguments of older writers like Aquinas and the others mentioned above (who would have had no truck with it), severely distorting contemporary readers' understanding of those arguments.

Until one sees that it is a distortion, though, one has not really understood classical theism and the arguments for it, much less refuted them. One has not earned the right to be a "post-theist." One is better described as a *pre*-theist.

References

Davies, Brian. (2004). *An Introduction to the Philosophy of Religion,* Third edition. Oxford: Oxford University Press.

Feser, Edward. (2009). *Aquinas*. Oxford: Oneworld Publications.

Feser, Edward. (2011). "Existential Inertia and the Five Ways." *American Catholic Philosophical Quarterly*, vol. 85, no. 2.

McGinn, Colin. 2012. "Why I Am an Atheist" *Theoretical and Applied Ethics*, vol. 1, no. 4.

9
The Road from Atheism

As most of my readers probably know, I was an atheist for about a decade—
roughly the 1990s, give or take. Occasionally I am asked how I came to reject atheism. I briefly addressed this in *The Last Superstition*. A longer
answer, which I offer here, requires an account of the atheism I came to reject.

I was brought up Catholic, but lost whatever I had of the Faith by the
time I was about 13 or 14. Hearing, from a non-Catholic relative, some of
the stock anti-Catholic arguments for the first time — "That isn't in the
Bible!", "This came from paganism!", "Here's what they did to people in
the Middle Ages!", etc.—I was mesmerized, and convinced, seemingly for
good. *Sola scriptura*-based arguments are extremely impressive, until you
come to realize that their basic premise—*sola scriptura* itself—has absolutely nothing to be said for it. Unfortunately it takes some people, like
my younger self, a long time to see that. Such arguments can survive even
the complete loss of religious belief, the anti-Catholic ghost that carries on
beyond the death of the Protestant body, haunting the atheist who finds himself sounding like Martin Luther when debating his papist friends.

But I was still a theist for a time, though that wouldn't survive my undergrad years. Kierkegaard was my first real philosophical passion, and his
individualistic brand of religiosity greatly appealed to me. But the individualistic *ir*religion of Nietzsche would come to appeal to me more, and for a
time he was my hero, with Walter Kaufmann a close second. (I still confess
an affection for Kaufmann. Nietzsche, not so much.) Analytic philosophy
would, before long, bring my youthful atheism down to earth. For the young
Nietzschean the loss of religion is a grand, civilizational crisis, and calls for
an equally grand response on the part of a grand individual like himself.
For the skeptical analytic philosopher it's just a matter of rejecting some bad
arguments, something one does quickly and early in one's philosophical education before getting on to the really interesting stuff. And that became my
"settled" atheist position while in grad school. Atheism was like belief in a

spherical earth—something everyone in possession of the relevant facts knows to be true, and therefore not worth getting too worked up over or devoting too much philosophical attention to.

But it takes some reading and thinking to get to that point. Kaufmann's books were among my favorites, serious as they were on the "existential" side of disbelief without the ultimately impractical pomposity of Nietzsche. Naturally I took it for granted that Hume, Kant, et al. had identified the main problems with the traditional proofs of God's existence long ago. On issues of concern to a contemporary analytic philosopher, J. L. Mackie was the man, and I regarded his book *The Miracle of Theism* as a solid piece of philosophical work. I still do. I later came to realize that he doesn't get Aquinas or some other things right. (I discuss what he says about Aquinas in *Aquinas*.) But the book is intellectually serious, which is more than can be said for anything written by a "New Atheist." Antony Flew's challenge to the intelligibility of various religious assertions may have seemed like dated "ordinary language" philosophy to some, but I was convinced there was something to it. Kai Nielsen was the "go to" guy on issues of morality and religion. Michael Martin's *Atheism: A Philosophical Justification* was a doorstop of a book, and a useful compendium of arguments. I used to wonder with a little embarrassment whether my landlord, who was religious but a nice guy, could see that big word "ATHEISM" on its spine — sitting there sort of like a middle finger on the bookshelf behind me—when he'd come to collect the rent. But if so he never raised an eyebrow or said a word about it.

The argument from evil was never the main rationale for my atheism; indeed, the problem of suffering has only gotten really interesting to me since I returned to the Catholic Church. (Not because the existence of suffering poses a challenge to the truth of classical theism—for reasons I've given elsewhere, I think it poses no such challenge at all—but because the role various specific instances of suffering actually play in divine providence is often really quite mysterious.) To be sure, like any other atheist I might have cited the problem of suffering when rattling off the reasons why theism couldn't be true, but it wasn't what primarily impressed me philosophically. What *really* impressed me was the evidentialist challenge to religious belief. If God really exists there should be solid arguments to that effect, and there just aren't, or so I then supposed. Indeed, that there were no such arguments seemed to me something which would itself be an instance of evil if God existed, and this was an aspect of the problem of evil that seemed really novel and interesting.

I see from a look at my old school papers that I was expressing this idea in a couple of essays written for different courses in 1992. (I think that when J. L. Schellenberg's book *Divine Hiddenness and Human Reason* appeared in 1993 I was both gratified that someone was saying something to that effect in print, and annoyed that it wasn't me.) Attempts to sidestep the evidentialist challenge, like Alvin Plantinga's, did not convince me, and still don't. My Claremont Graduate School Master's thesis was a defense of "evidentialism" against critics like Plantinga. I haven't read it in years, but I imagine that, apart from its atheism and a detail here or there, I'd still agree with it.

I was also greatly impressed by the sheer implausibility of attributing humanlike characteristics to something as rarefied as the cause of the world. J. C. A. Gaskin's *The Quest for Eternity* had a fascinating section on the question of whether a centre of consciousness could coherently be attributed to God, a problem I found compelling. Moreover, the very idea of attributing moral virtues (or for that matter moral vices) to God seemed to make no sense, given that the conditions that made talk of kindness, courage, etc. intelligible in human life could not apply to Him. Even *if* something otherwise like God did exist, I thought, He would be "beyond good and evil"—He would not be the sort of thing one could attribute moral characteristics to, and thus wouldn't be the God of Judaism, Christianity, and Islam. (Richard Swinburne's attempt to show otherwise did not work, as I argued in another school paper.) The Euthyphro problem, which also had a big impact on me, only reinforced the conclusion that you couldn't tie morality to God in the way that (as I then assumed) the monotheistic religions required.

Those were, I think, the main components of my mature atheism: the conviction that theists could neither meet nor evade the evidentialist challenge; and the view that there could be, in any event, no coherent notion of a cause of the world with the relevant humanlike attributes. What is remarkable is how much of the basis I then had for these judgments I still find compelling. As I would come to realize only years later, the conception of God I then found so implausible was essentially a modern, parochial, and overly anthropomorphic "theistic personalist" conception, and not the classical theism to which the greatest theistic philosophers had always been committed. And as my longtime readers know, I still find theistic personalism objectionable. The fideism that I found (and still find) so appalling was, as I would also come to see only later, no part of the mainstream classical theist tradition either. And while the stock objections raised by atheists against the traditional arguments for God's existence are often aimed at caricatures, some of them do have at least some force against some of the arguments of modern philosophers of religion. But they do not have force against the key arguments of the classical theist tradition.

It is this *classical* tradition—the tradition of Aristotelians, Neo-Platonists, and Thomists and other Scholastics—that I had little knowledge of then. To be sure, I had read the usual selections from Plato, Aristotle, Aquinas and Anselm that pretty much every philosophy student reads—several of Plato's dialogues, the Five Ways, chapter 2 of the *Proslogium*, and so forth. Indeed, I read a lot more than that. I'd read the entire *Proslogium* of Anselm, as well as the *Monologium*, the *Cur Deus Homo*, and the exchange with Gaunilo, early in my undergraduate years. I'd read Aquinas's *De Ente et Essentia* and *De Principiis Naturae*, big chunks of Plotinus's *Enneads*, Athanasius's *On the Incarnation*, Augustine's *Concerning the Teacher*, and Bonaventure's *The Mind's Road to God*. I'd read Russell's *History of Western Philosophy*—hardly an unbiased source, to be sure—but also a bit of Gilson. All while becoming an atheist during my undergrad years. And I still didn't understand the classical tradition.

Why not? Because to read something is not necessarily to understand it. Partly, of course, because when you're young, you always understand less than you think you do. But mainly because, to understand someone, it's not enough to sit there tapping your foot while he talks. You've got to *listen*, rather than merely waiting for a pause so that you can insert the response you'd already formulated before he even opened his mouth. And when you're a young man who thinks he's got the religious question all figured out, you're in little mood to listen—especially if you've fallen in love with one side of the question, the side that's new and sexy because it's not what you grew up believing. Zeal of the deconverted, and all that.

You're pretty much just going through the motions at that point. And if, while in that mindset, what you're reading from the other side are seemingly archaic works, written in a forbidding jargon, presenting arguments and ideas no one defends anymore (or at least no one in the "mainstream"), your understanding is bound to be superficial and inaccurate. You'll take whatever happens to strike you as the main themes, read into them what you're familiar with from modern writers, and ignore the unfamiliar bits as irrelevant. "*This* part sounds like what Leibniz or Plantinga says, but Hume and Mackie already showed what's wrong with that; I don't even know what the hell this other part *means*, but no one today seems to be saying that sort of thing anyway, so who cares …" Read it, read into it, dismiss it, move on. How far can you go wrong?

Very, *very* far. It took me the better part of a decade to see that, and what prepared the way were some developments in my philosophical thinking that seemingly had nothing to do with religion. The first of them had to do instead with the philosophy of language and logic. Late in my undergrad years at Cal State Fullerton I took a seminar in logic and language in which the theme was the relationship between sentences and what they express. (Propositions? Meanings? Thoughts? That's the question.) Similar themes would be treated in courses I took in grad school, at first at Claremont and later at UC Santa Barbara. Certain arguments stood out. There was Alonzo Church's translation argument, and, above all, Frege's wonderful essay "The Thought." Outside of class I discovered Karl Popper's World 3 concept, and the work of Jerrold Katz. The upshot of these arguments was that the propositional content of sentences could not be reduced to or otherwise explained in terms of the utterances of sentences themselves, or behavioral dispositions, or psychological states, or conventions, or functions from possible worlds, or anything else a materialist might be willing to countenance. As the arguments sank in over the course of months and years, I came to see that existing naturalistic accounts of language and meaning were no good.

Not that that led me to give up naturalism, at least not initially. A more nuanced, skeptical naturalism was my preferred approach—what else was there, right? My studies in the philosophy of mind reinforced this tendency. At first, and like so many undergraduate philosophy majors, I took the materialist line for granted. Mental activity was just brain activity. What could be more obvious? But reading John Searle's *The Rediscovery of the Mind* destroyed this illusion, and convinced me that the standard materialist theories were all hopeless. That Searle was himself a naturalist no doubt made this easier to accept. Indeed, Searle became another hero of mine. He was smart, funny, gave perfectly organized public lectures on complex topics *without notes*, and said whatever he thought whether or not it was fashionable. And he *wrote* so beautifully, eschewing the needless formalisms that give a veneer of pseudo-rigor and "professionalism" to the writings of too many analytic philosophers. "*That* is how I want to write!" I decided.

Brilliant as he was as a critic, though, Searle's own approach to the mind-body problem—"biological naturalism"—never convinced me. It struck me (and seemingly everyone else but Searle himself) as a riff on property dualism. But there was another major influence on my thinking in the philosophy of mind in those days, Michael Lockwood's fascinating book *Mind, Brain and the Quantum*. Lockwood was also a naturalist of sorts, and yet he too was critical of some of the standard materialist moves. Most importantly, though, Lockwood's book introduced me to Bertrand Russell's later views on these issues, which would have a major influence on my thinking ever afterward. Russell emphasized that physics really gives us very little knowledge of the material world. In particular, it gives us knowledge of its abstract structure, of what can be captured in equations and the like. But it gives us no knowledge of the intrinsic nature of matter, of the concrete reality that fleshes out the abstract structure. Introspection, by contrast, gives us direct knowledge of our thoughts and experiences. The upshot is that it is *matter*, and not mind, that is the really problematic side of the mind-body problem.

This was truly revolutionary, and it reinforced the conclusion that contemporary materialism was shallow and dogmatic. And that Lockwood and Russell were themselves naturalists made it once again easy to accept the message. I got hold of whatever I could find on these neglected views of Russell's—Russell's *The Analysis of Matter* and various essays and book chapters, Lockwood's other writings on the topic, some terrific neglected essays by Grover Maxwell, some related arguments from John Foster and Howard Robinson. David Chalmers and Galen Strawson were also starting to take an interest in Russell around that time. But once again I found myself agreeing more with the criticisms than with the positive proposals. Russell took the view that what fleshes out the structure described by physics were sense data (more or less what contemporary writers call qualia). This might seem to entail a kind of panpsychism, the view that mental properties are everywhere in nature. Russell avoided this bizarre result by arguing that sense data could exist apart from a conscious subject which was aware of them, and Lockwood took the same line. I wasn't convinced, and one of my earliest published articles was a criticism of Lockwood's arguments on this subject (an article to which Lockwood very graciously replied). Chalmers and Strawson, meanwhile, were flirting with the idea of just accepting the panpsychist tendency of Russell's positive views, but that seemed crazy to me.

My preferred solution was to take the negative, critical side of the Russellian position—the view that physics gives us knowledge only of the abstract structure of matter—and push a similar line toward the mind itself. *All* our knowledge, both of the external world described by physics and of the internal world of conscious experience and thought, was knowledge only of structure, of the relations between elements but not of their intrinsic nature. I would discover that Rudolf Carnap had taken something in the ballpark of this position, but the main influence on my thinking here was, of all people, the economist and political philosopher F. A. Hayek. The libertarianism I was then attracted to had already led me to take an interest in Hayek. When I found out that he had written a book on the mind-body problem, and that it took a position like Russell's only more radical, it seemed like kismet. Hayek's *The Sensory Order* and some of his related essays would come to be the major influences on my positive views.

But they were inchoate, since Hayek was not a philosopher by profession. That gave me something to do. Working out Hayek's position in a more systematic way than he had done would be the project of my UC Santa Barbara doctoral dissertation, "Russell, Hayek, and the Mind-Body Problem." This was, to be sure, a very eccentric topic for a dissertation. Russell's views were marginal at the time, and are still not widely accepted. Probably very few philosophers of mind even know who Hayek is, and fewer still care. But I thought their views were both true and interesting, and that was that. (If you want advice on how to climb the career ladder in academic philosophy, I'm not the guy to ask. But you knew that already.)

Spelling out the Hayekian position in a satisfactory way was very difficult. Lockwood had presented Russell's position as a kind of mind-brain identity theory in reverse: It's not that the mind turns out to be the brain, but that the brain turns out to be the mind. More precisely, visual and tactile *perceptions* of the brain of the sort a neurosurgeon might have do not tell us what the brain is really like, but present us only with a representation of the brain. It is actually *introspection* of our own mental states that tells us the inner nature of the matter that makes up the brain. It seemed to me that Hayek's position amounted to something like *functionalism* in reverse: It's not that the mind turns out to be a kind of causal network of the sort that might be instantiated in the brain, or a computer, or some other material system—understood naively, i.e., taking our perceptual experience of these physical systems as accurate representations of their intrinsic nature. Rather, introspection of our mental states and their relations is actually a kind of direct awareness of the inner nature of causation itself. We shouldn't reduce mind to causal relations; rather we should inflate our notion of causation and see in it the mental properties we know from introspection.

So I then argued, and wrote up the results both in the dissertation and in another article. But the views were weird, required a great deal of abstractive effort even to understand, and one had to care about Hayek even to try, which almost no philosophers of mind do. To be sure, Searle was interested in Hayek in a general way—when Steven Postrel and I interviewed him for *Reason* magazine, and when I talked to him about Hayek on other occasions, he even expressed interest in *The Sensory Order* in particular—but this interest never manifested itself in his published work. Chalmers very kindly gave me lots of feedback on the Hayekian spin on Russell that I was trying to develop, and pushed me to clarify the underlying metaphysics. But his own tendency was, as I have said, to explore (at least tentatively) the panpsychist reading of Russell.

And yet my own development of Hayek might itself seem ultimately to have flirted with panpsychism. For if introspection of our mental states gives us awareness of the inner nature of causation, doesn't that imply that causation itself—including causation in the world outside the brain—is in some sense mental? This certainly went beyond anything Hayek himself had said. In my later thinking about Hayek's position (of which I would give a more adequate exposition in my *Cambridge Companion to Hayek* article on Hayek's philosophy of mind), I would retreat from this reading and emphasize instead the idea that introspection and perception give us only representations of the inner and outer worlds, and not their intrinsic nature.

This, for reasons I spell out in the article just referred to, offers a possible solution to the problem that qualia pose for naturalism. But because the view presupposes the notion of representation, it does not account for *intentionality*. Here my inclinations went in more of a "mysterian" direction. I had long been fascinated by Colin McGinn's arguments to the effect that there was a perfectly naturalistic explanation of consciousness, but one we may be incapable in principle of understanding given the limitations on our cognitive faculties. I thought we could say more about consciousness than McGinn thought we probably could, but I also came to think that his mysterian approach was correct vis-à-vis the *intentional content* of our mental states. Lockwood and Hayek said things that lent plausibility to this.

I would later largely abandon the Hayekian position altogether, because it presupposes an indirect realist account of perception that I would eventually reject. (That took some time. The influence of indirect realism is clearly evident in my book *Philosophy of Mind*.) But I had come to some conclusions in the philosophy of mind that would persist. First, as Russell had argued, physics, which materialists take to be the gold standard of our knowledge of the material world, in fact doesn't give us knowledge of the intrinsic nature of matter in the first place. The usual materialist theories were not even clearly thought out, much less correct. Second, a complete naturalistic explanation of intentionality is impossible.

But I was still a naturalist. It was also while still a naturalist that I first started to take a serious interest in Aristotelianism, though at the time that interest had to do with ethics rather than metaphysics. Even before I became an atheist I had been introduced to the Aristotelian idea that what is good for us is determined by our nature, and that our nature is what it is whether or not we think of it as having come from God. After becoming an atheist, then, I became drawn to ethicists like Philippa Foot, who defended a broadly Aristotelian approach to the subject from a secular point of view. Her book *Virtues and Vices* and Alasdair MacIntyre's *After Virtue* were the big influences on my thinking about ethical theory during my atheist years.

One consequence of this was that I always took teleology seriously, because it was so clearly evident a feature of ordinary practical reasoning. (How did I reconcile this with naturalism? I'm not sure I then saw the conflict all that clearly. But in any event I thought that teleological notions could be fitted into a naturalistic framework in the standard, broadly Darwinian way—the function of a thing is to be cashed out in terms of the reason why it was selected, etc. I only later came to see that teleology ultimately had to be a bottom level feature of the world rather than a derivative one.)

After Virtue also taught me another important lesson—that a set of concepts could become hopelessly confused and lead to paradox when yanked from the original context which gave them their intelligibility. MacIntyre argued that this is what had happened to the key concepts of modern moral theory, removed as they had been from the pre-modern framework that was their original home. I would later come to see that the same thing is true in metaphysics—that the metaphysical categories contemporary philosophers make casual use of (causation, substance, essence, mind, matter, and so forth) have been grotesquely distorted in modern philosophy, pulled as they have been from the classical (and especially Aristotelian-Scholastic) framework in which they had been so carefully refined. As I argue in *The Last Superstition*, many of the so-called "traditional" problems of philosophy are really just artifacts of the anti-Scholastic revolution of the moderns. They flow from highly contentious and historically contingent metaphysical assumptions, and do not reflect anything about the nature of philosophical reflection per se. And the standard moves of modern atheist argumentation typically presuppose these same assumptions. But I wouldn't see that for years.

I was on my way to seeing it, however. Several crucial background elements were in place by the late nineties. Fregean and related arguments had gotten me to take very seriously the idea that something like Platonic realism might be true. (I would later see that *Aristotelian* realism was in fact the right way to go, but the basic anti-naturalistic move had been made.)

The arguments of Searle and others had shown that existing versions of materialism were no good. Russellian arguments had shown that modern science and philosophy had no clear idea of what matter was in the first place. Whatever it was supposed to be, though, it seemed it was not something to which one could assimilate mind, at least not if one wanted to avoid panpsychism. Naturalism came to seem mysterious at best. Meanwhile, Aristotelian ideas had a certain plausibility. All that was needed was some systematic alternative to naturalism.

Then, in the late nineties, while still a grad student, I was given an opportunity to teach a philosophy of religion course, followed by several opportunities to teach "intro to philosophy" courses. In the latter, I wanted to focus on topics that would be of interest to undergrads who might have no general interest in philosophy. Since everyone had some interest in religion (even if only, in some cases, a hostile interest), arguments for God's existence seemed a good topic for at least part of the course. Naturally, that was a topic for the philosophy of religion course too. So, I had a reason to revisit the subject after having given it relatively little thought for many years.

At first I taught the material the way so many professors do: Here are the arguments; here are the obvious fallacies they commit; let's move on. I never came across like Richard Dawkins, but I no doubt did come across like (say) philosophy popularizer Nigel Warburton: politely dismissive. And, as I gradually came to see, totally ill-informed. The "line 'em up, then shoot 'em down" approach was boring, and the arguments seemed obviously stupid. Yet the people who had presented them historically were obviously *not* stupid. So, it seemed to me that it would be interesting to try to give the arguments a run for their money, and to try to make it understandable to the students why anyone would ever have accepted them.

So I started to read and think more about them. I came to find William Rowe's approach to the Leibnizian sort of cosmological argument interesting and pedagogically useful. He didn't seem to accept the argument, but he made it clear that asking "What caused God?", "How do we know the universe had a beginning?", etc. weren't really serious objections. He also made it clear that the thrust of the argument had to do with what was a straightforward and undeniably serious philosophical question: Should we regard the world as ultimately explicable or not? If not, then the argument fails. But if so, then it does seem to make it plausible that something like God, or at least the God of the philosophers, must exist. And it didn't seem *silly* to wonder whether there might be such an explanation. Richard Taylor's clear, punchy chapter on natural theology in his little book

Metaphysics made the same point, and made for a useful selection for the students to read.

Naturally, I had already long been aware of this sort of argument. The difference was that when I had first thought about it years before I was approaching it as someone who had had a religious background and wanted to see whether there was any argument for God's existence that was really persuasive. Russell's retort to Copleston, to the effect that we can always insist that the universe is just there and that's that, had then seemed to me sufficient to show that the argument was simply not compelling. We're just not rationally forced to accept it. I had, as it were, put the argument on trial and it had been unable to establish its innocence to my satisfaction. But now I was approaching it as a naturalist who was trying to give my students a reason to see the argument as something at least worth thinking about for a class period or two. I was playing defense attorney rather than prosecution, but a defense attorney with the confidence of someone who didn't have a stake in his client's acquittal. Already being a confirmed naturalist, I could be dispassionate rather than argumentative, and could treat the whole thing as a philosophical exercise.

And from that point of view it started to seem that Russell's reply, while it had *rhetorical* power, was perhaps not quite airtight *philosophically*. Sure, you could always *say* that there's no ultimate explanation. And maybe there's no way to prove otherwise. But is it really true? Is it really even more *plausible* to think that than to think that there is an explanation? Guys like Rowe and Taylor, by no means religious fanatics or apologists but just philosophers entertaining a deep question, seemed to take the question pretty seriously. Interesting, I thought. Though for the time being, "interesting"—rather than correct or persuasive—was all I found it.

Then there was Aquinas. At the high tide of my undergrad Brash Young Atheist stage, I had taken a class on medieval philosophy with the late John Cronquist, an atheist professor at Cal State Fullerton who was absolutely contemptuous of Christianity. Campus apologists of the Protestant stripe were a frequent target of his ire, though he had a choice quip or two about Catholicism as well. He was one of the smartest and most well-read people I have ever known—the kind of guy you find intimidating and hope not to get in an argument with—and I liked him very much. One of the odd and interesting things about that course, though, was how respectfully Cronquist treated some of the medievals, especially Aquinas. He said that compared to them, contemporary apologists were "like a pimple on the ass of an athlete." (I remember him dramatically pointing to his own posterior as he said this, for emphasis.) He obviously didn't buy the Scholastic system for a moment, but he treated the material as worth taking a semester to try to understand. And he said a couple of things that stood out. First, for reasons I don't recall him elaborating on much, he seemed to think that the Third Way in particular might have something to be said for it. Second, he said that the mind-body problem, which he seemed to think was terribly vexing, really boiled down to the problem of universals. For years I would wonder what he meant by that. (I now think it must have had to do with the way our grasp of abstract concepts features in Aristotelian arguments for the immateriality of the intellect.)

At the time I filed these remarks away as curiosities (just as I had then regarded the material we covered in the class as mere curiosities). But I think his example made it easier for me, years later, to take a second look at Aquinas as I prepared course material. I look back at my first lectures on the Five Ways with extreme embarrassment. If you'd heard them, you'd have thought I was cribbing from an advance copy of *The God Delusion*, if not in tone then at least in the substance of my criticisms. But that started slowly to change as I read more about the arguments and began to work the material into my lectures. A good friend of mine, who had also gone from Catholicism to atheism and was a fellow grad student, was familiar with William Lane Craig's book *The Cosmological Argument from Plato to Leibniz*, and seemed to find it useful in preparing his own lectures on the subject. Our discussions of the arguments were very helpful. Furthermore, *Atheism and Theism* by J. J. C. Smart and John Haldane had recently appeared, with Haldane defending, and Smart treating respectfully, some old-fashioned Thomistic arguments for the existence of God. Such materials opened up a new world. The way I and so many other philosophers tended to read the Five Ways was, as I gradually came to realize, laughably off base.

The immediate effect was that I found a way to teach the Five Ways without seeming like I was putting fish in a barrel for the students to shoot at. I still didn't agree with the arguments, but at least teaching them was getting interesting. I recall one class period when, having done my best to try to defend some argument (the First Way, I think) against various objections, I finally stated whatever it was I thought at the time was a difficulty that hadn't been satisfactorily answered. One of my smartest students expressed relief: She had been worried for a moment that there might be a good argument for God's existence after all! (Anyone who thinks wishful thinking is all on the side of religious people is fooling himself.)

None of this undermined my commitment to naturalism for some time. I published my first several journal articles while still in grad school, and two of them were criticisms of the doctrine of the Trinity. (I'm now a staunch Trinitarian, of course. But once again, it turns out that I still more or less agree with the arguments I then presented. The *versions* of Trinitarianism I then attacked are, I continue to think, wrong. But Trinitarianism itself is true.)

But the language of act and potency, *per se* and *per accidens* causal series, and the like started to enter my lectures on Aquinas, and before long, my thinking. It was all very strange. Aquinas's arguments had a certain power when all of this metaphysical background was taken account of. And there was a certain plausibility to the metaphysics. There were *reasons* for distinguishing between actuality and potentiality, the different kinds of causal series, and so forth. Yet no one seemed to talk that way anymore— or, again, at least no one "mainstream." Could there really be anything to it all if contemporary philosophers weren't saying anything about it? And yet, precisely because they weren't talking about it, they weren't *refuting* it either. Indeed, when they did say anything about Aquinas's arguments at all, most of them showed only that they couldn't even be bothered to get him right, much less show why he was mistaken. Arguments from current philosophical fashion are bad enough. But when most philosophers not only do not accept a certain view, but demonstrate that they don't even understand what it is, things can start to smell very fishy indeed.

And so they did. I already knew from the lay of the land in the philosophy of language and philosophy of mind that the standard naturalist approaches had no solid intellectual foundation, and themselves rested as much on fashion as on anything else. Even writers like Searle, whom I admired greatly and whose naturalism I shared, had no plausible positive alternative. McGinn-style mysterianism started to seem like a dodge, especially given that certain arguments (like the Platonic realist ones) seemed to show that matter simply *is not* in fact all that there is, not merely that we can't *know how* it can be all that there is. Some secular writers were even toying with Aristotelian ideas anyway. The *only* reason for not taking Aquinas and similar thinkers seriously seemed to be that most other academic philosophers weren't taking them seriously. And yet as I had come to learn, many of them didn't even understand Aquinas and Co. in the first place, and their own naturalism was riddled with problems. Against Aquinas, for naturalism—the case increasingly seemed to come down to the consensus of the profession. And what exactly was that worth?

It isn't worth a damn thing, of course. Careerists might not see that, nor might a young man more excited by the "question what your parents taught you" side of philosophy than all that "objective pursuit of truth" stuff. But a grownup will see it, and a philosopher had sure as hell better see it.

I don't know exactly when everything clicked. There was no single event, but a gradual transformation. As I taught and thought about the arguments for God's existence, and in particular the cosmological argument, I went from thinking "These arguments are no good" to thinking "These arguments are a little better than they are given credit for" and then to "These arguments are actually kind of interesting." Eventually it hit me: "Oh my goodness, these arguments are *right* after all!" By the summer of 2001 I would find myself trying to argue my wife's skeptical physicist brother-in-law into philosophical theism on the train the four of us were taking through eastern Europe.

There's more to the story than that, of course. In particular, it would take an essay of its own to explain why I returned to the Catholic Church, specifically, as I would by the end of 2001. But I can already hear some readers protesting at what I have said. I don't mean the New Atheist types, always on the hunt for some *ad hominem* nugget that will excuse them from having to take the actual arguments of the other side seriously. (God Himself could come down from on high and put before such people an airtight ontological proof of His existence while parting the Red Sea, and they'd still insist that what *really* motivated these arguments was a desire to rationalize His moral prejudices. And that their own continued disbelief was just a matter of, you know, following the evidence where it leads.)

No, I'm talking about a certain kind of religious believer, the type who's always going on about how faith is really a matter of the heart rather than the head, that no one's ever been argued into religion, etc. It will be said by such a believer that my change of view was too rationalistic, too cerebral, too bloodless, too focused on a theoretical knowledge of the God of the philosophers rather than a personal response to the God of Abraham, Isaac, and Jacob.

But the dichotomy is a false one, and the implied conception of the relationship between faith and reason not only foolish but heterodox. As to the heterodoxy and foolishness of fideism, and the correct understanding of the relationship of faith and reason, I have addressed that set of issues elsewhere. As to the "heart versus head" stuff, it seems to me to rest on an erroneous bifurcation of human nature. Man is a unity, his rationality and animality, intellect and passions, theoretical and moral lives all ultimately oriented toward the same end. That is why even a pagan like Aristotle knew that our happiness lay in "the contemplation and service of God," whose existence he knew of via philosophical argumentation. That is why Plotinus could know that we "forget the father, God" because of "self-will." While the pagan may have no access to the *super*natural end that only grace makes possible, he is still capable of a *natural* knowledge of God, and will naturally tend to love what he knows.

As Plotinus's remark indicates, that does not mean that the will does not have a role to play. But that is true *wherever* reason leads us to a conclusion we might not like, not merely in matters of religion. And once you have allowed yourself to see the truth that reason leads you to, what reason apprehends is (given the convertibility of the transcendentals) as good and beautiful as it is real. If you find yourself intellectually convinced that there is a divine Uncaused Cause who sustains the world *and you* in being at every instant, and don't find this conclusion extremely strange and moving, something that leads you to a kind of reverence, then I daresay you haven't understood it. Of course, there are those whose heads and hearts are so out of sync that they cannot follow both at the same time. But we shouldn't mistake this pathology for an insight into human nature.

Speaking for myself, anyway, I can say this much. When I was an undergrad I came across the saying that learning a little philosophy leads you away from God, but learning a lot of philosophy leads you back. As a young man who had learned a little philosophy, I scoffed. But in later years and at least in my own case, I would come to see that it's true.

Philosophy of mind

10

Kripke, Ross, and the
Immaterial Aspects of Thought

I. Introduction

The late James Ross formulated a simple and powerful argument for the immateriality of our intellectual operations.[1] The gist of the argument is that: "Some thinking (judgment) is determinate in a way no physical process can be. Consequently, such thinking cannot be (wholly) a physical process."[2] Or as he puts it in a slightly less pithy summary:

> In a word: our thinking, in a single case, can be of a definite abstract form (e.g., $N \times N = N^2$), and not indeterminate among incompossible equally most particular forms … No physical process can be that definite in its form in a single case. Adding physical instances even to infinity will not exclude incompossible equally most particular forms (cf. Saul Kripke's "plus/quus" examples). So, no physical process can exclude incompossible functions from being equally well (or badly) satisfied … Thus, no physical process can *be* the whole of such thinking. The same holds for functions among physical states …[3]

To this contrast between the determinacy of thought and the indeterminacy of the physical, Ross added several related but distinct considerations in favor of the immateriality of thought, such as the contrast between the universality of thought and the particularity of physical processes.

---

1   The argument was first presented in his article "Immaterial Aspects of Thought," *Journal of Philosophy* 89 (1992), 136–50. It was restated in chapter 6 of Ross's book *Thought and World: The Hidden Necessities* (Notre Dame, IN: University of Notre Dame Press, 2008).
2   Ross, "Immaterial Aspects of Thought," 137.
3   Ross, *Thought and World*, 116–17.

Readers acquainted with ancient and medieval philosophy might perceive a family resemblance between Ross's argument on the one hand, and Plato's affinity argument[4] and Aquinas's argument from the universality of thought[5] on the other. But as the reference to Kripke indicates, whatever its classical antecedents, Ross's argument is one whose force he took to be evident from premises even contemporary philosophers should accept. Indeed, he regarded it as implicit in several of "the jewels of analytic philosophy," as he called them[6]: the "quus" argument of Kripke's book *Wittgenstein on Rules and Private Language*; the "gavagai" argument of W. V. Quine's *Word and Object*; and the "grue" paradox of Nelson Goodman's *Fact, Fiction, and Forecast*.[7] These famous indeterminacy results establish in Ross's view the indeterminacy of all *material* phenomena in particular. That our determinate thought processes are therefore *im*material is, he argues, a conclusion that can be avoided only at the cost of an outlandish and indeed self-defeating eliminativism.

Peter Dillard has recently criticized Ross's argument, and his use of Kripke in particular.[8] Dillard is, I think, correct to put special emphasis on the role Kripke plays in the argument, and as his critique shows, Ross's use of Kripke raises important questions those who sympathize with the argument need to answer (questions that are not raised by Ross's use of Quine and Goodman). Still, I maintain that Dillard's objections ultimately fail, and that Ross's argument emerges stronger once its relationship to Kripke's views is clarified.

What follows is an exposition and defense of Ross's argument, a defense against not only Dillard's objections but also other objections that might be raised against it. In the next section I lay some groundwork by explaining the difference between intellectual activity or thought in the strict sense and other aspects of the mind, which more commonly feature in the contemporary debate over materialism. We will see that Ross (like his ancient and medieval predecessors, and unlike modern critics of materialism)

---

4 *Phaedo* 78 b 4 – 80 e 1.
5 *Quaestiones disputatae de veritate* X.8. Cf. *Summa theologiae* I.75.5 and *De ente et essentia* 4.
6 Ross, "Immaterial Aspects of Thought," p. 137.
7 Saul A. Kripke, *Wittgenstein on Rules and Private Language* (Cambridge, MA: Harvard University Press, 1982); Willard van Orman Quine, *Word and Object* (Cambridge, MA: The MIT Press, 1960); Nelson Goodman, *Fact, Fiction, and Forecast*, Fourth edition (Cambridge, MA: Harvard University Press, 1983).
8 Peter Dillard, "Two Unsuccessful Arguments for Immaterialism," *American Catholic Philosophical Quarterly* 85 (2011): 269–86.

is *not* arguing for the immateriality of qualia or even of intentionality, as that is typically understood today. This will be crucial to understanding both why Ross's argument might seem to conflict with a key aspect of Kripke's position, and why it does not in fact do so. In the third section of the paper I provide a more detailed exposition of Ross's argument and its use of ideas drawn from Quine, Goodman, and (especially) Kripke. In the fourth section I address Dillard's objections, an objection raised by Brian Leftow, and an objection raised by Robert Pasnau against arguments similar to Ross's. In the fifth section I explain how Ross's position is perfectly compatible with what we know from modern neuroscience, and address a potential objection implicit in some recent work by Paul Churchland.

II. Intellectual and other mental phenomena

The materialist philosopher of mind Jerry Fodor sums up the challenge mental phenomena pose to materialism as follows:

> [S]ome of the most pervasive properties of minds seem so mysterious as to raise the Kantian-sounding question how a materialistic psychology is *even possible*. Lots of mental states are *conscious*, lots of mental states are *intentional*, and lots of mental processes are *rational*, and the question does rather suggest itself how anything that is material could be any of these.[9]

For Fodor, then, the difficulty facing the materialist is really a cluster of three problems: the problem of *consciousness*, the problem of *intentionality*, and the problem of *rationality*.

The first of these problems is generally understood within contemporary philosophy of mind to be a matter of explaining *qualia* in materialist terms. Qualia are the subjective, first-person features of a conscious experience, in virtue of which there is "something it is like" to have the experience. Examples would be the way heat and cold feel, the way red looks, the way a rose smells, the way a note sounds, and the way coffee tastes. The problem for the materialist is that there seems to be an unbridgeable logical and metaphysical gap between facts about brain chemistry, the wiring of

---

9   In his eponymously titled article "Jerry A. Fodor," in Samuel Guttenplan, ed., *A Companion to the Philosophy of Mind* (Oxford: Blackwell, 1994), 292–300, at 292. Emphasis in the original.

neurons, and the like on the one hand, and facts about qualia on the other. Hence, according to Frank Jackson's "knowledge argument," we could know all the facts of the former sort that there are to know, and still not know the facts about qualia[10]; and according to David Chalmers's "zombie argument," all facts of the former sort could obtain in the absence of any of the facts about qualia obtaining.[11] Hence facts about qualia seem to be non-physical facts, facts additional to all the facts about the material world.

Intentionality, as typically understood within contemporary philosophy, is the "aboutness" of a thought, its "directedness" onto an object. Here too the problem is that it seems that the neurophysiological and other physical facts could in principle be just as they are in the absence of any intentionality, so that no appeal to facts of that sort can suffice to explain intentionality.[12]

Arguments like these have tended to dominate the anti-materialist literature in modern philosophy, but they are not the sorts of arguments one finds in ancient and medieval critics of materialism like Plato, Aristotle, and Aquinas. In fact they presuppose a conception of the material world that was developed in opposition to the Aristotelian conception endorsed by Aquinas and other Scholastics. According to the "Mechanical Philosophy" put forward by Descartes, Hobbes, Locke and other early modern philosophers (which was essentially a revival of the Greek atomist view of nature that had been criticized by Aristotle) the material world is comprised of nothing more than colorless, odorless, soundless, tasteless particles in motion, governed entirely by efficient causes and devoid of any inherent teleology or final causality. Color, sound, heat, cold, and the like, at least as common sense understands them, are on this view to be regarded as mere projections of the mind, existing in our perceptual experience of the world rather than in the world itself. What correspond in objective physical reality to such qualities are only those features definable in terms of a purely "mechanical" picture of nature—surface reflectance properties of objects,

---

10 For Jackson's original essays on the argument as well as a variety of critical responses to it, see Peter Ludlow, Yujin Nagasawa, and Daniel Stoljar, eds., *There's Something About Mary: Essays on Phenomenal Consciousness and Frank Jackson's Knowledge Argument* (Cambridge, MA: The MIT Press, 2004).

11 See David J. Chalmers, *The Conscious Mind: In Search of a Fundamental Theory* (Oxford: Oxford University Press, 1997).

12 For a useful overview of the contemporary debate over intentionality, see Tim Crane, *The Mechanical Mind: A Philosophical Introduction to Minds, Machines, and Mental Representation*, Second edition (London: Routledge, 2003), especially chapters 1 and 5.

compression waves, molecular motion, and the like. Hence, when we say, for example, that a certain rose is red, if we mean by this that there is something in the rose that resembles the redness we perceive when we look at it, then what we are saying is false; but if we mean instead that, given its surface reflectance properties, light from the rose affects our senses in such a way that we will perceive it as having that redness, then what we are saying is true.

If one accepts this picture of matter, then qualia and intentionality naturally come to seem immaterial. In particular, if the matter that makes up a rose has nothing like the redness or fragrance that I experience it as having, but is red and fragrant only in the sense that it has, by virtue of its physical properties, the power to generate in me an experience with that qualitative character, then the matter that makes up my brain cannot plausibly be said to have these features either. Reddish and fragrant qualia must therefore be immaterial. Similarly, if matter is devoid of any inherent final causality or teleology, so that nothing in the material world is inherently "directed at" or "points to" anything beyond itself, then it is hard to see how the matter that makes up the brain can inherently be "directed at" or "point to" anything beyond itself, as it would have to do if it possessed intentionality. Intentionality too must therefore be a non-physical feature of the brain.

Now an Aristotelian who takes the redness we see really to exist in the rose, and who regards material processes to be inherently directed toward ends beyond themselves insofar as they are teleological, is not going to find such arguments compelling if intended as a completely general critique of materialism. What such arguments show is at most only that qualia and intentionality cannot be material *given the "mechanistic" conception of matter* the early moderns inherited from the Greek atomists. But the arguments do not show that these features cannot be material given some *other* conception of matter—and indeed, they *are* material on an Aristotelian conception of matter.

To be sure, the status of the so-called "secondary qualities" is a matter of controversy even among Aristotelians.[13] But those modern Aristotelians willing to allow that the redness we see in a rose is as subjective as a pain or a tickle would still regard the sensation of redness, like the pain and tickle, as a bodily feature of an organism. It is also true that the Aristotelian, unlike

---

13   For a brief discussion of the different opinions Neo-Scholastic writers held on this subject, see chapter XII of Celestine N. Bittle, *Reality and the Mind: Epistemology* (Milwaukee: Bruce Publishing Company, 1936).

the materialist, takes sentient organisms to differ in kind and not merely degree from non-sentient forms of life, just as he regards organic phenomena to differ in kind and not merely degree from inorganic phenomena. But for the Aristotelian these are distinctions within the material world, and do not mark a difference between material and immaterial phenomena.[14]

Similarly, the "directedness" in terms of which modern philosophers characterize intentionality does not for the Aristotelian mark a difference between the material and the immaterial. For instance, the phosphorus in the head of a match is entirely material, but given its chemical properties it is inherently "directed toward" or "points to" the generation of flame and heat; and in general, causal powers are for the Aristotelian "directed toward" or "point to" the manifestation of their typical effect or effects as toward an end or goal. Biology provides even more obvious examples of phenomena the Aristotelian regards as inherently directed toward ends or goals. But intentionality, at least as typically understood by contemporary philosophers—again, as a matter of something's being "directed" onto an object, or "pointing" beyond itself—is just a special case of this more general phenomenon of teleology or finality in nature. Indeed, the contemporary analytic philosopher George Molnar characterizes the causal powers even of inorganic phenomena as possessing "physical intentionality" insofar as these powers point to their typical effects, while another analytic philosopher, John Heil, speaks of the "natural intentionality" by virtue of which dispositional properties (such as the brittleness of a glass) point to their manifestations (such as the shattering of the glass).[15] And the biologist J. Scott Turner characterizes unconscious organic developmental processes as manifesting "intentionality" insofar as they point beyond themselves to a certain end state.[16] All of these phenomena are, for the Aristotelian no less than for the materialist, entirely material.

Of course, writers like Aristotle and Aquinas did regard certain aspects of intellectual activity as immaterial, and intellectual activity is certainly an

---

14 To be sure, the story is more complicated than this. As an anonymous referee rightly emphasizes, there is a sense in which, for Aquinas, sensation involves the reception of forms without matter. But Aquinas still regards sensation as involving material organs in a way that (for reasons of the sort we'll be examining) he thinks strictly intellectual activity does not.

15 George Molnar, *Powers: A Study in Metaphysics* (Oxford: Oxford University Press, 2003); John Heil, *From an Ontological Point of View* (Oxford: Oxford University Press, 2003).

16 J. Scott Turner, *The Tinkerer's Accomplice: How Design Emerges from Life Itself* (Cambridge, MA: Harvard University Press, 2007).

instance of intentionality. Indeed, contemporary philosophers typically regard beliefs as the paradigm instances of intentionality. But for Aristotle and Aquinas, that a belief is "directed toward" or "points to" its object is not what makes it immaterial; indeed, non-human animals have internal states that are "directed toward" objects—for example, a dog's desire for food is "directed toward" the food—but they do not have beliefs, certainly not in the sense we have them. The reason is that they do not have *concepts*; and it is the ability to form concepts, to combine them together into judgments, and to go from one judgment to another in accordance with the principles of logic, that not only marks the difference between human and non-human animals, but also the difference between a truly *immaterial* faculty and the purely material, sensory capacities we share with the lower animals.[17] Hence it is what Fodor calls the problem of *rationality*, rather than the so-called problems of consciousness and intentionality, that for Aristotelians and other classical and medieval philosophers poses the decisive challenge to materialism.

Unlike modern empiricists (though like modern rationalists) the Platonic and Aristotelian traditions insist on a rigid distinction between sensation and imagination on the one hand, and truly intellectual activity on the other. The concepts that are the constituents of intellectual activity are irreducible to sensations, to mental images or "phantasms," and for that matter to "mental representations" of the sort posited by contemporary cognitive

17 Tim Crane argues, plausibly enough, that in addition to "directedness" on to an object, what (following John Searle) he calls "aspectual shape" must also be regarded as essential to intentionality. For example, when you think about a certain object, you do not simply think about it full stop, but think about it *as an apple* (say), or *as a snack*. Your thought always has *this* "aspectual shape" rather than *that* one. [See Crane, "The Intentional Structure of Consciousness," in Quentin Smith and Aleksandar Jokic, eds., *Consciousness: New Philosophical Perspectives* (Oxford: Clarendon Press, 2003); and John R. Searle, *The Rediscovery of the Mind* (Cambridge, MA: The MIT Press, 1992, 155.] But it doesn't follow that "aspectual shape" must always involve the application of concepts. Indeed, Crane argues that pains and other bodily sensations are intentional and thus have aspectual shape. Yet non-human animals have pains and other sensations, even though (as already noted) they lack concepts. (I ignore the controversy over whether certain apes possess language, though I do not for a moment believe they do; that there are obviously *some* non-human animals which experience pain and other sensations yet lack concepts suffices to make the point.) Furthermore, Molnar argues that causal powers are "directed toward" their typical effects in a way that involves something like the referential opacity and "partial consideration" characteristic of the intentionality of the mental (Molnar, *Powers*, 62–66). Yet inorganic causes certainly do not possess concepts.

science (whether these are characterized as "sentences" encoded in the brain, as "distributed representations," or what have you). For concepts have features none of these things can have.

The feature most emphasized by writers in the Aristotelian-Scholastic tradition is the *abstract and universal* nature of concepts, as contrasted with the *concrete and particular* character of images or phantasms. As G. H. Joyce writes:

> A Concept is equally representative of all objects of the same character. Thus if I see a circle drawn on a black-board, the concept which I form of that geometrical figure will express not merely the individual circle before me, but all circles. The figure I see is of a definite size, and is in a particular place. But my mind by an act of abstraction omits these individual characteristics, and forms the concept of a circle as it is enunciated in Euclid's definition. This concept is applicable to every circle that ever was drawn. When however I form the phantasm of a circle, my phantasm must necessarily represent a figure of particular dimensions. In other words the concept of the circle is universal: the phantasm is singular. Similarly, if I form a concept of 'man,' my concept is applicable to all men. But a phantasm of a man must represent him as possessed of a certain height, with certain features, with hair of a definite colour, etc.[18]

Another crucial feature is the *clarity and distinctness* of many concepts as contrasted with the *vagueness and indistinctness* of their corresponding images or phantasms. Celestine Bittle provides an example:

> We can readily form a phantasm of five trees in a row. But to imagine fifty (not forty-nine or fifty-one) trees in a row will be for most people an impossible task. To imagine five thousand

---

18 George Hayward Joyce, *Principles of Logic*, Third edition (London: Longmans, Green, and Co., 1949), pp. 16–17. Cf. P. Coffey, *The Science of Logic*, Volume I (London: Longmans, Green, and Co., 1918), pp. 2–5; Michael Maher, *Psychology: Empirical and Rational*, Ninth edition (London: Longmans, Green, and Co., 1933), pp. 235–38; Celestine N. Bittle, *The Science of Correct Thinking: Logic*, Revised edition (Milwaukee: Bruce Publishing Company, 1951), pp. 24–28; and Raymond J. McCall, *Basic Logic*, Second edition (New York: Barnes and Noble, 1967), pp. 3–6.

(not more or less) trees in a row is an utter impossibility. But my idea of five thousand or five million trees is just as clear to my intellect as five or ten; I have no more difficulty in *understanding* the number 5,000,000 trees than I have in understanding the number 4,999,999 or 5,000,001.[19]

We might also think of Descartes' examples in the Sixth Meditation of the chiliagon (a polygon having 1,000 sides) and a myriagon (which has 10,000 sides). The intellect clearly and distinctly understands the difference between these figures, and the difference between them and either a circle or a figure having 1,002 sides. But we cannot form distinct mental images of these various figures. To the imagination they all appear vaguely the same.

Bittle goes on to suggest that a third difference between concepts and mental images is that "there are many things of which we have a very clear *idea*, but of which *no reasonable phantasm can be formed*," and gives examples like law, economics, soul, God, knowledge, ignorance, inference, conclusion, certainty, consistency, etc.[20] This is potentially misleading, since Aristotelian-Scholastic writers hold that while intellectual activity cannot be identified with or reduced to images or phantasms, it is always associated with them (a point to which we will have reason to return). Thus, while it is true that we cannot form a mental image of law or of certainty the way we can form a mental image of a circle or a man, we nevertheless can and do form mental images of *some* sort when we entertain these concepts—for instance, visual or auditory images of *words* like "law" and "certainty." Still, Bittle's point is well-taken insofar as the connection between these words and the corresponding concepts is entirely *arbitrary and conventional*, whereas the connection between the concepts of (say) a man or a circle and the corresponding mental images or phantasms is not arbitrary or merely conventional. A mental image of a man resembles a man in a way the word "man" does not; a mental image of a circle resembles a circle, and may even be said to instantiate circularity, while the word "circle" does neither. Words like "law" and "certainty," given their lack of any such natural or inherent connection to the concepts they name, are connected to their corresponding concepts only as a matter of contingent linguistic circumstance, and mental images of these words inherit this contingency. Given only their inherent properties, such images could have stood instead for anything at all.

19   Bittle, *The Science of Correct Thinking: Logic*, 26.
20   Ibid., p. 27. Emphasis in the original.

Bittle's point, then, is related to his earlier point that phantasms are vague or indistinct in a way concepts are not. In both cases the problem is one of *indeterminacy*: In the one case (illustrated by the tree and chiliagon examples) there is a relationship of *instantiation* between the image and the universal named by the concept, but the instantiation is too imperfect for the image *determinately* to instantiate the number of trees conceived of (in the one example) or to instantiate *being a chiliagon* as opposed to *being a myriagon* or *being a circle* (in the other example). In the case of Bittle's other point (illustrated by examples like the concept *law*), the connection between the image and the concept is even looser, since a mental image of the word "law" does not resemble law, does not instantiate the universal *law*, and indeed does not of itself have any determinate significance at all. The corresponding concepts themselves, by contrast, are entirely determinate. When I am thinking about a chiliagon, there is no question that that is what I am thinking about, even if the mental image I entertain at the same time could in principle be taken for a mental image of a circle or a myriagon (say, by someone who used a helmet similar to the one in the movie *Brainstorm* to gain quasi-introspective access to my mental imagery)[21]; and when I am thinking about law, there is no question that that is what I am thinking about, even if the visual or auditory image of the word "law" that I form while doing so could have been conventionally associated with some other concept.[22]

Now these points about indeterminacy, and the earlier point about the particularity of phantasms (as contrasted with the universality of concepts), apply to any material symbols cognitive scientists would purport to find in the brain no less than to images or phantasms. Suppose it turned out that when we thought about circles, the associated neural activity traced out a literally circular pattern in the brain. Just as with a circle drawn in ink on paper, this pattern would be merely one particular instantiation of circularity among others, with a size, spatial location, and material constitution it did not share with every other possible circle; and it would therefore lack the universality that the concept of a circle has. Like the circle drawn in ink on paper, it would also be less than perfectly circular and in other ways

21 I borrow the example from Daniel C. Dennett, "Quining Qualia," in Alvin I. Goldman, ed., *Readings in Philosophy and Cognitive Science* (Cambridge, MA: The MIT Press, 1993).

22 For useful summaries of contemporary discussion of the indeterminacy of imagery, see Crane, *The Mechanical Mind*, pp. 13–21, and Michael Tye, *The Imagery Debate* (Cambridge, MA: The MIT Press, 1991).

indeterminate; for instance, it would, given its physical properties alone, be indeterminate between an instance of *being circular* and an instance of *being oval* or an instance of *being a chiliagon*. Accordingly, it could not be identified with the concept of a circle, which is determinate.

Of course, the symbols posited by cognitive scientists are not typically of such a crude pictorial sort. They are instead sometimes modeled on maps,[23] or on linguistic symbols, as in Fodor's theory that thought is mediated by sentences encoded in the brain.[24] Indeed, whether even mental images themselves are best thought of as pictorial is a matter of dispute; some philosophers and cognitive scientists would argue that they are better thought of in linguistic terms, on the model of descriptions.[25] But in all these cases the indeterminacy is even more obvious. As with words like "law" and "certainty," the postulated linguistic symbols would bear no relation of resemblance or instantiation that might give them a natural connection to the concepts they are claimed to correspond to; and maps too differ from pictures precisely in less clearly or determinately resembling (much less instantiating) that which they are maps of, even if their difference from pictorial representations is not as great as that of linguistic symbols.

The materialist might suggest that the symbols in question are given a determinate content by virtue of their efficient causal relations to aspects of the external world. Thus, such-and-such a symbol encoded in the brain will signify *triangle* if and only if tokens of the symbol are typically caused by the presence of triangles; while another symbol will have a different content because of the different causal relations it bears to the external world. But there are many problems with causal theories of content, one of which is that they cannot account for the difference between concepts having exactly the *same* extension, as (for example) *triangle* and *trilateral* do. As the analytical Thomist philosopher John Haldane argues:

> Every triangle is a trilateral and vice versa, and in some manner possession of the one property necessitates possession of the other. Yet triangularity and trilaterality are not the same

23 David Braddon-Mitchell and Frank Jackson, *Philosophy of Mind and Cognition* (Oxford: Blackwell, 1996).

24 Jerry A. Fodor, *The Language of Thought* (Cambridge, MA: Harvard University Press, 1975).

25 For an overview of the debate between "pictorialist" and "descriptionalist" theories of imagery, see Ned Block, ed., *Imagery* (Cambridge, MA: The MIT Press, 1981), and Tye, *The Imagery Debate*.

attribute, and it takes geometrical reasoning to show that these properties are necessarily co-instantiated ... To the extent that he can even concede that there are distinct properties the naturalist will want to insist that the causal powers ... of trilaterals and triangulars are identical. Thus he cannot explain the difference between the concepts by invoking causal differences between the members of their extensions (as one might *seem* to be able to account for the difference between the concepts *square* and *circle*).[26]

As Haldane notes, the problem is completely general:

> For any naturally individuated object or property there are indefinitely many non-equivalent ways of thinking about it. That is to say, the structure of the conceptual order, which is expressed in judgments and actions, is richer and more abstract than that of the natural order, and the character of this difference makes it difficult to see how the materialist could explain the former as arising out of the latter.[27]

In short, any set of material facts, including facts about the efficient causal relations between material elements, is indeterminate between the different determinate ways in which we might conceptualize them; hence the former cannot suffice to account for the latter.

Now Ross too is concerned to argue that material processes are indeterminate in a way that thought or intellectual activity is not (or at least in a way that certain *aspects* of thought or intellectual activity is not, a qualification to which we will return); and as I have also noted, he takes the universality of thought to be a further feature which differentiates it from material processes. As this indicates, Ross's approach to the critique of materialism is classical rather than modern, and in particular it is in line with the Aristotelian-Scholastic tradition rather than the Cartesian tradition. He

---

26 J. J. C. Smart and J. J. Haldane, *Atheism and Theism*, Second edition (Oxford: Blackwell, 2003), pp. 106–07. I discuss various problems with causal theories of content in chapter 7 of *Philosophy of Mind* (Oxford: Oneworld, 2005), and in "Hayek, Popper, and the Causal Theory of the Mind," in Leslie Marsh, ed., *Hayek in Mind: Hayek's Philosophical Psychology*, special issue of *Advances in Austrian Economics*, Vol. 15 (2011).

27 Smart and Haldane, *Atheism and Theism*, 107.

is not concerned to argue for the immateriality of either qualia or intentionality (at least as the latter is typically understood in contemporary philosophy), but rather for the immateriality of our rational powers—our capacity to grasp concepts, combine them into judgments, and reason from one judgment to another in accordance with logical principles.[28] Qualia and the "directedness" contemporary philosophers regard as the core of intentionality are, after all, features of mental images or phantasms no less than of perceptual experiences. There is "something it is like" to have a mental image, and an image is "directed at" or "points to" that which it represents. But it is indeterminate for all that, and lacks the universality that concepts have. There is nothing in Ross's position that commits him to holding otherwise, and as we will see, this point is crucial for a proper understanding of his use of Kripke's "quus" example.

III. Exposition of Ross's argument

As Dillard notes, the basic structure of Ross's argument is as follows:

* All formal thinking is determinate.
* No physical process is determinate.
* Thus, no formal thinking is a physical process.[29]

The bulk of Ross's discussion is devoted to defending each of the premises. With regard to the first premise, it is important to note that Ross is quite clear that he takes *all* thinking to have a determinate and thus immaterial aspect, and not merely the kind we typically characterize as formal (viz. logic and mathematics).[30] But the determinacy is much easier to

---

28 We are now in a position to note, however, how the term "intentional" is used by Scholastics in discussions of cognition in a sense crucially different from, though not entirely unrelated to, that which is typical in contemporary philosophy of mind. On Scholastic usage, when we draw a circle on paper (for example) the form of circularity can be said to exist in the natural order; whereas when we conceptualize the object so drawn as a circle, the same form can be said to exist in the intentional order. But to say that it exists in the intentional order is not *merely* to say that we are in a state that is "directed at" or "points to" circularity. Also in view is the distinctively *conceptual* aspect of the mental act (which is not present in a dog which sees or imagines the circle, even though the dog might perceive it as a dog food bowl and thereby be in a state which "points to" it as an end to be pursued).

29 Dillard, "Two Unsuccessful Arguments for Immaterialism," p. 270.

30 Ross, "Immaterial Aspects of Thought," pp. 149–50. Cf. Ross, *Thought and World*, 123. As Ross indicates, even in the case of non-logical and non-mathematical examples, the determinacy of thought has to do with its form.

demonstrate in the case of logical and mathematical examples, and so they are the focus of his argument.

We'll return to the first premise. Ross's defense of the second is, as I have indicated, related to the points Scholastic writers often make about the indeterminacy of mental images. Evincing the Platonic origins of the type of critique of materialism that we are examining, such authors call attention to (say) the vagueness and particularity of mental images of geometrical figures as contrasted with the perfect determinacy and universality of the figures themselves, and therefore of our concepts of them.[31] It would follow that since anything material is as indeterminate and particular as mental images are, concepts can no more be identified with anything material than they can be identified with images. Similarly, Ross argues that "just as rectangular doors can approximate Euclidean rectangularity, so physical change can simulate pure functions but cannot realize them."[32] But it is indeed functions and the like that Ross focuses on, rather than geometrical figures, numbers, or the other sorts of examples the Scholastic writers cited earlier emphasize. This may reflect an intention directly to counter the functionalism dominant in contemporary materialist philosophy of mind, according to (one version of) which mental states are to be modeled on the functional states of a computer. It also reflects the centrality of Kripke's "quus" example to Ross's argument.

Now, Kripke was putting forward an interpretation of what he took to be the central argument of Wittgenstein's *Philosophical Investigations*, and his interpretation is famously controversial. But like many other commentators, Ross ignores questions of Wittgenstein exegesis and considers Kripke's ideas for their own intrinsic significance and interest. The line from Wittgenstein that forms the takeoff point for Kripke's discussion is the following:

> This was our paradox: no course of action could be determined
> by a rule, because every course of action can be made out to ac-
> cord with the rule.[33]

So, suppose you had never computed any numbers as high as 57, but are asked to compute "68 + 57." You answer "125," confident not only that this

31   Some readers might question the validity of the "therefore." But the inference is valid. I'll address this issue in the next section.
32   Ross, "Immaterial Aspects of Thought," p. 141.
33   Ludwig Wittgenstein, *Philosophical Investigations*, Third edition, translated by G. E. M. Anscombe (New York: Macmillan, 1968), sec. 201.

is the arithmetically correct answer, but also that it is correct in the sense that it accords with the way you have always used "plus," viz. to denote the addition function, which, when applied to the numbers you call "68" and "57," yields 125. But now, Kripke says, imagine that a bizarre skeptic asks how you can be certain that this is really what you meant in the past, and therefore how you can be certain that "125" is really the correct answer. Perhaps, he suggests, the function you really meant in the past by "plus" and "+" was not addition, but rather what Kripke calls the "quus" function, which can be defined as follows:

$$x \text{ quus } y = x + y, \text{ if } x, y < 57;$$
$$= 5 \text{ otherwise.}$$

Hence, perhaps you have always been carrying out "quaddition" rather than addition, since quadding and adding numbers will always yield the same result when the numbers are smaller than 57. That means that now that you are computing "68 + 57," the correct answer should be "5" rather than "125"; and perhaps you think otherwise because you are now misinterpreting all your previous usages of "plus." Obviously, this seems absurd. But how do you know the skeptic is wrong?[34]

Kripke argues that any evidence you could appeal to in order to prove that you meant addition is evidence that is consistent with your really having meant quaddition. For instance, it is no good to appeal to the fact that you have always *said* "Two plus two equals four" and never "Two quus two equals four," because what is at issue is what you *meant* by "plus." It could be, the skeptic says, that every time you said "plus" you meant "quus," and every time you said "addition" you meant "quaddition." But neither will it help to appeal to your memories of what was going on in your mind when you said things like "Two plus two equals four." Even if the words "I mean *plus* by 'plus,' and not 'quus'!" had passed through your mind, that would only raise the question of what you meant by *that*. So, Kripke's skeptic concludes, there is nothing that can possibly determine that it was indeed addition rather than quaddition that you had in mind when you used "plus" in the past. And in that case there really is no fact of the matter at all about what you meant.

Notice that it is irrelevant that most of us have in fact computed numbers higher than 57; for any given person there is always *some* number, even

---

34   Kripke, *Wittgenstein on Rules and Private Language*, pp. 7–9.

if extremely large, equal to or higher than which he has never calculated, and Kripke's skeptic can run the argument using that number instead. Notice also the skeptic's point can be made about what you mean *now* by "plus"; for all of your current linguistic behavior and what is now running through your mind, the skeptic can ask whether you mean by it addition or quaddition. Indeed, a similar point can be made about what you have meant in the past, and what you mean now, by *any* term, for a parallel skeptical scenario can be constructed for any term. It is always possible in principle that we are and always have really been following some rule for using a word other than the one we say we are following. But then there is no fact of the matter about what we mean by any word. The very notion of meaning seems to disintegrate.

In the next section we'll consider the solutions to this paradox that Kripke considers and rejects, and the "skeptical solution" he attributes to Wittgenstein. For the moment let's briefly consider the related arguments put forward by Quine and Goodman. The latter's "grue" paradox might not at first glance seem directly relevant to the issues Ross is concerned with, but Kripke's discussion of Goodman (which no doubt influenced Ross) shows how it is relevant. Goodman asks us to consider the predicate "grue," which applies to any thing before some time *t* just in case it is green, and to every other thing just in case it is blue. Any evidence we have prior to *t* that a thing is green is also evidence that it is grue.[35] Now Goodman's interest in this predicate has to do with the puzzle it raises about induction, which indeed is not something we are concerned with here. But as Kripke notes, the "grue" example provides an illustration of how what we mean when using color words is open to the same sort of skeptical doubt raised in the "quus" example. For just as all the evidence is (so the skeptic argues) compatible with the supposition that I have always meant quus when using "plus," so too is it compatible with the supposition that I have always meant grue when using "green."[36]

Quine's thought experiment involves a field linguist attempting to translate a native's utterance of "gavagai" in the presence of a rabbit. He could take the correct translation to be "Lo, a rabbit!," and might construct a manual of translation of the native's entire language that is consistent with this translation. But in principle he might replace "rabbit" with either "undetached rabbit part" or "temporal stage of a rabbit," and construct

---

35 Goodman, *Fact, Fiction, and Forecast*, p. 74.
36 Kripke, *Wittgenstein on Rules and Private Language*, pp. 20 and 58–59.

alternate manuals of translation each consistent with one of these possible translations.[37] Quine argues that there is nothing in the native's linguistic behavior that can determine which of these three alternative translation schemes is correct. But there is, in Quine's view, no evidence to go on other than the behavioral evidence. Hence there is *no fact of the matter* about which translation is correct, and the meaning of the utterance is indeterminate. The example is exotic, but the point applies equally well to the translation of anyone's speech. Indeed, as John Searle has emphasized, given Quine's behaviorist assumptions, there is no difference in principle between Quine's example and the first-person case in which one considers what one means by one's *own* words.[38] There will be alternative interpretations of one's own use of "rabbit" that are all equally compatible with one's behavioral dispositions. And in that case there is no fact of the matter about what one means.

Now as Kripke points out, a non-behaviorist could take this to be merely a *reductio ad absurdum* of Quine's behaviorist approach to language (as, indeed, Searle does).[39] By contrast, the upshot of the argument Kripke attributes to Wittgenstein, Kripke tells us, is that even an appeal to the introspection of one's mental states won't solve the problem raised by Quine.[40] For the evidence available from the "first-person" point of view, which Searle thinks suffices to refute Quine, is as indeterminate as the "third-person" behavioral evidence. In this way Kripke's indeterminacy results, being grounded in less controversial assumptions than those of Quine and more directly relevant to the subject at hand than those of Goodman, is more crucial to Ross's case. As I have said, Dillard, when criticizing Ross, is right to put special emphasis on the relevance of Kripke, and Ross could have been more careful in his use of all of these writers. Indeed, it might seem that Kripke's example *undermines* rather than supports Ross's argument. For again, Kripke emphasizes that the indeterminacy his skeptic wants to call our attention to applies to the *mental* realm no less than to our linguistic behavior. And doesn't Ross's entire case rest on the claim that the mental is determinate in a way the physical is not?

---

37 Quine, *Word and Object*, p. 51f.
38 John R. Searle, "Indeterminacy, Empiricism, and the First Person," in *Consciousness and Language* (Cambridge: Cambridge University Press, 2002). Cf. W. V. Quine, *Ontological Relativity and Other Essays* (New York: Columbia University Press, 1969), pp. 47–48.
39 Kripke, *Wittgenstein on Rules and Private Language*, 57.
40 Ibid., pp. 14–15 and 55–57.

But Ross's argument is not so easily undermined, though Ross himself could have been clearer about the reason why. Wittgenstein, and Kripke in interpreting him, are especially keen to emphasize the irrelevance of *private sensations* to the determination of linguistic meaning. For example, an appeal to a subjective sensation or mental image of green is not going to suffice to determine that it is indeed *green* rather than *grue* that one meant when using the expression "green." Now as Warren Goldfarb points out, this sort of point cuts no ice against an account of meaning like the one put forward by Gottlob Frege.[41] Frege emphasized that the sense of an expression is not a private psychological entity such as a sensation or mental image, any more than it is something material.[42] Thus he would hardly take an argument to the effect that meaning cannot be fixed either by sensations and mental images or by bodily behavior to establish that there is no determinate meaning at all. Now Frege conceived of the sense of an expression in Platonist terms, while Ross's position is Aristotelian. But he would no doubt say something similar in response. I noted above that Scholastic Aristotelian writers distinguished intellectual activity or thought in the strict sense from sensation and mental imagery, and that they regarded the latter as bodily. Ross, who is writing in the same tradition, would surely agree, and would thus be untroubled by Kripke's point that sensations and mental images do not suffice to fix the meaning of our thoughts and utterances. For they are not among the aspects of thought that he is arguing must be immaterial.

To be sure, Kripke also says some things intended to cast doubt on the suggestion that mental activity of some other kind might determine meaning. We'll come to that in the next section. To reinforce the claim that *material* processes cannot in any case determine meaning, Ross, again following Kripke, notes that there are no physical features of an adding machine, calculator, or computer that can determine whether it is carrying out addition or quaddition, no matter how far we extend its outputs.[43] As Kripke emphasized, appealing to the intentions of the programmer will not solve the problem, because that just raises the question of whether the programmer really had addition or quaddition in mind, as in the original paradox. But

---

41 Warren Goldfarb, "Kripke on Wittgenstein on Rules," *Journal of Philosophy* LXXXII (1985): 471–88. Cf. the discussion of Wittgenstein and Kripke in Jerrold J. Katz, *The Metaphysics of Meaning* (Cambridge, MA: The MIT Press, 1990), especially at pp. 158–61 and 164.

42 Gottlob Frege, "The Thought: A Logical Inquiry," *Mind* 65 (1956): 289–311.

43 Ross, "Immaterial Aspects of Thought," pp. 141–44; Kripke, *Wittgenstein on Rules and Private Language*, pp. 32–37.

Kripke makes a deeper point. No matter what the past behavior of a machine has been, we can always suppose that its *next* output—"5," say, when calculating numbers larger than any it has calculated before—might show that it is carrying out something like quaddition rather than addition. Now it might be said in response that if this happens, that would just show that the machine was *malfunctioning* rather than performing quaddition. But Kripke points out that whether some output counts as a malfunction depends on what program the machine is running, and whether the machine is running the program for addition rather than quaddition is precisely what is in question. We might find out by asking the programmer, but there is nothing in *the physical properties of the machine itself* that can tell us.[44]

Let's turn now to Ross's defense of the first premise of his basic argument, viz. the claim that *all formal thinking is determinate*. Adding, squaring, inferring via *modus ponens*, syllogistic reasoning, and the like are some of the examples of formal thinking Ross appeals to. Anyone who agrees that material processes are indeterminate in the way Kripke's and Quine's arguments imply but who wants to avoid the conclusion that thought is immaterial will have to deny that any of our thoughts is ever determinate in its content; and writers like Bernard Williams and Daniel Dennett essentially do deny this.[45] But then they will also have to deny that our thoughts are ever really determinate of any of the forms just cited. They will have to maintain that we only ever *approximate* adding, squaring, inferring via *modus ponens*, etc. "Now that," Ross says, "is expensive. In fact, the cost of saying we only simulate the pure functions is astronomical."[46]

In particular, Ross identifies four problems with the suggestion that we only ever approximate adding, squaring, *modus ponens*, etc. (Some of these

---

44 Kripke extended this line of argument into a critique of functionalism, though the critique was only developed in some unpublished lectures and is merely hinted at in *Wittgenstein on Rules and Private Language* (at pp. 36–37). For a useful discussion of this unpublished material, see Jeff Buechner, "Not Even Computing Machines Can Follow Rules: Kripke's Critique of Functionalism," in Alan Berger, ed., *Saul Kripke* (Cambridge: Cambridge University Press, 2011).

45 See Bernard Williams, *Descartes: The Project of Pure Inquiry* (London: Penguin Books, 1978), p. 300, and Daniel C. Dennett, "Evolution, Error, and Intentionality," in Dennett's *The Intentional Stance* (Cambridge, MA: The MIT Press, 1989). Cf. Dennett's *Darwin's Dangerous Idea* (New York: Simon and Schuster, 1995), chapter 14. In addition to Quine, Dennett identifies Paul and Patricia Churchland, Donald Davidson, John Haugeland, Ruth Millikan, Richard Rorty, Wilfrid Sellars, and Robert Stalnaker as philosophers who essentially take the same position.

46 Ross, "Immaterial Aspects of Thought," pp. 145–46.

are only hinted at, but what I will have to say in developing them is, I think, faithful to Ross's intentions.) The first is that it is just prima facie wildly implausible to suggest that whenever we have taken ourselves to add, square, draw a *modus ponens* inference, etc., we have been mistaken and have not really done so at all. Of course, Ross's critic might just dig in his heels and insist that we have to bite this particular bullet, but this would be plausible only if the considerations in favor of his bizarre position were more obviously correct than is our commonsense conviction that we do indeed often add, square, apply *modus ponens*, etc. And why should we believe that?

Second, it isn't just common sense that the critic's view conflicts with. The claim that we never really add, apply *modus ponens*, etc. is hard to square with the existence of the vast body of knowledge that comprises the disciplines of mathematics and logic. Nor is it just that mathematics and logic constitute genuine bodies of knowledge in their own right; they are also presupposed by the natural sciences. Now it is in the name of natural science that philosophers like Quine and Dennett draw the extreme conclusions about the indeterminacy of meaning that they do. But if natural science presupposes mathematics and logic and mathematics and logic presuppose that we do indeed have determinate thought processes, it is hard to see how they can consistently draw this conclusion.[47]

A third and related problem is that if we never really apply *modus ponens* or any other valid argument form, but at best only approximate them, then *none of our arguments is ever really valid*. That includes the arguments of those, like Quine and Dennett, who say that none of our thoughts is really determinate in content. Hence the view is self-defeating. Even if it were true, we could never be rationally justified in believing that it is true, because we couldn't be rationally justified in believing *anything*.

Fourth, the claim that we never really add, square, apply *modus ponens*, etc. is self-defeating in an even more direct and fatal way. For coherently to deny that we ever really do these things presupposes that we have a grasp of what it would be to do them. And that means having thoughts of a form as determinate as those the critic says we do not have. In particular, to deny that we ever really add requires that we determinately grasp what it is to add and then go on to deny that we really ever do it; to deny that we ever really apply *modus ponens* requires that we determinately grasp what it is to reason via *modus ponens* and then go on to deny that we ever really do that; and so forth. Yet the whole point of denying that we ever really add, apply *modus*

---

47   Cf. Maher, *Psychology: Empirical and Rational*, 238.

ponens, etc. was to avoid having to admit that we at least sometimes have determinate thought processes. So, to deny that we have them presupposes that we have them. It cannot coherently be done.

And so we have Ross's argument: Material processes cannot be determinate, as many materialists themselves acknowledge on the basis of arguments like those of Quine and Kripke; but at least some thought processes are determinate, as is evidenced by the fact that the very act of denying that they are commits us implicitly to affirming that they are; therefore, such thought processes are immaterial.

IV. The objections of Pasnau, Leftow, and Dillard

Robert Pasnau has raised an objection to one of Aquinas's arguments for the immortality of the human soul which might seem applicable to Ross's argument as well.[48] Aquinas writes:

> It is also evident that an intellective principle of this sort is not a thing composed of matter and form, because the species of things are received in it in an absolutely immaterial way, as is shown by the fact that the intellect knows universals, which are considered in abstraction from matter and from material conditions. The sole conclusion to be drawn from all this, then, is that the intellective principle, by which man understands, is a form having its act of existing in itself. Therefore this principle must be incorruptible.[49]

Pasnau claims that this passage commits what he calls the "content fallacy," which involves "conflating two kinds of facts: facts about the content of our thoughts, and facts about what shape or form our thoughts take in our mind."[50] A crude example of such a conflation would be reasoning from *Bob is thinking about a red sports car* to the conclusion that *Bob's thought is red*. In the passage at hand, Pasnau says, Aquinas's "conclusion pertains

---

48   Robert Pasnau, "Aquinas and the Content Fallacy," *The Modern Schoolman* LXXV (1998): 293–314; Cf. Pasnau, *Thomas Aquinas on Human Nature* (Cambridge: Cambridge University Press, 2002), pp. 315–16.

49   *Quaestiones disputatae de anima* XIV, as translated by John Patrick Rowan in *The Soul: A Translation of St. Thomas Aquinas's* De Anima (St. Louis: B. Herder, 1949), at p. 182.

50   Pasnau, "Aquinas and the Content Fallacy," p. 293.

to intellect's intrinsic qualities: being immaterial and hence incorruptible," and this is "inferred from intellect's intentional qualities: being 'concerned with universals.'"[51] In other words, Aquinas (so Pasnau seems to be claiming) is fallaciously inferring from the premise that *The intellect grasps universals, which are immaterial and incorruptible* to the conclusion that *The intellect is immaterial and incorruptible*. Now Ross might seem to be committing a similar fallacy. In particular, it might seem that he is reasoning from a premise like *Formal thought processes are about determinate functions like adding*, modus ponens, *etc., which are immaterial* to the conclusion that *Formal thought processes are immaterial*.[52]

But Ross is committing no such fallacy, and neither is Aquinas for that matter. Certainly there is a more charitable way to read them. I would suggest that they are both reasoning in something like the following way:

> The objects of thought have property X, which entails that they are immaterial.
> But thought itself also has property X.
> So thought must also be immaterial.

And this argument form is valid. For Aquinas, the X in question *universality*, and for Ross the X is *determinacy*. Aquinas can be read as saying that, just as the universal *circle* applies to every circle without exception, so too do the *thoughts* we have about circles (when doing geometry, say) apply to every circle without exception; and just as the former could not do so if it were material, neither could the latter. Ross can be read as saying that, just as the abstract form of inference *modus ponens* as studied in logic is determinate, so too do we have thoughts that are determinately of that form; and just as the former could not be determinate if it were material, neither could the latter.[53]

---

51 Ibid., p. 304.
52 To be sure, Pasnau does not accuse Ross of committing this fallacy. Indeed, a passing reference to Ross's argument in Pasnau's book *Thomas Aquinas on Human Nature* is positive, if noncommittal (411). But when I have cited Ross's argument in other contexts, Pasnau's "content fallacy" objection has sometimes been raised against it.
53 For somewhat different defenses of Aquinas against Pasnau's objection, see John Haldane, "The Metaphysics of Intellect(ion)," *Proceedings of the American Catholic Philosophical Association* 80 (2006): 39–55, at 51–53; and Gyula Klima, "Aquinas on the Materiality of the Human Soul and the Immateriality of the Human Intellect," *Philosophical Investigations* 32 (2009): 163–82, at 175–76.

Brian Leftow cites Ross's argument explicitly in the course of discussing Aquinas, and tentatively suggests a possible difficulty.[54] Quinean considerations of the sort raised by Ross do indeed imply, Leftow allows, that the content of our thoughts cannot be determined by physical processes in the brain. But a materialist who endorses an externalist theory of content could accept this consistent with maintaining his materialism: "Information not present in the brain could be present in a physical sum, the brain plus its physical environment."[55] One problem with this objection is that it fails to see that Quine himself has already addressed it insofar as he notes that a native's utterance of "gavagai" is indeterminate between alternative translations *even given* the facts about his environment that the field linguist has to go on. Scholastic writers of the sort considered earlier might point out in addition that even if we consider material reality as a whole, we will never find within it either a perfect instantiation of triangularity, or all possible instantiations of triangularity, or a symbol or set of symbols with a unique causal relationship to triangularity as opposed to trilaterality. Hence we will never find within it anything with the determinacy and universality of our concept *triangularity*.

A response to Leftow closer to Ross's own manner of arguing is suggested by Kripke's point about adding machines. For any such machine, we can always ask whether a given output is a malfunction. Perhaps what we take to be an output consistent with the machine's adding is really a malfunction in a machine that is "quadding" instead. Nothing in the physical aspects of the machine itself can tell us, and this will be true no matter how large or complex the machine is. But then, if we think of an individual's brain and the various parts of his environment as related like the parts of the machine, then even if that environment includes the entire physical universe, there will be nothing in the collection of these physical facts *itself* to tell us whether the individual's next utterance really is an expression of addition rather than a malfunction in a system that is really carrying out quaddition.[56]

---

54   Brian Leftow, "Soul, Mind, and Brain," in Robert C. Koons and George Bealer, eds., *The Waning of Materialism* (Oxford: Oxford University Press, 2010).

55   Ibid., p. 410.

56   Of course, an Aristotelian will not regard either the brain or a human being of which the brain is an organ as in every relevant respect comparable to a computer, since the latter is an artifact whose parts do not have the kind of organic relationship to one another that the parts of a living thing do. But we are not here comparing the brain or a human being to a computer, but rather the brain or human being *together*

Now Peter Dillard, as I have said, takes issue with Ross's use of Kripke, specifically. And as we have seen, there are aspects of Kripke's discussion whose relationship to Ross's argument could have been more directly and carefully addressed by Ross. But Dillard himself does not seem to have read Kripke, or Ross for that matter, as carefully as *he* could have. For instance, taking an example from computer science, Dillard says that there is a determinate difference between an and-gate, an or-gate, and other logic gates, which falsifies Ross's claim that physical phenomena are inherently indeterminate.[57] But this simply ignores Kripke's point that whether a machine has certain computational properties—in this case, whether a given electrical circuit really instantiates an and-gate or is instead malfunctioning—is not something that can be read off from the physical properties of the circuit itself, but depends on the intentions of the designer.[58] It also ignores the related Aristotelian point that a computer is an artifact, whose functional features are imposed from outside and not intrinsic to it in the way the teleological features of a natural substance are intrinsic to it. Dillard, who elsewhere calls attention to Ross's Aristotelian commitments, should have realized that such a reply is open to Ross.

Dillard also suggests that Kripke's point is epistemological rather than metaphysical — that his argument shows at most only that the claim that someone is thinking in accordance with a certain function (such as addition) is underdetermined by the physical evidence, and not that the physical facts are themselves indeterminate.[59] This is odd given that both Kripke and Ross explicitly insist that the points they are respectively making are metaphysical rather than merely epistemological.[60] Indeed, Kripke says that "not even what an omniscient God would know ... could establish whether I meant

with the various aspects of its physical environment to a computer. And those aspects of the environment are not related to an individual human being or his brain in the organic way that the parts of a living thing are related to one another.

57 Dillard, "Two Unsuccessful Arguments for Immaterialism," pp. 274–75.

58 Cf. John Searle's point that computational properties are not intrinsic to the physics of a system but are imposed on the physics from outside by designers and users. See John R. Searle, "Is the Brain a Digital Computer?" in *Philosophy in a New Century: Selected Essays* (Cambridge: Cambridge University Press, 2008); and chapter 9 of Searle's *The Rediscovery of the Mind* (Cambridge, MA: The MIT Press, 1992).

59 Dillard, "Two Unsuccessful Arguments for Immaterialism," p. 273.

60 Kripke, *Wittgenstein on Rules and Private Language*, pp. 21 and 39; Ross, *Thought and World*, pp. 119–20. In fairness to Dillard, it should be noted that he makes no reference to Ross's *Thought and World* and relies entirely on Ross's earlier discussion in "Immaterial Aspects of Thought."

plus or quus,"[61] because for the reasons given above, everything about my past behavior, sensations, and the like is compatible (not just compatible *as far as we know*, but compatible *full stop*) with my meaning either plus or quus. Nor does Dillard say anything to show otherwise.

A more interesting objection raised by Dillard is the suggestion that Ross's commitment to the Aristotelian-Scholastic view that causal powers as "directed toward" the generation of their typical effects (a view we had reason to discuss above) is inconsistent with his claim that physical processes are inherently indeterminate. For isn't (say) a match's tendency to produce flame and heat, specifically, an instance of a determinate physical process?[62] But the objection fails, in part for reasons Ross himself indicates. For the Aristotelian, a thing has the causal powers it has only because of its form. But forms don't exist in the material world as pristine Platonic universals; they are, for the Aristotelian, always individualized, with all the limitations and imperfections that that entails, and what is universal is only the form as abstracted by an intellect. And the same holds for pure functions, whether the sort we have already called attention to (adding, squaring, *modus ponens*, etc.) or the sort enshrined in the equations of the physicist. Ross writes:

> Physical phenomena often come close to our mathematizations that, of course, are invented to represent them. But those mathematizations are *idealizations* …[63]
>
> [N]ature is rich in intelligible, active structures for which humans have a natural abstractive aptitude. [But] such structures are materialized and not pure functions. Humans can find pure functions that many such processes *approximate*.[64]

Consequently, the causal powers a material thing possesses by virtue of instantiating a certain form or pure function are also approximations to an idealization, and thus indeterminate.

Dillard misses this point because, as with his remarks about Kripke, he fails to see that it is metaphysics rather than epistemology that is at issue, and insists that all that Ross can claim is that scientific theory is underdetermined

---

61 Kripke, *Wittgenstein on Rules and Private Language*, p. 21.
62 Dillard, "Two Unsuccessful Arguments for Immaterialism," p. 275.
63 Ross, *Thought and World*, p. 199, n. 20. Emphasis added.
64 Ibid., p. 198, n. 16; Cf. p. 121. Emphasis added.

by evidence.[65] But when your geometry teacher notes that perfect circularity does not exist in the material world, it would be absurd to suggest that the point is *epistemological*—that while the evidence underdetermines the thesis that there is such a thing as perfect circularity in the material world, perhaps it does exist there somewhere after all. Similarly, when Kripke points out that there is nothing in the physical properties of an adding machine that can tell us whether it is adding or quadding, and that we must appeal to the intentions of the programmer to find out, it would be absurd to suggest that *this* point is merely epistemological, a matter of underdetermination of theory by evidence rather than of indeterminacy. Ross's point about the relationship between concrete physical processes and the idealized pure functions they approximate is in the same way a metaphysical rather than epistemological point. As he says of the Kripkean argument about adding machines, "that's the same sort of reasoning that Plato used to argue that spatiotemporal things can only imitate, imperfectly copy, the ideal Forms."[66] Of course, the position Ross ends up with is Aristotelian rather than Platonic, but the point is that forms as idealized universals, whether conceived of as existing in a Platonic third realm or only as abstracted by an intellect, are determinate in a way concrete particular things are not. While the point has epistemological implications, it is not itself merely epistemological.

Another problem with Dillard's attempt to use the Aristotelian-Scholastic view of causal powers against Ross is one that Dillard himself inadvertently hints at when he alludes to the distinction between natural powers and rational powers.[67] For the Scholastic, a dog and a human being both looking

---

65 Dillard, "Two Unsuccessful Arguments for Immaterialism," pp. 273–74. In fairness to Dillard, Ross's reference in "Immaterial Aspects of Thought" to "underdetermination arguments" in the context of discussing the idealized character of equations (p. 145) facilitates this misunderstanding, since "underdetermination" is usually used in epistemological contexts to connote to a failure of evidence to support one theory to the exclusion of others. And Ross admittedly doesn't always make it sufficiently explicit how underdetermination of the sort he is interested in entails indeterminacy. But it is worth comparing the passage in "Immaterial Aspects of Thought" that exercises Dillard (which is at pp. 144–45 of Ross's article) with the later parallel passage in *Thought and World* (pp. 120–21). In the former, Ross does give the impression that it is underdetermination *rather than* the idealized nature of the physicist's equations that is relevant to his point. But this implication is absent in the latter, where the idealized character of the physicist's equations is clearly presented in support of Ross's argument. And as indicated above, Ross makes it clear that his point is "not just an epistemic claim" (*Thought and World*, p. 119).

66 Ross, *Thought and World*, p. 120.

67 Dillard, "Two Unsuccessful Arguments for Immaterialism," p. 275, n. 17.

at the same food are each in a perceptual state that is "directed at" the food. But there is a *conceptual* element to the human being's perceptual experience of the food that isn't present in the case of the dog. The dog's causal powers, however complex relative to those of non-sentient material substances, are nevertheless sub-rational. To borrow an example from Hilary Putnam, suppose it is suggested that a certain neural "data structure" evolved in dogs to facilitate their getting meat, and that this justifies us in attributing to them a concept or "proto-concept" of meat.[68] As Putnam points out, the dog will be satisfied and nourished whether it is given fresh meat, canned meat, or some textured vegetable protein that looks, smells, and tastes exactly like meat. For that reason, there is no fact of the matter about whether its putative "proto-concept" represents any one of these in particular, and thus no sense to be made of the question of whether the dog has a true belief about what it is eating when it eats the vegetable protein rather than meat. "Evolution didn't 'design' dogs' ideas to be true or false, it designed them to be successful or unsuccessful."[69] But in that case the suggestion that the dog really *has* a "proto-concept" of meat in the first place is groundless:

> [T]he whole idea that a unique correspondence between the data structure and meat is involved in this bit of natural selection is an illusion, an artifact of the way we described the situation. We could just as well have said that the data structure was selected for because its action normally signals the presence of something which has a certain smell and taste and appearance and is edible.[70]

In short, there is nothing in the situation described that entails that anything in the dog's brain corresponds to *meat* specifically, and thus there is nothing in the situation that entails that the dog has a *concept* (or "proto-concept") of meat. The point is completely general, applying to *any* concept. What a dog's neural wiring and corresponding perceptual experiences facilitate is survival, not truth or falsity. Hence we are not going to read off true or false beliefs from a dog's neural-cum-perceptual states, and neither will we read

68   Hilary Putnam, *Renewing Philosophy* (Cambridge, MA: Harvard University Press, 1992, pp. 27–33.

69   Ibid., p. 31.

70   Ibid.

off from them the *concepts* that true or false beliefs presuppose. It follows that, contra Dillard, the existence in purely material substances of causal powers which are directed toward certain outcomes does not suffice for the kind of determinacy characteristic of concepts.[71]

Now the solution to his "quus" paradox that Kripke himself takes the most seriously is the one he (controversially) attributes to Wittgenstein, the so-called "skeptical solution." The skeptical solution concedes that there is no fact of the matter about what we mean by "plus," and thus no way to give *truth-conditions* for the claim that by "plus" one means addition. It is then suggested that we can nevertheless give *assertibility-conditions* for this claim, and that these conditions are to be found in what a linguistic community actually agrees upon. That you mean addition rather than quaddition by "plus" is just a matter of your using "plus" in a way that the linguistic community counts as addition.[72] Dillard suggests that Ross's argument might be resisted simply by denying his first premise—that formal thinking is determinate—and embracing instead Kripke's skeptical solution, or the related Quinean view that to count a speaker's usage of "plus" as addition is just to note that his usage does not elicit "bizarreness reactions" in his fellow language users.[73]

Now as we have already seen, Ross argues that it is simply self-defeating to deny that our formal thought processes are determinate. Dillard offers no response to this other than the insinuation that by biting the bullet, the Kripkean or Quinean can stalemate Ross. But the views are *not* thereby left at a stalemate, for that would require that each view is at least internally consistent and thus as coherent as its rival, and neither Kripke's skeptical solution nor Quine's position *is* coherent. For one thing, and as John Searle has emphasized, both Kripke and Quine have implicitly to presuppose precisely what they deny. Even to get his "gavagai" scenario off the ground, Quine has to presuppose that we can understand the difference between meaning *rabbit* by "rabbit" and meaning *undetached rabbit part* by "rabbit," at least in our own case.[74] Something similar could be said about the

---

71 That directedness does not entail determinacy should be obvious enough from the existence of vague and ambiguous expressions. Such expressions "point" to a certain possible range of meanings—a large range in the case of vague expressions, a smaller one in the case of ambiguous ones—but not determinately to any particular meaning within the range.

72 Kripke, *Wittgenstein on Rules and Private Language*, chapter 3.

73 Dillard, "Two Unsuccessful Arguments for Immaterialism," pp. 277–78.

74 Searle, "Indeterminacy, Empiricism, and the First Person," p. 234.

difference between adding and quadding in Kripke's example. Indeed, Kripke himself insists that "the skeptical problem indicates no vagueness in the *concept* of addition ... or in the word 'plus', *granting* its usual meaning" and that, again, granting this meaning, "the word 'plus' denotes a function whose determination is *completely* precise."[75] (This is obviously related to Ross's point that we have to have a determinate grasp of what addition, *modus ponens*, etc. are even to deny that we have such a grasp.) And as Searle points out, Kripke's skeptical solution presupposes that I can know what I mean by "agreement" with the community (though given the skeptical paradox, *how* do I know that by "agreement" I really do mean *agreement* rather than *quagreement*?)[76]

For another thing, as Ross points out, to deny that our thoughts are ever determinate is to deny that we ever really reason validly. Now, both Kripke and Quine are eminent logicians, and paradigmatic analytic philosophers who would not be caught dead putting forward a bold philosophical thesis without claiming to be able to give a solid argument for it. And yet their position entails that there are no solid arguments for any philosophical position, including their own. How can it seriously be maintained that such a position stalemates Ross's?

As Thomas Nagel has argued, what Kripke's argument really amounts to is a *reductio ad absurdum* of the reductionist assumption that meaning must somehow be explicable in terms of something else—behavior, physiology, mental imagery, dispositions, or what have you.[77] Now Kripke has a response to the suggestion that meaning something by a word is *sui generis* and not to be assimilated to sensations, dispositions, or the like, and it is a response Dillard seems to think effectively rebuts Ross's argument:

> Such a move may in a sense be irrefutable ... But it seems desperate: it leaves the nature of this postulated primitive state—the primitive state of 'meaning addition by "plus"'—completely mysterious ... Such a state would have to be a finite object, contained in our finite minds ... Can we conceive of a finite state

---

75   Kripke, *Wittgenstein on Rules and Private Language*, p. 82.
76   John R. Searle, "Skepticism About Rules and Intentionality," in Searle's *Consciousness and Language* (Cambridge, MA: Cambridge University Press, 2002), p. 260. Thomas Nagel makes a similar point about "fact," "word," "mean," and other terms needed even to state the skeptical paradox and its solution. See *The Last Word* (Oxford: Oxford University Press, 1997), p. 44.
77   Nagel, *The Last Word*, pp. 41–47.

which *could* not be interpreted in a quus-like way? How could that be?[78]

Glossing Kripke's objection, G. W. Fitch characterizes the suggestion that meaning is *sui generis* as an appeal to a "brute fact."[79] Arif Ahmed suggests that Kripke's objections to explaining meaning by reference to sensations or mental images would apply to any appeal to a *sui generis* state as well.[80]

But all of this simply begs the question against the view that meaning is *sui generis*. Fitch's and Ahmed's claims presuppose that the *sui generis* state in question is one that could at least in principle come apart from meaning addition. They presuppose that there are *two* things in question here—the state itself and a certain content, where it is a "brute fact" that the two are conjoined in a particular case, and where we can imagine a case where the state exists with some different content instead. But that is precisely what the *sui generis* view denies. It holds that we should *not* think of meaning something by a word as an otherwise content-free mental state which has somehow been fitted with a detachable content. Similarly, when Kripke alleges that the view is "mysterious," he seems to assume that a *non*-mysterious view would be one that reduces meaning to something else—again, to behavior, sensations, dispositions, or what have you. And that too is just what the view of meaning as *sui generis* denies. Kripke and his commentators Fitch and Ahmed really offer no *argument* against the *sui generis* view. They merely express an undefended prejudice in favor of a reductionist approach, and pretend that it constitutes an objection.

It is, in any event, quite rich for someone who says that our thoughts never have any determinate content—and therefore implies that we never really add, square, reason in accordance with *modus ponens*, etc. but only seem to—to accuse the other side of mystery-mongering! The retort open to Ross is obvious: We *know* that there must be such a thing as a *sui generis* state of meaning addition by "plus" (or of meaning something else by another word), because arguments like Kripke's show that denying that there is reduces to absurdity. Even if we are left with a sense of mystery about the nature of meaning, mystery is different from, and far better than, the self-defeating incoherence that Ross's critic is forced into.

78 Kripke, *Wittgenstein on Rules and Private Language*, 51-2. Cf. Dillard, "Two Unsuccessful Arguments for Immaterialism," pp. 276, n. 20 and 279.

79 G. W. Fitch, *Saul Kripke* (Montreal and Kingston: McGill-Queen's University Press, 2004), p. 153.

80 Arif Ahmed, *Saul Kripke* (London: Continuum, 2007), p. 122.

That there is nothing arbitrary or ad hoc about the *sui generis* response to arguments like Kripke's and Quine's is evidenced by the fact that Scholastic philosophers took something like that view, on independent grounds, long before the arguments in question came on the scene. For instance, following the *Ars Logica* of John of St. Thomas, Francis Parker and Henry Veatch distinguish between *material* (or *instrumental*) signs and *formal* signs.[81] A material sign is "double-natured"; that is to say, it "is a sign and also something else, namely, an entity in its own right."[82] The smoke that we take to be a sign of fire, the red and white striped pole that functions as a sign of a barber shop, and written and spoken words are all material signs in that they can be characterized entirely apart from their status as signs—in terms of their chemical composition, say, or texture, or shape. Formal signs, by contrast,

> do not have traits which must be known before their significance is known. They are not *means*—things which *have* meaning. They are themselves meanings; they are signs and nothing but signs ... [They] have no nature other than their signifying nature ... [83]

Examples would be concepts and propositions. Neither a concept nor a proposition has any nature other than being about whatever it is about. It makes sense to suppose that a material sign might not have been about anything. But it makes no sense to suppose that a concept or proposition might not have been about anything. These are signs that are *nothing but* signs.

Notice that this a perfectly natural distinction to draw, and one which has been drawn for centuries, just given what we know pre-theoretically about the difference between words, material symbols, and the like on the one hand and concepts and propositions on the other. There is also, if there were really any doubt about whether there are any formal signs, a fairly intuitive argument for their existence, one suggested by Parker and Veatch.[84] Precisely because material signs and their content are separable, we cannot read off the content from the nature they have apart from their status as signs, and have to determine their meaning by reference to other signs (as we do when we check a dictionary to see how one word is defined by

81   Francis H. Parker and Henry B. Veatch, *Logic as a Human Instrument* (New York: Harper and Brothers, 1959), pp. 16–22.
82   Ibid., pp. 16–17.
83   Ibid., p. 18.
84   Ibid., pp. 19–20. What follows is my paraphrase of their argument.

reference to other words). But if every sign were a material sign, we would be led into a vicious regress. Hence there must be signs which *just are* their meanings, and which therefore need not be known by reference to other signs and can serve as the terminus of explanation of those signs which do need to be explained by reference to others.

Now this notion of a formal sign corresponds more or less exactly to what Kripke calls a *sui generis* conception of meaning, a conception in which there is simply no gap between a sign and its content of the sort Kripke's skeptic needs in order to get his skepticism off the ground. Whatever one thinks of the notion, it is motivated independently of the desire ("desperate" or otherwise) to find a response to arguments like Kripke's. And its very existence obviously bolsters Ross's case. Not only can he argue that the *sui generis* conception of meaning is unavoidable if we want to avoid the self-defeating incoherence of Ross's critic; he can argue that there is in the notion of formal signs a preexisting, independently motivated account of meaning that corresponds to the *sui generis* conception, already waiting there "on the shelf" as it were rather than being concocted ad hoc. We had good reason to accept it even apart from the arguments of Quine, Kripke, and Co. Their arguments show it to be not merely worthy of consideration, but unavoidable on pain of incoherence.

V. Churchland, neuroscience, and the rational soul

Dillard will still object that Ross's position opens up "an apparently unbridgeable gulf between thought and behavior."[85] And materialists will insist that it does not sit well with what we know from modern neuroscience. In response it must, first of all, be reiterated that the Aristotelian-Scholastic tradition Ross represents does not deny that in the normal case material processes are *necessary* for thought, but only that they are *sufficient* for it.

To see how a human thought has, in the normal case, material aspects as well as the immaterial aspects we have been considering so far, consider *sentences*. The English sentence "Snow is white" conveys the same proposition whatever material form it takes, whether spoken, written, or typed into a word processor. The spoken, written, or typed German sentence "Schnee ist weiss" also conveys the very same proposition, and that proposition could be conveyed too not only in some other natural language but in even more exotic ways—through Esperanto, say, or encoded in some

---

85 Dillard, "Two Unsuccessful Arguments for Immaterialism," p. 279.

computer language. So, the propositional content of a sentence cannot be reduced to any of its material or linguistic properties. All the same, we typically convey and entertain a proposition via the *medium* of a sentence. As Frege put it: "The thought, in itself immaterial, clothes itself in the material garment of a sentence and thereby becomes comprehensible to us. We say a sentence expresses a thought."[86] We do not "see" propositions "naked," as it were; they rarely if ever leave the house except in sentential garb. Thus while what we grasp when we grasp the proposition that snow is white is not *identical* with the English sentence "Snow is white," what we grasp is nevertheless grasped *through* that English sentence (or through the German sentence "Schnee ist weiss" or a sentence of some other language).[87]

Now when the sentence is spoken, written, or typed, the material medium will be compression waves in the air, ink marks, pixels, or the like. When it is entertained mentally, the medium will be a phantasm or mental image (whether visual or auditory), and the Aristotelian-Scholastic tradition regards that as something material. The conveying or entertaining of concepts without putting them together into complete thoughts will not involve the use of sentences but it will still involve the use of either individual words, or pictures, symbols, or the like, whether written, spoken, drawn, or imagined. In this way our intellectual activity, though it cannot in principle be entirely material, is nevertheless always conducted through material media. As Aquinas writes:

> Although the intellect abstracts from the phantasms, it does not understand actually without turning to the phantasms.[88]
>
> [I]t is clear that for the intellect to understand actually, not only when it acquires fresh knowledge, but also when it applies knowledge already acquired, there is need for the act of the imagination and of the other powers. For when the act of the

---

86 Frege, "The Thought: A Logical Inquiry," p. 292.
87 This is not to say that the mental imagery involved in entertaining propositions *must specifically* involve auditory or visual imagery of words or sentences. As David Clemenson has pointed out to me, that claim would require further argumentation. For present purposes, we need not rule out the possibility that propositions could be entertained via other sorts of imagery. The point is just that the conscious entertaining of a sentence provides a vivid illustration of the way in which a thought has both immaterial and material aspects.
88 *Summa theologiae* I.85.5, as translated by the Fathers of the English Dominican Province in St. Thomas Aquinas, *Summa Theologica* (Notre Dame, IN: Christian Classics, 1981).

imagination is hindered by a lesion of the corporeal organ, for instance in a case of frenzy; or when the act of the memory is hindered, as in the case of lethargy, we see that a man is hindered from actually understanding things of which he had a previous knowledge.[89]

[I]n the present state of life whatever we understand, we know by comparison to natural sensible things. Consequently it is not possible for our intellect to form a perfect judgment, while the senses are suspended, through which sensible things are known to us.[90]

From an Aristotelian-Scholastic point of view, then, it is hardly surprising that modern neuroscience has uncovered intimate correlations between neural activity and mental activity, or that damage to the brain can severely impair thought—any more than it is surprising that if we physically damage a sentence, its ability to convey its propositional content is diminished or destroyed despite that content's being irreducible to the sentence's physical properties. For the Aristotelian or Thomist to acknowledge that there is a physiological component to thought is not to make a desperate concession to modern scientific advances. On the contrary, it is merely to reaffirm something that Aristotle and Aquinas themselves already recognized.

It must also be kept in mind that for the Aristotelian-Scholastic tradition, human beings and their operations are, like other natural substances and processes, to be analyzed in terms of formal, material, efficient and final causes, which together form an irreducible unity. In the case of a thought (such as the thought that snow is white) the neural processes associated with the relevant phantasms might be regarded as the material cause of a single event of which the intellective activity of the rational soul is the formal cause. To be sure, the analysis of human thought and action in terms of the Aristotelian four-causal explanatory framework is a more complicated business than that suggests. But it is only if that framework is rejected that to acknowledge that there are immaterial aspects of thought can seem to open up what Dillard calls "an apparently unbridgeable gulf between thought and behavior." And to reject it without argument would simply be to beg the question against the Aristotelian-Scholastic view.[91]

---

89   *Summa theologiae* I.84.7.
90   *Summa theologiae* I.84.8.
91   I provide an exposition and defense of the Aristotelian four-causal explanatory framework in *Aquinas* (Oxford: Oneworld Publications, 2009).

Having said all that, an implicit neuroscientific refutation of the main argument of this paper might nevertheless seem to be suggested by the sub-title of Paul M. Churchland's recent book *Plato's Camera: How the Physical Brain Captures a Landscape of Abstract Universals.*[92] Can it be that neuroscience has after all finally shown that something with the determinacy and strict universality of a concept could be embodied in "muscle-manipulating *trajectories* of … collective neuronal activities" and the like?[93]

No, it cannot be, and Churchland does not actually try to show otherwise. Rather, what he does is to change the subject. He tells us that, contrary to what philosophers have supposed historically, the "fundamental unit of cognition" is not the judgment, with its susceptibility of truth or falsity and its logical relationships to other judgments, but rather "the *activation pattern* across a proprietary *population* of neurons."[94] Nor does "theoretical understanding" consist primarily in the grasp of sentences or propositions, but rather in "an *unfolding sequence of activation-vectors*" within the brain.[95] Nor does knowledge fundamentally involve justified true belief. Rather, a "conceptual framework" turns out to be "a hierarchically structured, high-dimensional activation space," and a "perceptual representation" turns out to be "a 10^6-element neuronal activation vector."[96] And Churchland tells us that while such neurological "representational vehicles … can have, or lack, sundry representational virtues," they "are not the sorts of things to which the notion of Tarskian truth even applies."[97]

Now little or nothing in the way of argument is actually given by Churchland for any of these claims. A general materialism is simply taken for granted, and it is insinuated that since processes of the sort Churchland describes are the ones neuroscientists are discovering within the brain, they must be what cognition essentially consists in. To his credit, Churchland sees that the properties in terms of which thought is typically characterized—propositional content, truth and falsity, logical interrelationships, and so forth—simply cannot intelligibly be ascribed to the brute physiological processes he is interested in. But in that case, what reason can there be to characterize such processes as embodying "cognition," "understanding," "knowledge," or the having of a "conceptual framework" in the first place?

92 Cambridge, MA: The MIT Press, 2012.
93 Ibid., p. 3.
94 Ibid., p. 4.
95 Ibid., pp. 22–23.
96 Ibid., p. 32.
97 Ibid.

When stripped of propositional content, truth or falsity, logical connections, and the like, how does a pattern of neural activity constitute a "cognition" any more than the flexing of a tendon or the secretion of bile constitutes a cognition? In fact Churchland is simply equivocating, using terms like "cognition," "concept," etc. in a novel way, as *stand-ins* for physiological descriptions. He is in no way *explaining* cognition in terms of physiology. He is instead simply *ignoring* (or even *eliminating*) cognition altogether and talking about physiology instead, using the vocabulary of cognition but in a way that is mostly contrary to its usual sense.

I say "mostly" rather than "entirely" contrary because it is crucial to Churchland's account that he retains the notion of "representation" in something like its traditional sense. Now he does nothing to *justify* his use of the notion of representation; again, why a neural process counts as a "representation" any more than the flexing of a tendon or the secretion of bile counts as a representation is something Churchland does not tell us. (Indeed, he is critical of existing materialist attempts to explain representation in terms of the causal relations between neural processes and properties of the external world, in part for indeterminacy reasons of the sort briefly canvassed above.[98]) Churchland simply *assumes* that the neural processes he describes constitute representations of a sort, and goes from there. In particular, he supposes that the brain embodies something like a "map" of the external world.

Now with this an Aristotelian-Scholastic writer like Ross can readily agree, at least for the sake of argument. But the map-like representations Churchland postulates do not amount to *concepts* of the sort Ross and other Aristotelian-Scholastic writers are concerned with. They are instead to be identified with *phantasms*, which such writers have always acknowledged to be physiological. And they are no less indeterminate and less than universal than phantasms as traditionally conceived of are. Churchland makes heavy use of the analogy of a road map, and of the notion that the "homomorphism" between such a map and the streets and highways it represents is a model for the homomorphism between the "maps" embodied in the brain and features of the external world. But of course, a road map is as indeterminate as any of the other material symbols and images we have considered. For instance, there is nothing in the material properties of the lines on a map that of themselves determine that an inch represents a mile (say) rather than ten miles; and a legend placed on the side of the map to explain

98   Ibid., pp. 97–98.

this will itself be comprised of material symbols that are *themselves* indeterminate in their meaning.

Churchland gives us no reason to think that any "map" encoded in the brain will be any less indeterminate. And thus his position is no challenge at all to the argument defended in this paper. To be sure, it is only fair to acknowledge that arguments like Churchland's may indeed help to elucidate the *material* aspects of thought, the role that phantasms and physiology play in cognition. But that there are also, and more importantly, *immaterial* aspects of thought is a thesis that no neuroscientific discovery has refuted or could refute. Ross has, perhaps more than any other recent philosopher, helped us to see why.[99]

99   For comments on an earlier draft of this paper I thank David Clemenson, an anonymous referee, and audience members at a symposium on the theme Creation and Modern Science held at the Dominican House of Studies in Washington, D.C. on April 14, 2012.

11

Hayek, Popper, and the Causal Theory of the Mind

I. Introduction

In late 1952, F. A. Hayek sent his friend Karl Popper a copy of his recently published book *The Sensory Order: An Inquiry into the Foundations of Theoretical Psychology*. In a letter dated December 2, 1952, Popper acknowledged receipt of the book and responded as follows to what he had read in it:

> I am not sure whether one could describe your theory as a causal theory of the sensory order. I think, indeed, that one can. But then, it would be also the sketch of a causal theory of the mind.
>
> But I think I can show that a causal theory of the mind cannot be true (although I cannot show this of the sensory order; more precisely, I think I can show the impossibility of a causal theory of the human language (although I cannot show the impossibility of a causal theory of perception).
>
> I am writing a paper on the impossibility of a causal theory of the human language, and its bearing upon the body-mind problem, which *must* be finished in ten days. I shall send you a copy as soon as it is & typed.[1]

In a later letter dated January 19, 1953, Popper added:

> As to my comments on your book, they are, as far as criticism is concerned, implicit in my paper. I think you have made a splendid effort towards a theory of the sub-linguistic

---

1   Karl Popper to F. A. Hayek, December 2, 1952, Hoover Institution, Hayek Archive, box 44, folder 1. Quoted with the permission of the estate of Karl Popper. I have left Popper's punctuation unaltered.

(= sub-human ((= descriptive)) language) level of mind; but I believe that no physiological approach (although most important) can be sufficient to explain the descriptive and argumentative functions of language. Or in other words, there can be no causal or physiological theory of reason.[2]

The paper Popper was referring to is his short article "Language and the Body-Mind Problem."[3] Hayek began a draft of a paper entitled "Within Systems and About Systems: A Statement of Some Problems of a Theory of Communication," which, as Jack Birner has suggested, appears to have been intended at least in part as a response to Popper's criticisms.[4] But it was never completed, and Hayek never addressed Popper's arguments in any of his published work.

The Sensory Order has, however unjustly, largely been forgotten outside the circles of Hayek specialists. Popper's brief paper is perhaps even less well-known. Neither Popper's letters to Hayek nor Hayek's unfinished draft have yet been published. So, this episode might seem rather insignificant in the history of thought, and indeed of little significance even to our understanding of either Hayek's thought or Popper's. But, as I hope to show in what follows, nothing could be further from the truth. With respect both to its general themes and to some of the specific philosophical moves made by each side, the brief, private dispute between Hayek and Popper foreshadowed a more prominent debate within twentieth-century analytic philosophy that began in the 1970s and continues to this day. Moreover, both the dispute between Hayek and Popper and the later debate reflect a deep tension that has lain at the heart of Western thought since the time of the scientific revolution. On the one hand, there is the "mechanical world picture"[5] according to which all natural phenomena can be explained entirely in terms of the mathematically describable behavior of matter in motion. On the other hand, there are rational human thought processes, including the philosophical and scientific theorizing that led to the

---

2   Karl Popper to F. A. Hayek, January 19, 1953, Hoover Institution, Hayek Archive, box 44, folder 1. Quoted with the permission of the estate of Karl Popper. Again, the punctuation is Popper's own.

3   First published in the *Proceedings of the 11ᵗʰ International Congress of Philosophy*, 7, 1953; reprinted as Popper, 1968.

4   The paper is still unpublished. The typescript is in the Hoover Institution, Hayek Archive, box 104, folder 22. Birner's thesis is cited in Caldwell, 2004, at pp. 300–01. The typescript is undated. Caldwell reports (p. 299) that in 1991 Hayek's secretary Charlotte Cubitt dated the paper to 1952, though if Birner's thesis is correct it was either begun or at least modified after Hayek's receipt of Popper's paper.

5   I borrow the expression from Crane, 2003.

mechanical world picture itself. It is far from obvious that the latter can be fitted comfortably into the former—that human rationality can be explained in terms of purely material processes—and from the time of Descartes until relatively recently, the dominant view was that it could not be. Hayek and Popper were writing at a time when this view began to give way to a new materialist orthodoxy. Hayek, though arguably more sensitive to the tension in question than most contemporary materialists, nevertheless thought it could be resolved in a way favorable to a broadly materialist or "naturalistic" understanding of the mind. Popper disagreed and believed the older, dualistic conception of the mind to be essentially correct; and as we will see, his reasons for doing so have in more recent years been regarded even by some non-dualist philosophers as posing a serious difficulty for materialism.

In the next section, I will set the stage for the discussion of Hayek and Popper with a brief account of the nature and origins of the mind-body problem (or "body-mind problem," as Popper preferred to call it). We will see that there are really at least three mind-body problems, and that while Hayek and most contemporary philosophers focus on the first of these, Popper was more concerned with the other two and believed that they pose a more serious difficulty for materialism than the former does. Section III will explain what a "causal theory of the mind" is and the respects in which Hayek's account can be regarded as a causal theory. Section IV will examine Popper's main criticism of causal theories, which will be elucidated by comparison with the views of contemporary philosopher Hilary Putnam, who (apparently independently) developed a line of argument that parallels and extends the one presented by Popper. Finally, in section V I will consider the possible response to Popper suggested both by Hayek's unpublished draft and by things Hayek had to say in some of his published work, relating it to the responses contemporary philosophers have given to arguments like those presented by Popper and Putnam. I will argue that none of these replies succeeds and that the Popperian critique remains a powerful and as yet unanswered challenge not only to dogmatic materialism but even to the more modest and critical form of materialism or naturalism defended by Hayek.

II. The mind-body problem

Jerry Fodor usefully sums up the mind-body problem as follows:

> [S]ome of the most pervasive properties of minds seem so mysterious as to raise the Kantian-sounding question how a

materialistic psychology is *even possible*. Lots of mental states are *conscious*, lots of mental states are *intentional*, and lots of mental processes are *rational*, and the question does rather suggest itself how anything that is material could be any of these. (Fodor, 1994, emphasis in original)

For Fodor, then, the mind-body problem is really a cluster of three problems: the problem of *consciousness*, the problem of *intentionality*, and the problem of *rationality*. Let us briefly consider why each of the phenomena in question is thought to be philosophically problematic.[6]

When light strikes your retinas, a complex series of neural processes is initiated which may result in one among a range of possible behaviors, such as taking steps to avoid an obstacle, sorting red apples from green ones, or saying "It's sunny outside." When light strikes an "electric eye" or photodetector of some sort, electrical processes are initiated which also may result in one among a range of possible behaviors, such as the setting off of an alarm; or, if the device is associated with a robot, perhaps behavior similar to the sort you might exhibit, such as avoiding an obstacle, sorting objects, or declaring (through a speech synthesizer) that it is sunny. In the case of the electric eye and its associated robot, what we can observe going on in the system is presumably all there is. The system would seem to have no "inner life" or conscious visual experience associated with the electrical activity and behavior. But we *do* have conscious awareness; we *do* have an "inner life." There is, as Thomas Nagel famously put it, "something it is like" for us to see things, whereas there is nothing it is like for the robot to "see" something (Nagel, 1979). Or as contemporary philosophers like to say, we have *qualia* while the robot appears not to. So, what accounts for this difference? It does not seem plausible to hold that it can be accounted for merely in terms of the greater complexity of the human brain, because the difference between conscious systems and unconscious ones seems clearly to be a difference in *quality* and not merely of quantity. Call this the *problem of consciousness*.[7]

---

6   For a detailed treatment of the mind-body problem in all its aspects, see Feser, 2006b.

7   I am, of course, aware that some philosophers would argue that the difference really is at the end of the day a matter of complexity, that a sufficiently complex robot would be conscious, and so forth. The point for now is just to describe what seems *prima facie* to be the case so as to give the uninitiated reader a sense of the problem, not to prejudice the issue of whether the *prima facie* judgments in question are correct.

Then there is the problem of *intentionality*, which concerns, not just intentions, but meaning in general. (The technical term "intentionality" derives from the Latin *intendere*, which means "to point at" or "to aim at," as a word or thought points to or aims at the thing that it means.) Suppose we say that within the robot of our example there is a symbolic representation that means that *it is sunny outside*. Though the representation has this meaning, it has it only because the designers of the robot programmed the system so that it would be able to detect weather conditions and the like. The electrical processes and physical parts of the system would have had no meaning at all otherwise. By contrast, the thoughts of the designers themselves have meaning without anyone having to impart it to them. As John Searle has put it, the robot's symbolic representations—like words, sentences, and symbols in general—have only *derived* intentionality, while human thought has *intrinsic* intentionality (Searle, 1992, pp. 78–82). What can account for the difference, especially if we assume that human beings are no less material than robots are? That, in a nutshell, is the *problem of intentionality*.

Consider also that we are able not only to have individual meaningful thought episodes, but also to infer to further thoughts, to go from one thought to another in a rational way. This is not merely a matter of one thought *causing* another; a lunatic might be caused to conclude that mobsters are trying to kill him every time he judges that it is sunny outside, but such a thought process would not be rational. Rather, we are able to go from one thought to another *in accordance with the laws of logic*. Now, it might seem that the robot of our example, and computers generally, can do the same thing insofar as we can program them to carry out mathematical operations and the like. But of course, *we* have had to program them to do this. We have had to assign a certain interpretation to the otherwise meaningless symbolic representations we have decided to count as the "premises" and "conclusion" of a given inference the machine is to carry out, and we have had to design its internal processes in such a way that there is an isomorphism between them and the patterns of reasoning studied by logicians. But no one has to assign meaning to *our* mental processes in order for them to count as logical. So, what accounts for the difference? How are *we* able to go from one thought to another in accordance, not just with physical causal laws, but in accordance with the laws of logic? That is the *problem of rationality*.[8]

---

8 Of course, some philosophers would deny the *prima facie* judgments on which these statements of the problems of intentionality and rationality rest. For example, some

As I indicated earlier, the origin of the mind-body problem(s) lies, at least in part, in the rise of the "mechanical world picture" inaugurated by early modern philosophers and scientists like Galileo, Descartes, Hobbes, Boyle, Locke, and Newton. Let us now consider how this is so.

On the medieval Aristotelian-Scholastic understanding of the natural world that these thinkers overthrew, qualities like color, sound, odor, taste, heat and cold were taken to exist in material substances more or less in just the way common sense supposes that they do. The moderns denied this; for them, the natural world is made up of intrinsically colorless, odorless, soundless, tasteless particles in motion, and the qualities in question exist only in the mind of the observer. To be sure, for purposes of physics, we can *redefine* heat and cold in terms of molecular motion, red and green in terms of the different surface reflectance properties of physical objects, sound in terms of compression waves, and so forth; but heat, cold, red, green, sounds and the like *as common sense understands them* exist only in our conscious experience of the world (as "qualia," to use the contemporary jargon). Now, since the brain is on this view made up of inherently colorless, odorless, tasteless particles no less than any other physical object, this seems inevitably to entail that conscious experiences, or at least their qualitative features or qualia, are not material features of the brain. That is, of course, exactly what Descartes, Malebranche, Locke, and other early modern thinkers concluded insofar as they embraced dualism in one form or another. And yet if these features are immaterial, how they get in any sort of causal contact with the material properties of the brain becomes mysterious. Therein lies the origin of what contemporary writers call the problem of consciousness.

The Aristotelian-Scholastic view also held that a kind of meaning, in the guise of teleology or goal-directedness, is built into the structure of the material world from top to bottom. This includes not just the usual examples—the functions of bodily organs and biological processes—but any causal regularity. For the Scholastics, if some cause A typically generates some specific effect or range of effects B—for instance, if striking a match typically generates flame and heat rather than the smell of lilacs, or if ice typically cools the liquid or air surrounding it rather than causing it to boil—this can only be

would argue that rationality *can* ultimately be explained in terms of the idea that the brain is a kind of computer. The point for now, again, is merely to give a rough idea of what the problems involve, not to prejudge the question of whether the materialist can solve them.

because A inherently "points to" or "aims at" B, specifically, rather than at C, or D, or no effect at all. Generating B is what Aristotelians would call the "final cause" of A, what A will tend *naturally* to do unless impeded; and it will do so by virtue of its "formal cause," that is, its essence or "substantial form." Now, the early modern thinkers eliminated formal and final causality too from their picture of the natural world. For them, ordinary natural substances possess no essences or substantial forms, and there is, accordingly, no teleology or goal-directedness built into matter either. There are only fundamental particles (or some other basic unit of matter) defined entirely in abstract mathematical terms, which exhibit law-like patterns of combination into more or less complex structures. That it is a "law" that events of such-and-such a kind are followed by events of some other kind is taken to be all an explanation of natural phenomena need be concerned with. *Why* such patterns hold—which becomes mysterious once the natural world is deemed to be devoid of essences or built-in teleology or goal-directedness—comes to be seen as a question for theology rather than philosophy or natural science, and perhaps one that is simply unanswerable. This eschewal of immanent teleology or final causality was and has remained the core of a "mechanistic" conception of nature, the one element of the early moderns' anti-Aristotelian revolution that has survived as other aspects of mechanism ("push-pull" models of causation, determinism, and so forth) have fallen by the wayside.[9]

Among the consequences of this new, anti-teleological conception of nature were the puzzles about causation and inductive reasoning famously raised by David Hume. If there is nothing in a cause A by virtue of which it *inherently* "points beyond itself" to the effect B that we typically associate with it, then there would seem to be no *objective* reason why A should be followed by B as opposed to C, or D, or no effect at all. Causes and effects become "loose and separate" and our belief in their essential connection comes to seem a mere projection of subjective expectations. Another consequence is that intentionality, like qualia, comes to seem essentially immaterial. For if nothing in the material world inherently "points to" or "aims at" anything beyond itself—devoid, as that world was now thought to be, of immanent final causes—then, since the brain is just one material object among others, it seems to follow that the intentionality of our thoughts, that

---

9   *The Cambridge Dictionary of Philosophy*, s.v. "mechanistic explanation." Cf. Crane, 2003, pp. 2–4. My description here of the historical transition from Aristotelian to modern attitudes toward teleology is, of course, oversimplified. For a more detailed treatment, see Feser, 2010.

by virtue of which *they* inherently "point to," "aim at," or mean something beyond themselves, cannot be any sort of material property of the brain. The problem of intentionality is thereby at least exacerbated by the anti-teleological approach of the moderns, and insofar as our rational thought processes exhibit intentionality, so too is the problem of rationality.[10]

Hayek recognized that the mind-body problem has its origins in the new conception of nature that informed the scientific revolution (though like so many modern writers, he takes it for granted that what was, in effect, a novel approach to the *methodology* of science amounted to an actual *discovery* of science—a highly challengeable assumption, as we will see). As he says in *The Sensory Order* vis-à-vis what we have called the problem of consciousness or qualia, "a precise statement of the problem raised by the existence of sensory qualities must start from the fact that the progress of the physical sciences has all but eliminated these qualities from our scientific picture of the external world" (Hayek, 1952, p. 2). He had written on this theme at greater length in "Scientism and the Study of Society," and there observed also that modern science regards appeals to allegedly "purposive" features of nature—final causality or teleology—as objectionably "anthropomorphic" or "animistic," and replaces the qualitative and teleological common-sense picture of the world with a new mode of description for which "the only appropriate language is that of mathematics."[11] Now, though this "objectivist approach" is appropriate to the natural sciences, Hayek famously criticized its application to the social sciences, where he regarded a "subjectivist approach" as legitimate and even necessary (Hayek, 1979a, p. 47). For an accurate representation of the human world must take account of the

---

10 To the extent that our intentional mental states have a *conceptual* structure and are connected by *logical* relations, the Scholastic tradition regarded them as necessarily immaterial in any event, for reasons related to the sort we will be examining when we turn to Popper. However, the Scholastics did not see this as generating a "mind-body problem." Following Aristotle, they took our intellectual capacities to be powers of the soul, and the soul in turn to be the form of the body. Hence, for them, thought is related to bodily action as its formal-cum-final cause. It was when formal and final causes were abandoned and mind and body were reinterpreted by the moderns as related instead by what Aristotelians call "efficient causation" that causal interaction between the mental and the physical came to be seen as problematic. For further discussion, see chapter 8 of Feser, 2006b, and chapter 4 of Feser, 2009.

11 The essay originally appeared in three parts in *Economica* between 1942 and 1944, and was reprinted as Part One of Hayek, 1979a, wherein the words quoted appear at pp. 29 and 33. The line about mathematics is one that Hayek is quoting approvingly from Stebbing, 1939, p. 107.

way things do in fact appear to us in everyday life, and they appear to us precisely under the categories physical science eschews. To that extent Hayek objected to the behaviorism of John B. Watson, the physicalism of Otto Neurath, and other varieties of materialism, and held that "for practical purposes ... we shall permanently have to be content with a dualistic view of the world" (Hayek, 1952, p. 179). But only for practical purposes, for *metaphysically* speaking, Hayek still regarded the human mind as nothing but an "order prevailing in a particular part of the physical universe—that part of it which is ourselves" and would "deny any ultimate dualism of the forces governing the realms of mind and that of the physical world" (Hayek, 1952, pp. 178–79). He regards the mind-body problem as essentially a problem of "showing that there can exist a system of relations between ... physiological events which is identical with the system of relations existing between the corresponding mental events" (Hayek, 1952, p. 2); and he believes that the theory presented in *The Sensory Order* solves that problem.

III. Hayek and the causal theory of the mind

According to David Armstrong, a causal theory of the mind holds "that mental states are states apt for the production of certain ranges of behavior and, in some cases, apt for being produced by certain ranges of stimuli" (Armstrong, 1993, p. xiv; cf. Armstrong, 1981). Such theories typically seek to show that causal relations of the sort in question *exhaust* the nature of mental states, that mental states have no features over and above their causal relations. Causal theories are generally regarded as materialist in intent even if consistent in principle with some forms of dualism. For if to be in a particular mental state is just to be in a state that is caused by certain kinds of stimuli and which in turn causes a certain kind of behavioral output, then while such a state might in principle be a state of an immaterial substance, Ockham's razor (so the argument goes) would favor instead the supposition that it is a state of a material substance, such as the brain.

Hayek is a causal theorist, and he evidently holds that each of the three aspects of the mind that we have identified can be accounted for in causal terms.[12] "There is," he says, "no problem of sensory qualities beyond the

---

12 Causal theories are closely related to functionalist theories of mind, which have dominated philosophy of mind since the 1970s, and Hayek can also be described as a kind of functionalist. I will stick to the label "causal theory" in the present paper, however, since it is closest to Hayek's and Popper's own usage. For discussion of Hayek's relationship to functionalism, see Feser, 2006a.

problem of how the different qualities differ from each other—and these differences can only consist of differences in the effects which they exercise in evoking other qualities, or in determining behavior" (Hayek, 1952, p. 19). "Sensory qualities" are more or less the same as what contemporary philosophers call "qualia," so that what Hayek is asserting here is that the problem of consciousness, as we have called it, can be solved in terms of a causal theory. Developing such a solution is what the bulk of *The Sensory Order* is devoted to, and when Popper says in the first of his letters to Hayek quoted above that he does not claim that a causal theory of the sensory order or of perception is impossible, he is essentially referring to the possibility of a causal theory of consciousness.[13]

But Hayek claims that "the principle used to explain [sensory] phenomena applies also to the so-called 'higher' mental processes such as the formation of abstract concepts and conceptual thought" (Hayek, 1952, p. 78; cf. Hayek, 1979a, pp. 82–83), as well as to "the processes of inference" (Hayek, 1952, p. 146); for there is, he says, "no justification for the sharp distinction between the direct sensory perception of qualities and the more abstract processes of thought," between "the operations of ... the senses and [those of] the intellect" (Hayek, 1952, p. 108). This is precisely to hold that both intentionality (of which "the formation of abstract concepts" is a paradigm) and rationality ("the processes of inference") are no less susceptible of a causal analysis than Hayek takes conscious experience to be. And this is where Popper demurs.

---

13   A word of caution is in order here. Since Hayek devotes only chapter 6 of *The Sensory Order* to the topic of "Consciousness and Conceptual Thought," it might seem odd that I should claim that the bulk of the book is devoted to solving the problem of consciousness. But the term "consciousness" can be used in a variety of ways, which need to be clearly distinguished. For instance, contemporary philosophers of mind often distinguish between "phenomenal consciousness"—the kind of consciousness exemplified by sensations and perceptual experiences, in which qualia feature centrally—and "access consciousness"—the paradigm of which would be the availability of the content of a thought for verbal expression. You can answer a question like "What did it taste like?" by virtue of being phenomenally conscious, and a question like "What are you thinking about?" by virtue of having access consciousness. (For an influential exposition of this distinction, see Block, 1997.) The "problem of consciousness" as it is usually understood by contemporary philosophers of mind is essentially concerned with phenomenal rather than access consciousness. Now, chapter 6 of *The Sensory Order* is devoted to the topic of what today would be called "access consciousness," and is the only part of the book so devoted. But the rest of the book is devoted to what would today be called "phenomenal consciousness," and in that sense the whole book is concerned with "the problem of consciousness," as that is understood today.

The controlling idea in Hayek's account is that of "classification"; for us to perceive, to think about, or to reason about events (whether events in the external world or those internal to the body) is just for our nervous systems to "classify" and "reclassify" those events.[14] Now, "classification" as ordinarily understood itself presupposes consciousness, intentionality, and rationality. For you to be able to classify the fruit in your grocery bag into categories like "apples," "oranges," "bananas," and the like, you first have to be conscious of the fruit, to grasp the concepts associated with the categories, and to infer from the attributes of a particular fruit which category it falls into. So, if Hayek were imputing to neural processes "classificatory" abilities in the ordinary sense of the term, he would be rather obviously guilty of committing the "homunculus fallacy"—the error of "explaining" some higher level psychological capacity by implicitly attributing to lower level neural processes the very capacity that is to be explained, which of course merely "passes the buck" and explains nothing.[15]

Hayek explicitly says, however, that "classification" as he uses it is to be understood as having "a special technical meaning," and connotes a certain kind of causal relation:

> By 'classification' we shall mean a process in which on each occasion on which a certain recurring event happens it produces the same specific effect, and where the effects produced by any one kind of such events may be either the same or different from those which any other kind of event produces in a similar manner. All the different events which whenever they occur produce the same effect will be said to be events of the same class, and the fact that every one of them produces the same effect will be

14 I speak of "events" rather than "objects" or the like because Hayek appears to reject what philosophers call a "substance ontology" in favor of an "event ontology" (Hayek, 1952, pp. 177–78). But nothing in what follows rides on this issue.

15 That the homunculus fallacy is rife within contemporary philosophy of mind and cognitive science is a major theme of the work of philosopher John Searle. See Searle, 1992, especially pp. 212–14. A similar position is developed at greater length in Bennett and Hacker, 2003, especially chapter 3. Bennett and Hacker prefer the label "mereological fallacy," because the mistake involves a certain kind of illegitimate move from a whole to its parts, not merely the treating of neural processes as if they were homunculi or "little men."

16 Hayek sometimes puts scare quotes around words like "learning," "experience," "symbol," etc. when using them to describe neural activity, which indicates that he

the *sole* criterion which makes them members of the same class.
(Hayek, 1952, p. 48)[16]

Hayek illustrates what he has in mind with examples of various machines—
one which moves balls into various receptacles depending on their size, another which rings different bells depending on which combinations of
electrical impulses it receives through various wires, and a third which generates different arrangements of cards depending on which patterns of holes
have been punched into them.

Similarly, the central nervous system amounts in Hayek's view to a
"kind of mechanism" capable of carrying out a "classificatory process"
along the same lines:

> We shall maintain that a classification of the sensory impulses
> which produces an order strictly analogous to the order of sen-
> sory qualities can be effected by a system of connexions through
> which the impulses can be transmitted from fibre to fibre; and
> that such a system of connexions which is structurally equivalent
> to the order of sensory qualities will be built up if, in the course
> of the development of the species or the individual, connexions
> are established between fibres in which impulses occur at the
> same time. (Hayek, 1952, pp. 51–52)

Elsewhere Hayek says that "'classifying' stands here … for a process of
channelling, or switching, or 'gating', of the nervous impulses so as to produce a particular disposition or set" (Hayek, 1969, p. 51). And in yet another
place he speaks of "conscious experience" as "the product of a superimposition of many 'classifications' of the events perceived" (Hayek, 1978, p.
36).

Considered in isolation, these summaries of Hayek's position might seem
frustratingly murky, but the basic idea is clear enough from the larger expositions in which they occur. Through stimulation of the sense organs, regular
causal relations are set up between events external to the body (or, in the case
of proprioception, internal to the body) on the one hand, and sets of neural
impulses on the other. The initial stage of "classification" of an external or
internal event involves the establishment of such a causal correlation between

is aware of the need to be careful with such language, so as to avoid fallacy. Whether
he *succeeds* in avoiding it is another question, to which we will return.

the stimulus event and a certain set of impulses—Hayek speaks of "stimuli evoking the impulses which 'represent' them in the central nervous system" (Hayek, 1952, p. 107). But an actual perceptual experience requires a "superimposition" or concurrence of various sets of impulses. We can illustrate the idea with a (deliberately oversimplified) example. Suppose A is a set of impulses correlated with a property like roundness; B a set correlated with solidity; C a set correlated with smoothness; D a set correlated with roughness; E a set correlated with whiteness; and F a set correlated with being orange. A concurrence or "superimposition" of A, B, C, and E might be said to underlie the perceptual experience of a cue ball on a pool table; whereas a superimposition of A, B, D, and F might underlie the perceptual experience of an orange. Hayek insists on "the primacy of the abstract" in consciousness, deliberately reversing the usual supposition that abstraction is a secondary phenomenon, following upon experience rather than preceding it. What he seems to have in mind is the notion that unless various neural processes *already* embodied "abstract categories" which might be "superimposed" so as to result in the "classification" of something specific—for example, something round, solid, smooth, and white, as a cue ball is—then a perceptual experience would not be possible (Hayek, 1978, p. 42).

As I say, the example is oversimplified. "Whiteness," "smoothness," and the like are not necessarily the sorts of stimuli we should be thinking in terms of—certainly not if we conceive of such attributes in terms of the "qualia" presented to us in conscious experience, since they are precisely what Hayek is trying to explain. A proper characterization of stimuli would have to be couched instead in the language of physics. Furthermore, Hayek emphasizes that there will not be a neat one-to-one match-up between stimuli and neural impulses; different stimuli might produce the same sorts of impulses, and the same stimulus might produce different sorts of impulses, depending on circumstances. Nor is "classification" confined to simple correlation between various stimuli on the one hand and "superimpositions" of sets of neural impulses on the other. Changes either in the (external or internal) stimuli or in the neural connections themselves may result in a "reclassification" of stimuli; and sets of neural impulses are also themselves the objects of higher-order "classifications," with the higher-order impulses being in turn the objects of "classifications" of yet a higher order, and so on. These complications and others are elaborated upon in *The Sensory Order*, and neuroscientists influenced by Hayek's work have developed views like his in a neurobiologically more up-to-date fashion (Edelman, 1987; Fuster, 2003).

However oversimplified, the example suffices for our purposes. For whatever the details, it is plain that Hayek regards "classification" as a matter of "impulses *representing* different parts of the environment" (Hayek, 1952, p. 125, emphasis added). He uses the terms "represent," "representing," and "representation" over and over again to describe the relationship between neural impulses and what they "classify."[17] That the nervous system embodies both a "map" and a "model" of the environment is also a key theme in Hayek's account, and these concepts obviously entail representation. Now, one might well ask how Hayek can help himself to this sort of language if his intention is to explain the human mind, since among our mental capacities are our powers of representation. Indeed, the notion of "representation" is in contemporary philosophy of mind regarded as more or less interchangeable with that of "intentionality," insofar as for one thing to "represent" another seems precisely for it to "point to" or be "directed at" the other. But if Hayek is implicitly *appealing* to intentionality in an attempt to *explain* intentionality, he hasn't really explained anything at all, and his account fails.

Hayek suggests that his notion of a "model" might be elucidated by comparison to "machines ... such as the predictor for anti-aircraft guns, or the automatic pilots for aircraft ... [which] show all the characteristics of purposive behaviour" and which "with regard to purposiveness ... differ from a brain merely in degree and not in kind" (Hayek, 1952, p. 126).[18] But such machines have the purposes they do only because human minds with representational powers designed them; their intentionality is *derived* rather than *intrinsic* (as Searle would put it) so that they *do* differ from human brains in kind and not degree. Since the intentionality of such machines needs to be explained by reference to that of human minds, we cannot coherently explain the intentionality inherent in the human mind by reference to such machines.

To be sure, Hayek is careful to note that "while using the conception of a model ... we must, of course, avoid the suggestion, originally connected with the word model, that it must be the creation of a thinking mind" (Hayek, 1952, p. 127). But by itself this cautionary note is not good enough, because we still need an account of exactly *how* "representation" (and thus intentionality) *does* enter the picture if it is not via some "thinking mind"

---

17 See Hayek, 1952, pp. 68–69, 72, 73, 89, 98, 99, 105, 109, 113–14, 115, 118, 120, 121, 124, 125, 126, and 166.

18 Cf. Armstrong's example of a homing rocket in Armstrong, 1981.

which imparts representational content to processes otherwise devoid of them (as the builder of a model in the everyday sense imparts representational content to it). I suggested above that the need to avoid concepts which smack of intentionality is the reason Hayek introduced his technical notion of "classification" rather than relying on the ordinary notion. But if the technical notion itself presupposes representation and thus intentionality, then the problem has merely been deferred rather than avoided. What Hayek needs is a way to *cash out* "classification," "representation," "modeling," "mapping," and related notions in terms that do not presuppose intentionality at all. Merely *shifting between* these notions doesn't solve the problem but only moves it around, like the pea in a shell game. The notions form a circle; the trick is to break out of the circle.

The solution evidently lies, in Hayek's view, in the idea that the right sort of causal relation suffices to *generate* intentionality or representational power:

> Since the different individual impulses will become members of a class through the fact that each of them evokes the same other impulses, it seems permissible to say that the latter *represent* the common attribute of the members of the class ... The classification is effected by the evocation of certain other impulses, and the latter serve, as it were, as the 'signs' or 'symbols' representing the class; the expression 'representative processes in the brain' ... can therefore appropriately be applied to them. (Hayek, 1952, pp. 68–69, emphasis in original.)

The notion of causation is generally thought to be non-intentional (i.e., not to presuppose intentionality). Hayek's position appears to be that we can derive the intentional from the non-intentional insofar as a set of impulses will "classify," "represent," "signify," or "symbolize" whatever causes or "evokes" it in a certain way. He does not elaborate on the idea; the bulk of *The Sensory Order* and of Hayek's other writings on the subject are devoted to spelling out the details of the causal processes Hayek takes to underline the mind. That is to say, it presupposes *that* causal processes can generate representational ones and goes from there, without explaining *how* they can do so.

Accordingly, much rides on the idea expressed in this brief passage. Indeed, Hayek's entire philosophy of mind rides on it. Obviously, his solution to the problem of intentionality does so. His solution to the problem of rationality clearly does as well, insofar as rational thought processes involve the transition from one thought to another, and the logical relations between thoughts are determined by their intentional or representational content. But even Hayek's solution to the problem of consciousness rides on it. For his account of *all* mental phenomena—sensation and perception no less than conceptual thought and rational inference—rests on his claim that neural processes can be said to "classify" and thereby "represent" events in the external and internal worlds.[19] Hence, if a causal theory of representation fails, so too does Hayek's theory of "the sensory order." Popper, who allowed that the latter might succeed even if the former does not, might have been too generous. Still, in suggesting that representation can be explained in terms of causation, Hayek does at least provide a way of breaking out of the (otherwise vicious) circle of intentional notions that is so crucial to his account. And while a suggestion is all he gives us, the idea of a causal theory of representation has since been developed by others in some detail.

Now we've seen that Hayek says little more than that neural impulses will "represent" (or constitute a "symbol" or "sign" of) whatever "evokes" them. But contemporary causal theorists are agreed that *merely* to say that *B will represent A when B is caused by A* is woefully inadequate. This is essentially what Fodor calls the "Crude Causal Theory," and there are several immediate problems with it (Fodor, 1987, p. 99). For example, suppose Grandma owns a cat and has the thought that *the cat is on the mat* whenever she thinks she sees the cat sitting on the mat. But suppose also that she has bad eyesight, and that unbeknownst to her, the cat is only on the mat half the times she thinks it is—the other times it is really the neighborhood dog, who has wandered in through the cat door, that is sitting on the mat. If the Crude Causal Theory were correct, the content of Grandma's thought should be the disjunctive proposition that *either the cat is on the mat or the dog is on the mat*, since both the cat and the dog cause the thought with the same regularity. But in fact she only ever has the thought that *the cat is on the mat*, and never thinks about the dog at all. How can a causal theory account for this? Call that the "disjunction problem." Or suppose that Grandma has never had a cat and that there are no cats in her neighborhood, but that she still thinks that *the cat is on the mat* whenever the neighborhood dog

---

19 In this respect, Hayek might be said to defend a version of what contemporary philosophers of mind call a "representational theory of consciousness," i.e., one which tries to explain consciousness (in one or more senses of that term) in terms of representation or intentionality. See, e.g., Dretske, 1995 and Tye, 1995.

wanders in, again because of her poor eyesight. This example too conflicts with the Crude Causal Theory, which falsely implies that she must be thinking about the dog, since it is only ever the dog that is causing her thought. This is the "misrepresentation problem."

These problems reflect different ways in which the causal factors in terms of which the causal theorist hopes to explain the meaning or intentional content of our thoughts seem *indeterminate* in a way the thoughts themselves are not: Grandma's thought is specifically about *the cat being on the mat*, and there does not seem to be anything in the causal facts appealed to that can explain why her thought has *exactly that content* and no other. The work of contemporary causal theorists like Fodor and Fred Dretske is devoted to solving such problems, and while their approaches are controversial, any serious attempt to defend a Hayekian theory of the mind will have to incorporate or improve upon the complexities they introduce into the causal theory in order to rescue it from these difficulties.[20]

IV. Popper's critique

This brings us to Popper's critique, which also raises problems of indeterminacy, but in an even more fundamental and (in Popper's view) decisive fashion. Popper begins by distinguishing four major functions of language (Popper, 1968, p. 295).[21] There is, first of all, the *expressive* function, which involves "an outward expression of an inner state" (Popper and Eccles, 1986, p. 58). Here language operates in a way comparable to the sound an engine makes when it is revved up, or an animal's cry when in pain. The second, *signaling* function adds to the expressive function the generation of a reaction in others. Popper compares it to the danger signals an animal might send out in order to alert other animals, and to the way a traffic light signals the possible presence of cars even when there are none about.

Popper allows that these two elementary functions of language might be explicable in causal terms. What he regards as inexplicable in such terms

---

20 See Drestke, 1981; Dretske, 1988; Fodor, 1987; and Fodor, 1990. Surveys of the debate over causal theories of representation can be found in chapter 5 of Crane, 2003 and chapter 7 of Feser, 2006b.

21 Popper borrows the distinction between the first three functions from psychologist Karl Bühler and adds to them the fourth. The distinction is developed at greater length in Popper, 1979, at pp. 235–38; in Popper and Eccles, 1986, at pp. 57–60; and in Popper, 1996, at pp. 84–92. Cf. W. W. Bartley's discussion of Popper's argument in Bartley, 1985, at pp. 174–78.

are the remaining two functions. The *descriptive* function of language involves the expression of a *proposition*, something that can be either *true or false*. The paradigm here would be the utterance of a declarative sentence, such as "Roses are red," "Two and two make four," or "There is a predator in the area." Notice that the latter example differs from an animal's cry of warning in having a *conceptual structure*. A bird's squawk might cause another bird to feel fear and take flight. What it does not do is convey an abstract concept like *eagle*, *predator*, or *danger*, and thus it does not convey the sort of propositional content that presupposes such concepts.[22] Finally, the *argumentative* function of language involves the expression of an inference from one or more propositions to another in a manner than can be said to be either *valid or invalid*, as when we reason from *All men are mortal* and *Socrates is a man* to the conclusion *Socrates is mortal*.

In Popper's view, a causal theory cannot in principle account even for a word's ability to function as the name of some object, which is the simplest example of a descriptive use of language; *a fortiori*, it cannot account for more complex descriptive (and argumentative) uses either. He states the basic argument as follows:

> Consider a machine which, every time it sees a ginger cat, says 'Mike'. It represents, we may be tempted to say, a *causal model* of naming, or of the name-relation ...
>
> We admit that the machine may be described as realizing what we may loosely call a 'causal chain' of events joining Mike (the cat) with 'Mike' (its name). But there are reasons why we cannot accept this causal chain as a representation or realization of the relation between a thing and its name.
>
> It is naive to look at this chain of events as beginning with the appearance of Mike and ending with the enunciation 'Mike'.
>
> It 'begins' (if at all) with a state of the machine prior to the appearance of Mike, a state in which the machine is, as it were, ready to respond to the appearance of Mike. It 'ends' (if at all) not with the enunciation of a word, since there is a state following this ... It is our *interpretation* which makes Mike and 'Mike'

---

22 Popper tentatively allows in Popper and Eccles, 1986, that at least some animal behavior "*may* perhaps" involve a descriptive component and not mere signaling, giving the bee's dance as a possible example (p. 58). I don't find this plausible myself, but nothing in what follows rides on the issue.

the extremes (or terms) of the causal chain, and not the 'objective' physical situation. (Moreover, we might consider *the whole process of reaction* as name, or only the last letters of 'Mike', say, 'Ike'.) Thus, although those who know or understand the name-relation may choose to interpret a causal chain as a model of it, it is clear that the name-relation is not a causal relation, and cannot be realized by any causal model. (Popper, 1968, pp. 297–98. I have removed Popper's paragraph numbers.)

As I understand it, what Popper is saying here is this. In order to explain representation or meaning in causal terms, we would need to be able to identify some specific, determinate cause *A* as "the beginning" of the relevant causal chain and therefore as that which is being represented, and some specific, determinate effect *B* as "the end" of the causal chain and therefore as that which does the representing. For a causal theory says that some effect *B* will represent whatever *A* causes it in just the right way (where what counts as "the right way" is going to be spelled out in terms of the sorts of complications a Dretske or Fodor would add to the Crude Causal Theory).

Now, objectively, as it is "in itself" and apart from human interests, the world contains an enormously complex network of causal chains. In the example at hand, there are the states and processes of the machine prior to the cat's appearance, the motion of the cat as it enters the room, the journey of the light from the cat's body to the electric eye affixed to the machine, the electrical current's passage from the eye to the machine's innards, the machine's emitting of the sound "Mike," the cat's perking up its ears on hearing this sound and perhaps fleeing the room as a consequence, and so forth. There are also all the events that occurred prior and subsequent to these ones, and the events occurring simultaneously which have some influence on them—the traveling of the electrical current from the wall socket to the machine it is powering, a mouse scurrying along the floor which the cat is hoping to catch, and so on and on. But what is it that makes any of this count as a "beginning" or an "end" of a causal chain? In particular, what is it that makes the *cat*, specifically—rather than the cat's surface or its motion, or the mouse, or the light traveling from the cat, or the electrical current, or one of a million other things—"the beginning" of some chain? What is it that makes the *sound "Mike,"* specifically—rather than the electrical current passing through the machine, or the sound "Ike" (i.e., the last part of the sound "Mike"), or the perking up of the cat's ears, or one of a million other things—"the end" of some chain?

The answer, Popper says, is that there is nothing in the objective physical facts *themselves* that determines which if any of these things is the "beginning" or "end" of a causal chain. Objectively there is just the complex network of causes extended forward and backward in time indefinitely. Rather, it is because *we* have an interest in this case in the cat and in the name "Mike"—an interest which, under the circumstances, we do not have in cat surfaces, or electrical current, or the mouse—that *we* pick out the cat and the utterance of the name as especially significant, and label the former "the beginning" of a causal chain and the latter "the end." But that means that the identification of the relevant causal chain *presupposes* our interpretive practices, and therefore *presupposes* our representational powers and the intentionality they embody. And in that case we cannot intelligibly appeal to such causal chains in order to *explain* our representational powers or intentionality.

Popper's argument might be elucidated by comparison with some considerations about the relationship between causation and the mental put forward by Hilary Putnam.[23] Criticizing Fodor's version of the causal theory of representation, Putnam notes that in everyday claims about causation, we typically distinguish between "contributory causes" or "background conditions," on the one hand, and "*the* cause" of an event on the other. For example, if we say that a stuck valve caused a certain pressure cooker to explode, we are treating the stuck valve differently than the way we treat (say) the lack of holes in the vessel of the pressure cooker, even though the latter also played a role in the explosion. The lack of holes we treat as a contributory cause or background condition; the stuck valve we treat as "*the* cause," as being of special significance. Putnam observes:

> Yet, in the physics of the explosion, the role played by the stuck valve is exactly the same as the role of [the lack of holes]: the absence of either would have permitted the steam to escape, bringing down the pressure and averting the explosion. (Putnam, 1987, pp. 37–38)
>
> For in fundamental physics, at least, one usually ignores the distinction between contributory causes and "the cause", and tries to provide a formalism which shows how all of the factors interact to produce the final result. (Putnam, 1992, p. 50)

---

23   See Putnam, 1992, especially chapter 3. Cf. Putnam, 1987, pp. 37–39; Putnam, 1990; and Putnam, 1994. Ideas similar to Putnam's are developed in Corbí and Prades, 2000.

Though it has no unique significance to the physics of the situation, we treat the stuck valve as special, Putnam says, because of our interests. We take it that

> the valve 'should have' let the steam escape—that is its 'function', what it was designed to do. On the other hand, the surface element [present where a hole might otherwise have been] was not doing anything 'wrong' in preventing the steam from escaping; containing the steam is the 'function' of the surface of which [this element] is a part. So when we ask 'Why did the explosion take place?', knowing what we know and having the interests we do have, our 'explanation space' consists of the alternatives:
>
> (1) Explosion taking place
> (2) Everything functioning as it should
>
> What we want to know, in other words, is why 1 is what happened *as opposed to* 2. We are simply not interested in why 1 is what happened *as opposed to* such alternatives as:
>
> (3) The surface element … is missing, and no explosion takes place. (Putnam, 1987, p. 38)

Now, insofar as the distinction between "*the* cause" and contributing or background conditions is in this way "interest-relative" and "context-sensitive," it *presupposes* the existence of our powers of representation or intentionality, for

> being interested in something involves, albeit in a slightly hidden way, the notion of "aboutness", that is, the central intentional notion. To be interested in something, in this sense, you have to be able to think about it—you have to be able to refer to it, in thought or in language. (Putnam, 1992, p. 50)

The reason this is significant is that the aim of a causal theory is to *explain* intentionality or representation in purely physical terms—terms that make no reference to concepts other than those recognized by physical science. Yet given their actual examples, causal theorists in fact help themselves to a "notion of things 'causing' other things [which] is not a notion … simply handed to us by physics"—namely, the everyday notion that presupposes the interest-relative distinction between "*the* cause" and contributing or background conditions (Putnam, 1992, p. 50). That is to say, they make reference to ordinary objects—cats, the valves on pressure cookers, and the like—in a way that gives them a causal significance they do not have in the sorts of explanations physics offers. Nor is it easy to see how these theorists can avoid doing this, given that their aim is precisely to explain how we can represent such everyday objects in thought and language. But in doing it they are subtly *presupposing* the existence of intentionality—the very phenomenon they are supposed to be explaining.

Popper presented his argument as a critique of "physicalistic" accounts of the mind, and if we read it in light of Putnam's similar but more thoroughly worked-out line of thought, we can see more clearly what he meant. The physicalist claims to be able to explain all phenomena entirely in terms drawn from physical science. The Popper-Putnam objection is that the specific causal notions the physicalist requires in order to account for intentionality are simply not available to him, given this constraint. As Putnam puts it, "Nature, or 'physical reality' in the post-Newtonian understanding of the physical, has no semantic preferences" (Putnam, 1990, p. 83). There is nothing in the physical facts so conceived that can determine why any particular causal chain "can be singled out as '*the*' relation between signs and their referents" (ibid., p. 89, emphasis added). What he has in mind can be understood by recalling what was said above about the anti-teleological, "mechanistic" character of the natural world as conceived of by the fathers of the scientific revolution. On the older, Aristotelian conception of nature championed by the medieval Scholastics, material substances and processes were inherently "directed towards" certain ends or "final causes" beyond themselves, given their "essences" or "substantial forms." The early modern philosophers and scientists defined themselves against this view. But as Putnam argues, causal theorists of intentionality, though officially committed to furthering the worldview of the anti-Scholastic founders of modern science, are implicitly beholden to "a notion according to which what is normal, what is an explanation, what is a bringer-about, is all in the *essence of things in themselves*"; and they are thereby beholden, in effect, to "a medieval notion of causation" (ibid., p. 88, emphasis added). For the idea that there is an "*intrinsic* distinction" between the cause of an event and mere background conditions "has much more to do with medieval (and Aristotelian) notions of 'efficient causation' than with post-Newtonian ones" (Putnam, 1987, p. 26). It presupposes an "Aristotelian conception of form"—of "self-identifying structures" which *objectively demarcate the ordinary objects of our experience from each other in a way they are not demarcated by modern physics* (Putnam, 1994, pp. 68–69).[24] And if we implicitly affirm such notions in the course of giving a causal account of intentionality, "then we abandon materialism without admitting that we are abandoning it" for in that case we "project into physical systems properties … that cannot be properties of matter 'in itself,'" at least not given the post-Newtonian conception of matter to which materialists are committed (Putnam, 1990, p. 90).

It is ironic that Hayek should be open to the Popper-Putnam critique, because Hayek himself had leveled a similar objection against behaviorism. Behaviorists claimed to describe human behavior "objectively," in terms of the categories of physical science rather than those of "naïve sense experience"; yet the way they characterized stimuli actually presupposed the latter rather than the former (Hayek, 1952, pp. 25–30; cf. Hayek, 1979a, pp. 78–80). If we followed out behaviorism seriously, then (in a line Hayek quotes from psychologist E. G. Boring) "green light of 505 millimicrons wavelength may be a stimulus but my grandmother is not a stimulus" (Hayek, 1952, p. 27). Consequently, Hayek is careful to insist that we characterize the stimuli which cause or "evoke" neural impulses in entirely physical and "objective" terms, rather than in terms of everyday, commonsense categories.

What Hayek does not realize is that the notion of causation or "evocation" that he needs is *itself* a further instance of a category that reflects the "naïve" commonsensical view of the world rather than the description given to us by physics. For however "objectively" he characterizes a particular stimulus considered *in isolation*, when characterizing *its relations to the neural impulses which it "evokes,"* he still needs to be able to distinguish it as *"the* cause" as opposed to a mere background condition, and nothing in the physics of the situation justifies that distinction. Hayek says that "behaviorism, from its own point of view, was not radical and consistent enough" (ibid.). Popper's objection is, in effect, that the same could be said of Hayek.[25]

---

24 Cf. the comparison of causal theories of reference to the notion of "substantial form" in Putnam, 1981, at p. 47.

25 If Popper is right, then the failure of Hayek's account of intentionality or representation will entail the failure of any Hayekian explanation of rationality as well, since the "argumentative" function of language presupposes the "descriptive" function. Popper later developed a further argument for the impossibility of a causal theory of rational argumentation, according to which no such theory can account for the

Hayek's response to Popper

In 1952 Hayek wrote to Popper about their disagreement, summing up what he took to be the main issues:

> If your argument were intended merely to prove that we can never explain why at a particular moment such and such sensations, mental processes, etc., take place I should agree. If, on the other hand, you were intending to deny that it can be explained how physical processes can be arranged in the general <u>kind</u> of order which is characteristic of mental phenomena, it would need a great deal to convince me. Of course, my analysis of a particular problem raises the most far-reaching philosophical problems. I am now for months puzzling about what just now seems to me the most general problem of all and which at the moment I describe for myself as the distinction between what we can say "within a system" and what we can say "about a system." I am convinced that this is a most important problem, since ever since I began to see it clearly I meet it constantly in all sorts of different connections, but though I have made some little headway it is one of the most difficult and elusive problems I have ever tackled. (Hayek, 1994, pp. 28–29)

Hayek's unfinished draft "Within Systems and About Systems" is a study of this problem, and as noted earlier, seems intended at least in part as a response to the difficulties raised by Popper. While he does not explicitly present it as such, he does say that he intends to reply to those who regard it as "futile" or "absurd" to analyze mental processes in terms of "causal systems," and that of the various mental phenomena his focus will be on "communication and particularly description"—the latter being precisely one of the phenomena Popper said could not be explained causally.[26]

difference between believing something on rational grounds and believing it as a result of such non-rational influences as intimidation, hypnosis, and the like. (See Popper and Eccles, 1986, pp. 75–81.) Given space limitations, we cannot consider this argument here, but for a brief discussion see Feser, 2006a, pp. 309–10. Cf. also the section on "The argument from reason" in chapter 6 of Feser, 2006b.

26 Hayek, "Within Systems and About Systems." The typescript in the Hoover Institution archive is organized into numbered paragraphs. The words quoted are in paragraphs 1 and 3. All quotations from Hayek's unpublished papers are made with the permission of the Estate of F. A. Hayek.

Moreover, he explicitly cites Bühler's distinction between functions of language, which Popper had borrowed and adapted for the purposes of his own argument.[27] Hayek's central claim is that:

> [F]or any causal system there is a limit to the complexity of other systems for which the former can provide the analogon of a description or explanation, and that this limit necessarily excludes the possibility of a system ever describing or explaining itself. This means that, if the human mind were a causal system, we would necessarily experience in discussing it precisely those obstacles and difficulties which we do encounter and which are often regarded as proof that the human mind is not a causal system.[28]

The impossibility of the mind's fully explaining itself is a recurring theme in Hayek's writings on our subject.[29] He takes it to follow from the complexity of any system capable of exhibiting mental properties, and in particular from the potentially infinite regress entailed by the mind's reflection on its own operations. For when one group of mental operations becomes an object of thought for another, understanding the latter will in turn require that it be made an object of thought for yet another, and so on *ad infinitum*, as each meta-level of thought becomes an object-level for another meta-level. The parallel with Gödel's incompleteness theorems, Cantor's set theory, and Russell's theory of types is obvious, and Hayek took puzzles of self-referentiality of the sort studied by such thinkers to provide the key to understanding why a material mind should seem to us to be inexplicable in material terms.[30]

The trouble with this sort of move, considered as a reply to Popper, is that it assumes that it is the "self" in self-referentiality that is the problem, when in fact it is the "referentiality" that is. Once we have a system capable of referring at all—capable, that is, of intentionality or representation—then yes, puzzles of *self*-referentiality are going to arise if the system becomes

---

27 Ibid., paragraph 39.
28 Ibid., paragraph 1.
29 See especially Hayek, 1979a, pp. 86; Hayek, 1952, pp. 184–90; and Hayek, 1969, pp. 60–63. For an exposition of Hayek's argument for this claim, see pp. 299–304 of Feser, 2006a.
30 Hayek explicitly cites Cantor and Gödel in this connection in Hayek, 1969, pp. 61–62.

sufficiently complex. But the question Popper is addressing is not whether a complex system *already* capable of intentionality can understand itself. The question he is addressing is whether a purely material system could exhibit intentionality of even a *rudimentary, non*-self-referential sort *merely* by virtue of bearing certain causal relations to other objects and events. Systems of the sort studied by Gödel, Cantor, and Russell are completely irrelevant to this question, as should be obvious when we consider that these systems already presuppose the existence of intentionality insofar as they presuppose minds capable of interpreting otherwise meaningless physical marks as symbols of logic and set theory. What we need to know is *how such intentionality enters the picture in the first place.*

That Hayek does not clearly understand what is at issue is evident from what he says in "Within Systems and About Systems." Much of the draft recapitulates the theory of *The Sensory Order*, and like the book makes free use of terms like "classification," "representation," "models," and "map"— terms the intentional connotations of which are precisely what need to be grounded. To be sure, Hayek says that he intends to explain "the property to which we refer by such terms as 'intention,' 'purpose,' 'aim,' 'need,' or 'desire'" and acknowledges that "we must not use any of these 'mental' terms until we have succeeded in adequately defining them in terms of our causal system."[31] Yet when he goes on to propose a definition of one of these notions in what he claims to be purely "causal terms" or "physical terms,"[32] this is what he says:

> By <u>intention</u> we shall mean such a state of a system that, whenever its classifying apparatus represents a chain of actions as producing a result which at the same time the internal state of the system singles out as appropriate to that state, it will perform that chain of actions.[33]

The problem with this definition is, of course, that it makes use of notions— "classifying," "represents," "singles out as appropriate"—which *themselves* have intentional connotations, notions he does not elsewhere define in purely causal, non-intentional terms. The argument of the draft—already

---

31 Hayek, "Within Systems and About Systems," paragraph 24. I have cleaned up Hayek's punctuation slightly.
32 Ibid., paragraphs 33 and 35.
33 Ibid., paragraph 34.

unfinished in any case—therefore presupposes the very phenomenon to be explained, and doesn't really answer Popper at all. As Putnam says in commenting on the work of a contemporary neuroscientist:

> If a philosopher asks what the nature of representation is, and one tells him or her that there are tens of millions of representations in the Widener Library, one has not answered the question. And if one tells him or her that there are tens of millions of representations in human brains, one has not answered the question either. (Putnam, 1992, pp. 22–23)[34]

Might a better response to Popper be at least implicit elsewhere in Hayek's oeuvre? Hayek does suggest that evolution plays a role in determining how the mind will "classify" the elements of its environment (Hayek, 1978, p. 42; cf. Hayek, 1988, pp. 21–23). And later writers have proposed that natural selection provides a solution to problems of the sort raised by Popper. In particular, philosophers like Ruth Millikan and Daniel Dennett have argued that the causal chains which underlie our representational powers have to be traced back farther than our immediate environment, indeed all the way back to the environment in which the brains of our ancestors were shaped by evolution (Millikan, 1984; Dennett, 1995).

But Hayek himself barely gestures in the direction of such arguments, and there are in any event serious difficulties facing them. For problems of indeterminacy of the sort discussed by Fodor, Dretske, Popper, and Putnam seem to arise for *any* causal account; whether the causal chains are traced only to the immediate environment or extend back to the time of our ancient ancestors is not to the point. To borrow an example from Putnam, suppose it is suggested that a certain neural "data structure" evolved in dogs to facilitate their getting meat, and that this justifies us in attributing to them a concept or "proto-concept" of meat (Putnam, 1992, pp. 27–33). As Putnam points out, the dog will be satisfied and nourished whether it is given fresh meat, canned meat, or some textured vegetable protein that looks, smells, and tastes exactly like meat. For that reason, there is no fact of the matter about whether its putative "proto-concept" represents any one of these in particular, and thus no sense to be made of the question of whether the dog

---

34   The neuroscientist in question is Gerald Edelman, but Putnam acknowledges that "Edelman himself is wary of trying to answer the philosophical question about the nature of reference" (p. 25).

has a true belief about what it is eating when it eats the vegetable protein rather than meat. "Evolution didn't 'design' dogs' ideas to be true or false, it designed them to be successful or unsuccessful" (ibid., p. 31). But in that case the suggestion that the dog really *has* a "proto-concept" of meat in the first place is groundless:

> [T]he whole idea that a unique correspondence between the data structure and meat is involved in this bit of natural selection is an illusion, an artifact of the way we described the situation. We could just as well have said that the data structure was selected for because its action normally signals the presence of something which has a certain smell and taste and appearance and is edible. (Ibid.)

In short, there is nothing in the situation described that entails that anything in the dog's brain corresponds to *meat* specifically, and thus there is nothing in the situation that entails that the dog has a *concept* (or "proto-concept") of meat. The point is completely general, applying to *any* concept. Natural selection favors survival value, not truth or falsity. Hence you are not going to get truth or falsity from natural selection, and neither will you get from it the *concepts* that thoughts and statements—the sorts of things that are *susceptible* of being either true or false—presuppose.

Indeed, the very idea that the evolutionary processes under discussion have anything to do with explaining the origin of intentionality in the first place is an illusion. After all, gazelles' legs were favored by natural selection because they allowed gazelles to run fast and thereby to escape predators. But no one suggests that this shows that a gazelle's leg has the concept of running fast, or the thought that *now would be a good time to run*. As Putnam writes:

> Isn't it with dogs as with gazelles? Dogs which tended to eat meat rather than vegetables when both were available produced more offspring (gazelles which ran faster than lions escaped the lions and were thus able to produce more offspring). Just as we aren't tempted to say that gazelles have a proto-concept of running fast, so dogs don't have a proto-concept of meat ... The "reference" we get out of this bit of hypothetical natural selection will be just the reference we put in our choice of a description. Evolution won't give you more intentionality than you pack into it. (Ibid., pp. 32–33.)

In other words, in order to make the evolution of certain neural structures relevant to the explanation of intentionality, a theorist like Millikan or Dennett has to *presuppose* that such neural structures "represent" the external world in the first place in a way that the gazelle's leg structure (say) does not. Like Hayek, these writers seem to be *reading intentionality into* the physical facts, not *deriving it from* them.

Now the materialist might at this point decide to bite the bullet and insist that if his position cannot account for the determinate content of our concepts and thoughts, then so much the worse for determinate content. That is to say, just as there is no fact of the matter about whether a dog's putative "proto-concept" refers to *meat* specifically or instead covers meat, textured vegetable protein, and what have you, so too (the materialist might say) there is no fact of the matter about what any of *our* concepts refers to. Indeed, some materialists take precisely this line—W. V. Quine is the best known example, and Dennett is another (Quine, 1960, chapter 2; Dennett, 1995, pp. 410–11).[35] Nor is it implausible to speculate that Hayek might have been open to such a position, given his emphasis on the role messy evolutionary processes play in the formation of our minds,[36] and given his view that the regress attending the mind's reflections on its own operations entails that "all we can talk about and probably all we can consciously think about presupposes the existence of a framework which determines its meaning ... but which we can neither state nor form an image of" (Hayek, 1969, p. 62)—though it would go beyond the evidence to assert flatly that Hayek *did* regard our concepts as inherently indeterminate.[37]

But there are grave problems with this strategy as well, problems which have been spelled out trenchantly by philosopher James Ross (Ross, 1992; Ross, 2008, chapter 6).[38] First, if we say that our concepts and thoughts are inherently indeterminate, that there is no objective fact of the matter about

35 As Putnam notes (1992, p. 101), Bernard Williams takes a similar line in Williams, 1990, at p. 300.

36 See again the pages from Hayek, 1988 cited above, and also the Epilogue to Hayek, 1979b.

37 One reason for caution here is that the remarks by Hayek that are relevant to the issue have an *epistemological* tenor, whereas the indeterminacy claims made by thinkers like Quine, Dennett, and Williams are *metaphysical* in import. Hayek says that we can't *know* everything that determines the content of our thoughts and statements, but the other writers make the stronger claim that there is *no objective fact of the matter in the first place* about what content they have.

38 Searle also presents an important related critique of Quine's indeterminacy thesis, in Searle, 2002.

what they mean or represent, then it would follow that there is no fact of the matter about whether we ever reason in accordance with valid modes of inference. It might seem to us that we are applying *modus ponens*, for example, when in reality there is no more reason to think we are doing so than to think that we are applying some different and invalid pattern of inference instead. But in that case we could never have any reason to believe that any of our inferences is rationally justified. Since this would include the inferences of materialists (including thinkers like Quine and Dennett) themselves, the materialist position would thus undermine itself.

Second, if we are intelligibly going to deny that the content of our thoughts is ever really determinate, we first have to understand what it is that we are denying. For example, if we are going to deny that there is a fact of the matter about whether we reason in accordance with *modus ponens*, or have thoughts about *meat*, specifically (as opposed to about *either meat or vegetable protein*) then we first have to be able to grasp *what it would be* for an inference to conform to *modus ponens*, and *what it would be* for a thought to be about meat, specifically, before going on to deny that there are any such inferences or thoughts. But in that case, we *do*, precisely in the act of grasping these concepts, have thoughts with determinate content of the sort we were supposed not to have. Again, the position in question undermines itself.

Obviously, these are deep issues; I do not claim to have settled them here. There is also the question of what alternative view one ought to take if one rejects Hayek's causal theory of the mind and any other essentially materialist position. Popper's response was to embrace Cartesian dualism. Putnam's is to opt for pragmatism, though he acknowledges that the considerations he raises against the causal theorist are "grist for the mill of a possible latter-day Aristotelian metaphysics" (Putnam, 1994, p. 69). My own view is that this is precisely what is called for—that the mind-body problem, whose origins lay in the early moderns' anti-Aristotelian revolution, can only be resolved (or dissolved) by a neo-Aristotelian restoration.[39] Naturally, I am talking about a return to Aristotelian *metaphysics*, not Aristotelian *science*. Unfortunately, not all writers on these issues are careful to make this distinction. As Putnam writes:

---

39 See Feser, 2009 for a defense of this approach. Nor is this position as eccentric as it might sound—neo-Aristotelianism is a growing force in contemporary philosophy. For an overview of its influence in philosophy of science, see Ellis, 2002; for an indication of its influence within contemporary metaphysics, see Tahko, 2012.

For the last three centuries a certain metaphysical picture suggested by Newtonian or Galilean physics has been repeatedly confused with physics itself ... Philosophers who love that picture do not have very much incentive to point out the confusion—if a philosophical picture is taken to be the picture endorsed by science, then attacks on the picture will seem to be attacks on science, and few philosophers will wish to be seen as enemies of science. (Putnam, 1992, p. 19)

Whatever one's position on the mind-body problem, we must be wary of this conflation of science with scientism—a conflation Hayek himself frequently warned us about. As he put it in "Scientism and the Study of Society":

The scientistic as distinguished from the scientific view is not an unprejudiced but a very prejudiced approach which, before it has considered its subject, claims to know what is the most appropriate way of investigating it. (Hayek, 1979a, p. 24)

Unfortunately, insofar as Hayek also took it for granted that the mind simply *must* be fitted somehow into a pinched, post-Newtonian "mechanical" conception of matter and causality, his own escape from scientistic prejudice was arguably less than complete.

References

Armstrong, D. M. (1981). The Causal Theory of the Mind. In: *The Nature of Mind*. Brighton: Harvester Press.

Armstrong, D. M. (1993). *A Materialist Theory of the Mind* (Rev. ed.). London: Routledge.

Bartley, W. W. (1985). *Wittgenstein*. La Salle, IL: Open Court.

Bennett, M. R. and P. M. S. Hacker (2003). *Philosophical Foundations of Neuroscience*. Oxford: Blackwell.

Block, Ned (1997). On a Confusion about a Function of Consciousness. In: Ned Block, Owen Flanagan, and Güven Güzeldere (Eds.), *The Nature of Consciousness. Philosophical Debates*. Cambridge, MA: The MIT Press.

Caldwell, Bruce (2004). *Hayek's Challenge. An Intellectual Biography of F. A. Hayek*. Chicago: University of Chicago Press.

Corbí, Josep E. and Josep L. Prades (2000). *Minds, Causes and Mechanisms. A Case Against Physicalism*. Oxford: Blackwell.

Crane, Tim (2003). *The Mechanical Mind* (2nd ed.). London: Routledge.

Dennett, Daniel (1995). *Darwin's Dangerous Idea*. New York: Simon and Schuster.

Drestke, Fred (1981). *Knowledge and the Flow of Information*. Cambridge, MA: The MIT Press.

Dretske, Fred (1988). *Explaining Behavior*. Cambridge, MA: The MIT Press.

Dretske, Fred (1995). *Naturalizing the Mind*. Cambridge, MA: The MIT Press.

Edelman, Gerald M. (1987). *Neural Darwinism. The Theory of Neuronal Group Selection*. New York: Basic Books.

Ellis, Brian (2002). *The Philosophy of Nature: A Guide to the New Essentialism*. Chesham: Acumen.

Feser, Edward (2006a). Hayek the cognitive scientist and philosopher of mind. In: Edward Feser (Ed.), *The Cambridge Companion to Hayek*. Cambridge: Cambridge University Press.

Feser, Edward (2006b). *Philosophy of Mind* (Rev. ed.). Oxford: Oneworld Publications.

Feser, Edward (2009). *Aquinas*. Oxford: Oneworld Publications.

Feser, Edward (2010). Teleology: A Shopper's Guide. *Philosophia Christi*, 12 (1), pp. 147–65.

Fodor, Jerry A. (1987). *Psychosemantics. The Problem of Meaning in the Philosophy of Mind*. Cambridge, MA: The MIT Press.

Fodor, Jerry A. (1990). *A Theory of Content and Other Essays*. Cambridge, MA: The MIT Press.

Fodor, Jerry A. (1994). Jerry A. Fodor. In: Samuel Guttenplan (Ed.), *A Companion to the Philosophy of Mind*. Oxford: Blackwell.

Fuster, Joaquín M. (2003). *Cortex and Mind. Unifying Cognition*. Oxford: Oxford University Press.

Hayek, F. A. (1952). *The Sensory Order. An Inquiry into the Foundations of Theoretical Psychology*. London: Routledge and Kegan Paul.

Hayek, F. A. (1969). Rules, Perception, and Intelligibility. In: *Studies in Philosophy, Politics, and Economics*. New York: Simon and Schuster.

Hayek, F. A. (1978). The Primacy of the Abstract. In: *New Studies in Philosophy, Politics, Economics, and the History of Ideas*. London: Routledge and Kegan Paul.

Hayek, F. A. (1979a). *The Counter-Revolution of Science*. Indianapolis: Liberty Press.

Hayek, F. A. (1979b). *Law, Legislation, and Liberty, Volume 3: The Political Order of a Free People*. Chicago: University of Chicago Press.

Hayek, F. A. (1988). *The Fatal Conceit*. Chicago: University of Chicago Press.

Hayek, F. A. (1994). *Hayek on Hayek. An Autobiographical Dialogue*, edited by Stephen Kresge and Leif Wenar. Chicago: University of Chicago Press.

Millikan, Ruth (1984). *Language, Thought, and Other Biological Categories*. Cambridge, MA: The MIT Press.

Nagel, Thomas (1979). What is it like to be a bat? In: *Mortal Questions*. Cambridge: Cambridge University Press.

Popper, Karl R. (1968). Language and the Body-Mind Problem. In: *Conjectures and Refutations. The Growth of Scientific Knowledge*. New York: Harper and Row.

Popper, Karl R. (1979). Of Clouds and Clocks. In: *Objective Knowledge*. Oxford: Clarendon Press.

Popper, Karl R. (1996). *Knowledge and the Body-Mind Problem*. London: Routledge.

Popper, Karl and John C. Eccles (1986). *The Self and Its Brain*. London: Routledge.

Putnam, Hilary (1981). *Reason Truth, and History*. Cambridge: Cambridge University Press.

Putnam, Hilary (1987). *The Many Faces of Realism*. La Salle, IL: Open Court.

Putnam, Hilary (1990). Is the Causal Structure of the Physical Itself Something Physical? In: *Realism with a Human Face*. Cambridge, MA: Harvard University Press.

Putnam, Hilary (1992). *Renewing Philosophy*. Cambridge, MA: Harvard University Press.

Putnam, Hilary (1994). Aristotle after Wittgenstein. In: *Words and Life*. Cambridge, MA: Harvard University Press.

Quine, W. V. (1960). *Word and Object*. Cambridge, MA: The MIT Press.

Ross, James (1992). Immaterial Aspects of Thought. *Journal of Philosophy*, (89) 3, pp. 136–50.

Ross, James (2008). *Thought and World*. Notre Dame, IN: University of Notre Dame Press.

Searle, John R. (1992). *The Rediscovery of the Mind*. Cambridge, MA: The MIT Press.

Searle, John R. (2002). Indeterminacy, Empiricism, and the First Person. In: *Consciousness and Language*. Cambridge: Cambridge University Press.

Stebbing, L. S. (1939). *Thinking to Some Purpose*. London: Pelican Books.

Tahko, Tuomas (Ed.) (2012). *Contemporary Aristotelian Metaphysics*. Cambridge: Cambridge University Press.

Tye, Michael (1995). *Ten Problems of Consciousness. A Representational Theory of the Phenomenal Mind*. Cambridge, MA: The MIT Press.

Williams, Bernard (1990). *Descartes: The Project of Pure Inquiry*. New York: Penguin Books.

12

Why Searle Is a Property Dualist

John Searle has tried to stake out a middle position between materialism and property dualism, which he calls "biological naturalism." To many of his critics (e.g., Nagel 1995, p. 96; Chalmers 1996, p. 370, n. 2), biological naturalism has seemed little more than property dualism in disguise. Searle insists that his view has been misunderstood, and has attempted in a series of writings (1984, 1991, 1992, 1997, 1998) to distinguish it from property dualism, most recently in his article "Why I Am Not a Property Dualist" (2002). But the critics are, as I will try to show, correct. Searle *is*, whether he realizes it or not, a property dualist.

The basic idea of "biological naturalism" is that mental states, though (contrary to materialism) not *identical to* the firing of neurons or any other brain processes, are nevertheless *caused by* such processes in a manner analogous to the way the solidity of an ice cube is caused by the state of the water molecules composing it. Consciousness and other mental phenomena are thus higher-order features of the brain, just as solidity is a higher-order feature of the system of water molecules constituting the ice cube. But just as solidity is nevertheless a physical property of a system of water molecules, so too (and contrary to property dualism) is consciousness a physical property of the system of neurons constituting the brain.

The reason this sounds to Searle's critics like property dualism is that there is—by Searle's own admission—a significant disanalogy between solidity and the like on the one hand and consciousness and other mental phenomena on the other. Solidity, like all uncontroversially physical properties, has what Searle calls a "third-person ontology" (2002, p. 60). That is, it is an entirely objective or "public" phenomenon, equally accessible in principle to every observer. The same is true of the water molecules which, when frozen, collectively manifest solidity. There is thus no mystery about how solidity can be a higher-order physical property of a system of water molecules. For, fully to describe the condition of water molecules at the temperature at which water freezes *just is* to describe them as solid. There is nothing more to solidity than that; it is *identical* to the configuration the molecules are in when the object they constitute is at freezing temperature. In any case, there is nothing about the nature of either water molecules or solidity—both of which are "third-person"—that excludes such an identification.

Neural processes also have by Searle's reckoning a third-person ontology. But consciousness and other mental phenomena do not; they have instead what he calls a "first-person ontology," being essentially subjective or "private," directly accessible only to the subject undergoing conscious experiences. There is thus an *essential* difference between conscious phenomena and all uncontroversially physical phenomena—the former, being essentially subjective, cannot be identified with or reduced to any subset of the latter, which are essentially objective. Searle, again, acknowledges this: "The property dualist and I are in agreement that consciousness is ontologically irreducible" (2002, p. 60). Consciousness is, unlike solidity, not identical to the microphysical structures which cause it. But then property dualism seems unavoidable. If the physical processes which cause consciousness are objective third-person phenomena, and consciousness and other mental phenomena are subjective or first-person in nature, it is reasonable to describe the latter as being of a *fundamentally different kind* than the former. That is, it is reasonable to say that there exists in the universe a *dualism* of properties. If what all uncontroversially physical properties have in common is precisely their objective or third-person character, it is reasonable too to regard that character as what is essential to being physical—in which case mental properties, being essentially subjective, would necessarily count as *non*-physical.

Such is the difficulty facing Searle's claim to have avoided property dualism. But Searle has presented four lines of argument (helpfully summarized in his most recent article (2002), but present also in his earlier writings), intended to demonstrate that the difficulty is illusory. As I hope to show, none of them succeeds.

The first line of argument is directed against the dichotomous physical/non-physical categorization implied by property dualism, a division Searle claims not to be committed to. "There are not two (or five or seven) fundamental ontological categories," Searle writes; "rather the act of categorization itself is always interest relative" (2002, p. 59). The claim is that the interest-relativity involved in our classificatory practices shows the dualist's division of the world into physical and non-physical spheres to be arbitrary, reflecting no objective difference in nature. But the problem with this as a criticism of property dualism is that the fact that *acts of categorization* are interest-relative does not entail that *categories themselves* have no objective validity. Being pet lovers with a penchant for zoology, we count dogs and cats as belonging to different categories, even though we can imagine a society whose inhabitants are uninterested in pets or scientific classification in which these animals were not so classified, but lumped together into one amorphous category of animals—"cogs," say. But this does not entail that there is no objective difference between dogs and cats, or that this classification is no more reflective of objective reality than would be an obviously artificial classification of all physical objects into those that are inside my office and those that are outside of it. Some classifications, however interest-relative our reasons for making them, clearly reflect objective features of reality. Searle, one of the staunchest contemporary defenders of metaphysical realism, would surely acknowledge this.

But the property dualist's classification seems clearly to be of this objective sort. Mental phenomena may be inherently "subjective," but as Searle has pointed out (1992, p. 94), this does *not* mean they are subjective in the sense of existing only relative to human interests—the reality of your experience of pain is not a matter of convention, and the pain exists whether or not we (or you) want it to. In *that* (interest-relative) sense of "subjectivity," the pain exists not subjectively but "objectively." The pain *is* subjective, however, in the different sense that it is, however objectively real, directly accessible only to you, from "within" your own mind. No other phenomena are like that; everything else in reality is objective in the sense of being in principle directly accessible to everyone. So the objective/subjective distinction—one Searle himself puts great emphasis on—surely reflects an objective difference between phenomena in the world. But it is precisely this distinction which marks the difference between the categories of physical and mental properties, on the property dualist's view. It is therefore hard to see how Searle can dismiss such a categorization as arbitrary.

It does not help to insist, as Searle does, that "we live in exactly one world" (2002, p. 59), for property dualism need not deny that, but need claim only that that one world contains two fundamentally different kinds of property. Nor does it help to point out that "in addition to electromagnetism, consciousness, and gravitational attraction, there are declines in interest rates, points scored in football games, reasons for being suspicious of quantified modal logic, and election results in Florida" (p. 59), as if this showed that reality can if desired be divided up into more than the dualist's two categories. For—as, again, Searle himself has argued (1995)—declines

in interest rates, points scored in football games, and the like are all phenomena which depend for their existence on human convention and the collective intentionality of countless human minds; so they hardly serve as
counterexamples to the claim that the mental and the physical are the two
ultimate ontological categories.

Furthermore, property dualism does not rest in the first place on the assumption that there are *only* two ultimate metaphysical categories. Many
dualists have argued that in addition to the mental and physical aspects of
reality, there is a "third realm" of abstract objects—mathematical entities,
Platonic forms, and the like. Property dualism as usually presented is a theory about the metaphysics of mind specifically, not a completely general
ontological theory; it claims that there are two fundamental kinds of property involved where *human nature* is concerned, but not necessarily that
there are only two fundamental kinds of property in all of reality. So, again,
it is no criticism of property dualism to note that there may be more than
two basic ontological categories.

Having said that, it is also implausible to suggest, as Searle does, that
we could just as easily divide the world up into "five or seven" or some
higher number of ontological categories. It is hard to imagine anything that
does not fall into one of the three categories just alluded to (though perhaps
God would count as being in a fourth category). Certainly Searle has not
provided any convincing examples of further irreducible categories. These
three (maybe four) categories seem the most basic; and while one can, of
course, dispute the reality of any of them, there is nothing *arbitrary* about
the distinction between them, as is evidenced by the fact that *all* the ontological disputes of the last 2,500 years always come down to disputes over
purported entities falling into one of precisely these categories.

The bottom line is that the distinction on which property dualism
rests—that between irreducibly subjective and objective phenomena—is
one that Searle himself is committed to as marking out two objective categories of phenomena in the universe. Whether or not there are any further
categories is beside the point, even if Searle's case were convincing that
such categories could be multiplied indefinitely. It is also beside the point
whether one wants to go on to label these two categories "non-physical"
and "physical"—this is a purely semantic issue, the distinction being real
whatever one chooses to call it. Searle chooses not to adopt these labels,
but given that (by Searle's own admission) every uncontroversially physical
phenomenon in the world is objective while mental phenomena alone are
subjective, it appears that it is Searle, in denying that this fact entails a

natural distinction between the physical and non-physical, who is more plausibly accused of arbitrariness than is the property dualist.

Searle's second line of argument suggests that his view differs from property dualism in acknowledging, as property dualism doesn't, that there is a sense in which consciousness is reducible to neural processes in the brain. To be sure, Searle acknowledges that consciousness is not "ontologically" reducible. But it is in his view nevertheless "causally reducible" to brain processes and thus not "something over and above its neurobiological base" (2002, p. 60), being instead "realized in" the latter (p. 57). The solidity of an object is caused by, and a higher-level feature of, the system of molecules comprising the object; and consciousness is caused by, and a higher-level feature of, the neural processes in the brain. But here again the alleged distinction between Searle's view and property dualism seems purely verbal. For by calling consciousness "causally reducible" to brain processes, all Searle means is that *brain processes cause consciousness*. But this is exactly what the property dualist believes, as Searle later acknowledges (p. 62)! So the *property dualist too* believes, in *Searle's* sense, that consciousness is "causally reducible." Nor does Searle's claim that consciousness is not something "over and above" the brain distinguish his view from property dualism. For all the property dualist means in holding that consciousness is something over and above the brain is that it is not *ontologically* reducible to neural processes—which Searle himself acknowledges! He acknowledges too that this ontological irreducibility distinguishes consciousness from features like solidity. So what the *point* is of appealing to solidity when Searle himself concedes that such examples fail to be analogous to consciousness in the very respect the property dualist takes to be crucial, is mysterious. When one gets clear on the meaning of the jargon Searle uses—"causally reducible to," which means nothing more than the property dualist's "caused by"; or "realized in the brain," which, given that Searle like the property dualist takes consciousness to be ontologically irreducible to neural processes, means nothing different from the property dualist's concession that consciousness is a "property of the brain"—the actual substance of Searle's position and property dualism turn out to be identical.

The impression that wordplay is all that Searle's case ultimately rests on is deepened by his third line of argument, wherein he insists that it is only the "inadequacy of the traditional terminology" of "the mental and the physical" that makes his biological naturalism seem identical to property dualism (2002, p. 61). Traditional philosophical usage takes "mental" to contrast *by definition* with "physical," so that taking the mental to be irreducible to the physical seems to imply taking it to be non-physical. But if we jettison this usage, Searle argues, the apparent commitment to property dualism disappears. The problem with this move is that it ignores the fact— a fact implicit in Searle's own position—that the distinction between mental and physical is obviously not *merely* a matter of arbitrary stipulative definition. As we've seen, mental phenomena are in Searle's view like the property dualist's *uniquely* subjective and therefore *uniquely* ontologically irreducible. *That* is the reason they are contrasted with physical phenomena, all uncontroversial or paradigm instances of which are objective and reducible. It is just not true that Descartes or anyone else decided one day capriciously to define "mental" to mean "non-physical," and then concluded, trivially, that some form of dualism must be true. It is rather that the dualist takes note of the objective, interest-independent fact that mental phenomena appear to differ from everything else in the world in being uniquely subjective and ontologically irreducible, and *then*, on *that* basis, concludes that they are non-physical. Of course, many philosophers would deny that they really are irreducibly subjective. But *Searle* does not do so, so it is hard to see how *he* can regard the suggestion that mental phenomena are inherently different from physical phenomena as resting on nothing more than terminological fiat.

If anything it is Searle who seems to be playing word games here, redefining "physical" so that it includes not only the objective phenomena usually counted as physical, but also the uniquely and irreducibly subjective phenomena that philosophers have had such trouble fitting into that objective physical world. Of course, he's free to use the word that way if he likes. But it does nothing to distinguish his position substantively from property dualism. The latter speaks of physical properties, which are objective, and non-physical properties, which are irreducibly subjective; Searle speaks of two kinds of physical properties, those which are objective and those which are subjective and irreducible to the other kind of physical properties. The words may be different, but the metaphysical pictures are identical.

This identity is made more evident when Searle writes that "consciousness ... has no cause and effect relations beyond those of its microstructural base" (p. 60). That is, the neural processes that cause consciousness, and to which consciousness is ontologically irreducible, are all that bear causal relations to other neural processes, behavior, etc.—consciousness *per se* has no such causal relations. But how does this differ from the epiphenomenalism Searle, like many other philosophers of mind, criticizes property dualism for (p. 59)? Searle's fourth line of argument is intended to answer this question, but it fails for the same reason his earlier arguments fail. Once again Searle appeals to the analogy with solidity, an analogy we've seen is imperfect in a way he elsewhere acknowledges. "[T]he solidity of the piston [of a car engine] has no causal powers in addition to its molecular base," Searle says, "but this does not show that solidity is epiphenomenal" (p. 61). But the *reason* it doesn't show this is precisely because solidity is ontologically reducible to the state of the piston's molecules. *Of course* there's no mystery about why solidity isn't epiphenomenal despite its lack of causal powers beyond those of its microstructural base—for solidity *is nothing but* the state of the microstructural base in the first place. They're *identical*! But consciousness, as Searle himself insists, is *not* identical to its base, *not* ontologically reducible to it. The analogy with the piston is therefore useless. For it's precisely this ontological irreducibility that threatens epiphenomenalism. The "microstructural base" of consciousness—the firing of neurons—would be just as it is, and in particular have just the causal powers it has, even in the absence of consciousness; so consciousness seems to add nothing to the causal story. Searle asks: "[W]hy would anyone suppose that causal reducibility implies epiphenomenalism?" (2002, p. 61) but the question is directed at a straw man, for no one does suppose this. What they do suppose is not that *causal reducibility* implies epiphenomenalism, but rather that *ontological ir*reducibility implies it. And Searle, who accepts ontological irreducibility, has done nothing to show that it doesn't. So he has, again, failed to distinguish his view from property dualism.

    The failure of this last of Searle's arguments manifests a problem plaguing his entire position, namely his refusal seriously to confront the fact that it is the ontological irreducibility of the mental, and the subjectivity that entails it, that are the basis of property dualism. Matters of terminology are ultimately irrelevant. If paradigmatically and uncontroversially physical phenomena are essentially objective, and paradigmatically and uncontroversially mental phenomena are irreducibly subjective, then it follows that they are of fundamentally different metaphysical kinds. It follows, that is, that property dualism—the claim that there are (at least) two metaphysically fundamental kinds of property in the universe—is true. Since Searle accepts the antecedent, he is committed also to the consequent, whether he realizes it or not and whether he wants to refer to that consequent by its usual label "property dualism," or instead by the label "biological naturalism."

    It is revealing that Searle, though he takes his biological naturalism to have "solved" the mind-body problem, also acknowledges that his position "raises a thousand questions of its own... [such as] how exactly do the elements of the neuroanatomy—neurons, synapses, synaptic clefts, receptors, mitochondria, glial cells, transmitter fluids, etc.—produce mental phenomena?" (1992, p. 1) and concedes that "we don't have anything like a clear idea of how brain processes, which are publicly observable, objective phenomena, could cause anything as peculiar as inner, qualitative states of awareness or sentience, states which are in some sense 'private' to the possessor of the state" (1997, p. 8). Since explaining all *that* is what most philosophers *mean* by "the mind-body problem," it is hard to see exactly what problem Searle thinks *he* has solved. Certainly it is no revelation to be told that brain processes cause mental processes – something everyone concerned with this question has known for decades if not centuries. In fact Searle's "solution" appears to be little more than to redefine the mind-body problem in such a way that the philosophical heart of it—the difficulty of fitting what is irreducibly subjective into the objective physical world—is arbitrarily re-classified as a problem for biology (1997, p. 3). I say "arbitrarily" because there is no reason whatever to believe that the methods of biology are any more likely to be able to deal with the objective/subjective divide than those of philosophy. Indeed, given the inherently *conceptual* nature of the problem, they are surely *less* likely to be able to do so. In any case, the problem remains, and remains just as difficult as it ever was, however we decide to label it. Once again, Searle's position appears to rest on little more than wordplay.

References

Chalmers, David (1996), *The Conscious Mind* (New York: Oxford University Press).

Nagel, Thomas (1995), *Other Minds* (New York: Oxford University Press).

Searle, John R. (1984), *Minds, Brains, and Science* (Cambridge, MA: Harvard University Press).

Searle, John R. (1991), "Response: The Mind-Body Problem" in Ernest Lepore and Robert van Gulick, eds. *John Searle and His Critics* (Oxford: Basil Blackwell).

Searle, John R. (1992), *The Rediscovery of the Mind* (Cambridge, MA: The MIT Press).

Searle, John R. (1995), *The Construction of Social Reality* (New York: Free Press).

Searle, John R. (1997), *The Mystery of Consciousness* (New York: The New York Review of Books).

Searle, John R. (1998), *Mind, Language, and Society* (New York: Basic Books).

Searle, John R. (2002), "Why I Am Not a Property Dualist" *Journal of Consciousness Studies* 9 (12), pp. 57–64.

Ethics

13
Being, the Good, and the Guise of the Good

I. Introduction

The aim of this paper is to put forward an exposition and defense of the Aristotelian-Thomistic (A-T) conception of the good, and in particular of the theses that goodness is convertible with being and that all action is directed at the good. The former thesis will be defended against the objection, longstanding within modern philosophy, that there is a "fact/value dichotomy" such that any attempt to derive claims about goodness from claims about the existence and nature of things commits a "naturalistic fallacy." The latter thesis will be defended against the recent criticisms of J. David Velleman. The application of the theses in question to the natural law approach to ethics and to natural theology will be noted in the course of the discussion.

II. Formal and final causes

The A-T conception of the good cannot be understood apart from the broader metaphysical context in which it is embedded. A-T is *essentialist* insofar as it holds that natural substances have essences or substantial forms that that are immanent to them and neither the inventions of the human mind nor mere artifacts of human language; and A-T is *teleological* insofar as it holds that natural substances have final causes or ends towards which they are directed inherently, by virtue of their essences or substantial forms. This commitment to immanent formal and final causes differentiates A-T from the broadly "mechanistic" conception of nature that supplanted Scholastic natural philosophy in the seventeenth century and that is simply taken for granted by most modern philosophers, including those critical of approaches to questions of value like the one associated with A-T.[1]

---

1   For more detailed discussion of the differences between the A-T conception of nature and the "mechanistic" conception, see my articles "Teleology: A Shopper's

Hence, David Hume famously argued that conclusions about what *ought* to be the case (statements about "value") cannot validly be inferred from premises concerning what *is* the case (statements of "fact"); and this Humean line has been pressed against Aquinas and other traditional natural law theorists by critics like Kai Nielsen and D. J. O'Connor.[2] From the A-T point of view, however, there is no "fact/value dichotomy" in the first place. More precisely, there is no such thing as a purely "factual" description of reality utterly divorced from "value," for "value" is built into the structure of the "facts" from the start. A gap between "fact" and "value" could exist only given a mechanistic understanding of nature, on which the world is devoid of any immanent essences or teleology.[3] No such gap, and thus no "fallacy" of inferring normative conclusions from "purely factual" premises, can exist given the A-T essentialist and teleological conception of the world. "Value" is a highly misleading term in any case, and subtly begs the question against critics of the "fact/value dichotomy" by insinuating that judgments about good and bad are purely subjective, insofar as "value" seems to presuppose someone doing the valuing. A-T writers (and other classical philosophers such as Platonists) tend to speak, not of "value," but of "the good," which on their account is entirely objective.

To see how, consider, to begin with, a simple example. It is of the essence or nature of a Euclidean triangle to be a closed plane figure with three straight

Guide," *Philosophia Christi*, Vol. 12, No. 1 (2010) and Feser, Edward, "Between Aristotle and William Paley: Aquinas's Fifth Way," *Nova et Vetera* Vol. 11, No. 3 (2013).

2   Kai Nielsen, "Religious Ethics Versus Humanistic Ethics," in his *Philosophy and Atheism* (Buffalo, NY: Prometheus Books, 1985), and D. J. O'Connor, *Aquinas and Natural Law* (London: Macmillan, 1968), p. 24. The hope of side-stepping this objection is part of the reason why Germain Grisez and John Finnis have sought to develop a "new" natural law theory which, unlike the traditional version, does not seek to ground morality in premises concerning the metaphysics of human nature. See Germain Grisez, "The First Principle of Practical Reason," in Anthony Kenny, ed., *Aquinas: A Collection of Critical Essays* (Garden City, NY: Doubleday, 1969) and John Finnis, *Natural Law and Natural Rights* (Oxford: Clarendon Press, 1980).

3   And maybe not even then, for the "fact/value distinction," though still affirmed by many contemporary philosophers, has been criticized by philosophers not necessarily sympathetic to A-T metaphysics. See, e.g., Hilary Putnam, *The Collapse of the Fact/Value Dichotomy and Other Essays* (Cambridge, MA: Harvard University Press, 2004). Criticisms on the part of writers who are sympathetic to A-T metaphysics include Christopher Martin, "The Fact/Value Distinction," in David S. Oderberg and Timothy Chappell, eds., *Human Values: New Essays on Ethics and Natural Law* (New York: Palgrave Macmillan, 2004) and David S. Oderberg, *Moral Theory: A Non-Consequentialist Approach* (Oxford: Blackwell, 2000), pp. 9–15.

sides, and anything with this essence must have a number of properties, such as having angles that add up to 180 degrees. These are objective facts that we discover rather than invent; certainly it is notoriously difficult to make the opposite opinion at all plausible. Nevertheless, there are obviously triangles that fail to live up to this definition. A triangle drawn hastily on the cracked plastic seat of a moving bus might fail to be completely closed or to have perfectly straight sides, and thus its angles will add up to something other than 180 degrees. Even a triangle drawn slowly and carefully on paper with an art pen and a ruler will contain subtle flaws. Still, the latter will far more closely approximate the essence of triangularity than the former will. It will accordingly be a *better* triangle than the former. Indeed, we would naturally describe the latter as a *good* triangle and the former as a *bad* one. This judgment would be completely objective; it would be silly to suggest that we were merely expressing a personal preference for straightness or for angles that add up to 180 degrees. The judgment simply follows from the objective facts about the nature of triangles. This example illustrates how an entity can count as an instance of a certain type of thing even if it fails perfectly to instantiate the essence of that type of thing; a badly drawn triangle is not a non-triangle, but rather a defective triangle. And it illustrates at the same time how there can be a completely objective, factual standard of goodness and badness, better and worse. To be sure, the standard in question in this example is not a *moral* standard. But from the A-T point of view, it illustrates a general notion of goodness of which moral goodness is a special case. And while it might be suggested that even this general standard of goodness will lack a foundation if one denies, as nominalists and other anti-realists do, the objectivity of geometry and mathematics in general, it is (as I have said) notoriously very difficult to defend such a denial.

Many contemporary thinkers are coming to see how difficult it is plausibly to deny the reality of essences in other domains. Consider an example that brings us closer to a specifically moral notion of goodness. Philippa Foot, following Michael Thompson, notes that living things can only adequately be described in terms of what Thompson calls "Aristotelian categoricals" of a form such as *S's are F*, where *S* refers to a species and *F* to something predicated of the species.[4] To cite Foot's examples, "Rabbits are

---

4   Philippa Foot, *Natural Goodness* (Oxford: Clarendon Press, 2001), chapter 2. The relevant paper of Thompson's is "The Representation of Life," in Rosalind Hursthouse, Gavin Lawrence, and Warren Quinn, eds., *Virtues and Reasons: Philippa Foot and Moral Theory* (Oxford: Clarendon Press, 1995).

herbivores," "Cats are four-legged," and "Human beings have 32 teeth" would be instances of this general form. Such propositions cannot be adequately represented as either existential or universal propositions, as these are typically understood by modern logicians. "Cats are four-legged," for instance, is not saying "There is at least one cat that is four-legged"; it is obviously meant instead as a statement about cats in general. But neither is it saying "For everything that is a cat, it is four-legged," since the occasional cat may be missing a leg due to injury or genetic defect. Aristotelian categoricals convey a *norm*, much like the description of what counts as a triangle. A particular living thing can only be described as an instance of a species, and a species itself can only be described in terms of Aristotelian categoricals stating at least its general characteristics.[5] If a particular *S* happens not to be *F*—if, for example, a particular cat is missing a leg—that does not show that *S*'s are not *F* after all, but rather that this particular *S* is a *defective* instance of an *S*.

In living things the sort of norm in question is, as Foot tells us, inextricably tied to the notion of teleology; as Aquinas writes, "all who rightly define *good* put in its notion something about its status as an end" (though as we shall see, Aquinas's point is meant to apply in non-biological contexts as well).[6] There are certain *ends* that any organism must realize in order to flourish as an organism of the kind it is, ends concerning activities like development, self-maintenance, reproduction, the rearing of young, and so forth; and these ends entail a standard of goodness. Hence (again to cite Foot's examples) an oak that develops long and deep roots is to that extent a good oak and one that develops weak roots is to that extent bad and defective; a lioness which nurtures her young is to that extent a good lioness and one that fails to do so is to that extent bad or defective; and so on. As with our triangle example, it would be silly to pretend that these judgments are in any way subjective or reflective of human preferences, or that the inferences leading to them commit a "naturalistic fallacy." For they simply

---

5   As Foot notes, questions about the evolutionary origin of a species can largely be set aside here, for the point of an Aristotelian categorical is to describe a species as it actually exists, whatever its origins. In general, from the A-T point of view questions about the origins of a natural substance are irrelevant to knowing its essence. For detailed discussion of this issue see chapter 9 of David Oderberg, *Real Essentialism* (London: Routledge, 2007).

6   *Quaestiones disputatae de veritate* 21.1, as translated by Robert W. Mulligan, James V. McGlynn, and Robert W. Schmidt in St. Thomas Aquinas, *Truth* (Indianapolis: Hackett Publishing Company, 1994), at p. 7 of Vol. III.

follow from the objective facts about what counts as a flourishing or sickly instance of the biological kind or nature in question, and in particular with an organism's realization or failure to realize the ends set for it by its nature. The facts in question are, as it were, *inherently laden* with "value" from the start. Or, to use Foot's more traditional (and less misleading) language, the goodness a flourishing instance of a natural kind exhibits is "natural goodness"—goodness *there in the nature of things*, not in our subjective "value" judgments about them.

What is true of animals in general is true of human beings. Like non-rational animals, we have various ends to which we are directed by nature, and these determine what is good for us. In particular, Aquinas tells us, "all those things to which man has a *natural inclination*, are naturally apprehended by reason as being good, and consequently as objects of pursuit, and their contraries as evil, and objects of avoidance."[7] It is important not to misunderstand the force of the expression "natural inclination" here. By "inclination" Aquinas does not necessarily mean something consciously desired, and by "natural" he doesn't mean something psychologically deep-seated, or even, necessarily, something genetically determined. What he has in mind are rather the *final causes* or *natural teleology* of our various capacities. For this reason, Anthony Lisska has suggested translating Aquinas's *inclinatio* as "disposition."[8] While this has its advantages, even it fails to make it clear that Aquinas is not interested in just any dispositions we might contingently happen to have, but rather in those that reflect nature's purposes for us. Of course, there is often a close correlation between what nature intends and what we desire. But like everything else in the natural order, our desires are subject to various imperfections and distortions. Hence, though in general and for the most part our desires match up with nature's purposes, this is not true in every single case. Habituated vice, peer pressure, irrationality, mental illness, and the like can often deform our subjective desires so that they turn us away from what nature intends, and thus from what is good for us. Genetic defect might do the same; just as it causes deformities like clubfoot and polydactyly, so too might it generate psychological and behavioral deformities as well.

7   *Summa theologiae* I-II.94.2, as translated by the Fathers of the English Dominican Province in St. Thomas Aquinas, *Summa Theologica* (Notre Dame, IN: Christian Classics, 1981). Emphasis added.
8   Anthony J. Lisska, *Aquinas's Theory of Natural Law: An Analytic Reconstruction* (Oxford: Clarendon Press, 1996), p. 104.

In general, "natural" in A-T philosophy does not mean merely "statistically common," "in accordance with the laws of physics," "having a genetic basis," or any other of the readings that a mechanistic, non-teleological and non-essentialist view of nature might suggest. It has instead to do with the final causes inherent in a thing by virtue of its essence, and which it possesses whether or not it ever realizes them or consciously wants to realize them. What is genuinely good for someone, accordingly, may in principle be something he or she does not want, like children who refuse to eat their vegetables, or like an addict convinced that it would be bad to stop taking drugs. From an A-T point of view, knowing what is truly good for us requires taking an external, objective, "third-person" point of view on ourselves rather than a subjective "first-person" view; it is a matter of determining what fulfills our *nature*, not our contingent desires. The good in question has *moral* significance for us because, unlike other animals, we are capable of intellectually grasping the good and freely choosing whether or not to pursue it.

Aquinas identifies three general categories of goods inherent in our nature. First are those we share in common with all living things, such as the preservation of our existence. Second are those common to animals specifically, such as sexual intercourse and the child-rearing activities that naturally follow upon it. Third are those peculiar to us as *rational* animals, such as "to know the truth about God, and to live in society," "to shun ignorance," and "to avoid offending those among whom one has to live."[9] These goods are ordered in a hierarchy corresponding to the traditional Aristotelian hierarchy of living things (i.e., those with vegetative, sensory, and rational souls respectively). The higher goods presuppose the lower ones; for example, one cannot pursue truth if one is not able to conserve oneself in existence. But the lower goods are subordinate to the higher ones in the sense that they exist for the sake of the higher ones. The point of fulfilling the vegetative and sensory aspects of our nature is, ultimately, to allow us to fulfill the defining rational aspect of our nature.

Naturally, the highest goods for non-human animals will be those definitive of their own natures, and the highest goods for plants will be those definitive of theirs. As what has already been said indicates, there is also a thin sense of "good" that applies even below the biological realm, and this will involve a kind of teleology as well. As Aquinas writes, "every agent acts for a good" insofar as efficient causes, including inorganic ones, point

9   *Summa theologiae* I-II.94.2.

beyond themselves to their typical effects as to an end or goal.[10] (More on this below.) The realization of an end versus the frustration of an end, and hence goodness versus badness, thus apply to inorganic processes no less than to organic ones. Hence when a medicine loses its potency we regard it as having "gone bad," whereas we say it is "still good" if we judge that it will work even though it is slightly past its expiration date. Nor are these judgments made merely relative to our ends as medicine users. The point is that the chemical properties of the medicine *by themselves* give it a tendency to generate a certain effect, and would do so *whether or not* we desired that effect. Hence when the medicine is no longer capable of realizing that tendency, there would still be a sense in which it has "gone bad" even if *we* no longer desired that it realize it.

Some A-T writers have suggested that different substantial forms, and thus irreducibly different kinds of thing, exist wherever we find irreducible causal powers in nature.[11] Hence if the causal powers of rational animals are irreducible to those of non-rational animals, then the former possess a substantial form that makes them an irreducibly different kind of substance than the latter (even if the former incorporates the powers of the latter). If water has causal powers that are irreducible to those of hydrogen and oxygen, then it possesses a substantial form that makes of it an irreducibly different kind of substance than they are (even if water is composed of hydrogen and oxygen in the sense that they are in it virtually and can be derived from it). And so forth. Given that these causal powers are directed toward the generation of their typical effects as to an end or goal, and that the realization of these ends constitutes a kind of success or goodness while a failure to realize them constitutes a kind of defectiveness, it would follow that to each of these irreducibly different kinds of substance there correspond different kinds of goods, and (correspondingly) different kinds of defectiveness or badness.

III. The transcendentals

The notions of formal and final causality are closely related to the A-T notions of *actuality* and *potentiality*. For a substantial form is what actualizes

---

10   *Summa contra gentiles* III.3, as translated by Anton C. Pegis, James F. Anderson, Vernon J. Bourke, and Charles J. O'Neil in Saint Thomas Aquinas, *Summa Contra Gentiles* (Notre Dame, IN: University of Notre Dame Press, 1975).

11   See e.g. Eleonore Stump, *Aquinas* (London: Routledge, 2003), p. 44. Cf. Edward Feser, "Between Aristotle and William Paley: Aquinas's Fifth Way."

otherwise formless matter to make of it a particular thing of a certain kind and to give it its distinctive potentialities; and a potentiality is always a potentiality *for* some actuality, toward which it is directed as to an end or final cause. Given the substantial form or essence of a lioness, she will have a potential to nurture lion cubs that other animals do not have; and to the extent to which she actualizes this potential, she will more perfectly realize that essence or be more perfectly lioness-like. Given the substantial form or essence of a tree, it will have a distinctive potential to sink roots into the soil; and to the extent to which it actualizes that potential, it will more perfectly realize that essence or be more perfectly tree-like. And so forth. In this way actuality and potentiality are also linked to the A-T conception of the good. As Eleonore Stump and Norman Kretzmann write:

> The substantial form … invariably includes at least one power, capacity, or potentiality, because every form … is a source of some activity or operation … [A] thing's form is perfected when and to the extent to which the thing performs an instance of its specific operation, actualizing its specifying potentiality. A thing's operation in accord with its specific power brings into actuality what was not actual but merely potential in that thing's form … [A] thing is good of its kind to the extent to which it is actual. Or, putting it another way, a thing is good of its kind (or perfect) to the extent to which its specifying potentiality is actualized, and bad of its kind (or imperfect) to the extent to which its specifying potentiality remains unactualized.[12]

But to be more fully *actualized* as a thing of a certain kind is more fully to have *being* as a thing of that kind. And that brings us to the convertibility of being and goodness.

Being is what is called in A-T metaphysics a *transcendental*, something above every genus, common to all beings and thus not restricted to any category or individual. The other transcendentals are *thing*, *one*, *something*, *true*, and *good*, and each is "convertible" with being in the sense that each designates one and the same thing—namely being—under a different aspect.

---

12 Eleonore Stump and Norman Kretzmann, "Being and Goodness," in Scott MacDonald, ed., *Being and Goodness: The Concept of the Good in Metaphysics and Philosophical Theology* (Ithaca: Cornell University Press, 1991), pp. 102–03. Cf. P. Coffey, *Ontology* (Gloucester, MA: Peter Smith, 1970), pp. 171–74.

(To put the point in terms made familiar by Frege, the transcendentals differ in *sense* but not in *reference*, referring to the same thing under different names just as "Superman" and "Clark Kent" do.[13]) This may be clearest in the cases of *thing* and *something*, since a "thing" is just a being of some kind or other, and "something" connotes either a being among other beings, or being as opposed to non-being or nothing. *One* (to oversimplify a bit) is meant in more or less the former of these senses of "something," as connoting one being distinct from others. The idea of convertibility is, for modern readers anyway, hardest to understand in the cases of *true* and *good*, since truth is usually understood by contemporary philosophers as an attribute confined to beliefs and propositions, and goodness is (as we have noted) often regarded as a matter of "value" rather than "fact."

With respect to truth, it is useful, in understanding the A-T view, to think of "true" in the sense of "real" or "genuine." A thing is true to the extent that it conforms to the ideal defined by the essence of the kind it belongs to. Hence the hastily drawn triangle of our earlier example is not as true a triangle as one drawn slowly and carefully, for since its sides will be less straight it will less perfectly instantiate the essence of triangularity; a lioness which lacks any impulse to nurture her young is not as true a lioness as the lioness which does have such an impulse; and so forth. Now for the A-T metaphysician, such essences, when considered as universals, exist only in the intellect; and following St. Augustine, the A-T tradition has tended to regard these universals as existing first and foremost in the divine intellect, as the archetypes according to which God creates the world.[14] Thus, in a sense, "the word 'true' ... expresses the conformity of a being to intellect,"[15] whether a human intellect which grasps a universal, or (ultimately) the divine intellect in which the universal exists eternally. Hence something *has being* as the kind of thing it is precisely to the extent that it is *a true instance* of that kind, as defined by the universal essence existing in the intellect; and in that sense being is convertible with truth.

This helps to elucidate the sense in which *good* is convertible with being. As we have seen, for the A-T tradition goodness is to be understood

---

13 A Scholastic way of putting the point would be to say that the distinction between the transcendentals is a "distinction of reason." For example, goodness is in itself not different from being, but is just being conceived of in relation to desire, in a sense to be explained below. Cf. George P. Klubertanz, *Introduction to the Philosophy of Being*, Second edition (New York: Appleton-Century-Crofts, 1963), p. 234.
14 Cf. Aquinas, *Summa Theologiae* I.15.1.
15 Aquinas, *Quaestiones disputatae de veritate* 1.1.

in terms of conformity to the ideal represented by a thing's nature or essence. Hence the well-drawn triangle is not merely a *true* triangle, but also a *good* triangle, and the poorly-drawn triangle a *bad* one—"good" and "bad" here understood in the sense in which we describe something as a good or bad specimen or example of a type of thing. As with *true*, then, something is *good* to the extent that it exists as, or has being as, an instance of its kind. As Aquinas says, "everything is perfect so far as it is actual. Therefore it is clear that a thing is perfect so far as it exists; for it is existence that makes all things actual."[16] Now it is also true that "the essence of goodness consists in this, that it is in some way desirable"; but "a thing is desirable only in so far as it is perfect," and thus to the extent that it is actual or exists.[17] "Hence," Aquinas concludes, "it is clear that goodness and being are the same really. But goodness presents the aspect of desirableness, which being does not present."[18]

This last part of the argument is liable to be badly misunderstood if it is not kept in mind that by "desirable" Aquinas does not mean that which conforms to some desire we happen contingently to have, nor even, necessarily, anything desired in a conscious way. Here as elsewhere, it is the notion of the final cause—the end or goal toward which a thing is directed *by nature*—that is key. As we have seen, a thing's final cause, and thus that which it "desires" (in the relevant sense), might be something of which it is totally unconscious, as in the case of inanimate natural objects and processes; in creatures with intellects, such as ourselves, it might even be something we consciously (if irrationally) try to avoid realizing. But given that the realization of a thing's good is what it is *by its nature* directed toward as its final cause, it follows that Aquinas's dictum (borrowed from Aristotle) that "goodness is that which all things desire"[19] is, when properly understood, not a dubious piece of armchair psychology, but rather (given his basic ontological commitments) a necessary truth of metaphysics.

The claim that being is convertible with goodness might nevertheless seem to be falsified by the existence of evil. For if evil exists, then (so it might be thought) it must have being; and since evil is the opposite of good, it would seem to follow that there is something having being that is nevertheless not good. But the A-T metaphysician would deny the first premise

16 *Summa theologiae* 1.5.1.
17 Ibid.
18 Ibid.
19 *Summa theologiae* I.5.4. Cf. Aristotle, *Nicomachean Ethics* I.1.

of this argument. Aquinas writes that "it cannot be that evil signifies being, or any form or nature. Therefore it must be that by the name of evil is signified the absence of good. And this is what is meant by saying that *evil is neither a being nor a good*. For since being, as such, is good, the absence of one implies the absence of the other."[20] Precisely because good is convertible with being, evil, which is the opposite of good, cannot itself be a kind of being but rather the absence of being. In particular, it is what the Scholastic philosophers called a *privation*, the absence of some perfection which should be present in a thing given its nature. Hence blindness (for example) is not a kind of being or positive reality, but rather simply the absence of sight in some creature which by its nature should have it. Its existence, and that of other evils, thus does not conflict with the claim that being is convertible with good.

Another way to put the point is in terms of the distinction between actuality and potentiality. Since a thing is a better instance of the kind of thing that it is the more fully it actualizes what Stump and Kretzmann call the "specifying potentialities" that follow upon its having the kind of substantial form it has, its being a *bad* instance is just a matter of its *failing* to actualize those potentialities. Again, badness or evil is the lack of something that should be there given a thing's nature, a privation. (It is because God is regarded in A-T natural theology as *pure actuality*, devoid of potentiality—and because He is, accordingly, regarded as *ipsum esse subsistens* or subsistent being itself rather than something which merely participates in being—that He is also, as a matter of metaphysical necessity, perfectly good.)

IV. Is A-T metaphysics still defensible?

It might, of course, be objected that the metaphysical foundations of the A-T account of the good are no longer defensible insofar as modern philosophy and science have shown both that we can do away with essences or substantial forms, and that apparently irreducibly teleological descriptions of natural phenomena can always be reduced to descriptions couched in non-teleological terms. But widespread though these assumptions are, there is surprisingly little in the way of actual argumentation in their favor, and much to be said against them. To be sure, Darwinian theory famously suggests a way of accounting for biological adaptation in a manner that dispenses with anything

---

20 *Summa theologiae* I.48.1.

like goal-directedness or final causality. But the adaptation of organisms to their environments is only one small (albeit important) aspect of the natural world, and the question is whether there is any reason to believe that teleology can be *entirely* or even *mostly* dispensed with in our understanding of nature. The answer, I would submit, is that it cannot be. Every attempt to eliminate teleology in one domain seems at most merely to relocate it elsewhere, leaving it "grinning residually up at us like the frog at the bottom of the beer mug," as J. L. Austin famously said of another problematic phenomenon.[21] And something similar can be said of the attempt to eliminate essences.

This is a large topic which I have addressed at length elsewhere.[22] Some general remarks will suffice for our purposes here. Certain common misconceptions about the nature of final causes form one of the main obstacles to acknowledging their reality. It is often thought, for example, that to attribute a final cause to something is necessarily to attribute to it something like thought or consciousness and/or something like a biological function. It is then concluded that anyone committed to the reality of final causes must believe such absurdities as that asteroids and piles of dirt (or whatever) somehow play a role within the larger universe that is analogous to the role a heart or kidney plays in an organism, and that they are at least dimly conscious of doing so. But this is a travesty of the A-T notion of final causality. In fact the A-T view has always been that most teleology is not associated with consciousness at all and that biological functions constitute only one kind of final causality among others.

The heart of the A-T "principle of finality" is, as Aquinas put it, that "every agent acts for an end."[23] This is just the idea, alluded to earlier, that anything that serves as an efficient cause—that which brings about a certain effect—is directed towards production of that effect as its natural end or goal. The cause "points to" that effect specifically, rather than to some other effect or to no effect at all; or in other words, when A is the efficient cause of B, that is only because the generation of B is the final cause of A. For example, the phosphorus in a match "points to" or is "directed at" the generation of flame and heat specifically, rather than frost and cold, or the smell

---

21   J. L. Austin, "Ifs and Cans," in his *Philosophical Papers*, Third edition (Oxford: Oxford University Press, 1979), at p. 231. Austin's topic was the analysis of the verb "can."

22   See *The Last Superstition* (South Bend, IN: St. Augustine's Press, 2008); *Aquinas* (Oxford: Oneworld Publications, 2009); "Teleology: A Shopper's Guide"; and "Between Aristotle and William Paley: Aquinas's Fifth Way."

23   *Summa Theologiae* I.22.2.

of lilacs, or a nuclear explosion. That is the effect it will naturally bring about when the match is struck unless prevented in some way, and even if it is never in fact struck it remains true that it is that specific effect that it always "aimed at." As Aquinas argued, unless we acknowledge the existence of finality in this sense, we have no way of explaining why it is that efficient causes have exactly the effects they do rather than other effects or no effects at all. In short, efficient causality becomes unintelligible without final causality.[24]

Notice that there is nothing in this that entails that matches or other efficient causes carry out "functions" in the biological sense. To say that final causality pervades the natural world is *not* to say that atoms and molecules or rocks and trees are somehow related to the world as a whole as biological organs are related to the organism whose organs they are. Functions of the sort that biological organs serve exist only where physical systems are organized in such a way that the parts of the system are ordered to the flourishing of the whole, as in living things. Most of the teleology that the A-T metaphysician would attribute to nature is not like this, but involves merely the simple directedness of a cause of a certain type towards the generation of a certain effect or range of effects. Notice also that there is no implication here that the causes in question are typically conscious (as the match of my example obviously is not). Other than human beings and animals, they typically are not conscious at all. The A-T claim is precisely that things can be directed towards certain ends or goals even if they are totally incapable of being conscious of this fact.

Now it is by no means only old-fashioned Aristotelians who would defend essences and teleology today.[25] One finds a hint of the latter even in the work of the materialist philosopher David Armstrong, who suggests that in order to explain intentionality—the human mind's capacity to represent the world beyond itself—his fellow materialists ought to consider the dispositions physical objects possess (such as the disposition glass has to break

---

24 That there is something to what Aquinas is saying here should be obvious to anyone familiar with the history of philosophical debate over causation since Hume. For a useful account of the historical transition from the Aristotelian-Scholastic understanding of causation to modern views like Hume's, see Walter Ott, *Causation and Laws of Nature in Early Modern Philosophy* (Oxford: Oxford University Press, 2009).

25 Though for an especially important contemporary statement and defense of the A-T position, see David Oderberg's *Real Essentialism* and "Teleology: Inorganic and Organic," in A. M. Gonzalez, ed., *Contemporary Perspectives on Natural Law* (Aldershot: Ashgate, 2008).

even if it never in fact shatters) as instances of a kind of "proto-intentionality" or "pointing beyond themselves" towards certain specific outcomes.[26] Metaphysician John Heil similarly attributes a "natural intentionality" to dispositions.[27] The late George Molnar defended the idea that the causal powers inherent in physical objects manifest a kind of "physical intentionality" insofar as, like thoughts and other mental states, they point to something beyond themselves, even though they are unlike thoughts in being unconscious.[28] In general, the question of whether there are irreducible "dispositional" properties in addition to "categorical" ones—essentially a revival of the A-T distinction between potentiality and actuality—has become the focus of a great deal of discussion in contemporary analytic metaphysics.[29] And the related notion that dispositions possess a kind of unconscious intentionality is essentially a revival of the A-T principle of finality.

Molnar was representative of a movement within the philosophy of science toward what Brian Ellis has called a "new essentialism," the view that the standard mechanistic and empiricist interpretation of physical science simply doesn't hold up in light of the actual discoveries of modern science and the facts of scientific practice.[30] Ellis and Nancy Cartwright, another prominent "new essentialist," are forthright about the neo-Aristotelian character of their position. Actual experimental practice, Cartwright argues, shows that the hard sciences are in the business of discovering, not mere Humean regularities, but the hidden natures or essences universal to, and the causal powers inherent in, things of a certain type. "The empiricists of the scientific revolution wanted to oust Aristotle entirely from the new learning," but, Cartwright judges, "they did no such thing."[31]

26   D. M. Armstrong, *The Mind-Body Problem: An Opinionated Introduction* (Boulder: Westview, 1999), pp. 138–40.

27   John Heil, *From an Ontological Point of View* (Oxford: Oxford University Press, 2003).

28   George Molnar, *Powers: A Study in Metaphysics* (Oxford: Oxford University Press, 2003).

29   For a useful overview, see Stephen Mumford, "Causal Powers and Capacities," in Helen Beebee, Christopher Hitchcock, and Peter Menzies, eds., *The Oxford Handbook of Causation* (Oxford: Oxford University Press, 2009).

30   See Brian Ellis, *Scientific Essentialism* (Cambridge: Cambridge University Press, 2001) and *The Philosophy of Nature: A Guide to the New Essentialism* (Chesham: Acumen, 2002).

31   Nancy Cartwright, "Aristotelian Natures and the Modern Experimental Method," in John Earman, ed., *Inference, Explanation, and Other Frustrations: Essays in the Philosophy of Science* (Berkeley and Los Angeles: University of California Press, 1992), at p. 70.

It should also be noted that the recent rise of the philosophy of chemistry as a sub-discipline within the philosophy of science has brought with it a reconsideration of the standard view that chemical phenomena are reducible to those described by physics.[32] For to affirm the reality of irreducible chemical kinds is to affirm at the level of chemistry at least a crucial component of the A-T notion of *substantial form*; while to affirm that what makes these kinds irreducible is the irreducibility of their causal powers—powers directed beyond themselves to certain characteristic outcomes—is to affirm a crucial component of the A-T notion of final causality.

Nor is it in physics and chemistry alone that we see hints of a return to Aristotelian categories. As the work of Foot and Thompson indicates, many contemporary thinkers are prepared to acknowledge the continuing applicability of Aristotelian concepts in biology. The philosopher of biology André Ariew has noted that even given that Darwinian evolution undermines William Paley's famous design argument, "it does not follow that Darwin has debunked natural teleology altogether," for "Aristotelian teleology is an entirely different sort."[33] Though natural selection might suffice to explain the adaptation of an organism to its environment, there is also the question of the internal development of an organism, and in particular of what accounts for the fact that certain growth patterns count as aberrations and others as normal. Here Aristotle would say that there is no way to make this distinction apart from the notion of an end toward which the growth pattern naturally points: normal growth patterns are those that reach this end, aberrations (clubfoot, polydactyly, and other birth defects, for example) are failures to reach it. Ariew seems to allow that there is nothing in Darwinism that undermines this sort of argument for final causes within biology. The biologist J. Scott Turner is even more explicit that accounting for the phenomena in question requires attributing an unconscious "intentionality" to biological processes.[34]

The persistence of teleological thinking within biology is perhaps most clearly evident from the way in which biologists describe DNA. Accounts of the function of this famous molecule regularly make use of such concepts as

---

32 For an overview of the relevant literature, see chapter 5 of J. van Brakel, *Philosophy of Chemistry* (Leuven: Leuven University Press, 2000). For a self-consciously A-T defense of the irreducibility of chemical kinds, see Oderberg, *Real Essentialism*.

33 André Ariew, "Teleology," in David L. Hull and Michael Ruse, eds., *The Cambridge Companion to the Philosophy of Biology* (Cambridge: Cambridge University Press, 2007), at p. 177.

34 J. Scott Turner, *The Tinkerer's Accomplice: How Design Emerges From Life Itself* (Cambridge: Harvard University Press, 2007).

"information," "code," "instructions," "data," "blueprint," "software," "program," and the like, and there seems to be no way to convey what DNA does without something like them. But every one of these concepts is suffused with intentionality—that is to say, with the notion of a thing's pointing to something beyond itself in the way our thoughts do, in this case to an organism's physiological and behavioral traits, including those determining the species or kind it belongs to. Of course, no one would claim that DNA molecules literally can be said to think. But the notion of something which points to some end or goal beyond itself despite being totally unconscious is just the Aristotelian notion of final causality. As the biophysicist and Nobel laureate Max Delbrück once wrote, if the Nobel Prize could be awarded posthumously, "I think they should consider Aristotle for the discovery of the principle implied in DNA" and "the reason for the lack of appreciation, among scientists, of Aristotle's scheme lies in our having been blinded for 300 years by the Newtonian [i.e. mechanistic or non-teleological] view of the world."[35] More recently, the physicist Paul Davies has complained of the contradiction implicit in biologists' use of informational concepts that entail meaning or purpose while purporting at the same time to be committed to a completely mechanistic picture of the world. Recognizing that such concepts are indispensible, his solution appears to be at least tentatively to suggest giving up mechanism, asking "Might purpose be a genuine property of nature right down to the cellular or even the subcellular level?"[36]

It should go without saying that human action is perhaps the most obvious example of a phenomenon that appears in principle impossible to account for in non-teleological terms.[37] Then there is human thought, which, even apart from the actions it sometimes gives rise to, manifests intention-

---

35 Max Delbrück, "Aristotle-totle-totle," in Jacques Monod and Ernest Borek, eds., *Of Microbes and Life* (New York: Columbia University Press, 1971), p. 55.

36 Paul Davies, *The Fifth Miracle: The Search for the Origin and Meaning of Life* (New York: Simon and Schuster, 1999), p. 122. Peter Godfrey-Smith is one philosopher of biology who resists the idea that genes encode for phenotypic traits, but even he concedes that they encode for the amino acid sequence of protein molecules in a way that involves semantic information. Though he does not draw the lesson, this would seem all by itself to concede the reality of something like Aristotelian teleology. See Godfrey-Smith's "Information in Biology," in David L. Hull and Michael Ruse, eds., *The Cambridge Companion to the Philosophy of Biology* (Cambridge: Cambridge University Press, 2007).

37 Two important recent defenses of this thesis are G. F. Schueler, *Reasons and Purposes: Human Rationality and the Teleological Explanation of Action* (Oxford: Oxford University Press, 2003) and Scott Sehon, *Teleological Realism: Mind, Agency, and Explanation* (Cambridge, MA: MIT Press, 2005).

ality or "directedness" toward something beyond itself and is thus as problematic for a mechanistic picture of the natural world as teleology is.[38]

Much more could be said in support of the classical teleological and essentialist picture of the natural world; and again, I have said much more in support of it elsewhere. Suffice it for present purposes to note that, given the philosophical and scientific trends I have described, there is at the very least a powerful case to be made for the view that ends or goals towards which things are directed by virtue of their essences pervade the natural order from top to bottom, from the level of human thought down to that of basic physical particles. It follows that defectiveness, "missing the mark," or failure to realize a natural end or goal also pervade the natural order—as does the opposite of this circumstance, namely that feature of things which Foot has aptly labeled their "natural goodness."

V. Human action

It is but a few short steps from natural goodness to the A-T understanding of natural law and of human action in general. Aquinas famously held that the fundamental principle of natural law is that "good is to be done and pursued, and evil is to be avoided" such that "all other precepts of the natural law are based upon this."[39] Now that "good is to be done etc." might at first glance seem to be a difficult claim to justify, and certainly not a very promising candidate for a first principle. For isn't the question "Why should I be good?" precisely (part of) what any moral theory ought to answer? And isn't this question notoriously difficult to answer to the satisfaction of the moral skeptic?

Properly understood, however, Aquinas's principle is not only plausible, but might seem trivially true. Aquinas is not saying that it is self-evident that we ought to be morally good. He is saying rather that it is self-evident that whenever we act we pursue something that we take to be good *in some way* and/or avoid what we take to be *in some way* evil or bad. And that seems clearly right. Even someone who does what he believes to be morally bad does so only because he is seeking something he takes to be good in the

---

38 My own view is that an explanation of intentionality in purely materialistic-cum-mechanistic terms is in principle impossible. See Edward Feser, *Philosophy of Mind* (Oxford: Oneworld Publications, 2005), chapter 7 for a survey and defense of various arguments for this position, and also chapters 5 and 6 of *The Last Superstition*.

39 *Summa theologiae* I-II.94.2.

sense of worth pursuing. Hence the mugger who admits that robbery is wrong nevertheless takes his victim's wallet because he thinks it would be good to have money to pay for his drugs; hence the drug addict who regards his habit as degrading nevertheless thinks it would be good to satisfy the craving and bad to suffer the unpleasantness of not satisfying it. Of course, these claims are true only on a very thin sense of "good" and "bad," but that is exactly the sense Aquinas intends.

Now, A-T metaphysics is not essential to seeing that this first principle is correct; it is supposed to be self-evident. But A-T metaphysics can help us to understand *why* it is correct. For like every other natural phenomenon, practical reason has a natural end or goal toward which it is ordered, and that end or goal is just whatever it is the intellect perceives to be good or worth pursuing. This brings us to the threshold of a conclusion that does have real moral significance. Given what has already been said, human beings, like everything else, have various ends the realization of which is good for them and the frustrating of which is bad, as a matter of objective fact. A rational intellect apprised of the facts will therefore perceive that it is good to realize these ends and bad to frustrate them. It follows, then, that a rational person will pursue the realization of these ends and avoid their frustration. In short, practical reason is directed by nature toward the pursuit of what the intellect *perceives* to be good; what is *in fact* good is the realization or fulfillment of the various potentials and ends inherent in human nature; and thus a correctly informed and rational person *will* perceive this and, accordingly, direct his actions towards the realization or fulfillment of those potentials and ends.

In this sense, good action is just that which is "in accord with reason,"[40] and the moral skeptic's question "Why should I do what is good?" has an obvious answer: Because to be rational *just is* (in part) to do what is good, to fulfill the ends set for us by nature. Natural law ethics as a body of substantive moral theory is just the formulation of general moral principles on the basis of an analysis of the various human potentialities and ends and the systematic working out of their implications. So, to take just one example, when we consider that human beings have intellects and that the natural end or function of the intellect is to grasp the truth about things, it follows that it is good for us—it fulfills our nature—to pursue truth and avoid error. Consequently, a rational person apprised of the facts about human nature will see that this is what is good for us and thus strive to attain truth and to avoid error. And so on for other natural human capacities.

---

40   *Summa theologiae* I-II.21.1; Cf. I-II.90.1.

Now things are bound to get more complicated than that summary perhaps lets on. Various qualifications and complications will need to be spelled out as we examine the various natural human potentialities and ends in detail, and not every principle of morality that follows from this analysis will necessarily be as simple and straightforward as "Pursue truth and avoid error." But this much is enough to give us at least a general idea of how A-T natural law theory determines the specific content of our moral obligations. It also suffices to give us a sense of the *grounds* of moral obligation, that which makes it the case that moral imperatives have categorical rather than merely hypothetical force. The hypothetical imperative *(1) If I want what is good for me then I ought to pursue what realizes my natural ends and avoid what frustrates them* is something which follows from the A-T metaphysics of the good. By itself, it does not give us a categorical imperative because the consequent will have force only for someone who accepts the antecedent. But that *(2) I do want what is good for me* is something true of all of us by virtue of our nature as human beings, and is in any case self-evident, being just a variation on Aquinas's fundamental principle of natural law. These premises yield the conclusion *(3) I ought to pursue what realizes my natural ends and avoid what frustrates them*. (3) does have categorical force because (2) has categorical force, and (2) has categorical force because it cannot be otherwise given our nature. Not only the content of our moral obligations but their obligatory character are thus determined by the A-T metaphysics of final causality or natural teleology. As the A-T natural law theorist Michael Cronin has written: "In the fullest sense of the word, then, moral duty is natural. For not only are certain objects natural means to man's final end, but our desire of that end is natural also, and, therefore, the necessity [or obligatory force] of the means is natural."[41]

VI. Sub specie boni?

Nevertheless, some contemporary philosophers writing on practical reason have challenged the thesis that all human action aims at the good. The objections of J. David Velleman have been particularly influential.[42]

Velleman's argument rests in part on what he takes to be a crucial contrast between *believing* and *desiring*. Like other contemporary theorists of

---

41 Michael Cronin, *The Science of Ethics, Volume 1: General Ethics* (Dublin: M. H. Gill and Son, 1939), p. 222.
42 J. David Velleman, "The Guise of the Good" in *The Possibility of Practical Reason* (Oxford: Oxford University Press, 2000).

practical reason, Velleman sees part of the difference between them to lie in their respective "directions of fit": A belief "is responsible for conforming itself to the world," whereas a desire "makes the world responsible for conforming itself to the attitude."[43] But there is more to it than that. Believing, assuming, or fantasizing that p, Velleman says, all involve regarding p as true. The difference between belief and these other cognitive attitudes is that in addition to regarding p as true, believing that p involves (as assuming and fantasizing that p do not) a concern that p really *is* in fact true.[44] Now desiring might seem to have a similar structure. In particular, Velleman says, desiring that p might seem to differ from other conative attitudes like wishing or hoping that p insofar as, while all three involve regarding p as something to be brought about, desiring that p involves (as wishing and hoping that p do not) a concern that p really *is* in fact something to be brought about.[45] In this way, Velleman says, desiring might seem to be inherently aimed at the good. But the appearance is deceiving, because desiring does not in fact have a structure that parallels the two-level structure of belief. In particular, Velleman says, what is distinctive about desiring that p cannot be that desiring involves approving p as something that is in fact to be brought about. For one cannot desire what is impossible or what has already come about, but one can approve of it. Desiring, Velleman suggests, instead has what is *attainable*, rather than what is good, as its constitutive aim.

There are several problems with this argument. To begin with, talk of desire's "direction of fit," at least as Velleman makes use of it, raises a number of questions. To say that a desire "makes the world responsible for conforming itself to the attitude" is obviously metaphorical, and the metaphor needs to be cashed out in literal terms before we can be confident that any argument that makes use of it is sound—something Velleman doesn't do. However we cash it out, though, the result would seem to be an account that makes "value" something subjective, after the fashion of Hume. In particular, it would seem to imply that objective states of affairs have "value" not in themselves but only insofar as they "fit" or conform themselves to an agent's desires. And in that case Velleman's argument simply begs the question against the A-T position. For A-T, since goodness is convertible with being, there is a clear sense in which desire, understood as aiming at the good, has a "direction of fit" similar to that of belief. In *both* cases the state in question, whether

---

43 Velleman, "The Guise of the Good," p. 111.
44 Ibid., p. 112.
45 Ibid., p. 115.

cognitive or conative, is "responsible" (to use Velleman's language) for con-forming itself to the world, to being—in the case of belief, under the guise of the true, and in the case of desire, under the guise of the good. Velleman's argument is at best the *expression* of an alternative account of the good and of desire, but not a (non-question-begging) *argument* against the A-T view.

Another problem is that Velleman's account of belief seems needlessly convoluted, so that the comparison with desire that his argument rests on is poorly motivated. Surely it is just wrong to say that believing, assuming, and fantasizing that *p* all involve regarding *p* as true, with belief distin-guished by a higher-order concern about the correctness of the first-order state. Rather, assuming and fantasizing that *p* don't involve regarding *p* as true at all, but instead merely treating it *as if* it were true. Belief, unlike these other states, *does* involve regarding *p* as true, and it is precisely this that differentiates it from them. There is no asymmetry between belief and desire of the sort Velleman postulates, then. In *neither* case do we have a constitutive second-order state, but only a first-order state—regarding *p* as true in the case of belief, and (for all Velleman has shown) regarding *p* as good in the case of desire.

Nor does Velleman's suggestion that desire aims at the attainable plau-sibly show otherwise. Being attainable is, after all, at most a *necessary* con-dition of an object of desire, not a *sufficient* one, as Velleman himself acknowledges.[46] For there are all sorts of things that an agent might be able to attain but which he does not desire. So, without providing an account of what else is constitutive of desire—which he does not try to do—Velleman can hardly claim to have shown that aiming at the good is not part of the story. And it is hard to see how it could fail to be, insofar as the difference between what is merely attainable and what is actually desired surely in-volves regarding the latter as an end that is worth pursuing in *some* respect that other attainable things are not—which for A-T suffices to make desire aim at the good, in the thin sense of "good." (As Candace Vogler has pointed out, Velleman is evidently assuming an inflated or "moralized" sense of "good" rather than this thin sense.[47])

It is in any event implausible to deny, as Velleman does, that what is impossible or what has already come about can be the object of desire. Such

46   Ibid., p. 117, n. 34.
47   Candace Vogler, *Reasonably Vicious* (Cambridge, MA: Harvard University Press, 2002), p. 258, n. 3. Bernard Williams makes a similar mistake in *Ethics and the Limits of Philosophy* (Cambridge, MA: Harvard University Press, 1985), at pp. 58–59.

desires would be *irrational*, but that does not entail that they are not true desires, any more than an irrational belief is a non-belief. Nor is Velleman correct to claim, as he does, that perverse desires would be impossible if desire aimed at the good. To be sure, Velleman seems correct to point out that not all perverse desires can plausibly be regarded as involving nothing more than a mistaken judgment about what is in fact good.[48] The Satan of *Paradise Lost*, for instance, desires evil precisely qua evil, not as a misperceived good. But what Velleman fails to consider is that the perversity of such a desire lies precisely in its *irrationality*. Velleman is evidently assuming the Humean view that reason as such is neutral as to ends, that there is nothing inherently irrational in desiring what is bad. Yet since that is precisely part of what is in dispute between the A-T position and the Humean view, it can hardly serve as a non-question-begging reason to reject the former in favor of the latter.

VII. Conclusion

Archaic as some contemporary philosophers might find it, then, the A-T conception of the good is still defensible today—and indeed many of its key components are *being* defended today, even by prominent writers with no specifically A-T ax to grind. Thus its return to the center of philosophical attention may require, on the part of contemporary philosophers, not a rediscovery of the past so much as a realization of what is already going on around them.

Bibliography

Aquinas, Thomas. *Summa Contra Gentiles*. Translated by Anton C. Pegis, James F. Anderson, Vernon J. Bourke, and Charles J. O'Neil. Notre Dame, IN: University of Notre Dame Press, 1975.

Aquinas, Thomas. *Summa Theologica*. Translated by Fathers of the English Dominican Province. New York: Christian Classics, 1981.

Aquinas, Thomas. *Truth*. Translated by Robert W. Mulligan, James V. McGlynn, and Robert W. Schmidt. Indianapolis: Hackett Publishing Company, 1994.

Ariew, André. "Teleology". In David L. Hull and Michael Ruse, eds., *The Cambridge Companion to the Philosophy of Biology*. Cambridge: Cambridge University Press, 2007.

48   Velleman, "The Guise of the Good," pp. 118–19.

Armstrong, D. M. *The Mind-Body Problem: An Opinionated Introduction*. Boulder: Westview, 1999.

Austin, J. L. "Ifs and Cans". In *Philosophical Papers*, Third edition. Oxford: Oxford University Press, 1979.

Cartwright, Nancy. "Aristotelian Natures and the Modern Experimental Method". In John Earman, ed., *Inference, Explanation, and Other Frustrations: Essays in the Philosophy of Science*. Berkeley and Los Angeles: University of California Press, 1992.

Coffey, P. *Ontology*. Gloucester, MA: Peter Smith, 1970.

Cronin, Michael. *The Science of Ethics, Volume 1: General Ethics*. Dublin: M. H. Gill and Son, 1939.

Davies, Paul. *The Fifth Miracle: The Search for the Origin and Meaning of Life*. New York: Simon and Schuster, 1999.

Delbrück, Max. "Aristotle-totle-totle". In Jacques Monod and Ernest Borek, eds., *Of Microbes and Life*. New York: Columbia University Press, 1971.

Ellis, Brian. *The Philosophy of Nature: A Guide to the New Essentialism*. Chesham: Acumen, 2002.

Ellis, Brian. *Scientific Essentialism*. Cambridge: Cambridge University Press, 2001.

Feser, Edward. *Aquinas*. Oxford: Oneworld, 2009.

Feser, Edward. "Between Aristotle and William Paley: Aquinas's Fifth Way". *Nova et Vetera* Vol. 11, No. 3 (2013).

Feser, Edward. *The Last Superstition: A Refutation of the New Atheism*. South Bend, IN: St. Augustine's Press, 2008.

Feser, Edward. *Philosophy of Mind*. Oxford: Oneworld Publications, 2005.

Feser, Edward. "Teleology: A Shopper's Guide". *Philosophia Christi* 12, no. 1 (2010): 142–59.

Finnis, John. *Natural Law and Natural Rights*. Oxford: Clarendon Press, 1980.

Foot, Philippa. *Natural Goodness*. Oxford: Clarendon Press, 2001.

Godfrey-Smith, Peter. "Information in Biology". In David L. Hull and Michael Ruse, eds., *The Cambridge Companion to the Philosophy of Biology*. Cambridge: Cambridge University Press, 2007.

Grisez, Germain. "The First Principle of Practical Reason". In Anthony Kenny, ed., *Aquinas: A Collection of Critical Essays*. Garden City, NY: Doubleday, 1969.

Heil, John. *From an Ontological Point of View*. Oxford: Oxford University Press, 2003.

Klubertanz, George P. *Introduction to the Philosophy of Being*, Second edition. New York: Appleton-Century-Crofts, 1963.

Lisska, Anthony J. *Aquinas's Theory of Natural Law: An Analytic Reconstruction*. Oxford: Clarendon Press, 1996.

Martin, Christopher. "The Fact/Value Distinction". In David S. Oderberg and Timothy Chappell, eds., *Human Values: New Essays on Ethics and Natural Law*. New York: Palgrave Macmillan, 2004.

Molnar, George. *Powers: A Study in Metaphysics*. Oxford: Oxford University Press, 2003.

Mumford, Stephen. "Causal Powers and Capacities". In Helen Beebee, Christopher Hitchcock, and Peter Menzies, eds., *The Oxford Handbook of Causation*. Oxford: Oxford University Press, 2009.

Nielsen, Kai. "Religious Ethics Versus Humanistic Ethics". In Kai Nielsen, *Philosophy and Atheism*. Buffalo, NY: Prometheus Books, 1985.

O'Connor, D. J. *Aquinas and Natural Law*. London: Macmillan, 1968.

Oderberg, David S. *Moral Theory: A Non-Consequentialist Approach*. Oxford: Blackwell, 2000.

Oderberg, David S. *Real Essentialism*. London: Routledge, 2007.

Oderberg, David S. "Teleology: Inorganic and Organic". In A. M. Gonzalez, ed., *Contemporary Perspectives on Natural Law*. Aldershot: Ashgate, 2008.

Ott, Walter. *Causation and Laws of Nature in Early Modern Philosophy*. Oxford: Oxford University Press, 2009.

Putnam, Hilary. *The Collapse of the Fact/Value Dichotomy and Other Essays*. Cambridge, MA: Harvard University Press, 2004.

Schueler, G. F. *Reasons and Purposes: Human Rationality and the Teleological Explanation of Action*. Oxford: Oxford University Press, 2003.

Sehon, Scott. *Teleological Realism: Mind, Agency, and Explanation*. Cambridge, MA: MIT Press, 2005.

Stump, Eleonore. *Aquinas*. London: Routledge, 2003.

Stump, Eleonore and Norman Kretzmann. "Being and Goodness". In Scott MacDonald, ed., *Being and Goodness: The Concept of the Good in Metaphysics and Philosophical Theology*. Ithaca: Cornell University Press, 1991.

Thompson, Michael. "The Representation of Life". In Rosalind Hursthouse, Gavin Lawrence, and Warren Quinn, eds., *Virtues and Reasons: Philippa Foot and Moral Theory*. Oxford: Clarendon Press, 1995.

Turner, J. Scott. *The Tinkerer's Accomplice: How Design Emerges From Life Itself*. Cambridge: Harvard University Press, 2007.

Van Brakel, J. *Philosophy of Chemistry*. Leuven: Leuven University Press, 2000.

Velleman, J. David. "The Guise of the Good". In *The Possibility of Practical Reason*. Oxford: Oxford University Press, 2000.

Vogler, Candace. *Reasonably Vicious*. Cambridge, MA: Harvard University Press, 2002.

Williams, Bernard. *Ethics and the Limits of Philosophy*. Cambridge, MA: Harvard University Press, 1985.

14

Classical Natural Law Theory, Property Rights, and Taxation

I. Introduction

The aim of this essay is to put forward an exposition and defense of a classical natural law theory of property rights and taxation. As the "natural law" label indicates, the view to be propounded holds that the right to private property is a natural right in the sense of being grounded in nature rather than human convention. The underlying natural law theory is a "classical" one in the sense that its understanding of nature is classical rather than modern. That is to say, it is *essentialist* rather than nominalist insofar as it holds that things instantiate natures or essences that that are neither the inventions of the human mind nor mere artifacts of human language; and *teleological* rather than mechanistic insofar as it holds that things have final causes or ends towards which they are naturally directed.

These metaphysical commitments are definitive of the "classical realist" tradition in philosophy represented by such thinkers as Plato, Aristotle, Augustine, and Aquinas along with many other Scholastic philosophers. The modern philosophical tradition inaugurated by the likes of Descartes, Hobbes, Locke, and Hume is defined more than anything else by its rejection of them in favor of a mechanistic and (usually) nominalistic conception of the natural world. Modern "natural law" theories are those which attempt to reformulate the idea of natural law in terms that either take on board, or at least do not challenge, this modern non-teleological and nominalistic conception of nature. Hence Locke, who is often classified as a natural law theorist but who vigorously rejects the Aristotelian metaphysics of the Scholastic tradition, grounds his doctrine of rights not in human nature or final causes, but in God's ownership of us.[1] Hence the "new natural law

---

1   See Edward Feser, *Locke* (Oxford: Oneworld Publications, 2007) for an account of the differences between Scholastic and Lockean conceptions of natural law.

theory" of contemporary writers like Germain Grisez, John Finnis, and Robert P. George eschews the Aristotelian-Thomistic metaphysics of the Neo-Scholastic natural law theorists of the late nineteenth and early twentieth centuries, in favor of an attempt to ground traditional natural law conclusions in a theory of practical reason that is neutral vis-à-vis the metaphysical dispute between classical and modern philosophers.[2] Other theories having no connection at all to the classical metaphysical tradition also sometimes go under the "natural law" label.[3] From the classical natural law theorist's point of view, all such theories appear to be "natural law" theories in name only, insofar as nature per se really plays no normative role in them (and couldn't, given that the moderns' conception of nature as devoid of teleology or final causes effectively strips it of any intrinsic value or purpose). Be that as it may, since these theories certainly differ radically from the classical theory in their basic metaphysical and methodological assumptions, it is important to keep these differences in mind when evaluating purportedly "natural law"-based arguments. Much confusion can and often does arise when critics of classical natural law theory unwittingly read into it metaphysical assumptions that only a modern natural law theorist would accept, and vice versa.

II. Metaphysical Foundations

One example of such confusion is the assumption that any natural law theory must commit the "naturalistic fallacy" by failing to take note of the "fact/value distinction." For there can only be a "fact/value distinction," and thus a "fallacy" in deriving normative conclusions from factual premises, given something like a modern mechanistic-cum-nominalistic conception

---

2 For a useful account of the differences between the classical and "new" natural law theories written from a classical point of view, see David S. Oderberg, "The Metaphysical Foundations of Natural Law," in H. Zaborowski, ed., *Natural Law and Contemporary Society* (Washington, D.C.: Catholic University of America Press, 2008).

3 For example, the libertarian theorist Randy Barnett characterizes his position as grounded in "natural law" because it takes account of general empirical facts or "natural laws" about human biology, psychology, and social organization. See *The Structure of Liberty: Justice and the Rule of Law* (New York: Oxford University Press, 1998), pp. 4–12. One problem with this characterization is that it makes the "natural law" label vacuous, since surely every moral theorist, including those who explicitly reject natural law theory, would claim to take account of such general empirical facts.

of nature.[4] No such distinction, and thus no such fallacy, exists given a classical essentialist and teleological conception of the world.

Consider, to begin with, a simple example. It is of the essence or nature of a triangle to be a closed plane figure with three straight sides, and anything with this essence must have a number of properties, such as having angles that add up to 180 degrees. These are objective facts that we discover rather than invent; certainly it is notoriously difficult to make the opposite opinion at all plausible. Nevertheless, there are obviously triangles that fail to live up to this definition. A triangle drawn hastily on the cracked plastic seat of a moving bus might fail to be completely closed or to have perfectly straight sides, and thus its angles will add up to something other than 180 degrees. Indeed, even a triangle drawn slowly and carefully on paper with a Rapidograph pen and a ruler will contain subtle flaws. Still, the latter will far more closely approximate the essence of triangularity than the former will. It will be a *better* triangle than the former. Indeed, we would quite naturally describe the latter as a *good* triangle and the former as a *bad* one. This judgment would be completely objective; it would be silly to suggest that we were merely expressing a personal preference for angles that add up to 180 degrees, say. Such a judgment simply follows from the objective facts about the nature or essence of triangles. This example illustrates how an entity can count as an instance of a certain type of thing even if it fails perfectly to instantiate the essence of that type of thing; a badly drawn triangle is not a non-triangle, but rather a defective triangle. And it illustrates at the same time how there can be a completely *objective, factual* standard of goodness and badness, better and worse. To be sure, the standard of goodness in question in this example is not a *moral* standard. But from the point of view of classical natural law theory, it illustrates a general notion of goodness of which moral goodness is a special case. And while it might be suggested that even this general standard of goodness will lack a foundation if one denies, as nominalists and other anti-realists do, the objectivity of

---

4   And maybe not even then, for the "fact/value distinction," though still (usually unreflectively) believed in by many contemporary philosophers, has been criticized by philosophers not necessarily sympathetic to classical metaphysics. See, e.g., Hilary Putnam, *The Collapse of the Fact/Value Dichotomy and Other Essays* (Cambridge, MA: Harvard University Press, 2004). Criticisms on the part of writers who are sympathetic to classical metaphysics include Christopher Martin, "The Fact/Value Distinction," in David S. Oderberg and Timothy Chappell, eds., *Human Values: New Essays on Ethics and Natural Law* (New York: Palgrave Macmillan, 2004) and David S. Oderberg, *Moral Theory: A Non-Consequentialist Approach* (Oxford: Blackwell, 2000), pp. 9–15.

geometry and mathematics in general, it is (as I have said) notoriously *very* difficult to defend such a denial.

Many contemporary philosophers (and not just philosophers) are coming to see how difficult it is plausibly to deny the reality of essences in other domains. Let us look at another simple example, one that brings us closer to the notion of a distinctly moral conception of goodness. Philippa Foot, following Michael Thompson, notes how living things can only adequately be described in terms of what Thompson calls "Aristotelian categoricals" of a form such as *S's are F*, where S refers to a species and F to something predicated of the species.[5] To cite Foot's examples, "Rabbits are herbivores," "Cats are four-legged," and "Human beings have 32 teeth" would be instances of this general form. Note that such propositions cannot be adequately represented in terms of either the existential or the universal quantifier. "Cats are four-legged," for instance, is obviously not saying "There is at least one cat that is four-legged." But neither is it saying "For everything that is a cat, it is four-legged," since the occasional cat may be missing a leg due to injury or genetic defect. Aristotelian categoricals convey a *norm*, much like the description of what counts as a triangle. Any particular living thing can only be described as an instance of a species, and a species itself can only be described in terms of Aristotelian categoricals stating at least its general characteristics.[6] If a particular S happens not to be F—if, for example, a particular cat is missing a leg—that does not show

---

5   Philippa Foot, *Natural Goodness* (Oxford: Clarendon Press, 2001), chapter 2. The relevant paper of Thompson's is "The Representation of Life," in Rosalind Hursthouse, Gavin Lawrence, and Warren Quinn, eds., *Virtues and Reasons: Philippa Foot and Moral Theory* (Oxford: Clarendon Press, 1995).

6   As Foot notes, questions about the evolutionary origin of a species can largely be set aside here, for the point of an Aristotelian categorical is to describe a species as it actually exists at a point in time, whatever its origins. One might still wonder, however (as Gerald Gaus did in commenting on an earlier version of this paper) whether the existence of such borderline cases as evolutionary transitional forms, which would seem to be indeterminate as to their essence, casts doubt on biological essentialism. But it does not. As David Oderberg points out, characterizing such forms as indeterminate presupposes a contrast with forms which are not indeterminate (such as the evolutionary ancestors and descendants of the forms in question), and thus does not entail that there are no biological essences at all. Furthermore, given the general arguments in favor of classical essentialism, there is no reason to doubt that even such borderline cases do in fact have essences of their own, different from the essences of the forms with which we are contrasting them. See Oderberg, *Real Essentialism* (London: Routledge, 2007), chapter 9 for detailed discussion of this issue.

that S's are not F after all, but rather that this particular S is a *defective* instance of an S.

In living things the sort of norm in question is, Foot tells us, inextricably tied to the notion of teleology. There are certain *ends* that any organism must realize in order to flourish as the kind of organism it is, ends concerning activities like development, self-maintenance, reproduction, the rearing of young, and so forth; and these ends entail a standard of goodness. Hence (again to cite Foot's examples) an oak that develops long and deep roots is to that extent a good oak and one that develops weak roots is to that extent bad and defective; a lioness which nurtures her young is to that extent a good lioness and one that fails to do so is to that extent bad or defective; and so on. As with our triangle example, it would be silly to pretend that these judgments of goodness and badness are in any way subjective or reflective of human preferences. They have rather to do with objective facts about what counts as a flourishing or sickly instance of the biological kind or nature in question, and in particular with an organism's realization or failure to realize the ends set for it by its nature.

It might, of course, be suggested that such teleological language can always be reduced to descriptions couched in non-teleological terms. But widespread though this assumption is, there is surprisingly little in the way of actual argumentation in its favor, and much to be said against it. To be sure, Darwinian theory famously suggests a way of accounting for adaptation in a manner that dispenses with anything like goal-directedness or final causality.[7] But

---

7   On one currently popular account of how this might work, to say (for example) that the kidneys existing in such-and-such an organism have the "function" of purifying its blood really amounts to something like this: Those ancestors of this organism who first developed kidneys (as a result of a random genetic mutation) tended to survive in greater numbers than those without kidneys, because their blood got purified; and this caused the gene for kidneys to get passed on to the organism in question and others like it. To say that an organ's function (now) is to do X is therefore shorthand for saying that it was selected for by evolution because its earliest ancestors did X. There are several well-known difficulties with this sort of account, however. For example, it seems to imply that an organ that did not arise through natural selection could not have a function; yet it is surely at least theoretically possible that organs with genuine functions could arise through means other than natural selection. Related to this, the account seems to imply that we cannot know the function of an organ until we know how it evolved; yet it is obvious, even to someone who knows nothing about evolution, what functions eyes, ears, and many other bodily organs serve. For further discussion of this issue, see Edward Feser, *The Last Superstition: A Refutation of the New Atheism* (South Bend, Indiana: St. Augustine's Press, 2008), pp. 248–57.

the adaptation of organisms to their environments is only one small (albeit important) aspect of the natural world, and the question is whether there is any reason to believe that teleology can be *entirely* or even *mostly* dispensed with in our understanding of nature. And the answer, I would submit, is that it cannot be. Every attempt to eliminate teleology in one domain seems at most merely to relocate it elsewhere, leaving it "grinning residually up at us like the frog at the bottom of the beer mug," as J. L. Austin famously said of another problematic phenomenon.[8]

This is a large topic which I have addressed at length elsewhere.[9] Some general remarks will suffice for our purposes here. Certain common misconceptions about the nature of final causes form one of the main obstacles to acknowledging their reality. It is often thought, for example, that to attribute a final cause to something is necessarily to attribute to it something like thought or consciousness and/or something like a biological function. It is then concluded that anyone committed to the reality of final causes must believe such absurdities as that asteroids and piles of dirt (or whatever) somehow play a role within the larger universe that is analogous to the role a heart or kidney plays in an organism, and that they are at least dimly conscious of doing so. But this is a complete travesty of the Aristotelian notion of final causality. In fact the Aristotelian view has always been that most teleology or final causality is not associated with consciousness or thought at all and that biological functions constitute only one kind of final causality among others.

The heart of the Aristotelian "principle of finality" is, as Aquinas put it, that "Every agent acts for an end."[10] What is meant by this is that anything that serves as what Aristotelians call an efficient cause—that which brings about a certain effect—is directed towards production of that effect as its natural end or goal. The cause "points to" that effect specifically, rather than to some other effect or to no effect at all; or in other words, when A is the efficient cause of B, that is only because B is the final cause of A. For example, a match "points to" or is "directed at" the generation of flame and heat specifically, rather than frost and cold, or the smell of lilacs, or a nuclear explosion. That is the effect it will naturally bring about when struck unless

8   J. L. Austin, "Ifs and Cans," in his *Philosophical Papers*, Third edition (Oxford: Oxford University Press, 1979), at p. 231. Austin's topic was the analysis of the verb "can."

9   See Edward Feser, *The Last Superstition,* and *Aquinas* (Oxford: Oneworld Publications, 2009).

10   *Summa Theologiae* I.22.2.

prevented in some way, and even if it is never in fact struck it remains true that it is that specific effect that it always "aimed at." As Aquinas argued, unless we acknowledge the existence of finality in this sense, we have no way of explaining why it is that efficient causes have exactly the effects they do rather than other effects or no effects at all. In short, efficient causality becomes unintelligible without final causality.[11]

Notice that there is nothing in this that entails that matches or other efficient causes carry out "functions" in the biological sense. To say that final causality pervades the natural world is *not* to say that atoms and molecules, rocks and trees, are somehow related to the world as a whole as biological organs are related to the organism whose organs they are. Functions of the sort that biological organs serve exist only where physical systems are organized in such a way that the parts of the system are ordered to the flourishing of the whole, as in living things. Most of the teleology that Aristotelians would attribute to nature is not like this, but involves merely the simple directedness of a cause of a certain type towards the generation of a certain effect or range of effects. Notice also that there is no implication here that the causes in question are typically conscious (as the match of my example obviously is not). Other than human beings and animals, they typically are not conscious at all. The Aristotelian claim is precisely that things can be directed towards certain ends or goals even if they are totally incapable of being conscious of this fact.

Now it is by no means only Neo-Scholastics and other old-fashioned Aristotelians who would defend essences and teleology today. One finds a hint of final causality even in the work of the materialist philosopher David Armstrong, who suggests that in order to explain intentionality—the human mind's capacity to represent the world beyond itself—his fellow materialists ought to consider the dispositions physical objects possess (such as the disposition glass has to break even if it never in fact shatters) as instances of a kind of "proto-intentionality" or "pointing beyond themselves" towards certain specific outcomes.[12] Similarly, the late George Molnar defended the idea that the causal powers inherent in physical objects manifest a kind of

---

11 That there is something to what Aquinas is saying here should be obvious to anyone familiar with the history of philosophical debate over causation since Hume. I would submit that Humean puzzles about efficient causality arose precisely because of the early modern philosophers' decision to abandon final causality. See the works cited in note 8 for elaboration of this suggestion.

12 D. M. Armstrong, *The Mind-Body Problem: An Opinionated Introduction* (Boulder: Westview, 1999), pp. 138–40.

"physical intentionality" insofar as, like thoughts and other mental states, they point to something beyond themselves, even though they are unlike thoughts in being unconscious.[13] Molnar was representative of a movement within the philosophy of science toward what Brian Ellis has called a "new essentialism," the view that the standard mechanistic and empiricist interpretation of physical science simply doesn't hold up in light of the actual discoveries of modern science or the facts of scientific practice.[14] Ellis and Nancy Cartwright, another prominent "new essentialist," are forthright about the neo-Aristotelian character of their position.[15] Actual experimental practice, Cartwright argues, shows that the hard sciences are in the business of discovering, not mere Humean regularities, but the hidden natures or essences universal to, and the causal powers inherent in, things of a certain type. "The empiricists of the scientific revolution wanted to oust Aristotle entirely from the new learning," but, Cartwright judges, "they did no such thing."[16]

As the work of Foot and Thompson indicates, many contemporary thinkers are prepared to acknowledge the continuing applicability of Aristotelian concepts in biology no less than in physics. To take another example, the philosopher of biology André Ariew has noted that even given that Darwinian evolution undermines William Paley's famous design argument, "it does not follow that Darwin has debunked natural teleology altogether," for "Aristotelian teleology is an entirely different sort."[17] Though natural selection might suffice to explain the adaptation of an organism to its environment, there is also the question of the internal development of an

---

13 George Molnar, *Powers: A Study in Metaphysics* (Oxford: Oxford University Press, 2003).

14 See Brian Ellis, *Scientific Essentialism* (Cambridge: Cambridge University Press, 2001) and *The Philosophy of Nature: A Guide to the New Essentialism* (Chesham: Acumen, 2002).

15 It should be noted that Ellis and Cartwright, unlike some of the authors to be cited later, do not extend their neo-Aristotelianism to biology, but confine it to physics. A more thoroughgoing Aristotelianism is defended in Oderberg, *Real Essentialism* and in Oderberg's "Teleology: Inorganic and Organic," in A. M. Gonzalez, ed., *Contemporary Perspectives on Natural Law* (Aldershot: Ashgate, 2008).

16 Nancy Cartwright, "Aristotelian Natures and the Modern Experimental Method," in John Earman, ed., *Inference, Explanation, and Other Frustrations: Essays in the Philosophy of Science* (Berkeley and Los Angeles: University of California Press, 1992), at p. 70.

17 André Ariew, "Teleology," in David L. Hull and Michael Ruse, eds., *The Cambridge Companion to the Philosophy of Biology* (Cambridge: Cambridge University Press, 2007), at p. 177.

organism from within, and in particular of what accounts for the fact that certain growth patterns count as aberrations and others as normal. Here Aristotle would say that there is no way to make this distinction apart from the notion of an end toward which the growth pattern naturally points: normal growth patterns are those that reach this end, aberrations (clubfoot, polydactyly, and other birth defects, for example) are failures to reach it. Ariew seems to allow that there is nothing in Darwinism that undermines this sort of argument for final causes within biology. The biologist J. Scott Turner is even more explicit that accounting for the phenomena in question requires attributing an unconscious "intentionality" to biological processes.[18]

The persistence of teleological thinking within biology is perhaps most clearly evident from the way in which biologists describe DNA. Accounts of the function of this famous molecule regularly make use of such concepts as "information," "code," "instructions," "data," "blueprint," "software," "program," and the like, and there is no way to convey what DNA does without something like them. But every one of these concepts is suffused with intentionality, that is to say, with the notion of a thing's pointing to something beyond itself in the way our thoughts do, in this case to an organism's physiological and behavioral traits, including those determining the species or kind it belongs to. Of course, no one would claim that DNA molecules literally can be said to think. But the notion of something which points to some end or goal beyond itself despite being totally unconscious *just is* the Aristotelian notion of final causality. As the biophysicist and Nobel laureate Max Delbrück once wrote, if the Nobel Prize could be awarded posthumously, "I think they should consider Aristotle for the discovery of the principle implied in DNA" and "the reason for the lack of appreciation, among scientists, of Aristotle's scheme lies in our having been blinded for 300 years by the Newtonian [i.e. mechanistic or non-teleological] view of the world."[19] More recently, the physicist Paul Davies has complained of the contradiction implicit in biologists' use of informational concepts that entail meaning or purpose while purporting at the same time to be committed to a completely mechanistic picture of the world. Recognizing that such concepts are indispensible, his solution appears to be at least tentatively to suggest giving up

18 J. Scott Turner, *The Tinkerer's Accomplice: How Design Emerges From Life Itself* (Cambridge: Harvard University Press, 2007).

19 Max Delbrück, "Aristotle-totle-totle," in Jacques Monod and Ernest Borek, eds., *Of Microbes and Life* (New York: Columbia University Press, 1971), p. 55.

mechanism, asking "Might purpose be a genuine property of nature right down to the cellular or even the subcellular level?"[20]

It should go without saying that human action is perhaps the most obvious example of a phenomenon that it appears in principle impossible to account for in non-teleological terms.[21] (As Alfred North Whitehead once said, "Those who devote themselves to the purpose of proving that there is no purpose constitute an interesting subject for study."[22]) Then there is human thought, which, even apart from the actions it sometimes gives rise to, manifests intentionality or "directedness" toward something beyond itself and is thus as problematic for a mechanistic picture of the natural world as teleology is.[23]

Much more could be said in support of the classical teleological and essentialist picture of the natural world; and again, I have in fact said much more in support of it elsewhere. To forestall irrelevant objections, I should perhaps also emphasize that the view in question has nothing whatsoever to do with "intelligent design" theory, creationism, or other such bogeymen. It is not William Paley, but Aristotle, who I would suggest stands vindicated by the philosophical and scientific trends I have been describing.[24] Given those

20 Paul Davies, *The Fifth Miracle: The Search for the Origin and Meaning of Life* (New York: Simon and Schuster, 1999), p. 122. Peter Godfrey-Smith is one philosopher of biology who resists the idea that genes encode for phenotypic traits, but even he concedes that they encode for the amino acid sequence of protein molecules in a way that involves semantic information. Though he does not draw the lesson, this would seem all by itself to concede the reality of something like Aristotelian teleology. See Godfrey-Smith's "Information in Biology," in David L. Hull and Michael Ruse, eds., *The Cambridge Companion to the Philosophy of Biology* (Cambridge: Cambridge University Press, 2007).

21 Two important recent defenses of this thesis are G. F. Schueler, *Reasons and Purposes: Human Rationality and the Teleological Explanation of Action* (Oxford: Oxford University Press, 2003) and Scott Sehon, *Teleological Realism: Mind, Agency, and Explanation* (Cambridge, MA: MIT Press, 2005).

22 Alfred North Whitehead, *The Function of Reason* (Princeton, NJ: Princeton University Press, 1929), p. 12.

23 My own view is that an explanation of intentionality in purely materialistic-cum-mechanistic terms is in principle impossible. See Edward Feser, *Philosophy of Mind: A Short Introduction* (Oxford: Oneworld Publications, 2005), chapter 7 for a survey and defense of various arguments for this position, and also chapters 5 and 6 of *The Last Superstition*.

24 Far from being Aristotelian in spirit, Paley's "design argument" and the "intelligent design" theories that have succeeded it essentially concede the idea that the physical universe is *inherently* mechanistic or non-teleological. Such arguments are thus as radically different from the theistic arguments of an Aristotelian like Aquinas as modern "natural law" theories are from classical natural law. See the works of mine cited in note 8 for discussion of this issue.

trends, there is at the very least a powerful case to be made for the view that ends or goals towards which things are directed by virtue of their essences pervade the natural order from top to bottom, from the level of human thought down to that of basic physical particles. It follows that defectiveness, "missing the mark," or failure to realize a natural end or goal also pervade the natural order—as does the opposite of this circumstance, namely that feature of things which Foot has aptly labeled their "natural goodness."

III. Natural Law

It is but a few short steps from natural goodness to natural law, as classically understood; and the other steps are very easily taken. Aquinas famously held that the fundamental principle of natural law is that "good is to be done and pursued, and evil is to be avoided" such that "all other precepts of the natural law are based upon this."[25] Now that "good is to be done etc." might at first glance seem to be a frightfully difficult claim to justify, and certainly not a very promising candidate for an axiom on which to rest an entire moral theory. For isn't the question "Why should I be good?" precisely (part of) what any moral theory ought to answer in the first place? And isn't this question notoriously hard to answer to the satisfaction of moral skeptics? Hasn't Aquinas therefore simply begged the most important question at the very start of the inquiry?

Properly understood, however, Aquinas's principle is not only *not* difficult to justify, but is so obviously correct that it might seem barely worth asserting. Aquinas is not saying that it is self-evident that we ought to be morally good. He is saying rather that it is self-evident that whenever we act we pursue something that we take to be good *in some way* and/or avoid what we take to be *in some way* evil or bad. And he is clearly right. Even someone who does what he believes to be *morally* bad does so only because he is seeking something he takes to be good in the sense of worth pursuing. Hence the mugger who admits that robbery is evil nevertheless takes his victim's wallet because he thinks it would be good to have money to pay for his drugs; hence the drug addict who knows that his habit is wrong and degrading nevertheless thinks it would be good to satisfy the craving and bad to suffer the unpleasantness of not satisfying it; and so forth. Of course, these claims are obviously true only on a very thin sense of "good" and "bad," but that is exactly the sense Aquinas has in mind.

25 *Summa Theologiae* I-II.94.2

Now you don't need the metaphysics of natural goodness described in the previous section to tell you that Aquinas's principle is correct. Again, it is just obviously correct, as everyone knows from his own experience. But that metaphysics does help us to understand *why* it is correct. Like every other natural phenomenon, practical reason has a natural end or goal toward which it is ordered, and that end or goal is just whatever it is the intellect perceives to be good or worth pursuing. This claim too is obvious, at least if one accepts the metaphysical view in question. And now we are on the threshold of a further conclusion that does have real moral bite. For if the metaphysical view described earlier is correct, then like everything else in the world, human beings have various capacities the realization of which is good for them and the frustrating of which is bad, as a matter of objective fact. A rational intellect apprised of the facts will therefore perceive that it is good to realize these capacities and bad to frustrate them. It follows, then, that a rational person will pursue the realization of these capacities and avoid their frustration. In short, practical reason is directed by nature toward the pursuit of what the intellect perceives to be good; what is *in fact* good is the realization or fulfillment of the various capacities and potentials definitive of human nature; and thus a *rational* person will perceive this and, accordingly, direct his actions towards the realization or fulfillment of those capacities and potentials. This, in essence, is what the moral life consists in. Natural law ethics as a body of substantive moral theory is just the formulation of general moral principles on the basis of an analysis of the various human capacities in question and the systematic working out of their implications. So, for example, if we consider that human beings have intellects and that the natural end or function of the intellect is to grasp the truth about things, it follows that it is good for us—it fulfills our nature—to pursue truth and avoid error. Consequently, a rational person apprised of the facts about human nature will see that this is what is good for us and thus strive to attain truth and to avoid error. And so on for other natural human capacities.

Things are more complicated than that summary perhaps lets on. Various qualifications and complications will need to be spelled out as we examine the various natural human capacities in detail, and not every principle of morality that follows from this analysis will necessarily be as simple and straightforward as "Pursue truth and avoid error." But this much is enough to give us at least a general idea of how natural law theory determines the specific content of our moral obligations. It also suffices to give us a sense of the *grounds* of moral obligation, that which makes it the case that moral imperatives have categorical rather than merely hypothetical force. The hypothetical imperative *(1) If I want what is good for me then I ought to pursue what fulfills my natural capacities and avoid what frustrates them* is something whose truth is revealed by the metaphysical analysis sketched in the previous section. By itself, it does not give us a categorical imperative because the consequent will have force only for someone who accepts the antecedent. But that *(2) I do want what is good for me* is something true of everyone by virtue of his nature as a human being, and is in any case self-evident, being just a variation on Aquinas's fundamental principle of natural law. Thus the conclusion *(3) I ought to pursue what fulfills my natural capacities and avoid what frustrates them* is unavoidable. It does have categorical force because (2) has categorical force, and (2) has categorical force because it cannot be otherwise given our nature. Not only the content of our moral obligations but their obligatory force are thus determined by natural teleology.[26] As the natural law theorist Michael Cronin has written, "In the fullest sense of the word, then, moral duty is natural. For not only are certain objects natural means to man's final end, but our desire of that end is natural also, and, therefore, the necessity of the means is natural."[27]

IV. Natural Rights

We are rationally obliged, then, to pursue what is good for us and avoid what is bad, where "good" and "bad" have, again, the senses described in our discussion of the metaphysical foundations of classical natural law theory. Hence we are obliged (for example) to pursue the truth and avoid error, to sustain our lives and our health and to avoid what is damaging to them, and so on and so forth (ignoring as irrelevant to our present purposes the various complications and qualifications a fully developed natural law theory would have to spell out). The force and content of these obligations derive from our nature as human beings.

26 Hence, from a classical natural law point of view, the problematic status of moral obligation in modern moral philosophy is a symptom of the moderns' abandonment of final causes. In general, from a classical point of view, many philosophical problems often characterized as "perennial" or "traditional" (e.g., the mind-body problem, the problem of personal identity, puzzles about causation, and many others) are in fact merely byproducts of the moderns' adoption of a mechanistic philosophy of nature, and do not arise, or at least do not arise in so puzzling a form, on a classical metaphysical picture. See Feser, *The Last Superstition*, chapter 5 for development of this idea.

27 Michael Cronin, *The Science of Ethics, Volume 1: General Ethics* (Dublin: M. H. Gill and Son, 1939), p. 222.

It is part of that nature that we are *social* animals, as Aristotle famously noted. That is to say, we naturally live in communities with other human beings and depend on them for our well-being in various ways, both negative (such as our need not to be harmed by others) and positive (such as our need for various kinds of assistance from them). Most obviously, we are related to others by virtue of being either parents or children, siblings, grandparents and grandchildren, cousins, and so forth. Within the larger societies that collections of families give rise to, other kinds of relationships form, such as that of being a friend, an employee or an employer, a citizen, and so forth. To the extent that some of these relationships are natural to us, their flourishing is part of what is naturally good for us.

For example, as Foot writes, "like lionesses, human parents are defective if they do not teach their young the skills that they need to survive."[28] It is part of our *nature* to become parents, and part of our *nature* that while we are children we depend on our own parents.[29] Accordingly, it is simply an objective fact that it is good for us to be good parents to our children and bad for us to be bad parents, just as it is (even more obviously) an objective fact that it is good for children to be taken care of by their parents. The satisfaction good parents often feel and the sense of failure and frustration bad parents feel obviously give us confirmation of this judgment, but it is important to emphasize that classical natural law theory does not regard the often fluctuating subjective feelings and desires of individuals to be what is most fundamental to an analysis of what is good for them. To be sure, there is at least a rough and general correlation between what is good for us and what we want or find pleasant, and on a classical natural law analysis, our tendency to find some things pleasurable and other things unpleasant is one of nature's ways of getting us to do what is good for us and avoid what is bad. Still, feelings and desires are not infallible. It is good for us to eat, which is why we like to do it, but obviously this doesn't entail that it is good for us to follow just every impulse we have to eat; the heroin addict finds it pleasurable to take drugs, but it doesn't follow that it is good for him to give in to his desire to take them; and so forth. For a variety of reasons—ignorance, stubbornness, irrationality, peer pressure, addiction, habituated vice, genetic defect, mental illness, and so on—people sometimes do not want

---

28   Foot, *Natural Goodness*, p. 15.

29   As a fully worked out natural law account of the matter would show, this does not entail that every human being is under an obligation to become a parent, but it does entail that if someone does become a parent, he is obligated to be a good one, with everything that that implies.

what is in fact good for them, and even want what is not in fact good for them, their natural desire for the good being oriented away from its proper object. The fact remains that what really is good for them is defined by their nature as human beings, and thus by the sorts of biological and metaphysical considerations summarized earlier. Subjective feelings that would incline us to act contrary to our nature must themselves be judged defective, something we have a moral duty to strive against and try to overcome. Hence the existence of sadistic parents or the occasional "deadbeat dad" who has no regrets does nothing to undermine the truth of the judgment that their behavior is contrary to their nature and thus bad for them, just as the existence of a sickly squirrel who has been conditioned to prefer sitting in a cage eating toothpaste on Ritz crackers to scampering about the woods looking for acorns does not undermine the judgment that the squirrel's behavior is contrary to its nature and thus bad for it.

Now if it is good for a parent to provide for his children, then given that we are obliged to do what is good for us, it follows that a parent has an obligation to provide for them. Similarly, since given their need for instruction, discipline, and the like, it is good for children to obey and respect their parents, it follows that they have an obligation to obey and respect them. But an obligation on the part of a person A toward another person B entails a right on the part of B against A.[30] It follows in turn, then, that children have a *right* to be provided for by their parents, and parents have a *right* to be obeyed and respected by their children. And since the obligations that generate the rights in question are obligations under *natural* law (rather than positive law) it follows that they are *natural* rights, grounded not in human convention but in human nature. Other obligations we have under natural law toward various other human beings will similarly generate various other natural rights. At the most general level, we are all obliged to refrain from interfering with others' attempts to fulfill the various moral obligations placed on them by the natural law. For as Austin Fagothey puts it, "man cannot have such obligations unless he has a right to fulfill them, and a consequent right to prevent others from interfering with his fulfillment of them."[31] The most *basic* natural right is the right to do what we are obligated to do by the natural law. Hence everyone necessarily has a natural right not to be coerced into doing evil. There

---

30 Though the weaker the obligation is, the weaker the right generated by it. (Cf. the distinction between perfect rights and imperfect rights discussed below.)

31 Austin Fagothey, *Right and Reason*, Second edition (St. Louis: The C. V. Mosby Company, 1959), p. 250. Cf. Oderberg, *Moral Theory*, pp. 53–63.

are also many things that are naturally good for us even if we are not strictly obligated to pursue them, such as having children. This particular example is, according to classical natural law theory, the foundation for the natural right to marry.[32] And of course we cannot pursue any good or fulfill any obligation at all if our very lives could be taken from us by others as they saw fit, so that the natural law entails that every human being (or at least every innocent human being) has a right not to be killed.[33]

If classical natural law theory entails the existence of natural rights, it also entails that there are very definite limits on those rights. To be sure, a right to a significant measure of personal liberty is clearly implied by the natural law, given that the natural differences between individuals in terms of their interests, talents, upbringing, and other personal circumstances, and in general the complexities inherent in the human condition, entail that there are myriad ways in which human beings might concretely realize the capacities and potentials inherent in their common nature, and each person will need to be free to discover for himself which way is best for him. But this freedom cannot possibly be absolute, for while there is much that the natural law allows, there is also much that it forbids as absolutely contrary to the human good, and rights only exist to allow us to fulfill the human good. Thus, as one classical natural law theorist has put it, "the rights of all men are limited by the *end* for which the rights were given"[34]; and therefore, to cite another, "there can never be a right to that which is immoral. For the moral law cannot grant that which is destructive of itself."[35] Natural rights have a *teleological* foundation, and cannot exist except where they further the purposes they serve.

It is important to emphasize that this does not entail the institution of a totalitarian "morality police." As Aquinas famously emphasized, that the

---

32 Explaining exactly how and why (and what the implications are for the debate over "same-sex marriage") would require an excursus into the classical natural law approach to sexual morality, which is beyond the scope of this paper. Readers interested in an exposition of this approach are directed to chapter 4 of Feser, *The Last Superstition.*

33 Famously, for classical natural law theory this rules out abortion and euthanasia but not capital punishment or just wars. For a useful recent explanation of why this is the case, see David S. Oderberg, *Applied Ethics: A Non-Consequentialist Approach* (Oxford: Blackwell, 2000).

34 Celestine N. Bittle, *Man and Morals* (Milwaukee: Bruce Publishing Company, 1950), p. 293. Emphasis mine.

35 Thomas J. Higgins, *Man as Man: The Science and Art of Ethics*, Revised edition (Milwaukee: Bruce Publishing Company, 1959), p. 231.

natural law *morally* prohibits something does not suffice to show that governments should *legally* prohibit it.[36] The point is rather that no one can coherently justify his indulgence of some vice on the grounds that he has a *natural right* to indulge in it, or that it would be *intrinsically unjust* to prevent him from doing so. The idea of a "natural right to do wrong" is an oxymoron. But there still might be many reasons of a prudential or even moral sort for government to tolerate certain vices; for instance, enforcing laws against them may be practically impossible, or inadvertently do more harm than good.

Both the existence of natural rights and their limitations derive from their teleological foundation, and neither can be made sense of apart from it. From a classical natural law point of view, this is precisely why the very notion of natural rights has been so problematic in modern philosophy, given its mechanistic or anti-teleological metaphysical orientation. For example, Locke, famously critical of Aristotelian Scholasticism, cannot give natural rights an essentialist-cum-teleological foundation, and so must appeal directly to God's will for us. His famous thesis of self-ownership turns out to be a kind of shorthand for talk about the leasehold rights over ourselves that God has granted us, with God ultimately being our true "owner." The result is that Locke's "defense" of natural rights is really a denial of them: Strictly speaking, for Locke it is God who has all the rights, not us, and our obligation not to harm others derives not from any rights they have, but rather from our duty not to damage what belongs to God. As we will see, Locke's rejection of final causes poses particular problems for his theory of property.[37]

Contemporary Lockeans, who eschew Locke's theology, are even more hard-pressed to find a way to justify the claim that we have rights that are in some interesting sense "natural." For instance, Robert Nozick's notion of self-ownership, though more robust than Locke's, is also (and notoriously) even less well-grounded.[38] Certainly self-ownership cannot by itself serve as the foundation of a theory of natural rights, since the concept of ownership *presupposes* the notion of rights. Nozick's appeal to Kant's principle

36   *Summa Theologiae* I-II.96.2
37   It causes him many other problems too, for discussion of which see Feser, *Locke*.
38   Robert Nozick, *Anarchy, State, and Utopia* (New York: Basic Books, 1974). Edward Feser, *On Nozick* (Belmont, CA: Wadsworth, 2004), chapter 3 offers a sympathetic discussion, though it was written at a time when I believed (as I no longer do) that Nozick's theory of rights could be grounded in a classical natural law approach to moral theory.

of respect for persons only raises the question of *why* we should respect persons as such, and while the classical natural law theorist can answer this question in terms of a robust metaphysics of human nature, those who reject that metaphysics (as Nozick, and indeed Kant himself, would) have no clear answer—at least, again, if their intention is to show that our basic rights are truly *natural* rights.

If the existence of natural rights becomes problematic for Locke and Lockeans, it is in the work of Hobbes and his successors that we see most clearly how the limitations the classical natural law theorist would put on our rights are undermined when a teleological metaphysics is abandoned. In the Hobbesian state of nature, everyone has a right to do anything he wants, without any limitations whatsoever. Of course, that is precisely because Hobbesians do not see us as *naturally* having "rights" in the moral sense at all, morality being the result of a kind of contract between rationally self-interested individuals. Even when the contract is made, though, the rights that result seem inevitably to have very little in the way of restrictions upon them, at least in the thinking of contemporary contractarians inspired by Hobbes.[39] The reason is that it is not any objective natural end that our rights are meant to further on a contractarian account, but rather whatever subjective desires or preferences we happen to have, whether or not these desires or preferences are in line with any purported natural ends. The contract that rationally self-interested individuals would agree to, then, is essentially a non-aggression pact, each party granting the others the "right" to be left alone to do whatever they want to so long as they are willing to reciprocate. If such a right has very little in the way of restrictions on it, however, that is, again, precisely because it is not natural but (in the relevant sense) conventional.

Of course, contractarians themselves would not regard either the conventional status of rights or the lack of restrictions as a problem for their theory. But contractarian theories also famously face the problems of explaining why we should attribute even conventional rights to the weakest members of society (who have nothing to offer the stronger parties to the proposed "contract" in return for being left alone) and why we should suppose that even every rationally self-interested individual would sincerely agree to such a contract in the first place (since some might prefer to take their chances in a Hobbesian war of all against all, or opt for the life of a

---

39　See, e.g., Jan Narveson, *The Libertarian Idea* (Philadelphia: Temple University Press, 1988).

free-rider who benefits from others' abiding by the contract while he secretly violates it whenever he knows he can get away with doing so). Contractarians have offered various responses to these difficulties, which typically involve inventive appeals to various less obvious ways in which the strong might benefit from leaving the weak alone, or in which even a rational misanthrope might benefit from sincerely abiding by the terms of the contract. At the end of the day, however, the contractarian can give no *rational* criticism of someone who fully understands the benefits that would accrue to him by agreeing to the social contract and treating others as if they had rights, but nevertheless refuses to do so. The most the contractarian can say is "Better keep an eye on *that* guy, then," for he might do the rest of us harm. He does not do *himself* harm, though, on a contractarian analysis, and in denying others their rights he does not deny them anything they really had objectively in the first place.

For the classical natural law theorist, by contrast, such a sociopath *does* do himself harm as well as fails to perceive the objective facts about others. As Foot puts it, "free-riding individuals of a species whose members work together are just as *defective* as those who have defective hearing, sight, or powers of locomotion."[40] If we look at the evident facts of human experience through the lens of an essentialist metaphysics, we can see that a certain measure of fellow-feeling is, like bipedalism or language, natural to human beings and thus objectively good for every human being simply by virtue of being human, whether or not certain specific individuals fail for whatever reason to realize this.

V. Property Rights

Much more could be said about the classical natural law theory of natural rights, but our interest here is in the right to private property in particular, so let us turn at last to that. The best known defenses of private property in contemporary philosophy, those of Locke and Nozick, start with some version of the thesis of self-ownership and work from it to a defense of private property in general, their strategy being to show that if as self-owners we own our own labor, then we must also have a right to the fruits of our labor. Does classical natural law theory recognize anything like the thesis of self-ownership?

Yes and no. On the one hand, if the thesis of self-ownership is taken (as

---

40   Foot, *Natural Goodness*, p. 16. Emphasis in the original.

it seems to be by Nozick) to entail the virtually unlimited right to do with ourselves just anything we want, then classical natural law theory obviously cannot endorse the thesis. For if, as classical natural law theorists would typically hold, illicit drug use, prostitution, suicide, and other so-called "victimless crimes" are inherently immoral, then for reasons stated already there can be no natural right to do such things. Moreover, as Fagothey has argued, "since in the exercise of any right the subject always subordinates the matter [i.e., that which the right is a right to] to himself and uses it as a means to his own end, it follows that the matter of a right can never be a person."[41] Fagothey's point is that since every human being already has certain ends set for him by nature, he cannot possibly be entirely subordinated to the ends of another, which he would be if he were owned by another; and his immediate aim is to argue against the legitimacy of chattel slavery.[42] But this argument might seem to rule out self-ownership as well, since if each human being has certain ends set for him by nature, he not only could not legitimately use another person, but also could not use himself, for just *any* ends he happens to have, as it seems he could do if he could be said to be his own property.

On the other hand, it is hardly unusual to speak of someone as owning something even if it is also said that he cannot do just whatever he likes with it. Though I have no right to stab you with my knife, it doesn't follow that the knife is not my property. Though I have no right to conduct dangerous experiments on radioactive materials in my garage, lest I accidentally blow up the neighborhood, it doesn't follow that I don't own my garage. Similarly, even if there are limits on what I can legitimately do with myself, it wouldn't follow from that fact alone that there is no sense in which I own

---

41 Fagothey, *Right and Reason*, p. 243.
42 It is sometimes claimed that classical natural law theory supports the moral legitimacy of slavery, but this is highly misleading at best and at worst slanderous. What natural law theorists have held is that, since it is obviously morally unproblematic for one person to come to owe another this or that particular service as a matter of right, it is in principle possible that someone could come legitimately to owe another service for some prolonged period of time, perhaps even a lifetime. For example, such servitude might be imposed as a punishment for a crime. But this is a far cry from chattel slavery, slave hunting, allowing children to be born into slavery, etc., all of which are condemned by natural law theory as intrinsically immoral. (Hence the African slave trade could not be justified in terms of classical natural law theory.) Moreover, the consensus among recent classical natural law theorists is that even the more limited form of servitude natural law allows in principle is so morally hazardous that in practice it cannot be justified.

myself.[43] Ownership involves the possession of various rights over a thing—the right to use it, the right to sell it, the right to exclude others from it, and so forth—and even if someone does not have every possible right one could have over a thing, it will still be plausible to say that he owns it as long as he possesses a sufficient number of these rights. Of course, as it stands, that is somewhat vague. But it suffices to make the point that as long as natural law theory allows that an individual has over himself and his faculties certain key rights, such as the right to decide how to employ his labor, the right to life and to bodily integrity, the right to a significant measure of personal liberty, and so forth—and the theory would affirm rights of this sort—then perhaps this will suffice to show that natural law theory entails that individuals are, in *some* significant sense, self-owners.

However, given the qualifications we have seen would have to be put on self-ownership from a natural law point of view, it is also probably true that the idea of self-ownership ceases to be very interesting. For that idea is, of course, most commonly employed by libertarians seeking to undermine every form of paternalistic morals legislation and redistributive taxation in one fell swoop, as violations of the right of self-ownership; and such a strategy obviously becomes impossible on classical natural law theory. The point isn't that natural law theory entails that all or even any redistributive taxation is legitimate—we have yet to address that issue—nor, as I have already noted, is it to say that the theory necessarily entails that there should be laws against vices indulged in privately. The point is rather that given the qualifications the theory would place on self-ownership, the concept of self-ownership can no longer serve as a "magic bullet" that *automatically* takes down everything the libertarian wants to rule out. If self-ownership is far from absolute in the first place, then to know whether I either have a moral right to do this or that, or ought at least to be allowed legally to do it whether or not it is immoral, it will not suffice to shout "I own myself!" One will have to investigate, on a case by case basis, how the act in question either helps, hinders, or is neutral vis-à-vis the realization of what natural law entails is good for me; whether a law against it would, even if it is bad for me, do more harm than good all things considered; and so forth. That I own my home doesn't by itself settle whether I can sink a well

43 Indeed, even Locke says that we cannot legitimately commit suicide or sell ourselves into slavery despite our ownership of ourselves, though in his case this is precisely because talk of "self-ownership" is for Locke really a kind of shorthand for talk of our leasehold rights over what is ultimately God's property rather than ours.

in my back yard, tear my house down and build a skyscraper on the lot, put up a guard tower manned with sentries carrying grenades and machine guns, and so on. Private property rights are simply more complicated than that. Similarly, even if there is some sense in which I can be said to own myself, that doesn't *by itself* show that I can inject myself with heroin, become a prostitute, sell my bodily organs for profit, or whatever.

So, from a natural law point of view, self-ownership per se would not seem to be a promising basis on which to build a political philosophy, including a theory of private property rights. Still, like Locke and Nozick, many classical natural law theorists have argued that a right to private property follows from a consideration of (among other things) our natural powers and labor specifically. Indeed, to a large extent the classical natural law case for private property overlaps with that made by classical liberal and libertarian property theorists. The difference—and it is a significant one—is in the way this case is informed by a classical essentialist-cum-teleological metaphysics and by the moral implications we have already seen to follow from that metaphysics.

Now, by nature human beings obviously need natural resources in order to survive. But that fact is consistent with holding that they ought to be allowed only the use of natural resources rather than ownership of them, or with the view that natural resources ought to be collectively owned. Of course, there are very serious and well-known practical problems both with a situation where natural resources are left in the commons and with any system of collective ownership à la socialism and communism. But that would by itself show only that private property has certain practical advantages, not that there is a natural right to it. So how does classical natural law theory show that such a right does in fact exist?

The case begins by noting that the institution of private property is something toward which we are both *naturally suited* and even *require* for our well-being.[44] With respect to the former point, we can note first that an individual human being's intellect and will make it possible for him (unlike the lower animals) to take permanent occupation and control of a resource and to use it for his personal benefit; and such occupation, control, and use

---

44 A particularly thorough presentation of the classical natural law case for private property can be found in Michael Cronin, *The Science of Ethics, Volume 2: Special Ethics* (Dublin: M. H. Gill and Son, 1939), chapter 4, which has informed my discussion here. (In addition, chapters 5–8 contain a lengthy critique of socialism.) Also useful are Bittle, *Man and Morals*, chapters 16 and 17; Fagothey, *Right and Reason*, chapters 28 and 29; and Higgins, *Man as Man*, chapters 17 and 18.

is precisely what private property consists in.[45] Furthermore, in doing so the individual inevitably imparts something of his own personality to the resources he transforms, insofar as the particular properties a resource takes on as a result of his use and transformation of it reflect his personal intentions, knowledge, talents, and efforts. As Cronin colorfully puts it, considered just as such, "a machine is very little more than crystallized human thought and energy."[46] In our very use of external resources, then, we tend unavoidably to put into them something that is already ours (which is, of course, something Locke also emphasizes in his talk of "mixing our labor" with external resources).

So our inherent faculties naturally orient us toward private ownership. But such ownership is also necessary for us. It is necessary for us first of all as individuals. An individual's personal capacities and potentials cannot be exercised and realized, respectively, without at least some stable body of resources on which to bring his efforts to bear; the freedom of action required in order to do this cannot exist unless he has permanent access to at least some of those resources; and as the experience of individuals in even the most egalitarian societies attests, human beings have a natural desire for at least something to call their own, and cannot be happy if this desire is frustrated.

Ownership is also necessary for us as families. We are naturally ordered toward the having of children, and as we have seen, for classical natural law theory this entails an obligation to provide for whatever children we have, not only materially but spiritually, that is, with respect to their moral upbringing, education, and the like. Furthermore, as is well-known, classical natural law theory entails that large families will inevitably tend to be the norm given what the natural law tells us with respect to sexual morality (though this is, again, not something there is space to get into here). As children grow to adulthood and have families of their own, they tend to need assistance from parents in starting out; there are other relatives (aunts and uncles, cousins and the like) to whom in some circumstances we might also owe some assistance under natural law, even if our obligations here are not

---

45 Classical natural law theorists also typically add that since what is less perfect exists for the sake of what is more perfect, inanimate resources, plants, and animals exist for the sake of man. But the hierarchical conception of reality this presupposes is an aspect of classical metaphysics that I do not have space here to expound or defend. For a general account, see Feser, *Aquinas*.

46 Cronin, *Special Ethics*, p. 120. Of course the "little more," namely the natural resources out of which a machine is made, are important too. More on this presently.

as strong as to our own children; and there are always emergencies that need to be planned for as far as possible. As the fundamental social arrangement, for the sake of which others (such as states) exist, it is also crucial that the family maintains a significant measure of independence. These considerations entail that heads of families need to be able to amass large amounts of wealth to which they have permanent rights of use and transfer.[47]

Finally, private ownership is necessary for the good of the larger societies that tend naturally to form out of groups of families. Here the sorts of considerations favoring private property famously adduced by Aristotle and Aquinas become particularly relevant. The incentives to labor are massively reduced where the laborer is not allowed to reap its fruits, which drastically limits the amount of wealth available for the use of society at large; economic and social planning are far more efficient when individuals are able to look after their own property than when things are held in common (a point Mises and Hayek have developed in illuminating detail); and social peace is more likely when individuals each have their own property than when they must debate over how best to use what is held in common.[48]

If our natural capacities are ordered toward private ownership, and if the fulfillment of those capacities and of our moral obligations under natural law requires such ownership, then it follows, given the justification of natural rights outlined above, that the natural law entails a natural right to private property. So far, though, this establishes only the general institution of private property. We need to say something more to determine how a title to this or that *particular* resource can come to be acquired by this or that *particular* individual. That is to say, we need a theory of "original appropriation" or "initial acquisition."

The tendency of classical natural law theorists of property is to find the origin of such appropriation in first occupation. Taking occupation of a previously unowned resource is *necessary* for ownership because unless one first takes hold of a resource, nothing else can be done with it at all, including the carrying out of any other procedure that might be claimed to be necessary for appropriation. In particular, one cannot "mix one's labor" with a resource until one has first taken hold of or occupied it, for which reason

---

47 As Cronin notes, it is irrelevant that some individuals might not in fact have families, for the conclusions of natural law follow from the normal case, from what our nature inclines us to. Thus, insofar as even those who happen not to have children nevertheless have an inherent or natural tendency toward family life, they will retain whatever natural rights flow from this particular aspect of human nature.

48 Cf. Aquinas, *Summa Theologiae* II-II.66.2.

classical natural law theorists tend to reject Locke's theory of appropriation at least as an account of the *fundamental* means by which ownership gets started. Taking occupation is also (apart from a qualification to be noted presently) *sufficient* for ownership because it suffices to enable one to fulfill the ends for which natural law theory tells us the right to property exists in the first place.[49]

Though not as fundamental as first occupation, labor nevertheless also has a crucial role to play in the story of how property comes into being. For as noted above, for classical natural law theory, to labor over a resource is, as it were, to put into it an impress of one's own personality, and thus something one already has a right to. Furthermore, most of the value that comes to exist in a transformed resource derives not from the resource per se but from the labor put into transforming it. As Cronin puts it, "with the exception of a mere fraction of our present wealth, the riches of the world are entirely a result of human labour" (where he is clear that what he has in mind is "labour in its broad sense—not mere manual labour").[50] Hence the more one has put one's labor into a previously unowned resource of which he takes first occupation, the *stronger* or more *complete* is his property right to that resource.

This naturally brings us to the question of the limits on the right to private property, which are implied by the suggestion that a property right can be more or less strong or complete. As with natural rights in general, the right to private property has a teleological basis, namely the role it plays in enabling us to realize our natural capacities and fulfill our obligations under natural law; and as with natural rights in general, this right is limited by the very teleological considerations that ground it. As what has already been said clearly implies, the right to private property, like our other natural rights, cannot possibly be so strong that it would justify us in doing what is contrary to the natural law. Hence there can be no *natural* right to use our property for intrinsically immoral purposes. As before, this doesn't by itself entail that government must or even should regulate our private exercise of our rights so that it conforms to the standards of natural law. But it does entail that there can be no natural law basis for libertarian arguments to the

49   What *counts* as first occupation? Does an explorer who merely sets foot on the edge of a vast continent thereby come to occupy the whole thing? I would argue that the mark of genuine occupation of a resource is some significant measure of *control* over it. Cf. my discussion of this issue in "There is No Such Thing as an Unjust Initial Acquisition," *Social Philosophy and Policy* 22, no. 1 (2005).

50   Cronin, *Special Ethics*, p. 127.

effect that outlawing strip clubs and drug dens (or whatever) is *necessarily* a violation of the natural right to private property.

But there is another limitation on the right to private property, one that is more directly related to its specific teleological grounding. As we have seen, for classical natural law theory, property exists in the first place in order to allow individuals to realize their natural capacities and moral obligations by bringing their powers to bear on external resources. Hence if property rights were so strong that they would justify some people in using their property in a way that undermined the possibility for others to fulfill their natural ends and moral obligations, then the very point of the institution of private property would be undermined. To take an extreme but clear example, if some one person or group of persons acquired a monopoly over some crucial resource (such as land or water) and refused those who did not have this resource access to it, or allowed them access only under onerous conditions, then it is obvious that the institution of private property would allow some individuals to fulfill their natural ends at the expense of the ability of others to fulfill theirs. Clearly, then, the right to private property cannot be so strong as to justify such a circumstance.

What does this limitation imply in practice? The most obvious implication is that individuals in circumstances of what Cronin calls "absolute distress" have a right to the use of the resources of others, where the paradigm examples would be the starving man in the woods who takes food from a cabin, or a window washer who grabs a flagpole to break his fall from a building, or someone fleeing robbers who can only escape by running through someone else's back yard.[51] Someone in circumstances like these is not guilty of theft or the like, because for actions like the ones in question to count as theft etc., the cabin owner or flagpole owner or homeowner would have to have such an *absolute* right to his property that he could justly refuse to allow others to use it even in the circumstances in question, and according to natural law theory, no one could possibly have so absolute a property right. For the same reason, if some resource (the only remaining source of water in an area stricken by drought, say) became "absolutely necessary ... to save the community or part of it from extinction," then any individual who had heretofore privately owned that resource would have an obligation in justice to relinquish it.[52]

---

51   Ibid., p. 135.
52   Ibid., p. 136. Given the improvements an owner might have made to a resource, or his personal economic stake in it, compensation might be called for in such a case.

Here classical natural law theory is committed to something analogous to what the libertarian philosopher Eric Mack calls the "self-ownership proviso" on the use of resources, which "requires that persons not deploy their legitimate holdings, i.e., their extra-personal property, in ways that severely, albeit noninvasively, disable any person's world-interactive powers."[53] I say "analogous" rather than identical both because, for reasons already stated, classical natural law theory is probably not best thought of as basing its theory of property rights on self-ownership per se, and because it isn't clear that Mack would allow for a case where an owner would have to relinquish his property, as opposed to merely allowing others to use it (though the distinction between taking and merely using blurs in the case of something like a source of water, which people use precisely by taking some of it). Like Mack, though, natural law theory is less concerned with the initial appropriation of resources (the focus of Locke's famous provisos) than with how they are used after acquired.[54] And as for Mack, the key to the issue for classical natural law theory is the possibility of bringing what he calls our "world-interactive powers" to bear on the world, since the point of the institution of private property is precisely to allow us to fulfill the natural end of these powers.

In this connection we should note that classical natural law theorists would argue that their metaphysical commitments allow them to make sense of what they and Lockeans (like Mack) have in common in a way that strict Lockeans cannot. For to speak (as Mack does) of our "powers" as "essentially" "world-interactive" is to say something that naturally suggests an Aristotelian essentialist-cum-teleological metaphysics; certainly it is hard to see how we could *literally* have "powers" that are of their essence oriented or directed toward the external world on a modern mechanistic or anti-teleological metaphysics, and if this talk is not meant literally then its import needs to be explained. Similarly, Jeremy Waldron has noted that it is hard to see why Locke should think that putting one's labor into a resource would give one a property right in that resource, any more than dropping one's diamond into a

---

53 Eric Mack, "The Self-Ownership Proviso: A New and Improved Lockean Proviso," *Social Philosophy and Policy* 12, no. 1 (1995). See Feser, "There is No Such Thing as an Unjust Initial Acquisition," for a development and defense of Mack's proviso, though I would now qualify much of what I said in that paper in light of the views expressed in this one.

54 Though Cronin indicates that a person could not justly appropriate for himself a previously unowned resource that was known *in advance* to be necessary for the continued existence of the community.

vat of cement would give one a property right in the cement, unless we think in teleological terms.[55] But how could Locke appeal to the teleology of labor, or of natural resources, when he denies the existence of Aristotelian final causes? Indeed, how can he even ground a *natural* right to property by appeal to the concepts of labor, natural resources, etc. when for Locke the essences of things (including, if he is to be consistent, of labor, natural resources, and indeed of human beings themselves) are man-made or conventional rather than natural? The mechanistic metaphysical picture of the world to which Locke and his successors tend explicitly or at least implicitly to be committed seems to undermine the foundations of their political philosophy. Yet to try to avoid these difficulties by adopting an Aristotelian metaphysics would entail committing oneself to the classical natural law theory that flows from it, and thus to cease to be a Lockean—or so I would argue.[56]

VI. Taxation

The question of the limits classical natural law theory would put on the right to private property naturally brings us at last to the issue of taxation. There is no way this subject can be treated adequately without discussing the natural law understanding of the nature of the state and the basis of its authority, and that is obviously beyond the scope of this paper. Suffice it to say that classical natural law theory rejects the classical liberal idea that the state is artificial, a product of human convention, and regards it instead as a natural institution to which we owe allegiance whether or not we consent to it. At the same time, natural law theory regards the state as existing only to serve the interests of its citizens, and only with respect to those functions that private citizens cannot carry out on their own. Hence the natural law theorist is committed to the idea of limited government, though given what was said earlier the limitations in question would no doubt not be severe enough to satisfy contemporary libertarians. In any event, whatever taxes would be required to fund the legitimate functions of government are taxes the classical natural law theorist would hold us to be obligated in justice to pay.[57]

---

55 Jeremy Waldron, *God, Locke, and Equality* (Cambridge: Cambridge University Press, 2002), p. 159. Nozick famously gives a similar example in *Anarchy, State, and Utopia* (at p. 175), though without drawing the teleological lesson.

56 Again, see Feser, *Locke*.

57 From this and what is said below it should be clear that I have moved away considerably (though not completely) from the position I defended in "Taxation, Forced Labor, and Theft," *The Independent Review* 5, no. 2 (2000).

Beyond this some further general remarks can be made in light of the theory of property rights sketched above. Other than those limits on the use of one's property that are entailed by one's general obligation not to employ what one owns for evil purposes (e.g., as a drug den or brothel or whatever), we saw that the main limitation, and the one that entails the possibility that one might under certain circumstances be morally required to relinquish (or at least allow others to use) one's property, had to do with cases where a more absolute right to ownership would undermine the very point of the institution of private property. But how can we be required *in justice* (not merely in charity) to give up our property rights even in these cases, especially since, as we have seen, it is our talents and energies that are primarily responsible for the existence of the objects owned in the first place, and since in using our talents and energies we have put something of ourselves into the products of our labor? As Cronin argues, the answer to this question must lie in the fact that we are never *entirely* responsible in the first place for the existence of the things we produce, since we must always make use of natural resources which we did not create and which start out unowned by anyone.[58] For if others have at least *some* claim over these preexisting resources even before we transform them with our labor, that claim will persist even after we do so, and even though the claim is so weak that it will require us to relinquish our property rights only under certain exceptional conditions. That others do have such a claim is entailed by the reason for which property rights exist in the first place, viz. to allow us to bring our capacities to bear on external natural resources so that we might fulfill the ends and obligations set for us by natural law.[59]

These various considerations would appear to suggest what we might call a *Natural Law Proviso* on the use of property, according to which an individual has a natural right to use whatever property he acquires either via first occupation or by trade, gifts, wages, inheritance, etc.[60] in any way

58 Cronin, *Special Ethics*, p. 135.
59 Hence the claim that natural resources start out unowned needs to be qualified; everyone has at least this minimal claim over them. But this does not entail anything like initial common ownership of resources, because it does not entail that we all collectively have all the rights constitutive of ownership, such as the right to exclude others from a resource, the right to sell it, the right to transform it, the right to destroy it, and so forth. These rights only come into existence with respect to specific resources once they are acquired via occupation by specific individuals.
60 The "transfer" of property via such means, as Nozick famously calls it to distinguish buying, inheriting, etc. from what he describes as the "initial acquisition" of previously unowned resources, does not appear to be considered more problematic by

he wishes provided that (i) he does not use it in a manner that is directly contrary to the general moral obligations imposed on us by the natural law, and (ii) he allows those who lack resources sufficient even for the possibility of the fulfillment of their own natural capacities and obligations to use or take ownership of it *to the extent and in the manner that* their particular circumstances (and his own) dictate.

This is a very rough formulation; a more complete treatment would no doubt require some tightening up, such as the addition of further qualifying phrases. But it seems to me that it is a useful first approximation, and that it gives us a basis for determining the grounds and limitations set by natural law for taxation and for governmental regulation of the use of private property. What sort of regulation and taxation might this proviso justify, at least in principle? Much more than libertarians would be happy with but also, it seems to me (and contrary perhaps to first appearances), much less than egalitarians would be happy with.

The implications of the first clause should be evident from what has been said already. If there can be no natural right to use one's property for intrinsically immoral purposes, then it seems at least in principle allowable for government to regulate property to prevent this, at least where such use might have a dramatic negative impact on public morality. (Again, whether this is advisable in practice in any particular case is a separate issue.) The qualification that its uses that are "directly" contrary to natural law that are ruled out by the proviso is added to forestall governmental interventions that are so draconian that they would effectively undermine the institution of private property. So, for example, it is reasonable (if one accepts the standard natural law attitude towards illicit drug use and sexual morality, anyway) to hold that no one has a natural right to use his property as a public opium den or brothel. And it would be absurd to suggest that a government that forbade such uses was totalitarian, or threatened the very institution of private property. But it is another thing altogether to hold that no one has a natural right to sell a home or rent an apartment to someone he believes will be carrying out this or that immoral activity in it *in private*, or to suggest

classical natural law theorists than it is by Nozick, since once a resource is justly acquired it would seem to follow automatically that an owner precisely *qua* owner can transfer it to others in any way he wishes. (In general, anyway, though see note 58 below.) This is no doubt because, like Nozick, classical natural law theorists are uninterested in preserving any overall *pattern* of wealth distribution per se, even if they are more inclined than Nozick is to see in this or that particular case of economic distress the possibility of injustice.

that a government could enforce a prohibition on such selling or renting practices without endangering the integrity of the institution of private property.[61] Such selling or renting practices would of themselves involve at most *indirect* cooperation in immorality, which natural law theorists regard as sometimes permissible in light of the principle of double effect.[62]

The second clause of the proposed proviso is what would justify the starving man in the woods taking food from a cabin and similar uses or seizures of another's property in emergency situations. It is also what would justify the taxation required for the necessary functions of government (defense, courts of law, etc.), since from a classical natural law point of view the very existence of the community, and thus the possibility of its members fulfilling the ends set for them by nature, depend on the state's performance of these functions. Again, though, an adequate treatment of this issue would require a detailed exposition of the natural law theory of the state.

It seems clear that the second clause of the proviso would also justify taxation for the purposes of funding some measure of public assistance for those in absolute distress who are incapable either of finding work or getting help from family members and friends. For these circumstances would seem to be relevantly similar to those in which the starving man in the woods finds himself. Bureaucratic inefficiency, fraud, and welfare dependency are potential problems here, but they are problems of practical implementation rather than moral principle. Governmental regulation to prevent monopolies on natural resources crucial to the existence of the community (such as water) would also seem obviously justifiable, and though there are, here as elsewhere, practical problems the solution of which requires a sound understanding of economics, they do not entail that such regulation would be unjust per se.[63]

---

61   I do not mean that owners have no *right* to refuse to rent or sell to such a person. They may refuse if they see fit. The claim is rather that there is no *absolute obligation* to refuse to sell or rent to him.

62   For a recent defense of the principle of double effect argued from a classical natural law point of view, see Oderberg, *Moral Theory*, pp. 86–126.

63   There is also the thorny question of the "just wage," a concept central to classical natural law thinking about economics and social justice. This is too big a topic to deal with here, but two general points can be made. First, the natural law conception of property rights definitely entails that it is *in principle* possible for the market wage to diverge from the just wage. To take the most obvious sort of example, someone who legally buys up all the land and businesses in some geographical region, making it impossible for others to support themselves through farming and the like and leaving himself the only possible employer, would be committing an injustice

Would the second clause of the Natural Law Proviso require a more extensive system of "welfare rights," such as government provision of health care, education, and the like? It does not seem to me that it would, at least not by itself. Property as we know it is the result of two factors, natural resources on the one hand (such as land, water, plants, animals, minerals, etc.) and the labor and ingenuity of specific individuals on the other. Following Cronin, I have suggested that it is the fact that everyone has at least a general claim to the former that justifies putting some limitation on the right to private property. But there is no general claim to the latter; that is to say, no one has a claim in justice to the labor, ingenuity, etc. of a particular individual except that particular individual himself (as well as those to whom he has certain specific obligations under natural law, such as his children). Now what a human being needs in order to stay alive and thus to have the possibility of fulfilling his natural capacities and obligations—namely food, water, basic shelter and clothing and the like—are included among natural resources, or at least require only the most rudimentary effort to produce. As a Lockean might say, these things exist even in a state of nature, before property rights have been established and even before anyone has exerted much or any labor or ingenuity at all. Hence it is plausible to hold that those with no access to these basic resources have a right to public assistance to the extent needed to feed, clothe, and shelter themselves until they can once again become economically self-sufficient. But education and health care are *not* naturally existing resources like food, water, etc. They exist only because of the highly specialized labor and ingenuity of particular individuals. But in that case they are not among the natural resources to which everyone has a general claim under natural law, and thus they are not the sort of thing access to which could plausibly be guaranteed as a matter of justice by the Natural Law Proviso.[64]

against those whom he employed at mere subsistence wages, even if they "freely" consented to these wages. Second, what this entails *in practice* is not at all obvious. For real world conditions are almost never anywhere close to this cartoonish example, and the further they diverge from it the less clear it is that the market wage really has diverged from the just wage. So while the moral principle that the market wage and the just wage can diverge seems to me obviously correct, it seems equally obvious that *by itself* this principle tells us very little where practical policy measures are concerned.

64 Would the proviso entail that natural resources beyond food, water, etc.—in particular land, raw materials, and the like—should be redistributed so that as many people as possible might become as self-sufficient as they might have been in the state of nature, as the "distributism" of Hilaire Belloc and G. K. Chesterton would seem

Now there is, to be sure, a *weaker* right to these things under natural law, as to economic and other assistance more generally. Given that we are social animals by nature, we have various obligations to one another that derive not only from family ties, but also from being friends, fellows citizens, or even just fellow human beings. Hence, just as others have a right to be treated by us with courtesy, respect, and the like in our everyday dealings with them, so too do they have a right to our assistance when they are in distress, simply by virtue of being friends, fellow citizens, and fellow human beings (with the strength of these rights increasing the closer the relationship we bear to the people in question and decreasing the less close it is). But it doesn't follow from this that our obligations here are the sort that ought to be met through taxation for the purposes of funding extensive social programs, any more than the fact that everyone has a right to be treated courteously entails that government has a duty to throw me in jail if I am rude to someone. There is a distinction traditionally drawn in rights theory between *perfect* rights, those which uphold the very possibility of morality, entail absolute obligations, and are paradigmatically the sorts of rights governments ought to enforce; and *imperfect* rights, which tend merely to support morality, entail only some lesser degree of obligation, and which governments need not enforce. The right of an innocent person not be killed is obviously a perfect right, while the right to be treated courteously is obviously only an imperfect right. And while there is obviously a strong case to be made for the claim that we have an imperfect right to be aided by others when in distress vis-à-vis health care, education, and the like, the Natural Law Proviso does not seem to entail that we have a perfect right to such assistance.[65]

to require? No, for at least two reasons. First, if such resources are susceptible of being redistributed as often as doing so would allow yet more people to be self-sufficient, it is hard to see how those holding them could really be said to have private ownership of them. Second, as David Schmidtz has emphasized, appropriation of natural resources is not a zero-sum game. While it diminishes the stock of raw materials that can be "initially acquired" (in Nozick's sense) it increases the stock of wealth that can be owned, and it is the latter which matters with respect to self-sufficiency. Hence though a starving farmer whose crops have failed and cattle have died due to drought may own his land outright and a middle class office worker may live his entire life well-fed in a rented apartment, it does not seem plausible to suggest that the former is more self-sufficient than the latter. See Schmidtz, "The Institution of Property," *Social Philosophy and Policy* 11, no. 2 (1994).

65 When Aquinas famously says that the ownership of property ought to be private but its use common (*Summa Theologiae* II-II.66.2), what he seems to mean is not that those in need of assistance have (in general) a perfect right to my property, but

It is also important to keep in mind that in a society whose ethos is deeply influenced by the principles of classical natural law, families will tend to be much larger and more stable, religious and other social institutions intermediate between the family and government will be stronger and have a greater role in people's everyday lives, and in general the "individualist" mentality of modern liberal societies will be absent. The circumstances in which individuals would be unable to find assistance from sources other than government would accordingly be extremely rare. But this raises another possible justification of a right to at least minimal assistance when in distress vis-à-vis health care and the like. I have argued that the Natural Law Proviso does not imply an obligation in justice for government to provide such assistance; our rights against others to assistance in obtaining these specific things are at most imperfect. But suppose the ethos of a society is informed by natural law principles in the way I just described. Suppose in particular that the individuals who make up such a society are in general so united in their basic values that the majority of them are willing to accept taxation for the purposes of aiding those relatively rare individuals who have no recourse to family, friends, etc. in obtaining decent health care, education, and the like. Again, they are not *obligated* in justice to accept such taxation. But *may* they do so? It seems to me that they may, even if there is a minority of individuals who would not agree to such taxation, but who are "outvoted." For even this minority has an imperfect obligation to provide assistance; and while the usual reason for not enforcing imperfect obligations is that doing so would be impractical or draconian, that consideration does not seem to apply in this case. For the policy in question would not be like a policy of punishing rude people through force of law, which, far from making ordinary life more pleasant, would make it intolerable. The policy in question would simply be one of collecting a relatively small amount of extra tax money to aid a relatively small group of people in unusually difficult circumstances. That is surely workable.

A further possible justification of a right to assistance when in distress vis-à-vis health care and education would be to hold that such assistance falls under the "public good" that the state is obliged to provide for under natural law. The operative principle here is that of *subsidiarity*, according to which the more central authorities within a society should not carry out

rather that they have an imperfect right to it. For if they had a perfect right to it, it is hard to see in what sense ownership would be truly private. Cf. Cronin, *Special Ethics*, p. 134.

any functions that can be performed by less central ones, though it should carry out those which cannot be performed by the less central ones. To the extent that those in distress vis-à-vis health care and education simply have no other recourse, a right to assistance would arguably follow, if not from the Natural Law Proviso by itself, then at least from that proviso together with the classical natural law theory conception of the state and its proper functions.

The *extent* of governmental assistance such a right would justify is another question, and here I will end with three points. First, what classical natural law theory strictly requires and strictly rules out in the way of practical policy is much less than many partisans of various political persuasions would like. What it does strictly require is a system of private property rights that are robust but not absolute. What it strictly rules out, accordingly, are socialism at one extreme and *laissez-faire* libertarianism at the other. Between these extremes, though, there is wide latitude for reasonable disagreement among classical natural law theorists about how best to apply their principles, and these disagreements can largely be settled only by appeal to prudential matters of economics, sociology, and practical politics rather than fundamental moral principles.

Second, it would be a mistake to conclude from this that a classical natural law theorist ought always to favor policies that fall exactly midway between these extremes. As any good Aristotelian knows, though any virtue is a mean between opposite extremes, one extreme can sometimes be a more serious deviation from virtue than the other is. Now natural law theory takes the family to be the fundamental social unit, which puts it at odds with both the excessive individualism of the libertarian and the collectivism of the socialist. But the family is obviously closer to the level of the individual than it is to the level of the "community" or "society" as the socialist tends to understand those terms, viz. as referring to the entire population of a modern state. Furthermore, while classical natural law theory is concerned both with affirming the right to private property and meeting the needs of those who lack resources of their own, there is a clear sense in which the former concern is analytically prior, at least where questions of justice (as opposed to charity) are concerned. For the theory starts by affirming the right to property and only afterward addresses the question of how that right might be limited. There is a presumption in favor of a person's having a right to what he owns even if that presumption can sometimes be overridden. In these ways, it seems clear that the classical natural law approach to property rights is at least somewhat closer to the libertarian or individualist end of the contemporary political spectrum than it is to the socialist or collectivist end.[66]

Third, it needs to be emphasized that the sort of assistance through taxation that I have countenanced here essentially involves *emergency aid to those in distress*, not only in cases where the Natural Law Proviso strictly requires such aid (e.g., for someone in danger of death by starvation) but also where it merely allows it or where the "public good" functions of government kick in (e.g., for someone unable to afford education or health care). It does *not* follow from this that government could legitimately provide education and health care to its citizens *in general* either through cash payments funded via taxation or (even less plausibly) by directly providing educational and health services itself. While the issues involved here are complex, it seems clear that given its emphasis on private property, the independence of the family, and subsidiarity, there is at the very least a strong *presumption* implicit in classical natural law theory against the social democratic approach to these matters and in favor of private enterprise.

VII. Conclusion

Though the devil is in the empirical details, then, the classical natural law approach to private property does give us substantial moral principles to guide our economic, sociological, and political-scientific inquiries. And in its essential conservatism, it is, I should think, exactly what we would expect from a theory rooted in Aristotelianism: A mean between extremes. Moderate. Unexciting. And true.[67]

---

66 This seems clear at least where questions of *economic justice* are concerned. On non-economic questions most libertarians and socialists are probably equally distant from classical natural law theory. And where charity rather than justice is concerned, I suppose socialists might claim to be closer than libertarians are to classical natural law theory, though in my view it is by no means obvious that socialism is really motivated by charity.

67 I thank Ellen Frankel Paul and the other contributors to the volume in which this essay first appeared for their comments on an earlier version.

15

Self-ownership, Libertarianism, and Impartiality

I.

Impartiality is a central theme of contemporary liberal political philosophy, and certainly of the work of John Rawls, the most significant recent theorist of liberalism. The Kantian principle that persons are "ends in themselves" and thus moral equals entitled to impartial concern underlies the argument of Rawls's *A Theory of Justice*.[1] His later book *Political Liberalism* empha-sizes another kind of impartiality important to liberals, namely the neutrality they think basic social institutions ought, as far as possible, to exhibit vis-à-vis the competing "reasonable comprehensive doctrines" existing within a pluralistic society, and whose adherents these institutions are to govern.[2] Rawls is also keen to argue, in that same book, that his conception of justice is impartial or neutral in a third sense too, insofar as it can be defended philosophically without having to appeal to controversial moral or meta-physical premises peculiar to some specific comprehensive philosophical doctrine. Rawls's "political liberalism" might be defined in terms of these three components: it is "liberal" insofar as it seeks to ensure an equal and impartial concern for all persons as a matter of justice; and it is a "political" conception rather than a "comprehensive" one insofar as it attempts to fulfill this ambition in a way that is neutral both between the diverse moral and religious worldviews prevailing among citizens of the sort of society it is to govern, and between the various alternative philosophical doctrines (liberal and non-liberal) individual political theorists who could support it might be personally committed to. It rests instead on an "overlapping consensus" be-tween doctrines, while nevertheless sustaining a shared sense of justice be-tween them, rather than a mere *modus vivendi* or truce between hostile factions.

Libertarianism, which is commonly interpreted as a variant of

---

1   John Rawls, *A Theory of Justice* (Cambridge, MA: Harvard University Press, 1971).
2   John Rawls, *Political Liberalism* (New York: Columbia University Press, 1996).

liberalism,[3] shares the liberal's concern for treating persons as ends in themselves, though it understands this to entail a higher estimation of free markets and a lower estimation of government action than other modern liberals tend to exhibit. This is certainly true of Rawls's critic Robert Nozick, who explicitly appeals to Kant's principle in defense of *laissez faire* capitalism and the minimal state, and in criticism of Rawls's difference principle.[4] Libertarianism also appears to be concerned with impartiality; indeed, the view of libertarians seems to be that theirs is the most impartial of all political philosophies, in each of the three senses mentioned above:

I. With respect to our rights and duties as individuals: As usually interpreted, libertarianism is committed to a doctrine of universal full self-ownership, on which (as Nozick's critic G. A. Cohen summarizes it) "each person enjoys, over herself and her powers, full and exclusive rights of control and use, and therefore owes no service or product to anyone else that she has not contracted to supply."[5] In Nozick's work, this principle is apparently understood as a concomitant of the Kantian principle of respect for persons; that is to say, to treat someone as an end in himself seems in Nozick's view to entail treating him as a self-owner.[6] And the principle of self-ownership seems, in turn, to entail that, at least as a matter of strict justice, we can have no positive obligations to other human beings—including not only the destitute, but even our own family members and friends—apart from those that we explicitly consent to take on. Justice requires only that we respect each individual's (negative) right to be left alone. This is impartiality with a vengeance. In any event, it is in the view of libertarians a more impartial doctrine than Rawlsian liberalism is, given that Rawls's difference principle entails (they would argue) discriminatory treatment of the rich and powerful as resources to be used for the benefit of the least well off members of society.

---

3 Though for a different interpretation, see Samuel Freeman, "Illiberal Libertarians: Why Libertarianism Is Not a Liberal View," *Philosophy & Public Affairs* 30, no. 2 (2001): 105–51.

4 Robert Nozick, *Anarchy, State, and Utopia* (New York: Basic Books, 1974).

5 G. A. Cohen, *Self-Ownership, Freedom, and Equality* (Cambridge: Cambridge University Press, 1995), p. 12.

6 Though Nozick is not clear about exactly what he takes the relationship between these principles to be. See Edward Feser, *On Nozick* (Belmont, CA: Wadsworth, 2003), pp. 43–45 for discussion. Some libertarians are less inclined to regard the principle of self-ownership as a useful way of formulating or grounding libertarianism. See, e.g., Douglas B. Rasmussen and Douglas J. Den Uyl, *Norms of Liberty* (University Park, PA: University of Pennsylvania Press, 2005), ch. 9.

2. With respect to the various comprehensive doctrines prevailing within a pluralistic society: Libertarianism claims to provide, in Nozick's words, a "framework for utopia," an "environment in which utopian experiments may be tried out [and] in which people are free to do their own thing."[7] Adherents of any comprehensive doctrine and the vision of life it embodies may within a libertarian polity live according to its dictates, even if those dictates are radically non-libertarian, so long as no one else is forced to do likewise. A hippie commune, Puritan commonwealth, Muslim *umma*, and Buddhist *sangha* can all co-exist within the boundaries of the minimal state, and can require of their members any degree of submission to their rules that they like, provided that membership in them is voluntary. Here too libertarians claim to be more impartial than other liberals insofar as their view does not require such private organizations to adhere to some egalitarian standard of admission. From the libertarian point of view, modern liberals' promotion of anti-discrimination laws of various sorts imposes on all, in the name of neutrality, what is in fact nothing more than one particular comprehensive doctrine among others.

3. With respect to philosophical foundations: Libertarianism has been defended by philosophers committed to a wide variety of moral theories. Nozick, as we have seen, appeals to Kant's principle of treating people as ends in themselves. Other libertarians have appealed to utilitarianism, contractarianism, Aristotelianism, natural law theory, Lockean natural rights theory, Ayn Rand's "Objectivist" philosophy, and Habermasian discourse ethics. Yet others eschew moral theory *per se* and emphasize economic arguments. Libertarian conclusions thus seem derivable from widely divergent premises. Nor is this surprising, libertarians might argue, given that their conception of justice is a very "thin" one, requiring, again, only that everyone leaves everyone else alone. This is a polity (so the argument goes) that everyone, whatever the moral, religious, or philosophical premises he is committed to, can find reason to endorse.

It is not surprising, then, that some libertarians have even tried to make a case for their view on Rawlsian grounds.[8] For example, some have suggested that the unfettered free market best fulfills the egalitarian demands of Rawls's difference principle, as a rising tide lifts all boats. More relevant

---

7 Nozick, *Anarchy, State, and Utopia*, pp. 297 and 312.
8 See, e.g., Loren Lomasky, "Libertarianism at Twin Harvard," *Social Philosophy and Policy* 22, no. 1 (2005): 178–99.

to our purposes here, some libertarians have also suggested that it is their view that most fully realizes the neutrality Rawls sought to enshrine in his ideal of "political liberalism." "Political *libertarianism*," in their estimation, thus constitutes a superior vision of a just, liberal, and pluralistic society. Law professor Randy Barnett seems to be the most prominent libertarian to have defended this view, in a recent essay entitled "The Moral Foundations of Modern Libertarianism."[9]

In what follows, I will argue that the purported impartiality of libertarianism is illusory, in each of the three senses of "impartiality" described above. Barnett's account will be my primary target, though what I will say is intended to apply to libertarian theories generally. For some libertarians, it may not matter whether their view really is as impartial or neutral as some have claimed; their commitment to libertarianism *per se* as a "comprehensive" moral and political vision of the world may trump the desire to appeal to non-libertarians by suggesting that they need not give up anything essential to their own creeds by agreeing to accept a libertarian polity. Still, much of the rhetorical force of libertarian arguments lies in their suggestion that the libertarian worldview is compatible with any number of particular moral, religious, and philosophical systems. If many who would otherwise accept libertarianism were to conclude that they could not in fact do so consistent with their own deeper moral, religious, or philosophical commitments, the theory would lose much of its attraction.

II.

Taking last things first, let us begin with the third sense in which some libertarians would regard their position as impartial or neutral, i.e., with respect to alternative moral-theoretic foundations. Barnett devotes almost half of his essay to defending this idea, which is reasonable given that, for reasons that will become evident, if this claim cannot be sustained, it is hard to see how libertarianism can possibly be neutral in either of the other senses in question. His focus is on the distinction between what he calls "moral rights" and "consequentialist" defenses of libertarianism, where by the former he has in mind natural rights approaches of the sort favored by Nozick, Rand,

---

9   In Peter Berkowitz, ed., *Varieties of Conservatism in America* (Stanford, CA: Hoover Institution Press, 2004). See Barnett's *The Structure of Liberty: Justice and the Rule of Law* (New York: Oxford University Press, 1998) for a more thorough statement of his conception of a libertarian theory of justice.

and Murray Rothbard, and by the latter, the economics-oriented arguments of writers like F. A. Hayek and Milton Friedman. As Barnett recounts, the history of libertarian political theory is partly a history of debate over whether these approaches are compatible, with libertarian rights theorists sometimes accusing consequentialist libertarians of being compromisers willing to trade liberty for economic well-being, and consequentialists accusing the rights theorists of utopian dogmatism.

In Barnett's estimation, this debate is misconceived. Rights and consequentialist theories are in his view best interpreted, not as rival claimants to ultimate moral truth, but rather as "fallible" and complementary "modes of analysis," "useful heuristics," or "problem-solving devices," which by virtue of their "creative tension" together afford us a more nuanced picture of the social world. In particular, rights theories make us attentive to the possible effects of our actions and policies on the private sphere of the individual, while consequentialist theories force us to consider the public sphere as well. The different theories also provide an "analytic check" on one another: to the extent that they tend to converge on the same results, this should increase our confidence in those results; to the extent that they diverge, this could indicate a problem at the level of theory or application that calls for a reconsideration of some of our working assumptions. Moreover, their ultimate significance in Barnett's view is as ways of refining our understanding of the deliverances of a third "problem-solving device," namely the gradual evolution of the legal norms enshrined in the common law. It is from these norms that moral rights and consequentialist theories "get their starting points"; and since legal decision-making is "casuistic," it takes account of more of the details of real-world circumstances than either philosophical or economic analysis are able to, and thus (Barnett seems to imply) has analytic priority over these other methods. Since the theories in question are "means, not ends," and specifically means of improving our "conventional legal principles," there need be no conflict between them. In this sense—and insofar as they tend to lead to similarly libertarian conclusions in any case—libertarianism can be said to be neutral between them.

Barnett's account seems to me to have a number of serious problems. The first is that the idea that natural rights and consequentialist theories are merely alternative "problem-solving devices" that provide "analytic checks" on one another is a non-starter. It certainly isn't the way most actual rights theorists or consequentialists understand their own theories. And as usually understood the theories are indeed flatly incompatible. Suppose a rights theorist claims that I have an absolute right to X. Then in his view, no consideration of consequences could justify violating that right; indeed, any violation of that right would *just be* a bad consequence. For a consequentialist, on the other hand, there can be no such thing as an *absolute* right in the first place. So the theories are just at cross purposes. Since they differ fundamentally in their conceptions of the basic moral facts, they don't agree on what we should be "checking" *for*, and thus can hardly be construed as "devices" or "checks" or "modes of analysis: aimed at solving the same problems.

That Barnett doesn't take seriously enough the self-understanding of actual natural rights and consequentialist theorists is also evident from his remarks about the limits he sees in these theories. The problem with rights theories, he says, is that they demand that justice be done 'though the heavens fall,' while the problem with consequentialist theories is that they are too ready to sacrifice individual liberty for the sake of the greater good. Now of course, these might well be good objections to each of these theories. But each objection is obviously only going to be valid from the point of view of the competing theory, or from the point of view of some third alternative theory. For a natural rights theorist might think that justice *should* sometimes be done though the heavens fall, while a consequentialist might say that liberty *should* sometimes be sacrificed for the greater good. From the natural rights or consequentialist perspective, these are not "problems" at all. How, then, can a perspective which insists that these are problems for these theories be said to be "neutral" between them? Surely what such a perspective really involves is just the belief that both theories are *wrong*, and ought to be replaced by some new theory, albeit one that incorporates certain elements of the ones superseded.

At bottom, what Barnett really seems to be saying is not that "moral rights" and "consequentialist" libertarian theories are compatible, but rather that although they are incompatible as they stand, they can and ought to be *reinterpreted*—specifically, in an instrumentalist "problem-solving" fashion—so that the incompatibilities disappear. But the "neutrality" between moral theories that results is bogus, in two respects. First, it is not a neutrality between existing moral theories—which is surely what matters if libertarianism is to be impartial in some interesting sense—but only between theories that Barnett thinks should exist in the place of the ones that actually exist. Second, it appears surreptitiously to favor consequentialism over natural rights theories, since a piecemeal or "problem-solving" approach to moral problems seems more in harmony with the consequentialist's interest in maximizing some good or other (where the means of doing so are less important than that it is done) than with the interest of rights theories (as usually understood anyway) in respecting certain deontic constraints regardless of whether this conduces to problem-solving.

A second problem with Barnett's account is that the suggestion that the alternative theories in question converge on the same (libertarian) results, and thus confirm those results, is ambiguous. On one interpretation of this claim, it is true but trivial, while on another it is non-trivial but obviously false. To take the latter interpretation first, if Barnett means to say that consequentialism and natural rights theory *per se* tend to converge on libertarianism—or, for that matter, that Aristotelianism, natural law theory, etc. *as such* converge on it—then this is just clearly not true, since the vast majority of consequentialists, natural rights theorists, Aristotelians, natural law theorists, et al. are not libertarians. But if he means instead to say only that those consequentialists, natural rights theorists, Aristotelians, and so forth who happen also to be libertarians tend to converge in their arguments on libertarianism, then while true, the claim is (for obvious reasons) uninteresting. That some theorists (and a small minority at that) think that libertarianism can be defended by means of these various theories hardly suffices to show that the theories themselves necessarily have a tendency to converge on the same conclusions (libertarian or otherwise) much less that libertarianism is neutral between these theories (most of whose proponents are probably hostile to libertarianism, and on grounds they would derive from the theories themselves).

Finally, it is hard to see how Barnett's advocacy of what he calls the "rule of law" approach—taking the deliverances of the evolution of the common law to be the source of the norms that other approaches, including natural rights theory and consequentialism, must take as their starting points, and which it is their *raison d'être* to refine—can be anything other than the promotion of one "comprehensive" philosophical doctrine over others. This is only more evident when we consider that Barnett is here endorsing and developing a set of ideas he derives in part from Hayek, ideas that some other libertarian theorists (whose views Barnett claims to be adjudicating in a neutral way) would object to. Of course, that doesn't show that Barnett's preferred Hayekian conception of the foundations of libertarian theory is mistaken. But it does show that it is implausible to present it as if it were a "neutral" framework that favored no particular comprehensive philosophical doctrine (including no particular way of giving philosophical foundations to libertarianism) over any other.

Barnett's legal emphasis also smuggles in the common liberal conception of morality (or at least of justice, in Barnett's case) as ultimately a matter of interpersonal conflict resolution—a conception that is by no means "neutral" between alternative moral theories, and certainly not compatible with the Aristotelian and classical natural law approaches some libertarians claim to follow.[10] But this brings us to his treatment of the idea that libertarianism is neutral or impartial in the second sense we have identified, i.e., neutral between the various comprehensive doctrines prevailing within modern pluralistic societies. So let us now turn to that.

III.

A further objection to Barnett's account as summarized so far would be that his claim that the various alternative moral theories (consequentialist, rights-based, or what have you) are valuable insofar as they help us to improve existing legal conventions presupposes some standard by reference to which something counts as an improvement, and that this standard is unlikely to be a neutral one. This is an objection Barnett raises himself, and his answer is to reiterate the suggestion that the various comprehensive theories in question be interpreted, not as embodying competing ends (one of which gets to provide the criteria for improvement that the others must meet), but rather as "devices" for solving a problem that is to be defined independently of any these particular doctrines. That problem is providing for the possibility of "social order," in the sense of conditions wherein individuals can pursue their own happiness in a way that is consistent with others doing the same. Indeed, this, Barnett asserts, is what justice is ultimately concerned with.

Now the first thing to say about this is just to reemphasize two points made already. First, insofar as Barnett's attempt to be neutral between competing moral-theoretic foundations for libertarianism requires that these theories be reinterpreted in a way their adherents might not approve of, the "neutrality" thus achieved is specious. Second, Barnett's insinuation that the end of providing for "social order" in the sense he describes is definable apart from some particular comprehensive doctrine is dubious, especially given that he characterizes it as nothing less than the end of justice itself. For this characterization is distinctively liberal, and thus merely one conception of justice among others.

---

10 Libertarian theorists Rasmussen and Den Uyl acknowledge that the glib assimilation of morality to rules for avoiding interpersonal conflict is a common foible of liberal theorizing, a foible they strive to avoid. See *Norms of Liberty*, ch. 3.

Now in fairness to Barnett, it must be noted that he does acknowledge that his conception of justice is liberal, indeed libertarian, and thus controversial. So when he says that justice-as-social-order is an end that does not favor one comprehensive doctrine over another, what he presumably means, given the immediate context, is that it does not favor any particular *libertarian* comprehensive doctrine (rights-based, consequentialist, or whatever) over another. But again, this just raises the question of how Barnett's conception of justice can provide a neutral framework for all the various non-libertarian moral, philosophical, and religious doctrines that prevail within a modern pluralistic society. In dealing with this question, Barnett acknowledges, as Rawls does, that no framework, even a merely "political" rather than "comprehensive" one, can be *entirely* neutral. Rawls claimed only that his own brand of liberalism is neutral between what he called "reasonable" comprehensive doctrines, and Barnett also acknowledges that his position is bound to rule out any vision of the good that is incompatible with the possibility of "the pursuit of happiness of each person living in society with others."[11] Nazis and jihadists, then, are simply out of luck within a libertarian social order, but that's a failure of neutrality that the rest of us can happily endorse.

So far so good. The question, though, is whether Barnett's proposed framework can nevertheless be neutral *enough* to encompass all of the reasonable people within modern pluralistic societies who deeply disagree with each other but who do *not* believe in settling their disputes by murdering the opposition. In particular, we need to ask whether it can accommodate: both those who believe that abortion is a basic human right and those who believe it is tantamount to murder; both those who believe that a right to view pornography is a corollary of the right of free speech and those who believe (on either feminist or traditional moral grounds) that pornography ought to be curtailed for the good of society; both those who believe that laws against discrimination in hiring, renting, admission to private associations, and the like are a requirement of basic justice, and those who believe such laws violate a natural right to freedom of association; both those who believe that the legalization of same-sex marriage is required by justice and those who regard it as an affront to the moral order that makes justice possible; both those who believe that religion ought to be kept out of public institutions and debate lest the rights of non-believers be threatened, and those who believe that public acknowledgement of at least a generic theism is a

11 "The Moral Foundations of Modern Libertarianism," p. 70.

prerequisite of the very intelligibility of "rights" talk; and so on and so forth. These examples represent some of the most contentious debates within modern pluralistic societies, the very sorts of debates that motivate Rawlsian liberals and their libertarian fellow travelers to seek a framework enshrining a sense of justice shared in common between alternative comprehensive doctrines. So if it turns out that Barnett's framework isn't neutral even between the sorts of views just described, it is hard to see how it can be neutral in any interesting sense at all. Hence, again, we need to ask: *Is* it neutral between them?

To answer this question, let us first consider how Barnett fleshes out the libertarian conception of social order.[12] First, he says, it acknowledges "the existence and value of individual persons." Second, it values "the ability of all persons to live and pursue happiness." Third, it recognizes that "only the protection of actions, rather than a guaranty of results, can potentially be afforded to everyone." Fourth, it emphasizes that the actions of any one person "may have both positive and negative effects on others." Fifth, it insists that a set of "ground rules" are possible that would "provide all, or nearly all, persons living in society the opportunity to pursue happiness without depriving others of the same opportunity."

Again, so far so good. There isn't much on this list that many people would object to, though some egalitarians might raise questions about the third point. Though even there, Rawlsians, at least, would be happy with a purely procedural conception of justice, since they regard their egalitarian difference principle as a constraint upon action rather than a guarantee of any particular result. But there's the rub. For libertarians, obviously, would *not* regard Rawls's difference principle as something that ought to inform the framework within which adherents of competing comprehensive doctrines operate. They would regard it instead as the imposition of one particular, egalitarian, comprehensive doctrine on all. And yet Rawlsians would regard it as nothing of the kind. The trouble is that the idea that a neutral framework should entail only "the protection of actions, rather than a guaranty of results" is itself susceptible of radically divergent interpretations. And so too are all of the other points Barnett lists.

Take the first point, about "the existence and value of individual persons." The import of this principle obviously depends on what we count as a "person." Do slaves count as persons? Could a slaveholder in antebellum Virginia plausibly endorse Barnett's "neutral" libertarian framework and

---

12   Ibid., p. 64.

still keep his slaves, on the grounds that they are not (in his view) full persons and that anyone who claimed otherwise would be imposing some comprehensive moral or metaphysical doctrine on him? Presumably not, and Barnett would no doubt be untroubled by this limit on the neutrality of his system. Well and good; and the question is purely academic in any case, given that apologists for slavery are thin on the ground these days. But what about fetuses? If they count as persons, and if one remains unpersuaded by Judith Jarvis Thomson's view that the question is irrelevant to the legitimacy of abortion, then quite obviously a practice that is now very common in Western pluralistic societies would have to be outlawed in any truly libertarian society. To fail to outlaw it on the grounds that not everyone thinks abortion is immoral would simply be to impose a particular comprehensive moral doctrine (i.e., a "pro-choice" one) on unborn persons. On the other hand, if fetuses are in fact not persons at all, then it would seem that abortion must remain legal, and that it is those who want to restrict abortion who are trying to impose their comprehensive doctrine on others. Either way, it seems obvious that no polity, including Barnett's purportedly neutral libertarian one, can possibly be "neutral" between the "pro-life" and "pro-choice" sides on the abortion debate. Any polity will either regard abortion as tantamount to murder or not so regard it, and those who disagree with the view that prevails can quite plausibly complain that a certain contentious view about the nature of "persons" is being imposed on all. When we add to the mix other contemporary controversies over matters of life and death— euthanasia, capital punishment, the treatment of animals, and so forth—it becomes even more obvious that to cite a recognition of 'the existence and value of individual persons' does nothing to give content to the suggestion that libertarianism provides an impartial framework between comprehensive doctrines. For what *matters* – what (some of) these different frameworks disagree about – is what counts as a person, and what counts as valuing a person, in the first place.

Of course, Barnett might say that one side or the other in the debate over abortion (or capital punishment, euthanasia, or whatever) is just "unreasonable," in the Rawlsian sense, and that his view, like Rawls's, is not intended to be neutral between "reasonable" and "unreasonable" comprehensive doctrines. But if he does say this, then the "neutrality" of his system would be useless for the project of providing a framework within which the competing comprehensive doctrines that actually exist within contemporary pluralistic societies might abide by a shared sense of justice rather than an uneasy *modus vivendi*. For it would then appear that Barnett's system is "neutral" only between those comprehensive doctrines that are "reasonable" in the sense of being consistent with the moral and metaphysical presuppositions that Barnett and those of like mind happen to consider reasonable. Those who do not share these presuppositions—surely millions of Barnett's fellow citizens—would simply be written off as beyond the political pale, rather than (as we would expect from a view claiming to provide an interesting way of reconciling the hostile factions that characterize contemporary politics) accommodated within a more encompassing set of common principles. Here we see manifested a dilemma that I think afflicts Barnett's entire project: either he keeps the statement of the principles guiding his favored polity extremely vague, so as to preserve a genuine neutrality between the main competing doctrines actually prevailing within existing pluralistic societies; or he makes them so determinate that they effectively marginalize a great many of these doctrines as "unreasonable." In either case, the "neutrality" that results seems uninteresting and anticlimactic.

A similar result follows from a consideration of Barnett's condition that a liberal social order respects "the ability of all persons to live and pursue happiness"—not only because what counts as a "person" is just as problematic here as in the previous case, but also because what counts as "pursuing happiness" is problematic. What is "happiness," after all? Is it a matter of "getting what you want"?[13] Is it a matter of maximizing pleasure and minimizing pain, as Bentham and Mill held (albeit in different ways)? On these conceptions, happiness seems to be definable in terms of the subjective states of the agent. On an Aristotelian or classical natural law conception, though, it is something objective, a matter of living in accordance with one's nature, understood as a fixed essence entailing a natural end or purpose. Other conceptions are also possible. Now, on several subjectivist conceptions of happiness, it seems plausible that the sort of libertarian polity Barnett favors would be a just one. If we concede the libertarian argument that the unfettered free market maximizes the satisfaction of individual preferences, then it would seem that libertarianism does indeed promote the pursuit of happiness in the sense that it best allows people to "get what they want." Perhaps it even maximizes pleasure and minimizes pain, at least in Bentham's crude sense of "pleasure" and "pain." It isn't so clear, however, that it maximizes pleasure and minimizes pain in Mill's more refined senses of "pleasure" and "pain." And it is very difficult to believe that it best

13   For a critique of this conception, see Bob Brecher, *Getting What You Want? A Critique of Liberal Morality* (London: Routledge, 1998).

promotes happiness in Aristotle's sense of the term. For the market maximizes the satisfaction, not of all preferences, but rather of those backed by the most spending power. It is bound, then, to cater to the most vulgar tastes and passions—which are, by definition, the most common and thus the ones most people will pay to satisfy—rather than to more refined sensibilities. And since on an Aristotelian conception an individual's moral character—his characteristic habits and sensibilities—is inevitably deeply influenced by the character types and sensibilities prevailing in the society around him, it follows that a commercial society is one in which the sort of refined moral character that most fully manifests the realization of human potentialities, and thus most fully guarantees human happiness, is bound to be very rare and difficult to achieve. But then, since on a classical Aristotelian or natural law view, a society cannot be just unless it makes the attainment of virtue a realistic possibility, a libertarian society would seem to be deeply *un*just. It certainly isn't *neutral* between an Aristotelian or classical natural law conception of justice and other conceptions.

Moreover, since the conception of happiness operative in many religious traditions is far closer to the Aristotelian or natural law conception than it is to any subjectivist conception, a libertarian polity would also seem to be anything but neutral between these traditions either, at least where respecting "the ability of all persons to live and pursue happiness" is concerned. If a society characterized by an unfettered free market is bound to be one in which all sorts of behaviors considered sinful from a religious point of view are prominent and celebrated, then from a religious point of view such a society cannot fail to be seriously unjust, since it will tend greatly to reduce the likelihood that individuals living within it will be able to lead virtuous lives and thus attain salvation and true happiness, whether this be conceived of in terms of the beatific vision, paradise, nirvana, moksha, or what have you.

Barnett's remaining principles—that a liberal society recognizes that individual actions "may have both positive and negative effects on others" and aims to "provide all, or nearly all, persons living in society the opportunity to pursue happiness without depriving others of the same opportunity"—are no less problematic than the ones already discussed, and for the same reasons. For what counts as a "negative effect" on others, and what counts as "depriving others of the opportunity to attain happiness," depend on which comprehensive doctrine one is committed to. For the pro-choice advocate, one woman's decision to have an abortion has no negative effect on anyone else, since others are free not to have abortions. But for the pro-life advocate, to have an abortion is to have the most negative effect imaginable on another person, since it involves a kind of murder. The pornographer claims to hurt no one since those who disapprove of his product are free not to purchase it. But many feminists, and people with traditional moral and religious views, would argue that when pornography becomes widespread and socially acceptable it creates what economists call a "negative externality," insofar as it radically alters the average person's perception of women and of the meaning of sex, and effectively makes certain moral virtues extremely difficult or impossible to achieve on anything but the smallest of scales. And so forth.

Now Barnett maintains that whatever failings traditional moralists and others might see in a libertarian society, such failings do not count as *injustices* and thus do not evidence a failure of neutrality on the part of a libertarian polity vis-à-vis the comprehensive doctrines in question. Thus he claims, for example, that while a libertarian society may not guarantee respect for the "imperfect rights" we might be said to have as moral beings aiming to realize some vision of the good (i.e., rights that others cannot legitimately be forced to respect, even if they should respect them), it does guarantee the "perfect (i.e., enforceable) rights" we have not to be harmed by others, and this is sufficient for justice.[14] Hence while it may in some sense violate my rights as a pursuer of moral perfection to have someone tempt me to view women as sex objects (for example), the rights in question are not perfect or enforceable rights, and thus the fact that their violation might be tolerated or even celebrated in a libertarian society does nothing to show that such a society is unjust. Furthermore, to try to promote the pursuit of moral virtue and other "spiritual goods" via the coercive power of government would threaten to undermine the very "social order" that is a prerequisite to their successful pursuit.[15] It would lead to a "war of all against all" insofar as those who "seek to impose by force their conception of the good" on others are bound to be resisted by those with different conceptions.[16]

The problem with this reply is that it begs all the important questions. The rigid distinction between the right and the good or between matters of justice and matters of virtue, and the related assumption that perfect rights and duties exactly correlate with the former and imperfect ones with the latter, are precisely what Aristotelians, classical natural law theorists, and many religious believers tend to reject. On their view, rights and justice are

14 "The Moral Foundations of Modern Libertarianism," p. 69.
15 Ibid., pp. 70–71.
16 Ibid., p. 73.

grounded in the good, and part of their very *raison d'etre* is to aid us in realizing moral virtue. For this reason, while most of what government does
in securing justice and rights will involve merely keeping people from killing
and stealing from each other and the like, government may, and sometimes
should, step in to prevent at least large-scale threats to "private" morality. As
if in reply to this objection, Barnett complains that "many conservatives assume, usually implicitly, that force is justified whenever human conduct is
found to be bad or immoral," and that "for comprehensive moralists of the
Right or Left, using force to impose their morality on others might be their
first choice among social arrangements."[17] But surely no thinker of the Right
or Left actually believes that force is justified *whenever* human conduct is
bad or immoral, or is even advisable as a general policy. Even from a conservative point of view, literally sending the police into people's bedrooms
might be seen as counterproductive and indeed unjust. Even from a left-wing
point of view, it might be unwise and unjust to try to force everyone to love
people of other races. It is possible consistently to hold both that government
should refrain from interfering in the small-scale, day-to-day private moral
choices of individual citizens and also that it may and sometimes should in-
terfere with business activity that may have a large-scale effect on the overall
moral tenor of society—such as the marketing of narcotics or pornography,
a refusal to cater to customers of a certain race, or what have you.

The point is not to defend any particular piece of right-wing or left-
wing morals legislation. The point is rather to note that certain conceptions
of justice incorporate the idea that it is part of justice (even if not the whole
of it) to guarantee the preconditions of the attainment of moral virtue, or at
least of minimal public decency, so that any polity that rules this out *a priori*
can hardly be said to be neutral between comprehensive moral doctrines or
plausibly defensible from the point of view of an "overlapping consensus"
of such doctrines. Nor will it do for Barnett to pretend that only libertarianism can save us from the "war of all against all" that must result if adherents
of competing doctrines are allowed to 'impose' them on others—as if libertarianism alone existed above the fray of competing conceptions of justice,
and as if libertarians cannot plausibly be seen by their critics as attempting
to "impose" their view of justice on non-libertarians. From the point of view
of a traditional moralist, say, or a socialist, the libertarian is interested in
nothing less than "imposing" his idiosyncratic moral views on society as a
whole—by refusing to allow government to defend the rights of the unborn,

17   Ibid., pp. 72–73, 74.

for example, or by denying to every citizen the equal share of the overall social product to which he is (in the view of some socialists) entitled as a matter of justice. Yes, the libertarian holds that these conceptions of justice are mistaken.[18] But then, that is precisely the point: Because he does take them to be mistaken, he cannot plausibly claim that his view is neutral in any interesting sense, or that it does not involve an imposition on others of a moral view at odds with their own. To be sure, Barnett's "political libertarianism" might differ from such conceptions of justice in *aiming* to be neutral and in *claiming* not to involve any such imposition—that is not in dispute. What is in dispute is whether the aim can actually be realized and whether the claim can be sustained, and Barnett gives us no reason to answer either question in the affirmative.

Once again, Barnett might well reply by arguing that any comprehensive doctrine that has implications of the sort I've described is to that extent not only mistaken but "unreasonable" (in the Rawlsian sense) and thus not a doctrine to which his analysis is meant to apply in the first place. But to do so would be to make manifest that his purportedly "neutral" framework is really neutral only between comprehensive doctrines that have already incorporated into themselves the liberal premises definitive of the very sort of comprehensive liberalism that Barnett, like others who seek a "neutralist" liberalism *a la* Rawls, claim not to be imposing on the various other comprehensive doctrines prevailing in modern pluralistic societies. Worse, it would be to make manifest that the resulting system is one that leaves out in the political cold enormous numbers of Barnett's fellow citizens—indeed, probably a majority of them—who are committed to some variation or other of the moral and religious views in question. As I've argued, the "neutrality" thus achieved would be bogus, and certainly useless for solving the problem of showing that a shared sense of justice, and not merely a *modus vivendi*, is possible between adherents of rival comprehensive doctrines under conditions of pluralism.

IV.

We turn finally to the question of whether libertarianism is truly an "impartial" view in the remaining sense of respecting all persons equally. Here too, I think, the impartiality that libertarianism can be said to exhibit is either

---

18　Some libertarians allow that abortion can legitimately be outlawed under certain circumstances, but the majority of libertarians seem to take a "pro-choice" view.

trivial or specious, certainly in Barnett's version and in any "political" brand of libertarianism that aims to be neutral in the other two senses we've discussed. Part of the reason for this might be obvious from what has been said already. Libertarianism claims to treat all persons as self-owners. But as we have seen, what counts as a "person" is itself a matter of contention. Do fetuses, antebellum slaves, and people in "persistent vegetative states" count as "persons" and thus as self-owners? Depending on the answer the libertarian gives, his view is bound to sound less than impartial from some points of view. Should he say, for example, that fetuses do not count as persons, then opponents of abortion will say that his view is not impartial between born and unborn persons. Should he say that fetuses are persons and should be protected by law accordingly, then people who seek abortions, or who want to become pregnant via in vitro fertilization (which typically entails the death of unneeded embryos), or who favor experimentation on embryos in the hope of finding new cures and the like, will say that his view is not impartial toward them, since it interferes with their liberty in the interests of upholding some controversial religious or metaphysical doctrine. Similarly, if the libertarian does not regard those in "persistent vegetative states" as persons, euthanasia opponents will accuse him of discriminating against persons simply on the (in their view irrelevant) grounds that they are no longer capable of consciousness. While if he does regard them as persons, other critics will say that he is not truly impartial toward those whom he would burden with the care of human beings who (in their view) can no longer benefit from care and lack any entitlement to it. The libertarian could, of course, decide not to answer such questions at all, but if he does his view will lose much of its interest: If he refuses to tell us what counts as a person, his assurance that all persons must be treated as self-owners is of limited use.

One problem with the claim that libertarianism upholds an impartial concern for all persons, then, is the same problem afflicting Barnett's proposal that libertarianism be interpreted as a "political" doctrine that is neutral between different possible philosophical justifications and competing comprehensive doctrines: It sounds plausible only if we keep the key concepts vague or indeterminate, and thus philosophically uninteresting and practically useless. Might not the claim be salvaged, though, if the idea of libertarianism as a "neutral" or "political" doctrine is abandoned and some rich comprehensive libertarian theory is put forward in its place?

This might seem possible on some versions of libertarianism—for example, if Nozick's very sketchy attempt to ground libertarianism in Kant's principle of treating persons as ends in themselves could be fleshed out successfully, or if an old-fashioned Lockean natural rights theory could be revitalized.[19] One problem, though, is that these deontological approaches to libertarianism do not seem to have many defenders today. Contractarian and consequentialist approaches appear to be favored by most contemporary libertarian theorists. This is certainly true of Barnett, who, as we've seen, interprets all libertarian theories as merely alternative heuristics or tools for refining conventional and evolving legal principles whose point is to coordinate the behavior of individuals as each pursues his own happiness. Barnett acknowledges that his approach is "consequentialist" insofar as it provides only "hypothetical imperatives" which, he thinks his analysis shows, we ought as a matter of empirical fact to follow *if* we happen to value the goal of allowing each individual to pursue "happiness, peace, and prosperity" in harmony with others.[20] Obviously, it is bound to be much harder to sustain the claim that libertarianism enshrines an impartial respect for all persons as such if the theory contains no deontic component.[21] For only if we are already impartially concerned with the happiness of all persons as such might we care to consider Barnett's suggested method for securing it. By itself, Barnett's consequentialist version of libertarianism gives us no reason to adopt such a concern, any more than a description of how to engineer a functioning bridge, however accurate, gives us a reason to construct one. Those who think, for example, that some groups have an inherent right to rule over others can simply thank Barnett for his advice but reply that they are not interested in it, given that they are not seeking the happiness of all but rather the aggrandizement of a special few. Barnett would rightly disapprove of this, but by his own admission he has given us no grounds for doing so.

Things are even worse for impartiality where contractarian approaches to libertarianism are concerned.[22] The contractarian takes all moral

---

19 But see Cohen, *Self-Ownership, Freedom, and Equality*, pp. 238–43 for problems with the first strategy, and Jeremy Waldron, *God, Locke, and Equality* (Cambridge: Cambridge University Press, 2002) for problems with the second.

20 *The Structure of Liberty*, chapter 1.

21 Barnett does tentatively suggest at p. 24 of *The Structure of Liberty* that his theory might be "deontological" to the extent that he thinks the analysis he gives provides the necessary conditions for each individual's being able to pursue happiness in society with others. But since he does not claim to show that we ought to pursue this goal, the fact (if it is a fact) that his theory shows us the only way to attain it does not make the theory a deontological one.

22 See, e.g., James Buchanan, *The Limits of Liberty* (Chicago: University of Chicago Press, 1975) and Jan Narveson, *The Libertarian Idea* (Philadelphia: Temple University Press, 1988).

obligations to derive from a tacit agreement to abide by certain norms in the interests of furthering the mutual advantage of the parties to the agreement. Since in general we all benefit from others' leaving us alone in the pursuit of our own aims, it is to that extent to our advantage to agree to a general policy of leaving others alone, in the hope that they will extend to us the same courtesy. Notoriously, though, to the extent that some individuals cannot realistically benefit us at all, not even by leaving us alone (since they are too weak to threaten us anyway), it is hard for a contractarian to show that we have any grounds for treating them other than any way we feel like treating them. And those who are not parties to the agreement—either because they never entered into it in the first place or because they have broken it—can indeed be treated in principle any way we like. Contractarians have attempted to come up with various ways of avoiding the very nasty implications this view of morality seems to have (most of them ad hoc and unconvincing in the view of the theory's critics), but the bottom line is that the theory does entail that we do not owe persons as such our impartial concern. They are owed concern only to the extent that it can be shown that a policy of treating them with concern somehow accrues to our benefit.

Even on a deontological version of libertarianism, though, it is not at all clear that the view can plausibly claim to enshrine an impartial respect for persons as such. The reasons are threefold, and have to do, paradoxically, with the very strong conception of individual rights definitive of libertarianism. So literal is the standard libertarian conception of persons as their own property that it seems to allow that a person has the right to sell himself into slavery. (Nozick is explicit about this, though in fairness it must be noted that Barnett rejects the idea.[23]) As Samuel Freeman points out, this would entail that any agreement to become another person's slave is one that a libertarian government would have to enforce just as dutifully as it enforces any other contract.[24] But it is surely odd to think of a government that forces someone to become another's slave as one that is impartial between persons. The fact that the agreement was entered into voluntarily does not seem to mitigate this point. Surely only someone who was stupid, insane, or in a state of total desperation would make such an agreement, and most of them would inevitably come deeply to regret having done so. Any

---

23   See *Anarchy, State, and Utopia*, pp. 58, 283, and 331 for Nozick's endorsement of the possibility of voluntary slavery and *The Structure of Liberty*, pp. 78–82 for Barnett's rejection of it.

24   "Illiberal Libertarians," p. 132.

political system that would enforce such agreements thus seems partial to the intelligent, sane, and fortunate. Moreover, it is hard to see how the considerations that lead us to think persons worthy of impartial concern in the first place—the fact that they are rational, possess free will, are capable of formulating a life plan, and so forth—could plausibly be thought to entail a polity on which these very attributes could be practically nullified as a matter of justice.

A second and related point concerns the libertarian commitment to absolute property rights in external resources, which leaves open the possibility that some person or persons could justly acquire all those resources that are necessary for bare survival and refuse to allow others access to them even in return for payment or labor. The chilling upshot for these others is (as Herbert Spencer put it) that "save by the permission of the lords of the soil, they can have no room for the soles of their feet."[25] Of course, libertarians argue, not implausibly, that such a consequence is extremely unlikely to occur in the actual world and that the market can adequately guarantee almost all persons the means to provide for themselves at well above subsistence level. The point, though, is that the theory does allow that in principle someone could *justly* be allowed by government to starve to death simply because he was too stupid, mad, or just plain unfortunate not to get hold of enough resources to sustain himself and could find no one willing voluntarily to help him. Once again, a libertarian polity would seem partial to the intelligent, sane, and fortunate. And once again, it is at least questionable whether the considerations that lead us to think persons entitled to impartial concern could entail property rights that are *so* strong that the very small level of taxation required to fund even temporary assistance to those destitute through no fault of their own is ruled out as a grave injustice.

Finally, and as Freeman again points out, the libertarian conception of political power is one on which such power is merely a special case of the furtherance of private economic interests. The minimal state advocated by Nozick is essentially a private security firm which has (for morally legitimate reasons, in Nozick's view) taken it upon itself to decide whether and how its clients can be punished for alleged offenses committed against others, and which compensates those others for this inconvenience. It owes its clients protection only insofar as they have contracted for it, and only at the level at which they have agreed to pay for it; it owes those who accuse its clients of wrongdoing and whom it does not allow to exact justice on their

25 *Social Statics* (New York: Robert Schalkenbach Foundation, 1995), p. 104.

own initiative only protection against said clients and not against anyone else who might seek to violate their rights; and it owes nothing to anybody else. The libertarian minimal state is clearly not impartial to all those who live under its jurisdiction, then, any more than any other private corporation is impartial to all those who might benefit from its services. It favors paying customers, and favors most those who can afford to pay the most. Those who do not pay get no protection at all, and this is, on the libertarian view, perfectly just, even if the reason they do not pay is that they are stupid, mad, or just cannot afford to do so. Once again, the intelligent, sane, and fortunate have the advantage in a libertarian polity.

V.

All told, libertarian claims to impartiality prove, upon analysis, to be devoid of interesting content. A libertarian theory of justice is neutral between various comprehensive political philosophies—as long as they more or less share the same premises as the libertarian writer who happens to be presenting said theory of justice. A libertarian polity is neutral between the various comprehensive moral and religious doctrines that prevail in a pluralistic society—as long as they are willing to incorporate into themselves a basically libertarian conception of rights and justice. A libertarian society treats all its citizens equally—but the intelligent, sane, and fortunate are more equal than the stupid, mad, and unfortunate. As J. L. Austin famously put it, "there's the bit where you say it and the bit where you take it back."[26]

---

26   J. L. Austin, *Sense and Sensibilia* (Oxford: Oxford University Press, 1962), p. 2.

16

In Defense of the Perverted Faculty Argument

I. Introduction

"Perverted faculty" arguments were a commonplace in Neo-Scholastic manuals of ethics and moral theology in the period prior to Vatican II. They were
applied to various moral issues, but no doubt their best known application
was to the critique of contraceptive intercourse and other sexual behaviors
at odds with Catholic moral teaching. Indeed, to this day, when asked to explain the grounds of the Church's objection to contraception, most people
would probably respond with some version (albeit oversimplified) of the
perverted faculty argument.

They would also probably regard the argument (again, in oversimplified
form) as a paradigmatic exercise in natural law reasoning. This seems to
annoy no one so much as "New Natural Law" theorists, who have typically
been as harsh in their criticism of the argument as secularist critics of
Catholic teaching have been. Germain Grisez alleges that its defenders
"have exposed Catholic moral thought to endless ridicule and surely have
caused harm in other ways" (1964, p. 31). John Finnis dismisses the argument as "ridiculous" (1980, p. 48). Robert P. George and Patrick Lee characterize it as "easily disposed of" (1999, p. 161). Accordingly, "New Natural
Lawyers" are at pains to correct those who think that any natural law argument against contraception or homosexual behavior (say) *must* be a perverted faculty argument (George 1999, responding to Posner 1992; George
2006, responding to Sullivan 2006).[1]

However, the New Natural Lawyers' two main contentions—that the
perverted faculty argument is a bad argument, and that natural law theorists
in any event need make no use of it in order to show why contraception, homosexual acts, and the like, are wrong—are false, or so I will argue. In fact

---

1   In the interests of full disclosure I should note that the views Prof. George distances
     himself from in responding to Sullivan are, specifically, mine—and (it is only fair
     to acknowledge) that he does so very politely.

the argument, rightly understood, is correct, and certainly isn't undermined by the standard objections. "New Natural Law" theorists think otherwise because, like liberal critics of the argument, they direct their objections at straw men, or at least fail to consider the most plausible reconstructions of the argument. And in fact there are no serious alternative arguments for the intrinsic immorality of contraception, homosexual acts, etc. (apart, that is, from sheer appeals to the authority of scripture, tradition, or the Magisterium). "New Natural Law" arguments against these practices (and other arguments, such as personalist arguments) are all at least implicitly committed to the basic thrust of the perverted faculty argument, and can be rescued from the charge of obscurantism only when this is recognized.

Properly to understand perverted faculty arguments in general and their application to sexual morality in particular requires a fair bit of stage-setting. In the next section I provide an exposition and defense of the "old" natural law theory, viz. natural law theory as Aquinas understood it and as the manualists of the Neo-Scholastic period understood it.[2] In the third section I explain the general approach to sexual morality that follows from natural law theory so understood. In section four, the perverted faculty argument itself, as applied to sexual morality, is then developed and defended against various objections raised by "New Natural Lawyers" and other critics. Finally, in the fifth section I show how the arguments of "New Natural Lawyers" and others who purport to defend Catholic sexual morality without adverting to the perverted faculty argument are in fact implicitly beholden to it.

II. The old natural law theory

Among the features that crucially distinguish the "old" natural law theory from the "new" is the former's grounding of ethics in specifically Aristotelian-Thomistic metaphysical foundations. In particular, natural law theory as Aquinas and the Neo-Scholastics understand it presupposes an *essentialism* according to which natural substances possess essences that are objectively real (rather than inventions of the human mind or mere artifacts of language) and immanent to the things themselves (rather than existing in a Platonic third realm); and a *teleologism* according to which the

---

2   Of course, "New Natural Lawyers" have sometimes claimed that their own position can be found in Aquinas and that the manualists' approach to natural law departs from that of Aquinas in essential respects. For rebuttals, see Veatch (1990), McInerny (1992), Lisska (1996), and Paterson (2006).

activities and processes characteristic of a natural substance are "directed toward" certain ends or outcomes, and *inherently* so, by virtue of the nature of the thing itself (rather than having a "directedness" that is purely extrinsic or entirely imposed from outside, the way artifacts do).[3]

The "old" natural law theory is, in other words, committed to formal and final causes of the sort that were central to the Scholastic tradition in opposition to which modern, post-Cartesian philosophy has largely defined itself. Modern philosophers have generally adopted instead a "passivist" and "mechanistic" conception of nature according to which there are no *immanent* natures or substantial forms (but only "laws" which determine the behavior of things "from outside," as it were) and no "directedness," teleology, or finality *inherent to* natural substances and processes as such (so that teleology is either entirely non-existent in nature or must be imposed from without on otherwise purposeless matter, after the fashion of a watchmaker who imposes a time-telling function on material parts that would otherwise in no sense have it).[4] Some objections to the "old" natural law theory rest on a failure to understand its Aristotelian-Thomistic metaphysical background, and a tendency to read into it modern metaphysical assumptions of precisely the sort defenders of the theory would challenge.

One such objection (famously raised by "New Natural Lawyers" as well as by secularist critics) is the charge that that the "old" natural law theory commits a "naturalistic fallacy" by failing to take note of the "fact/value distinction." For from the Aristotelian-Thomistic point of view, there simply is no "fact/value distinction" in the first place. More precisely, there is no such thing as a purely "factual" description of reality utterly divorced from "value," for "value" is built into the structure of the "facts" from the start. A gap between "fact" and "value" could exist only given a mechanistic understanding of nature of the sort commonly taken for granted by modern philosophers, on which the world is devoid of any immanent essences or

3   Naturally, Thomists would affirm that natural teleology ultimately requires a divine cause, as Aquinas does in the Fifth Way. But this is no more incompatible with holding that the teleology of a natural substance is immanent to it (contra writers like William Paley who would assimilate natural substances to artifacts, whose finality is entirely extrinsic) than affirming God as first cause is incompatible with affirming the reality of secondary causes (contra occasionalism, which attributes all causality to God). For further discussion see Feser 2010.

4   For useful discussions of the difference between the Aristotelian conception of nature and the modern "passivist" and "mechanistic" conception that replaced it, see Ellis 2002 and Osler 1996.

natural ends.[5] No such gap, and thus no "fallacy" of inferring normative conclusions from "purely factual" premises, can exist given an Aristotelian-Thomistic essentialist and teleological conception of the world. "Value" is a highly misleading term in any case, and subtly begs the question against critics of the "fact/value distinction" by insinuating that morality is purely subjective, insofar as "value" seems to presuppose someone doing the valuing. Aristotelians and Thomists (and other classical philosophers such as Platonists) tend to speak, not of "value," but of "the good," which on their account is entirely objective.

Consider, to begin with, a simple example. It is of the essence or nature of a Euclidean triangle to be a closed plane figure with three straight sides, and anything with this essence must have a number of properties, such as having angles that add up to 180 degrees. These are objective facts that we discover rather than invent; certainly it is notoriously difficult to make the opposite opinion at all plausible. Nevertheless, there are obviously triangles that fail to live up to this definition. A triangle drawn hastily on the cracked plastic seat of a moving bus might fail to be completely closed or to have perfectly straight sides, and thus its angles will add up to something other than 180 degrees. Indeed, even a triangle drawn slowly and carefully on paper with an art pen and a ruler will contain subtle flaws. Still, the latter will far more closely approximate the essence of triangularity than the former will. It will be a *better* triangle than the former. Indeed, we would quite naturally describe the latter as a *good* triangle and the former as a *bad* one. This judgment would be completely objective; it would be silly to suggest that we were merely expressing a personal preference for angles that add up to 180 degrees. It would be equally silly to suggest that we have somehow committed a fallacy in making a "value" judgment about the badness of the triangle drawn on the bus seat on the basis of the "facts" about the essence of triangularity. Given that essence, the "value judgment" follows *necessarily*. This example illustrates how an entity can count as an instance of a certain type of thing even if it fails perfectly to instantiate the essence of that type of thing; a badly drawn triangle is not a non-triangle, but rather a defective triangle. It illustrates at the same time how there can be a completely *objective, factual* standard of goodness and badness, better and worse. To

5   And maybe not even then, for the "fact/value distinction" has also been criticized by philosophers who are not sympathetic to Aristotelian-Thomistic metaphysics. (See, e.g., Putnam 2004.) Criticisms on the part of writers who are sympathetic to Aristotelian-Thomistic metaphysics include Martin 2004 and Oderberg 2000, pp. 9–15.

be sure, the standard in question in this example is not a *moral* standard. But from an Aristotelian-Thomistic point of view, it illustrates a general notion of goodness of which moral goodness is a special case.

Living things provide examples that bring us closer to a distinctively moral conception of goodness, as has been noted by several contemporary philosophers who, though not Thomists, have defended a neo-Aristotelian position in ethics. For instance, Philippa Foot, following Michael Thompson, notes how living things can only adequately be described in terms of what Thompson calls "Aristotelian categoricals" of a form such as *S's are F*, where *S* refers to a species and *F* to something predicated of the species (Foot 2001, chapter 2; Thompson 1995). To cite Foot's examples, "Rabbits are herbivores," "Cats are four-legged," and "Human beings have 32 teeth" would be instances of this general form. Note that such propositions cannot be adequately represented in terms of either the existential or the universal quantifier. "Cats are four-legged," for instance, is obviously not saying "There is at least one cat that is four-legged." But neither is it saying "For everything that is a cat, it is four-legged," since the occasional cat may be missing a leg due to injury or genetic defect. Aristotelian categoricals convey a *norm*, much like the description of what counts as a triangle. Any particular living thing can only be described as an instance of a species, and a species itself can only be described in terms of Aristotelian categoricals stating at least its general characteristics. If a particular *S* happens not to be *F*—if, for example, a particular cat is missing a leg—that does not show that *S's* are not *F* after all, but rather that this particular *S* is a *defective* instance of an *S*.

In living things the sort of norm in question is, as Foot also notes, inextricably tied to the notion of teleology. There are certain *ends* that any organism must realize in order to flourish as the kind of organism it is, ends concerning activities like development, self-maintenance, reproduction, the rearing of young, and so forth; and these ends entail a standard of goodness. Hence (again to cite Foot's examples) an oak that develops long and deep roots is to that extent a good oak and one that develops weak roots is to that extent bad and defective; a lioness which nurtures her young is to that extent a good lioness and one that fails to do so is to that extent bad or defective; and so on. As with our triangle example, it would be silly to pretend that these judgments of goodness and badness are in any way subjective or reflective of human preferences, or that the inferences leading to them commit a "naturalistic fallacy." They simply follow from the objective facts about what counts as a flourishing or sickly instance of the biological kind or nature in question, and in particular from an organism's realization or failure to realize the ends set for it by its nature. The facts in question are, as it were, inherently laden with "value" from the start. Or to use Foot's more traditional (and less misleading) language, the goodness a flourishing instance of a natural kind exhibits is "natural goodness"—the goodness is there *in the nature of things*, and not in our subjective "value" judgments.

What is true of animals in general is true of human beings. Like the other, non-rational animals, we have various ends inherent in our nature, and these determine what is good for us. In particular, Aquinas tells us, "all those things to which man has a natural inclination, are naturally apprehended by reason as being good, and consequently as objects of pursuit, and their contraries as evil, and objects of avoidance" (*Summa Theologiae* I-II.94.2).[6] It is crucial not to misunderstand the force of Aquinas's expression "natural inclination" here. By "inclination" he does not necessarily mean something consciously desired, and by "natural" he doesn't mean something merely psychologically deep-seated, or even, necessarily, something genetically determined. What he has in mind is rather the *natural teleology* of our capacities, their inherent "directedness" toward certain ends. For this reason, Anthony Lisska has suggested translating Aquinas's *inclinatio* as "disposition" (1996, p. 104). While this has its advantages, even it fails to make it clear that Aquinas is not interested in just any dispositions we might contingently happen to have, but rather in those that reflect nature's purposes for us.

Of course, there is often a close correlation between what nature intends and what we desire. Nature wants us to eat so that we'll stay alive, and sure enough we tend to want to eat. Given that we are social animals, nature intends for us to avoid harming others, and for the most part we do want to avoid this. And so forth. At the same time, there are people (such as anorexics and bulimics) who form very strong desires not to eat what they need to eat in order to survive and thrive; and at the other extreme there are people whose desire for food is excessive. Some people are not only occasionally prone to harm others, but are positively misanthropic or sociopathic. Desires are nature's way of prodding us to do what is good for us, but like everything else in the natural order, they are subject to various imperfections and distortions. Hence, though in general and for the most part our desires match up with nature's purposes, this is not true in every single case. Habituated vice, peer pressure, irrationality, mental illness, and the like can often

---

6 ˊ All quotes from the *Summa* are taken from the translation in Aquinas 1948.

deform our subjective desires so that they turn us away from what nature intends, and thus from what is good for us. Genetic defect might do the same; just as it causes deformities like clubfoot and polydactyly, so too might it generate psychological and behavioral deformities as well.

Here as elsewhere, it is crucial in understanding the "old" natural law theory that one keeps the background Aristotelian-Thomistic metaphysical theses always in mind. "Natural" for the Aristotelian-Thomistic philosopher does not mean merely "deeply ingrained," "in accordance with the laws of physics," "having a genetic basis," or any other of the readings that a non-teleological view of nature might allow. It has instead to do with the final causes inherent in a thing by virtue of its essence, and which it possesses whether or not it ever realizes them or consciously wants to realize them. What is genuinely good for someone, accordingly, may in principle be something he or she does not consciously want, like children who refuse to eat their vegetables, or an addict convinced that it would be bad to stop taking drugs. For the "old" natural law theory, knowing what is truly good for us requires taking an external, objective, "third-person" point of view on ourselves rather than a subjective "first-person" view; it is a matter of determining what fulfills our *nature*, not our contingent desires.

Aquinas identifies three general categories of goods inherent in our nature. First are those we share with all living things, such as the preservation of our existence. Second are those common to animals specifically, such as sexual intercourse and the child-rearing activities that naturally follow upon it. Third are those peculiar to us as *rational* animals, such as "to know the truth about God, and to live in society," "to shun ignorance," and "to avoid offending those among whom one has to live" (*Summa Theologiae* I-II.94.2). These goods are ordered in a hierarchy corresponding to the traditional Aristotelian hierarchy of living things (viz. the vegetative, sensory, and rational forms of life, respectively). The higher goods presuppose the lower ones; for example, one cannot pursue truth if one is not able to conserve oneself in existence. But the lower goods are subordinate to the higher ones in the sense that they exist for the sake of the higher ones. The point of fulfilling the vegetative and sensory aspects of our nature is, ultimately, to allow us to fulfill the defining rational aspect of our nature.

Now these various goods have *moral* significance for us because, unlike other animals, we are capable of *intellectually grasping* what is good and *freely choosing* whether or not to pursue it. And that brings us from "natural goodness" (as Foot calls it) to natural law. Aquinas famously held that the fundamental principle of natural law is that "*good is to be done and pursued, and evil is to be avoided*. All other precepts of the natural law are based upon this," where the content of those precepts is determined by the goods falling under the three main categories just mentioned (*Summa Theologiae* I-II.94.2). Now that "good is to be done etc." might at first glance seem to be a difficult claim to justify, and certainly not a very promising candidate for a first principle. For isn't the question "Why should I be good?" precisely (part of) what any moral theory ought to answer? And isn't this question notoriously hard to answer to the satisfaction of the moral skeptic?

Properly understood, however, Aquinas's principle is not only not difficult to justify, but is so obviously correct that it might seem barely worth asserting. Aquinas is not saying that it is self-evident that we ought to be morally good. Rather, he is saying that it is self-evident that whenever we act we pursue something that we take to be good *in some way* and/or avoid what we take to be *in some way* evil or bad. And he is clearly right. Even someone who does what he believes to be morally bad does so only because he is seeking something he takes to be good in the sense of worth pursuing. Hence the mugger who admits that robbery is evil nevertheless takes his victim's wallet because he thinks it would be good to have money to pay for his drugs; hence the drug addict who knows that his habit is wrong and degrading nevertheless thinks it would be good to satisfy the craving and bad to suffer the unpleasantness of not satisfying it; and so forth. Of course, these claims are obviously true only on a very thin sense of "good" and "bad," but that is exactly the sense Aquinas has in mind.

Though acceptance of the Aristotelian-Thomistic metaphysics of natural goodness is not necessary in order to see that Aquinas's principle is correct, it does help us to understand *why* it is correct. For like every other natural phenomenon, practical reason has a natural end or goal toward which it is ordered, and that end or goal is just whatever it is the intellect perceives to be good or worth pursuing. Now given what has already been said, human beings, like everything else in nature, have various capacities and ends the fulfillment of which is good for them and the frustrating of which is bad, as a matter of objective fact. A rational intellect apprised of the facts will therefore perceive that it is good to realize these ends and bad to frustrate them. It follows, then, that a rational person will pursue the realization of these ends and avoid their frustration. In short, practical reason is directed by nature toward the pursuit of what the intellect perceives to be good; what is *in fact* good is the realization of the various ends inherent in human nature; and thus a *rational and correctly informed* person will perceive this and, accordingly, direct his actions towards the realization or fulfillment of those ends. In this sense, good action is just that which is "in accord with reason" (*Summa Theologiae* I-II.21.1; cf. *Summa Theologiae* I-II.90.1), and the moral skeptic's question "Why should I do what is good?" has an obvious answer: Because to be rational *just is* (in part) to do what is good, to fulfill the ends set for us by nature. Natural law ethics as a body of substantive moral theory is the formulation of general moral principles on the basis of an analysis of the various human capacities and ends and the systematic working out of their implications. So, to take just one example, when we consider that human beings have intellects and that the natural end or function of the intellect is to grasp the truth about things, it follows that it is good for us—it fulfills our nature—to pursue truth and avoid error. Consequently, a rational person apprised of the facts about human nature will see that this is what is good for us and thus strive to attain truth and to avoid error. And so on for other natural human capacities.

Of course, things are much more complicated than that summary lets on. Various qualifications and complications will need to be spelled out as we examine the various natural human capacities in detail, and not every principle of morality that follows from this analysis will necessarily be as simple and straightforward as "Pursue truth and avoid error." But what has been said so far suffices to give us at least a very general idea of how natural law theory determines the specific content of our moral obligations. It also suffices to give us a sense of the *grounds* of moral obligation, that which makes it the case that moral imperatives have categorical rather than merely hypothetical force. The hypothetical imperative (1) *If I want what is good for me then I ought to pursue what realizes my natural ends and avoid what frustrates them* is something whose truth follows from the metaphysical analysis sketched above. By itself, it does not give us a categorical imperative because the consequent will have force only for someone who accepts the antecedent. But that (2) *I do want what is good for me* is something true of all of us by virtue of our nature as human beings, and is in any case self-evident, being just a variation on Aquinas's fundamental principle of natural law. These premises yield the conclusion (3) *I ought to pursue what realizes my natural ends and avoid what frustrates them*. It does have categorical force because (2) has categorical force, and (2) has categorical force because it cannot be otherwise given our nature. Not only the content of our moral obligations but their obligatory force are thus determined by natural teleology. As the Neo-Scholastic natural law theorist Michael Cronin (whose account of obligation has influenced my own presentation) writes, "In the fullest sense of the word, then, moral duty is natural. For not only are certain objects natural means to man's final end, but our desire of that end is natural also, and, therefore, the necessity of the means is natural" (1939, p. 222).[7]

It goes without saying that a complete defense of the "old" natural law theory requires a defense of the controversial metaphysical assumptions that underlie it. This is not the place for such a defense, but I have provided it elsewhere (Feser 2008, Feser 2009), and Aristotelian-Thomistic metaphysics has in recent years attracted a growing number of able advocates. (See, e.g., the essays collected in Haldane 2002, and, for an outstanding full-length defense, Oderberg 2007. Oderberg 2010 addresses the metaphysical foundations of natural law, specifically.) Nor need one sympathize with Thomism or natural law theory to endorse a broadly Aristotelian metaphysics; neo-Aristotelianism is a small but growing movement within contemporary academic philosophy more generally. (See the articles collected in Tahko 2012 and Groff and Greco 2013 for some representative examples.) Those who would dismiss the old natural law theory on the grounds that its basic metaphysical presuppositions are no longer taken seriously within mainstream philosophy are not only guilty of a fallacy of relevance, but operating from assumptions that are themselves out of date.

III. General sexual ethics

When we apply the "old" natural law theory to sexual morality, the first step is to identify the natural end or ends of our sexual faculties. For if what is good for us is determined by what realizes the ends inherent in our nature, then what is good for us in the sexual context can only be what realizes the ends of our sexual faculties. Now for Aquinas and other natural law theorists

---

7 Notice that no mention has been made here either of divine command as the source of obligation or of rewards and punishments in the hereafter as motivation for moral behavior—contrary to what one would expect from Grisez's description of "conventional natural law theory," which he wrongly accuses of having a "voluntaristic" conception of obligation (1964, pp. 46–53). Grisez fails to take note of a crucial distinction between what Cronin calls the "ultimate ground" and the "proximate ground" of moral obligation (Cronin 1939, p. 213). Just as God's being the first cause is perfectly consistent with the reality of secondary causes (contra the occasionalist), so too is God's being the *ultimate* source of obligation consistent with there being a *proximate* ground of obligation in the will's having the good as its natural end (contra the voluntarist). Hence the "old" natural law theory does not (contra Grisez) have to appeal to natural theology in order to make obligation intelligible (even if a *complete* account of obligation—as with a complete account of causality, or of anything else for that matter—will make reference to natural theology). See Feser 2009, pp. 188–92 for further discussion.

who build on an Aristotelian metaphysical foundation, to be a human being is to be a *rational animal*. That we are *animals* of a sort entails that the vegetative, sensory, locomotive, and appetitive ends that determine what is good for non-human animals are also partially constitutive of our good. That we are *rational* entails that we also have as our own distinctive ends those associated with intellect and volition. Like other animals, in order to flourish we must take in nutrients, go through a process of development from conception through to maturity, reproduce ourselves, and move ourselves about the world in response to inner drives and the information we take in through sense organs. But on top of that we have to exercise the rational capacities to form abstract concepts, put them together into judgments, and reason from one judgment to another in accordance with the laws of logic; and we have to choose between alternative courses of action in light of what the intellect knows about them.

Now these latter, higher, rational activities do not merely constitute distinctive goods; they also alter the nature of the lower, animal goods. For example, both a dog and a human being can have a visual perception of a tree. But there is a *conceptual* element to normal human visual perception that is not present in the dog's perception. The dog perceives the tree, but not in a way that involves conceptualizing it *as* a tree, forming a judgment like *that tree is an oak*, or inferring from the presence of the tree and the tree's status as an oak that *an oak is present*.[8] In man, the animal, sensory element is fused to the distinctively human, rational element in such a way as to form a seamless unity. Hence while perception is a good for both non-human animals and human beings, that perception in our case participates in our rationality makes of it a different and indeed higher sort of good than that of which non-human animals are capable. Other goods we share in common with animals similarly participate in our rationality and are radically transformed as a result. Thus, *meals* have a social and cultural significance that raises them above mere feeding; *games* have a social import and conceptual content that raises them above the play of which other mammals are capable; and so forth.

Our sexual faculties are no different, and this is the key to understanding why they have a *unitive* as well as a *procreative* end, and why these ends are inseparable. Take the latter first. That sex considered from a purely

---

8   For discussion of the crucial differences between intellectual activity in the strict sense and the exercises in sensation and imagination of which non-human animals are capable, see Feser 2013.

biological point of view exists for the sake of procreation is uncontroversial. This is true even though people have sexual relations for various reasons other than procreation, since we are talking about *nature's* ends here, not ours. In particular, it is true even though sex is pleasurable and human beings and animals are typically drawn to sex precisely because of this pleasure. For giving pleasure is not *the* end of sex, not that *for the sake of which* sex exists in animals. Rather, sexual pleasure has as its own natural end the getting of animals to engage in sexual relations, so that they will procreate. This parallels the situation with eating: Even though eating is pleasurable, the biological point of eating is not to give pleasure, but rather to provide an organism with the nutrients it needs to survive. The pleasure of eating is just nature's way of getting animals to do what is needed to fulfill this end. When analyzing the biological significance of either eating or sex, to emphasize pleasure would be to put the cart before the horse. Pleasure has its place, but it is secondary.

Notice also that nature makes it very difficult to indulge in sex without procreation. There is no prophylactic sheathe issued with a penis at birth, and no diaphragm issued with a vagina. It takes some effort to come up with these devices, and even then, in the form in which they existed for most of human history they were not terribly effective. Moreover, experience indicates that people simply find sexual relations more pleasurable when such devices are not used, even if they will often use them anyway out of a desire to avoid pregnancy. Indeed, this is one reason pregnancy is (even if often cut short by abortion) very common even in societies in which contraception is easily available: People know they could take a few minutes to go buy a condom, but go ahead and engage in "unprotected" sex anyway. As this indicates, sexual arousal occurs very frequently and can often be very hard to resist even for a short while. And that last resort to those seeking to avoid pregnancy—the "withdrawal" method—is notoriously unreliable. Even with the advent of "the pill," pregnancies (though also abortions) are common; and even effective use of the pill—which has existed only for a very brief period of human history—requires that a woman remember to take it at the appointed times and be willing to put up with its uncomfortable side effects.

So, sex exists in animals for the sake of procreation, and sexual pleasure exists for the sake of getting them to indulge in sex, so that they will procreate. And we're built in such a way that sexual arousal is hard to resist and occurs very frequently, and such that it is very difficult to avoid pregnancies resulting from indulgence of that arousal. The obvious conclusion is that the natural end of sex is (in part) not just procreation, but procreation in large numbers. Mother Nature clearly wants us to have babies, and lots of them. Nor can this be written off as just so much rationalization of prejudice. Apart from the Aristotelian jargon, everything said so far about the natural ends of sex and sexual pleasure could be endorsed by the Darwinian naturalist as a perfectly accurate description of their biological functions, whether or not such a naturalist would agree with the moral conclusions natural law theorists would draw from it.

Now in light of all this, it does seem that Mother Nature has put a fairly heavy burden on women, who, if "nature takes its course," are bound to become pregnant somewhat frequently. She has also put a fairly heavy burden on children too, given that unlike non-human offspring they are utterly dependent on others for their needs, and for a very long period. This is true not only of their biological needs, but of the moral and cultural needs they have by virtue of being little rational animals. They need education in both what is useful and what is right, and correction of error. In human beings, procreation—generating new members of the species—is not just a matter of producing new organisms, but also of forming them into persons capable of fulfilling their nature as distinctively *rational* animals. So, nature's taking its course thus seems to leave mothers and offspring pretty helpless, or at any rate it would do so if there weren't someone ordained by nature to provide for them. But of course there is such a person, namely the father of the children. Fathers obviously have a strong incentive to look after their own children rather than someone else's, and they are also, generally speaking, notoriously jealous of the affections of the women they have children with, sometimes to the point of being willing to kill the competition. Thus Mother Nature very equitably puts a heavy burden on fathers too, pushing them into a situation where they must devote their daily labors to providing for their children and the woman or women with whom they have had these children; and when "nature takes its course" these children are bound to be somewhat numerous, so that the father's commitment is necessarily going to have to be long-term. Even considered merely from the point of view of its animal, procreative aspects, then, the natural teleology of sex points in the case of human beings in the direction of at least something like the institution of marriage. Here too nothing has been said that couldn't be endorsed by secular social scientists or evolutionary psychologists, whatever moral lessons they may or may not draw.[9]

9   This account of the purely biological functions of sex and marriage is of course just common sense, and it is also more or less the account Aquinas gives in *Summa*

That is the big picture view of the natural teleology of sex considered merely in its animal and procreative aspects. Let's turn now momentarily to the small picture, focusing on the sexual act itself. If we consider the structure of the sexual organs and the sexual act as a process beginning with arousal and ending in orgasm, it is clear that its biological function, its final cause, is to get semen into the vagina. That is why the penis and vagina are shaped the way they are, why the vagina secretes lubrication during sexual arousal, and so forth. The organs fit together like lock and key. The point of the process is not just to get semen out of the male, but also into the female, and into one place in the female in particular. This too is something no one would deny when looking at things from a purely biological point of view, whatever moral conclusions may or may not follow from it. Of course, there is more going on here than just plumbing. Women can have orgasms too, sexual pleasure can be had by acts other than just vaginal penetration, and all sorts of complex and profound passions are aroused in a man and woman during the process of lovemaking that go well beyond the simple desire to get semen into a certain place. But from the point of view of the animal, procreative side of sex, all of this exists for the sake of getting men and women to engage in the sexual act, so that it will result in ejaculation into the vagina, so that in turn offspring will be generated at least a certain percentage of the time the act is performed, and so that father and mother will be strengthened in their desire to stay together, which circumstance is (whatever their personal intentions and thoughts) nature's way of sustaining that union upon which children depend for their material and spiritual well-being. Every link in the chain has procreation as its natural end, whatever the intentions of the actors.

Whatever else sex is, then, it is *essentially* procreative. If human beings did not procreate, then while they might form close emotional bonds with one another, maybe even exclusive ones, they would not have *sex*—that is to say, they would not be *man* and *woman*, as opposed to something asexual or androgynous. (The claim is not that procreation entails sex—there is in the biological realm such a thing as asexual reproduction—but rather that

---

Contra Gentiles III.122-126. Even Posner, whose views are otherwise very far from the ones defended here, affirms that from a biological point of view sex functions both to procreate and to bind a man to the mother of his children (1992, pp. 226–27). See Wright 1995 for a useful survey of the things evolutionary psychologists say about sex and a sense of the ways in which, descriptively if not prescriptively, they confirm what common sense and natural law thinkers like Aquinas would say.

sex entails procreation in the sense that procreation is *the reason* sex exists in the first place, even if sex does not in every case result in procreation and even if procreation could have occurred in some other way.)

Unlike other sexually reproducing animals, though, we *know this* about ourselves, we *know* that qua male or female each of us is in some unusual way incomplete; and that is why, in human beings, the procreative end of sex is by no means the end of the story. Human beings *conceptualize* their incompleteness, and *idealize* what they think will remedy it. It is important to note that this is as true of human sexuality at its most "raw" and "animal" as it is of its more refined manifestations. Dogs don't worry about the size of breasts and genitalia; nor do they dress each other up in garters and stockings, or in leather and leashes for that matter. The latter are *adornments*—some perfectly innocent, some not—and reflect an *aesthetic* attitude toward the object of desire of which non-rational animals are incapable. Animals also do not conceptualize the desires and perceptions of their sexual partners, as human beings do even in the most immoral sexual encounters. Like the sexual organs, then, our sexual psychology is "directed at" or "points to" something beyond itself, and in particular toward what alone can complete us, *emotionally* as well as physiologically, given our natures. The human soul is directed to *another soul*—and not merely toward certain organs—as its complement, man to woman and woman to man. (And that some people do not have a desire for the opposite sex, and in some cases lack sexual desire altogether, is as irrelevant to the *natural* end of our psychological faculties as the existence of clubfeet is to telling us what nature intends feet for.)

Now the nature of this psychological "other-directedness" is complex. In his chapter on romantic love in *The Four Loves* (1988), C. S. Lewis usefully distinguishes *Eros* from *Venus*. Venus is sexual desire, which can be (even if it shouldn't be) felt for and satisfied by any number of people. Eros is the longing associated with being in love with someone, and no one other than that one person can satisfy it. Obviously, Venus can and very often does exist without Eros. Eros typically includes Venus, but it not only focuses Venus specifically on the object of romantic longing, but carries that longing to the point where Venus itself, along with everything else, might be sacrificed for the sake of the beloved if necessary. *Sexual release* is the object of Venus; *the beloved* is the object of Eros.

As Lewis wisely notes, it is an error to think that Venus without Eros is *per se* morally suspect. We might wish that every husband and wife felt for each other as did Tristan and Isolde, or Romeo and Juliet, or Catherine and

Heathcliff; or maybe not, given the tragic ends of these couples. Needless to say, real human life is rarely like that, and very frequently it does not even rise to the level of a more sober approximation. Arranged marriages were common for much of human history; modern marriages for love often lose their passion and settle into routine, or at least have their ups and downs, but without the disappearance of Venus; and some people simply do not have Erotic temperaments (in the relevant sense) in the first place, but still have normal sexual desires and wish to marry. Eros is too unstable and outside our control to think it essential to the moral use of Venus. Sometimes mere affection (which, like Venus itself, can be felt for any number of people) has to suffice to civilize Venus.

All the same, there is a reason Eros is commonly regarded as an *ideal*, and is indeed often achieved at least to some extent, even if passion inevitably cools somewhat. Like Venus, Eros is natural to us. It functions to channel the potentially unruly Venus in the monogamous and constructive direction that the stability of the family requires. Of course, a respect for the moral law, fear of opprobrium, and sensitivity to the feelings of a spouse can do this too, but unlike Eros the motivations they provide can all conflict with the agent's own inclinations, and are thus less efficacious. A decent man *will* confine the gratification of his sexual appetites to the marriage bed; a man who is in love with his wife *wants to* confine them to the marriage bed. Eros also brings us out of ourselves more perfectly than Venus can, and thus raises Venus not only above the merely animal but even above the merely social. As Lewis writes, the sheer selflessness of Eros at its most noble, and its fixation on the beloved to the exclusion of everything else, make it an especially fitting model for the sort of love we are to have for God.

Venus and Eros, then, considered in terms of their natural function, might best be thought of not as distinct faculties, but as opposite ends of a continuum. Venus tells us that we are incomplete, moving us toward that procreative action whose natural end—the generation of new human beings — requires the stability of marital union for its success. Eros focuses that desire onto a single person with whom such a union can be made and for whom the Erotic lover happily forsakes all others and is even willing to sacrifice his own happiness. Eros is the perfection of Venus; mere Venus is a deficient form of Eros. Human experience seems to confirm this insofar as it is the rare Lothario who does not at some point desire something more substantial, and the rare Erotic lover who is willing entirely to forego Venus.

Eros is itself perfected in what psychologist Robert Sternberg (1988) calls "consummate love," which adds to romance the interpersonal bonds of which other relationships are also capable. Sternberg's influential "triangular theory" of love distinguishes between intimacy, commitment, and passion, and six kinds of suboptimal love, each of which involves only one or two of these elements. Intimacy by itself involves the kind of closeness typical of friendship. Commitment by itself is characterized by Sternberg as "empty" love, a bloodless sort of thing that might suffice for an arranged marriage, at least initially. Passion by itself amounts to mere infatuation (and seems to correspond to Lewis's notion of Eros, and perhaps in its less intense manifestations to lower points on the continuum I have proposed exists between Venus and Eros). What Sternberg calls "companionate love" combines commitment with the intimacy of friendship but is devoid of passion. "Romantic love" combines passion with intimacy, as in a relationship that begins with infatuation and leads to friendship or vice versa. "Fatuous love" combines passion and commitment, as in a marriage which was entered into suddenly on the basis of passion before true intimacy has developed. "Consummate love," Sternberg says, combines all three of the basic kinds of love—commitment, the intimacy of friendship, and the passion that begins with mere infatuation but develops into something more stable. It is difficult to achieve, but is commonly regarded as definitive of the best marriages.

One needn't endorse all the details of Lewis's or Sternberg's views to see that Erotic love's perfection of Venus, and "consummate" love's perfection of Eros, are not only ideals toward which human beings are in fact generally drawn, but are also highly conducive to the realization of sex's procreative end understood in the broad sense that includes not just the generation of new human beings but also their upbringing, and thus requires a stable union of sexual partners. Indeed, though families are often stable enough to function even when the parents fall far short of Sternberg's "consummate love," it is hard to see how marriage and family as institutions could survive unless Erotic and consummate love were generally honored at least as ideals, and approximated at least to some significant extent in most marriages. In short, the *procreative* end of sex points, in human beings, given their rational nature, to a *unitive* end. And once again, with this much a secular social scientist or Darwinian evolutionary psychologist could readily agree.

When we read all this in light of the Aristotelian-Thomistic metaphysics underlying the "old" natural law theory, however, we are bound to draw some conclusions with which many secularists will not agree. First of all, the unitive end of sex builds on the procreative in just the way the conceptual structure of human perceptual experience builds on the sensory element. That means that, as in the latter case, our rationality raises our animality to a higher level without in any way negating it. A human visual experience is a seamless unity of the rational and the animal; that we (unlike non-human animals) conceptualize what we receive through sensation does not make a perception *less* than sensory, even if it makes it more than *merely* sensory. Similarly, that the physiology of sexual arousal is in human beings associated with various complex other-directed psychological states of which non-human animals are not capable not does make our sexual acts *less* than procreative in their natural end, even if they are more than *merely* procreative. A human sexual act is a seamless unity of the procreative and the unitive, directed at the same time toward both biological generation and emotional communion.

Hence there is no such thing as a sexual act which *of its nature* is *merely* unitive and in no way procreative, any more than there is such a thing as a human perceptual experience which *of its nature* is merely conceptual and in no way sensory. Of course, a particular sexual act may in fact be incapable of resulting in conception because the sexual organs have been damaged or worn out by age, but that no more changes what they and their activities are *by nature* than the fact that the visual apparatus might be damaged to the point of reducing the sensory content largely or even entirely (as in "blindsight") changes what visual perception is by nature, or any more than the fact that there are dogs which, due to injury, have fewer than four legs, shows that it is not of the nature of a dog to have four legs. In all three cases we have deviation from the norm expressed in an Aristotelian categorical: "Sexual acts are both unitive and procreative" is like "Human visual perceptual experiences have both conceptual and sensory content" and "Dogs have four legs."

Nor is there any such thing as a sexual act which *of its nature* (as opposed to a particular individual's personal motivation) exists for the sake of pleasure alone and not for either the procreative or unitive end of sex. For as with the pleasure associated with the purely procreative sex of which animals are capable, the pleasure associated with human sexual relations exists for the sake of the natural ends of those relations — in this case, unitive as well as procreative—rather than for its own sake. It is precisely *because* sex involves the lovers' taking intense pleasure in each others' bodies and most intimate feelings that it is capable of uniting them as it does.[10] Without either the unitive or procreative ends there would be no reason for nature to make sex pleasurable, and (at least for the Aristotelian-Thomistic metaphysician) nature does nothing in vain.

Now, since the natural ends of our sexual capacities are simultaneously procreative and unitive, what is good for human beings vis-à-vis those capacities is to use them only in a way consistent with these ends. This is a *necessary* truth, given the background metaphysics. It *cannot possibly* be good for us to use them in a way contrary to these ends, whether or not an individual person thinks it is, any more than it can possibly be good for a diseased or damaged tree to fail to sink roots into the ground. This is true *whatever* the reason is for someone's desire to act in a way contrary to nature's purposes—intellectual error, habituated vice, genetic defect, or whatever—and however strong that desire is. That a desire to act in such a way is very deeply entrenched in a person only shows that his will has become corrupted. A clubfoot is still a clubfoot, and thus a defect, even though the person having it is not culpable for this and might not be able to change it. And a desire to do what is bad is still a desire to do what is bad, however difficult it might be for someone to desire otherwise, and whether or not the person is culpable for having a tendency to form these desires (he may not be).

What has been said so far clearly supports a general commendation of confining sexual activity to marriage and the having of large families, and a general condemnation of fornication, adultery, contraception, homosexual acts, bestiality, masturbation, pornography, and the like. For fornication threatens to bring children into the world outside of the marital context they need for their well-being; adultery undermines the stability of that context; contraceptive acts directly frustrate the procreative end of sex altogether; homosexual acts and bestiality have no tendency toward procreation at all, and the emotions associated with them direct the unitive drive, which can by nature be fulfilled only by a human being of the opposite sex, toward an improper object; and masturbation and pornography are also contrary to

---

10   It is thus silly to speak, as some well-meaning people do, as if sex exists for the sake of expressing love *as opposed to* for the sake of giving pleasure. For it is only because sex is pleasurable in just the intense and intimate way it is that it is capable of being an expression of love in the first place. (No one ever suggests: "Let me rub your elbows in order to express my love. It will be an especially pure expression, since it won't give either of us much if any pleasure.") What such moralists should say is that the pleasure exists for the sake of the expression of love rather than for its own sake.

this inherently other-directed unitive drive insofar as they turn it inward toward a fantasy world rather than outward toward another human being, like an arrow pointed back at the archer.

But this might still seem to fall short of establishing the *absolute* moral claims made by Catholic teaching. Consider a devout Mormon couple who have a large family of nine children, but who have occasionally used contraception so as to space their children evenly, or to avoid pregnancy in circumstances where the wife's health or life might be endangered. Or consider someone who has to be away from his or her spouse for a prolonged period of time and who, during this time, indulges the temptation to masturbate, but who only ever fantasizes about his or her spouse while doing so and who otherwise has a normal marital sex life and a large family. It might seem that these people are fulfilling both the procreative and unitive ends of sex. It would certainly seem strained and even unjust to accuse them of having a "contraceptive mentality," of being insufficiently "open to life," or of being otherwise insensitive to the "personalist" dimensions of sex, insofar as their attitude toward sex is obviously different from those who regard sex as mere recreation and children as an inconvenience to be avoided. Of course, one could object that it can in practice be difficult to know where to "draw the line" before indulgence in such contraceptive and masturbatory acts starts to impede the procreative and unitive ends of sex, but that does not by itself show that it is *always and in principle* wrong to indulge in them.

So, what has been said so far might, from the point of view of Catholic teaching, seem not to have proved enough. It may also seem to have proved too much. For if it is good for us to pursue the procreative and unitive ends of sex and bad for us to frustrate them, wouldn't it follow that it is wrong to refrain from marrying if one had the opportunity to do so? And if the unitive and procreative ends must go together, wouldn't it follow that it is wrong for sterile and aged married couples to have sexual intercourse?

In fact these conclusions do not follow, any more than the fact that private property is good for us shows that it is always wrong to give our goods away to the poor, or any more than the fact that truth-telling is good for us shows that it is always wrong to keep embarrassing information to ourselves, or any more than the fact that food is good for us shows that it is always wrong to fast. With sex as with these other goods, while identifying their natural ends is the crucial first step to determining their role in a morally well-ordered life, it does not by itself answer every question we might have about them. For human life is complicated and requires the pursuit of many different goods, not all of which can be pursued at the same time. Sometimes one good can be sacrificed for the sake of a higher good, as when one sacrifices marriage and family for the sake of the priesthood or religious life. Sometimes a good cannot be pursued because of circumstances, as when a suitable marriage partner is simply not available, or as when a married couple's indulging the desire for intercourse might lead to a dangerous pregnancy.

If there is to be an *absolute* moral prohibition on contraceptive acts, masturbatory acts, and the like as such, even though there is no such prohibition on merely refraining from sex or on sex between sterile spouses, then there must be something about the nature of the former acts that makes them *inherently* contrary to the good for us, apart from their circumstances and apart from their relation to goods higher than sex, in a way that the latter sorts of act are not. This is where the perverted faculty argument comes in.

IV. The perverted faculty argument defended

The basic idea of the perverted faculty argument is fairly simple, though a precise formulation of its key premise requires the kind of semi-formal style beloved of analytic philosophers. I would state it as follows:

> Where some faculty F is natural to a rational agent A and by nature exists for the sake of some end E (and exists in A precisely *so that* A might pursue E), then it is *metaphysically impossible* for it to be good for A to use F in a manner contrary to E.

This thesis, I maintain, follows from the general Aristotelian-Thomistic metaphysics of the good described above. The good for a thing is determined by the end which it has by nature. F exists for the sake of E, and agents like A naturally possess F precisely so that they might pursue E. Hence (given the underlying metaphysics) it cannot possibly be good for A to use F *for the sake of* preventing the realization of E, or *for the sake of* an end which has an inherent tendency to frustrate the realization of E.

It is important to be clear about exactly what this premise says and what it does not say. Note first of all that it is describing what is good *for a rational agent*. For morality is essentially about what it is good for rational agents, given their nature, not what is good for plants, animals, or inanimate objects. (That is not to say that morality does not have implications for the latter, but they are derivative from morality's implications for the good for rational agents.) Hence there is nothing in the premise that implies that it is wrong for a rational agent to use a plant or animal in a way that is contrary to what is good for *it* by nature, or to use an artifact in a way that is contrary to its function.

Note secondly that the premise does not entail that a faculty *F* cannot have more than one natural end, and neither does it entail that it cannot be good for *A* to use *F* for an end *other than E*. For "*different* from *E*" and "*other* than *E*" do not entail "*contrary* to *E*." Nor does it entail that we *have* to use *F* at all. Indeed, since *F*, which is a part of *A*, exists for the sake of the agent *A* as a whole, it is even perfectly consistent with the premise to destroy *F* if doing so is the only way to preserve *A*, as when one has cancerous organs surgically removed. (This is known as the "principle of totality," which is justified on precisely the same teleological grounds that underlie the perverted faculty argument.) The premise says only that if *A* is actually going to *use F*, then even if he uses it for some reason other than *E*, it cannot be good for him to use it for the sake of *actively frustrating* the realization of *E* or in a manner which of its nature tends actively to frustrate the realization of *E*.

Nor does the thesis entail that *A* must *consciously intend* to try to realize *E*, even as part of his aim, whenever he uses *F*. It entails only that, whether or not he intends when using *F* to try to realize *E*, he cannot intend *actively to frustrate* the realization of *E*. Nor does the premise entail that *A* cannot use *F* when he knows its end *E* won't in fact be achieved; for in that case he is not using *F for the sake of* frustrating the realization of *E*, and he is not himself *attempting* to frustrate the realization of *E* in the course of using *F*. To *foresee* that *F*'s end *E* won't in fact be realized is not the same thing as using *F in a way that will prevent E* from being realized, any more than foreseeing that something will happen is the same as causing it to happen.

Nor does the premise entail that to use man-made devices is *per se* to frustrate the natural end of *F*. On the contrary, man-made devices can sometimes restore natural function (as with eyeglasses) or enhance it (as with binoculars). And one could frustrate the end of a faculty without using man-made devices (for example, if one gouged out one's eyes using only one's bare hands). Being *contrary to nature*, here and in the "old" natural law theory more generally, has nothing to do with whether a thing is "artificial" in the sense of man-made but rather with whether it actively frustrates the end toward which a faculty is naturally "directed."

Nor, it is worth emphasizing again, is the premise in any way undermined by the possibility that someone might have a deep-seated and perhaps even genetically-based desire to use *F* in a way contrary to *E*. That someone is born with a clubfoot doesn't mean that his feet have a different natural end than those of people with normal feet. It means that while his feet have the same natural end, they are defective in a way that makes them less capable of realizing that natural end. That someone is born with a predication toward alcoholism does not mean that the realization of his natural ends, unlike those of other human beings, requires drinking to excess. It means instead that while he has the same natural ends as other human beings, the realization of which requires avoiding drinking to excess, he has a psychological defect that makes it harder for him to realize those ends.

Nor is there anything in the premise that entails a "physicalistic" emphasis on brute physiology alone. For there are psychological faculties as well as physiological faculties, and the former have ends for which they exist by nature just as much as the latter do. At the same time, the premise does not reduce morality to the question of whether one misuses a certain faculty, whether physiological or psychological. It tells us only that certain actions are inherently contrary to the good and thus (as the argument as a whole will go on to show) for that reason ruled out. But that is not to deny that there are many other considerations to be brought to bear when developing a systematic account of morality, sexual or otherwise.

Now, when applied to sexual morality, there is a wide range of action which this key premise of the perverted faculty argument leaves open. For example, it is perfectly consistent with the premise for someone to refrain from sex for the sake of the priesthood or the religious life, or even just to avoid pregnancy. For the premise does not say that there is anything *necessarily* contrary to nature in *not* using a faculty, only that there is something contrary to nature in *using* it *in a way that actively frustrates the end* of the faculty. (Of course, there may be other moral reasons why it would be wrong to seek to avoid pregnancy or in some other way to avoid using a faculty, but that is another question. The point is that *refraining from using* a faculty, whatever the reason one refrains, is not the same as *perverting* the faculty.)

Nor does the premise imply that there is anything inherently wrong with having sex during pregnancy, or during infertile periods, or with a sterile spouse, or after menopause, or in general under circumstances in which it is foreseen that conception will not result. For none of this involves using one's sexual faculties in a way that *actively frustrates* their natural end. *Foreseeing* that a certain sexual act will in fact not result in conception is not the same thing as *actively altering* the relevant organs or the nature of the act in a way that would make it impossible for them to lead to conception even if they were in good working order. To use organs that *happen to be* damaged, worn out, or otherwise non-functional to the extent that they will not realize their end, is not to pervert them; *actively to try* to damage them or prevent them from functioning for the sake of making sure their use will not result in the realization of their end *is* to pervert them.

Nor does the premise imply that a couple has to intend or even want to conceive when engaging in intercourse, but only that they cannot intend actively to alter the nature of the act or the relevant organs in a way that would make them incapable of realizing conception even if they were in good working order. Nor does the premise imply that a couple cannot stimulate each other's sexual organs in various ways, including manually and orally, within the overall context of an act of sexual intercourse that climaxes with the husband's ejaculating within his wife's vagina.

It is worth pausing over this point briefly so as to forestall simplistic interpretations of what it is to "pervert" a faculty (which will be important for responding to certain objections later on). Part of the reason stimulation of the sort in question is not ruled out by the premise is that, as long as it does not result in premature ejaculation, manual and oral stimulation of the genitals does not involve using them in a way that is *contrary to* their natural function, but at most for something that is only *other than* their natural function. But even saying that such use is for something "other than" their natural function is not quite right and presupposes too crude an understanding of natural function. For there is nothing in the natural end of the sexual act that requires a businesslike immediate penetration and swift climax, any more than there is anything in the natural end of eating that requires ingesting a bland meal as quickly as possible. Just as enhancing the gustatory and aesthetic pleasures of food is not only consistent with, but can facilitate the realization of, the natural end of eating, so too is enhancing the pleasures of lovemaking not only consistent with, but can facilitate the realization of, the natural ends of sex. As Ford and Kelly note in their well-known manual on sexual morality, modern Catholic moralists have generally affirmed the moral justifiability of oral-genital stimulation within the overall context of marital intercourse at least to the extent that it is "necessary or useful to the achievement of satisfactory sexual relations" (1963, p. 229). Now, physiologically speaking, manual or oral stimulation can obviously prepare the organs for intercourse (and for many wives is the only way they can achieve orgasm); while psychologically speaking, such stimulation can enhance a couple's delight in one another and in their marital relations (though of course this might depend on the couple). In that sense manual or oral stimulation of the genitals is not really use of the organs for something "other than" their natural ends but in fact can actively enhance the realization of the procreative and unitive ends of the sexual act. (Of course, hedonistic excess is possible, here as in the case of eating. But as with eating, that does not show that the acts in question are inherently bad.)[11]

Similarly, there nothing in the key premise of the perverted faculty argument that rules out the use of artificial means *per se* in the context of the sexual act. For example, it would not rule out the use of drugs to treat a husband's impotence, or the use of a vibrator by the couple during the context of intercourse as a means of treating a wife's inability to achieve orgasm. To be sure, there might be other moral objections to such practices (for example, if they reflected nothing more than hedonism) but they would not *per se* involve the frustration of the natural ends of the sexual act.

So, the perverted faculty argument is not nearly as simplistic or restrictive in its implications as its critics seem to suppose. All the same, it does rule out exactly the sorts of practices it has traditionally been deployed in criticizing. For example, use of the birth control pill, or of condoms, or of any other contraceptive devices, would obviously involve using the sexual faculties while actively frustrating the realization of their procreative end.

---

11 Despite the general agreement that now exists among Catholic moralists on the justifiability of such acts, one occasionally hears moral objections to them, though in my estimation the objections are uniformly feeble. For instance, it is sometimes claimed that such acts involve "simulating" acts which result in ejaculation outside the vagina, and are for that reason morally suspect. But this is like saying that surgery is morally suspect because it involves "simulating" stabbing someone to death. With a married couple as with a surgeon, there is "simulation" only if the act is *intended* as a simulation; and as with the surgeon, if no such simulation is intended then there is no moral problem. Another objection holds that the mouth is not a proper receptacle for sexual organs. But this is like objecting to passionate marital kissing on the grounds that the mouth was made for food and is not the proper receptacle for someone else's lips, tongue, or saliva. In neither case is the natural function of the relevant organs being frustrated and, in the case of oral-genital foreplay even *more* than in the case of kissing, the relevant fluids are not being prevented from ending up in their proper receptacle. It is also sometimes objected that acts of oral-genital stimulation are undignified. But *how* are they undignified, and why would that have any moral significance anyway? (Is eating chili dogs undignified? Dressing up like a clown at the circus? Standing on one's head so as to amuse a child? Passing gas or blowing one's nose? Or, for that matter, engaging in straightforward marital intercourse? In some sense each of these acts is undignified, and yet they are all also perfectly innocent.) To answer that the acts in question are objectionably undignified insofar as they pervert the natural functions of sex would be to beg the question; while the answer that it is just intuitively obvious that they are objectionably undignified is hard to distinguish from a sheer appeal to one's subjective prejudices, which is no argument at all.

And it is this active frustration, rather than the artificiality of the means, that makes them in the relevant sense "contrary to nature." That is why the withdrawal method, or manual or oral stimulation of the husband's genitals taken to the point of orgasm, are also contrary to nature in the relevant sense even though no artificial means are employed. For these acts too involve using the sexual faculties in a way that actively frustrates their natural procreative end.

Masturbatory acts involve a twofold frustration of the natural ends of sex. For one thing, they frustrate the procreative end insofar as the natural end of the physiological process in the male leading from arousal to ejaculation is not only to get semen out of the male but into the vagina, while the natural end of the physiological process of arousal in the female is to prepare the vagina for reception of semen. But these acts also frustrate the unitive end insofar as arousal is "other-directed" in a *psychological* sense no less than a physiological sense. Male sexual arousal is of its nature *woman-oriented*, and female sexual arousal is of its nature *man-oriented*. In each case realization of the natural end requires connecting emotionally as well as physically with *another person*. Masturbatory acts involve the active taking of the process of arousal to a climax that does *not* involve another person, and thus turns it against its natural end.

Homosexual acts and bestiality are also twofold in their frustration of the natural ends of sex. They both frustrate the procreative end insofar as they involve the active taking of the physiological processes associated with sexual arousal toward a climax in which conception would be impossible even in principle, even when all of the faculties of the parties involved are in good working order. They also frustrate the unitive end insofar as they involve actively taking the psychological process of arousal through to an emotional climax that involves an object other than the one toward which nature has directed it—in the one case toward a person of the wrong sex, in the other toward an object that isn't even a person.

When we add to these considerations Aquinas's fundamental principle of natural law—that practical reason has as it natural end the pursuit of what is good and the avoidance of what frustrates the realization of the good—we have the ingredients for a formal presentation of the perverted faculty argument as applied to the use of our sexual faculties. It can be stated as follows:

1.   Where some faculty F is natural to a rational agent A and by nature ex
     ists for the sake of some end E (and exists in A precisely *so that A* might

pursue E), then it is metaphysically impossible for it to be good for A to use F in a manner contrary to E.

2. But our sexual faculties exist by nature for the sake of procreative and unitive ends, and exist in us precisely so that we might pursue those ends.

3. So it is metaphysically impossible for it to be good for us to use those faculties in a manner that is contrary to their procreative and unitive ends.

4. But contraceptive acts, masturbatory acts, homosexual acts, and acts of bestiality involve the use of our sexual faculties in a manner that is contrary to their procreative and/or unitive ends.

5. So it is metaphysically impossible for it to be good for us to engage in contraceptive acts, masturbatory acts, homosexual acts, or acts of bestiality.

6. But it can be rational to engage in an act only if it is in some way good for us and never when it frustrates the realization of the good.

7. So it cannot be rational to engage in contraceptive acts, masturbatory acts, homosexual acts, or acts of bestiality.

The answers to the standard objections to the argument might be obvious from what's been said already, but it is worthwhile addressing them explicitly. Paul Weithman summarizes several of them (1997, pp. 236–37). He claims, first, that the argument depends on "a principle forbidding interference with the reproductive organs' performance of their natural function," which is open to "obvious counterexamples" insofar as even natural law theorists allow that a diseased uterus and ovaries might legitimately be removed even though this impedes their function. But the problems with this objection are, first, that it rests on an imprecise formulation of the perverted faculty argument's key premise, and second, that it ignores the role the principle of totality plays in justifying the alleged "counterexample." For one thing, the perverted faculty argument does not object to "interference" with a natural faculty as such. Again, enhancement of a natural faculty (such as the use of eyeglasses or binoculars) is perfectly consistent with the argument, even though it involves a kind of "interference." So too is removal of a diseased organ, on the grounds that the organ exists precisely for the sake of the human being as a whole and therefore can be removed if this is necessary to save the human being. In both of these cases, it is precisely the *realization* of the natural ends inherent in human nature that is being furthered—in the one case by enhancing the natural faculties, and in the other by preserving the life of the whole person, so that at least some of his natural ends might still be realized even if others no longer can be. (Removal of a *healthy* organ could *not* be given such a teleological justification.) And in the latter case, precisely because the diseased faculty is being removed it is not being *used* at all. By contrast, contraception, homosexual acts, and the like *do* involve the *use* of a faculty but precisely in a way that *actively frustrates* the natural ends of such use rather than *facilitating* the realization of those ends. That is what makes such acts *perverse* in a way that the enhancement of healthy organs or removal of diseased organs is not. And it is this perverse sort of *use*—actively directing a faculty to an end positively contrary to its natural one—rather than "interference" as such, that the argument rules out.

Weithman also says that the perverted faculty argument "seems to be motivated by a crudely physicalist understanding of sexual morality" and fails adequately to explain "why facts about the natural functions of the reproductive organs are even morally *relevant*, let alone morally *decisive*." But we have already seen that there is absolutely nothing in the perverted faculty argument that entails that it is only *physiological* or otherwise "physicalistic" faculties that are important to sexual morality. And to allege that the argument fails to explain why facts about natural function are relevant simply ignores, without answering, the general Aristotelian-Thomistic metaphysics of the good that underlies the argument. (To his credit, however, Weithman explicitly declines to endorse Finnis's allegation that the perverted faculty argument commits a "naturalistic fallacy"—an allegation which, as I have already noted, simply begs the question against the Aristotelian-Thomistic metaphysics that underlies the argument.)

Finally, Weithman claims that the perverted faculty argument "seems suspiciously *ad hoc*" and fails to draw "a principled distinction between the reproductive organs, whose frustration the principle forbids, and other organs whose operation it is permissible to impede." But what is truly suspicious is how consistently imprecise, prone to caricature, and incapable of giving a charitable reading critics of the perverted faculty argument seem to be. Weithman offers no examples of *ad hoc* allowances for "organs whose operation it is permissible to impede," but it is easy enough to find alleged examples in the literature. Grisez cites the use of earplugs; "walking on one's hands [which] interferes at least temporarily with their proper function"; "smoking [in which] we use the respiratory system in a way which does frustrate its proper function to a considerable extent"; "hanging rings in one's ears or nose, [which] by stretching them out of shape, may lessen

their effectiveness"; "ingest[ing] some food and drink by mouth for satisfaction although for medical reasons the stomach constantly is pumped so
that nothing is digested"; and "lactation" in which "there is excess milk and
it is pumped out of the breasts and thrown away" even when the infant is
fed artificially during such times (1964, pp. 28–30). Other alleged examples
sometimes given by critics are shaving, chewing gum, using antiperspirant,
and even damming rivers.

Such examples are often presented as obviously devastating, when in
fact they have no force whatsoever against the argument when it is properly
understood. Here it is important to keep four points in mind.

First, it cannot be repeated too often—if only because some critics seem
to want to attack nothing but straw men—that the perverted faculty argument does *not* entail that there is anything wrong with the use of man-made
devices, or the use of a faculty for something merely *other than* its natural
function, or the interference with natural processes where plants, non-human
animals, or inanimate objects and processes are concerned. Nor is there anything *ad hoc* about this, for the whole point of the argument is simply to
draw out the implications of the Aristotelian-Thomistic position that what
is good *for us* can in principle only be what is consistent with the realization
of our natural ends. And neither artificial devices, nor the pursuit of ends
other than our natural ends, nor interference with non-human natural
processes are inherently contrary to the realization of our natural ends.
Hence examples like chewing gum (which is merely *other than*, rather than
contrary to, the natural end of our digestive faculties) or the use of earplugs
(which though artificial facilitate the realization of our natural ends insofar
as they protect the ears from excessive noise, facilitate sleep, etc.) and the
damming of rivers (which doesn't even concern human faculties in the first
place) simply miss the point of the argument. (Cf. Jensen 2010, pp. 245–46
and Smith 1991, p. 345 n. 13.)

Second, for any of these examples to be true counterexamples, they
have to be cases that really do involve the frustration of a natural end, and
with at least some of them that is simply not even prima facie plausible.
Grisez never explains exactly how earrings or nose-piercings might "lessen
[the] effectiveness" of the ears or nose, and of course those who do sport
these decorations rarely complain of any resulting difficulty in hearing or
smelling. (And if someone *did* so mutilate the ears or nose that their function
was impaired, this would not be a *counterexample* to the perverted faculty
argument but rather exactly the sort of thing the "old" natural law theory
would condemn.) Nor is it clear how walking on one's hands frustrates their

natural end even "temporarily." A hand is evidently a "general purpose" organ, without the sort of specificity of function that eyes, ears, and genitals have. Even if it is insisted that they are for *grasping* things, specifically, there is no specific sort of thing they are made to grasp and no specific sort of occasion or length of time that they are intended by nature to be grasping things. Walking on them no more frustrates their natural end than leaving them hanging by one's sides does. It is clearly at worst in the "other than" rather than "contrary to" category. Eating food that one will for *medical* reasons out of one's control not be able safely to keep down is also not a plausible candidate for something that is contrary to the natural end of eating any more than removing a diseased organ is. One arguably has to go out of one's way to avoid a charitable reading of the perverted faculty argument to think these examples pose any serious difficulty. (It is hardly a *stretch* for the "old" natural law theorist to claim that sex is for procreation and interpersonal emotional bonding, while it is *quite* a stretch to say that nature intends for us always to be grasping things!)

A third point to keep in mind is that there are crucial differences between, on the one hand, an *individual deliberate act* of using a bodily faculty and, on the other, an *ongoing and involuntary physiological process*. Use of the sexual organs is an example of the former whereas hair growth, breathing, perspiring, and lactating are examples of the latter. Now the former has a specific end-state or climax, while the latter do not. In particular, the former has as its physiological end a specific emission (or reception) of semen, while the latter have as their end the continual generation of hair, sweat, and milk and the continual oxidation of the blood. There is no specific individual event that initiates the latter processes and there is no specific individual event that culminates any of them either. It is oxidation *in general*, hair production *in general*, sweat production *in general*, and milk production *in general* that is their natural end. And those general outcomes are not frustrated by any individual act of smoking, shaving, breast-pumping, or putting on antiperspirant. By contrast, the process that begins with arousal and ends with ejaculation within the vagina is episodic rather than ongoing, and its outcome, which *is* a specific event, *is* frustrated by contraception, masturbation, and the like.

It is certainly not plausible, then, to suggest that breast-pumping *as such* interferes with the natural end of lactation or that smoking *as such* interferes with the natural end of breathing (as if smokers qua smokers had to hold their breath any longer than is required by activities like speaking). Nor is the small area of the body to which antiperspirant is typically applied crucial to perspiration's realizing its natural end of cooling the body down (any more than the fact that some semen tends to leave the vagina after inter-course is incompatible with the procreative end—and no natural law theorist holds that a woman should go out of her way to prevent this from happen-ing). And while many people shave and some even remove most of the hair on their bodies without this plausibly being immoral, it is not clear that body hair in humans serves any non-ornamental function in the first place.

To be sure, smoking to excess clearly *does* frustrate the natural end of breathing, and *refraining altogether* from breastfeeding one's children ar-guably frustrates the natural end of lactation, especially if we factor in the bonding between mother and child that is facilitated by nursing. But then, precisely for these reasons, people are inclined to raise at least a mild moral objection to smoking to excess, and even gently to recommend that it is, all things considered, better for mothers to breastfeed their children. In this way, common sense clearly tracks the "old" natural law theory's insistence that there is a connection between what is good for us and what is consistent with the realization of the ends nature has set for us.

But this brings us to a fourth point, which is that it is crucial to under-stand that the "old" natural law theory, given its Aristotelian-Thomistic foundations, does not draw the sort of rigid distinction between matters of ethics and matters of practicality, good mental and physical health, etc. that modern moral theorists tend to draw. Ethics, for Aristotelians, Thomists, and other classical thinkers, is a matter of *how to live well*, in *all* aspects of life. Anything that enters into living well—from avoiding stress to avoiding disease to avoiding murder and adultery—is part of the moral life, broadly construed. At the same time, by no means is *every* failure to live well a grave error or mortal sin. Many such failures—including some failures to respect the natural ends of our faculties—are merely minor lapses. There is, accord-ingly, a bit of question-begging sleight-of-hand in objections to the perverted faculty argument that pretend that it would be an embarrassment if it turned out that the argument entailed that failure to breastfeed one's infants (say) or cleaning too much of the wax out of one's ears were contrary to what is good for us. The "old" natural law theorist would say, or certainly should say: *Yes, of course such things might be contrary to what is good for us, as even your doctor will tell you. And that is all that the perverted faculty ar-gument is claiming. It does not follow that every frustration of a natural end is a grave sin. That depends on how crucial to the good for us as rational animals is the faculty in question is, and that is determined by such consid-erations as how fully it participates in our distinctively rational faculties, how significant it is to our nature as social animals, and so forth.*

Hence self-abuse and pornography, which turn sexual pleasure away from its natural end of leading a person intensely to delight in and thereby bond emotionally with another individual human being and reduces it to a kind of recreational virtual reality, are bound to be far more seriously damaging to realizing the good for us as rational, social animals than is (say) overuse of cotton swabs to clean one's ears. The former can seriously distort one's ability to find sexual fulfillment in a spouse; the latter can cause a mere ear infection. It would be silly to pretend that the latter is a grave moral fault, but it would be equally silly to deny that it is at least a mild lapse in a virtue like prudence.

A genuine counterexample to the perverted faculty argument's key premise would have to involve an action that *both* involved *the active frustration* of the natural end of a faculty and yet which was *in no way* contrary to what is good for us, not even in a minor respect. I submit that there are no such counterexamples, and that there could not be any given an Aristotelian-Thomistic metaphysics of the good.

V. There is no alternative

That the perverted faculty argument is essentially correct is implicit in the arguments of those among its critics who accept the moral conclusions it is typically deployed in defense of (the immorality of contraception, masturbation, homosexual acts, and the like) but who purport to offer an alternative non-theological justification of those conclusions. For there is no such alternative justification. Unless one accepts something like a perverted faculty argument—in particular, an argument that grounds the good in an essentialist and teleological metaphysics and analyzes the good use of our sexual capacities in terms of consistency with their natural ends—then one will have no grounds, apart from a sheer appeal to divine authority, for condemning the sexual behaviors in question as intrinsically immoral. The would-be alternatives to the perverted faculty argument do indeed presuppose such an account of the good use of our sexual capacities, and would have no force if they did not.

The two main purported alternatives are personalist or phenomenological arguments and "new natural law" arguments. In the former, special emphasis is put on the interpersonal psychological aspects of sex, and in particular on the idea that the sexual act ought to be an expression of mutual "self-donation" of the spouses rather than the "using" of each other for mere selfish pleasure-seeking. Now as Grisez notes in criticizing phenomenological arguments, "the psychological consideration of the sexual act is just as much a functional interpretation of it as is the ordinary natural-law approach" (1964, p. 36). As we have already seen, there is nothing in the perverted faculty argument or the "old" natural law theory in general that requires an exclusive focus on the physiology of sex, so that to emphasize the psychological ends is by itself in no way to put forward an *alternative* to a perverted faculty argument.

As Grisez also points out, it is hard to see how a phenomenological approach rules out homosexual acts or contraception (1964, p. 37). Why couldn't a committed same-sex couple or spouses using contraception regard their non-procreative sexual behavior as an affectionate expression of "mutual self-giving"? Here the personalist will appeal to the "language of the body" or the "nuptial meaning" of sexual intercourse as indicating that it has a specifically procreative and heterosexual nature. But there are three problems with this sort of move considered as an *argument* against contraception, homosexual acts, etc. (as opposed to a mere *expression* of independently justified moral disapproval of them). First, if the body's "nuptial meaning" or "language" is put forward merely as a phenomenological description, then it can at most tell us how the sexual act is *experienced* by us (and even then only by some people, not all). And that by itself is insufficient to justify claims about what makes it good or bad as a matter of *objective fact*. Second, if it *is* instead meant as a description of the objective facts about the nature of the body and the sexual act, then the problem is that it is a metaphorical description that needs to be cashed out in literal terms if it is to provide us with the basis of a convincing argument (since there is no literal "language" or "meaning" of a semantic sort in the body or in the sexual act).

And this brings us to the third problem, which is that if the talk of the body's inherently heterosexual and procreative "language" and "meaning" is a roundabout way of describing the immanent teleology of sex that follows from the essence or nature of our sexual faculties—as it surely is—then the personalist argument is, once again, not an *alternative* to the "old" natural law theorist's perverted faculty argument at all, but merely a more flowery (and less precise) way of stating that argument.

The arguments of "New Natural Lawyers" are open to similar objections. They insist that sexual acts can be good only if they foster a "one-flesh unity" of persons (Grisez 1993, p. 568, n. 43). And why exactly do homosexual sodomy and marital intercourse in which the wife has been taking birth control pills fail to foster such a "one-flesh unity"? (The fleshy bits of the participants in such acts are, after all, as snugly fitted together as they are in heterosexual procreative sexual acts, and the partners can also be just as passionate in their emotional commitment to one another.) The answer, we are told, is that it is only "sexual acts of the reproductive type" that can foster such a unity (George and Bradley 1999, p. 139), for only a man and woman engaged in non-contraceptive sex are "unite[d] ... biologically" in a way that makes them "one reality," a "biological (and therefore personal) unit" (Finnis 1994, pp. 1066–67)—indeed, "the copulating male and female," Grisez assures us, make up "one organism" (Grisez 1996, p. 28; cf. Lee and George 2008, Chapter 6). Homosexual acts, meanwhile, involve "the partners ... treating their bodies as instruments to be used in the service of their consciously experiencing selves," and such use "disintegrates each of them precisely as acting persons" (Finnis 1994, p. 1067). And masturbation "alienate[s] one's body from one's conscious subjectivity" and not only thereby damages "self-integration" but also "violat[es] the body's capacity for self-giving" in marital sex (Grisez 1993, pp. 650–51).

As with personalist arguments, what we have here is essentially a set of metaphors, and more obscure ones at that. For instance, in no literal sense are a copulating man and woman "one organism." Grisez claims that "though a male and a female are complete individuals with respect to other functions—nutrition, sensation, locomotion—with respect to reproduction they are only potential parts of a mated pair, which is the complete organism capable of reproducing sexually" (1996, p. 28). This is like saying that people engaged in conversation or competitive games make up one organism, since qua individuals they cannot carry out these essentially social activities. (Or are playing solitaire and delivering a soliloquy on all fours with self-abuse? And does the deliberate cessation of copulation constitute the suicide of the "one organism" that the copulating pair make up? Is it therefore a mortal sin to stop copulating once you have started?)

Where the metaphors can be cashed out intelligibly, they will show what the "New Natural Lawyers" want them to show only insofar as they reflect an Aristotelian-Thomistic metaphysics of formal and final causes and the accounts of substance and value that these notions enter into. In what sense does the "acting person" engaged in sodomy or masturbation "alienate" and "instrumentalize" his body and thereby become "disintegrated"? And exactly why is this bad? The Aristotelian-Thomistic philosopher would say that the parts of a thing make up a genuine substance (including an organic substance) only insofar as they are united by a substantial form rather than an accidental form; that the parts' being so united involves an inherent directedness toward the flourishing of the whole of which they are a part; and that this teleological aspect makes the unity or integration of the whole intrinsically good in a way the unity of an accidental collection of things is not. In the case of our sexual faculties, the Aristotelian-Thomistic "old" natural law theorist would add that the realization of their natural end requires another human being of the opposite sex and that directing them toward another object frustrates this end and thus the good of the whole organism of which they are a part. Now if all of this is what the "New Natural Lawyers" have in mind with their talk of "self-integration," the badness of "instrumentalizing" the body for mere pleasure-seeking, the copulating pair forming a "biological unit," etc., then what they are saying is intelligible, though it is really just a much less rigorous and straightforward way of saying what every "old" natural law theorist already knows. And if it is not what the "New Natural Lawyers" are saying, then whatever it is they *are* saying is completely mysterious.

To be sure, George and Bradley tell us that "the concept of a reproductive-type act is biological-functional" (1999, p. 153, n. 5)—with no hint of irony, let it be noted, despite the fact that the charge of "physicalism" or "biologism" is ritualistically flung at the perverted faculty argument!—and Grisez, Finnis, and other "New Natural Law" adepts also rely heavily on the notion of biological integrity. But this only reinforces the point that their position cannot be made intelligible without an essentially Aristotelian metaphysical foundation. For it is no good *merely* to appeal to facts of the sort one might find in a biology textbook, as if the metaphysical import of these facts was not itself a matter of controversy. (Are the "New Natural Lawyers" aware that there is an entire academic subfield called the "philosophy of biology"?) Biological reductionists and eliminativists would be unimpressed by the appeal to "integrity" and "acts of the reproductive type," since their position entails that biological phenomena have only what Aristotelians would call an "accidental" rather than "substantial" unity, and they would deny that there is any inherent and irreducible teleology in nature. And to show that they are wrong would *just be* to show that something like an Aristotelian metaphysics of biological substances is correct.

As it happens, Grisez himself acknowledged in his early work his own indebtedness to the perverted faculty argument despite his having "severely" criticized it (1964, p. 100). His aim was essentially to extract its analysis of our sexual faculties from its "conventional natural law" framework and integrate it instead into his "new natural law" theory and its account of practical reason. He writes that "our argument uses the principle of the perverted-faculty argument only after limiting it to the sexual faculty," and without putting the emphasis on the "natural teleology" of the "generative power" (1964, pp. 100–01).

I have already argued that the objections Grisez, Finnis, et al. have leveled against the "old" natural law theory are without force, and others (including the other contributors to this volume) have exposed the grave philosophical and theological problems with the "New Natural Law" alternative. What remains is just to note how Grisez and his followers, like so many revolutionaries, are guilty of precisely the faults charged to those they sought to overthrow. Traditional natural law theory is routinely accused of being a set of *ad hoc* rationalizations of claims whose true motivation is theological, and rationalizations that would lead to absurd conclusions if followed out consistently. Neither of these charges is just. In fact the basic claims of the "old" natural theory follow quite naturally from the Aristotelian-Thomistic metaphysics which underlies it, which is independently motivated. One can quibble over this or that detail, but it cannot reasonably be denied that given a metaphysics of essentialism and immanent teleology, the good for us is determined by the natural ends of our faculties. Nor, as I have argued, do the absurd conclusions many have claimed to find implicit in this account of the good really follow from it.

The "New Natural Lawyers," by contrast, are wide open to both charges. Rather than working out the implications of an ancient and independently motivated metaphysical tradition, their theory was invented by Grisez only fifty years ago precisely in an attempt to find a novel secular justification for the claims of Catholic sexual morality. And in struggling to work out such a justification in a way that will disassociate them from the "old" natural law theory they happily joined the secularists and liberals in bashing, they have been led into increasingly *ad hoc*, obscure, and indeed bizarre lines of argument that have surely served to "expos[e] Catholic moral thought to endless ridicule," as Grisez accused defenders of the perverted faculty argument of having done (1964, p. 31). The "natural law" of Grisez and Co. is new, yes, but not improved.

References

Aquinas, Thomas. 1975. *Summa Contra Gentiles, Book 3: Providence, Part II.* Translated by Vernon J. Bourke. (Notre Dame: University of Notre Dame Press).

Aquinas, Thomas. 1948. *Summa Theologica.* Translated by the Fathers of the English Dominican Province. (New York: Benziger Bros.).

Cronin, Michael. 1939. *The Science of Ethics, Volume 1: General Ethics* (Dublin: M. H. Gill and Son).

Ellis, Brian. 2002. *The Philosophy of Nature: A Guide to the New Essentialism.* (Chesham: Acumen).

Feser, Edward. 2008. *The Last Superstition: A Refutation of the New Atheism.* (South Bend, IN: St. Augustine's Press).

Feser, Edward. 2009. *Aquinas.* (Oxford: Oneworld Publications).

Feser, Edward. 2010. "Teleology: A Shopper's Guide," *Philosophia Christi* 12: 142–59.

Feser, Edward. 2013. "Kripke, Ross, and the Immaterial Aspects of Thought," *American Catholic Philosophical Quarterly* 87: 1-32.

Finnis, John. 1980. *Natural Law and Natural Rights.* (Oxford: Clarendon Press).

Finnis, John. 1994. "Law, Morality, and 'Sexual Orientation,'" *Notre Dame Law Review* 69: 1049–76.

Foot, Philippa. 2001. *Natural Goodness.* (Oxford: Clarendon Press).

Ford, John C. and Gerald Kelly. 1963. *Contemporary Moral Theology, Volume II: Marriage Questions.* (Westminster, MD: The Newman Press).

George, Robert. 1999. "Can Sex Be Reasonable?" In Robert P. George, *In Defense of Natural Law.* (Oxford: Oxford University Press).

George, Robert. 2006. "A Walking Contradiction," *The New Criterion* 25

George, Robert P. and Gerard V. Bradley. 1999. "Marriage and the Liberal Imagination." In Robert P. George, *In Defense of Natural Law.* (Oxford: Oxford University Press).

George, Robert P. and Patrick Lee. 1999. "What Sex Can Be: Self-Alienation, Illusion or One-Flesh Union." In Robert P. George, *In Defense of Natural Law.* (Oxford: Oxford University Press).

Greco, John and Ruth Groff, eds. 2013. *Powers and Capacities in Philosophy: The New Aristotelianism.* (London: Routledge).

Grisez, Germain G. 1964. *Contraception and the Natural Law.* (Milwaukee: Bruce Publishing Company).

Grisez, Germain. 1993. *The Way of the Lord Jesus, Volume 2: Living a Christian Life.* (Franciscan Herald Press).

Grisez, Germain. 1996. "The Christian Family as Fulfillment of Sacramental Marriage," *Studies in Christian Ethics* 9: 23–33.

Haldane, John, ed. 2002. *Mind, Metaphysics, and Value in the Thomistic and Analytical Traditions.* (Notre Dame: University of Notre Dame Press).

Jensen, Steven J. 2010. *Good and Evil Actions: A Journey through Saint Thomas Aquinas.* (Washington, D.C.: Catholic University of America Press).

Lee, Patrick and Robert P. George. 2008. *Body-Self Dualism in Contemporary Ethics and Politics.* (Cambridge, MA: Cambridge University Press).

Lewis, C. S. 1988. *The Four Loves*. (New York: Harcourt, Brace, Jovanovich).

Lisska, Anthony. 1996. *Aquinas's Theory of Natural Law*. (Oxford: Oxford University Press).

Martin, Christopher. 2004. "The Fact/Value Distinction." In David S. Oderberg and Timothy Chappell, eds., *Human Values: New Essays on Ethics and Natural Law* (New York: Palgrave Macmillan).

McInerny, Ralph. 1992. *Aquinas on Human Action*. (Washington, D.C.: Catholic University of America Press).

Oderberg, David S. 2000. *Moral Theory: A Non-Consequentialist Approach* (Oxford: Blackwell).

Oderberg, David. 2007. *Real Essentialism*. (London: Routledge).

Oderberg, David. 2010. "The Metaphysical Foundations of Natural Law." In H. Zaborowski, ed., *Natural Law and Contemporary Society* (Washington, D.C.: Catholic University of America Press).

Osler, Margaret J. 1996. "From Immanent Natures to Nature as Artifice: The Reinterpretation of Final Causes in Seventeenth-Century Natural Philosophy," *The Monist* 79: 388–407.

Paterson, Craig. 2006. "Aquinas, Finnis, and Non-Naturalism." In Craig Paterson and Matthew S. Pugh, eds., *Analytical Thomism: Traditions in Dialogue*. (Aldershot: Ashgate).

Posner, Richard. 1992. *Sex and Reason*. (Cambridge, MA: Harvard University Press).

Putnam, Hilary. 2004. *The Collapse of the Fact/Value Dichotomy and Other Essays*. (Cambridge, MA: Harvard University Press).

Smith, Janet E. 1991. *Humanae Vitae: A Generation Later*. (Washington, D.C.: Catholic University of America Press).

Sternberg, Robert J. 1988. *The Triangle of Love: Intimacy, Passion, Commitment*. (New York: Basic Books).

Sullivan, Andrew. 2006. *The Conservative Soul*. (New York: HarperCollins).

Tahko, Tuomas, ed. 2012. *Contemporary Aristotelian Metaphysics*. (Cambridge: Cambridge University Press).

Thompson, Michael. 1995. "The Representation of Life." In Rosalind Hursthouse, Gavin Lawrence, and Warren Quinn, eds., *Virtues and Reasons: Philippa Foot and Moral Theory* (Oxford: Clarendon Press).

Veatch, Henry B. 1990. "Natural Law and the 'Is'-'Ought' Question: Queries to Finnis and Grisez." In Henry B. Veatch, *Swimming Against the Current in Contemporary Philosophy*. (Washington, D.C.: Catholic University of America Press).

Weithman, Paul J. 1997. "Natural Law, Morality, and Sexual Complementarity." In David M. Estlund and Martha C. Nussbaum, eds., *Sex, Preference, and Family*. (Oxford: Oxford University Press).

Wright, Robert. 1995. *The Moral Animal*. (New York: Vintage Books).